D1414881

AL QAEDA
IN EUROPE

LORENZO VIDINO

AL QAEDA IN EUROPE

The New Battleground of International Jihad

FOREWORD BY

Steven Emerson, Director of the Investigative Project

 Prometheus Books

59 John Glenn Drive
Amherst, New York 14228-2197

Published 2006 by Prometheus Books

Inquiries should be addressed to
Prometheus Books
59 John Glenn Drive
Amherst, New York 14228–2197
VOICE: 716–691–0133, ext. 207
FAX: 716–564–2711
WWW.PROMETHEUSBOOKS.COM

09 08 07 06 05   5 4 3 2 1

Library of Congress Cataloging-in-Publication Data

Vidino, Lorenzo.
    Al Qaeda in Europe : the new battleground of international jihad / by Lorenzo Vidino ; foreword by Steven Emerson.
        p. cm.
    Includes bibliographical references and index.
    ISBN 1–59102–433–1 (hardcover : alk. paper)
    1. Qaida (Organization) 2. Terrorists—Europe. 3. Muslims—Europe. 4. Jihad.
5. Islamic fundamentalism. I. Emerson, Steven. II. Title.

HV6433.E852Q358 2005
320.5'57094—dc22

2005024234

TO MY PARENTS AND TO JESSICA,
FOR THEIR LOVE AND SUPPORT

CONTENTS

PART III: AL QAEDA'S MAIN STATION HOUSE IN EUROPE AND THE IRAQI JIHAD

PART IV: MADRID, VAN GOGH, AND THE NEW FACE OF AL QAEDA

APPENDIX: ISLAMIC EXTREMISM IN EUROPE

ACKNOWLEDGMENTS

I am gratefully indebted to many people who, over the last few years, have helped me research and understand terror networks operating in Europe. First and foremost, I am especially thankful to Steven Emerson, without whose support, advice, and patience this book would not have come to light. I have had the fortune of working for Steve for more than three years, and the passion with which he runs the Investigative Project is a continuous source of inspiration. The current and past staff members of the Investigative Project represent a unique group whose dedication and hard work reflect Steve's commitment. Among them, I would like to express my most sincere appreciation to Josh Lefkowitz, Tamar Tesler, Kim Beck, Jason Mintz, and Cynthia Dachowitz.

I am also grateful to Alive Falk, Guido Olimpio, Emerson Vermaat, Antonio Oppi, Muriel Nellis, and everybody at Literary & Creative Artists. Michael Wildes deserves a separate mention for his support and dedication to national security.

Finally, I owe a special measure of gratitude to two good friends with whom I have the privilege of sharing passions and interests: Andrea Morigi and Evan Kohlmann.

FOREWORD

Rallies calling for jihad. Fatwas calling for killing Americans and Jews. Islamic organizations condemning democracy and the West. Islamic clerics demonizing the United States and Europe. Terrorist leaders operating freely and planning operations. Fund-raising for terrorist groups. "Enemies of Islam" targeted for assassination. Hundreds of innocent civilians marked for death. Young Muslims volunteering and training for jihad.

No, this is not the Middle East. It is far closer to home, and it has been going on for years in London, Paris, Madrid, Milan, Rome, Bonn, Strasbourg, Amsterdam, Oslo, Copenhagen—throughout the European continent. The jihad battlefront is everywhere nowadays, present throughout the capitals of Europe. The war that Europe has so assiduously tried to avoid since being ravaged in World War II is now suddenly at its doorstep.

For more than a dozen years, the jihad has been simmering throughout Europe, with regimes studiously unwilling to pay attention to, let alone clamp down on, the Islamic terrorists organizing on European soil. Even the horrific attacks of 9/11 in the United States—pivotally organized from the sanctuary of Europe by the free-wheeling lieutenants of Osama bin Laden—did not jar Europe out of its slumber. Only when the streets of Europe began running red with the blood of its citizens—with the brutal execution of filmmaker Theo Van Gogh, the murder of 197

Spanish train travelers, and the killing of fifty-two British citizens—did European leaders and governments begin to address the jihad problem on their own turf.

But is it too late? Is Europe doomed to become Eurabia? Has the concentration of radical Muslims reached levels that cannot be rolled back? Has Europe essentially ceded sovereignty over its increasingly radical Islamic populations to extremist organizations that have successfully implanted themselves? Is Europe destined to become the target of even *more* lethal attacks? And will Europe continue to serve as a staging ground for American targets in the Middle East or, worse yet, on American soil? And if radical Islamic populations dominating European cities is the future, is the United States facing the same course of disaster?

Lorenzo Vidino exposes the jihad network on European soil in frightening and meticulous detail, revealing the organizational networks, terrorist plots, and radical infrastructure operating for years throughout the European continent. As one of the senior investigators and researchers at the Investigative Project on Terrorism, Vidino, in the span of only a few short years, earned a reputation at the highest levels of the US government as perhaps the top expert on al Qaeda and radical Muslim cells in Europe. He has an unparalleled ability to take massive amounts of information—tens of thousands of documents, Muslim Web sites, court records, and interviews—and distill them into a brilliant narrative that tells a gripping story. This book is the cumulative result of years of research and investigation, much of it never publicly revealed, into the extremist networks in Europe.

For those who want to know more than what the headlines or thirty-second sound bites reveal—for anyone concerned about the future of Europe and the United States—this book *must* be read. It will teach you; it will frighten you; it will mobilize you; it will anger you; it will educate you more than anything you have ever read on how the Muslim radicals have been transformed from "foreign" to "domestic" cells within Europe. With the rapid growth of radical Muslim populations, and with young Muslims having been subject to a steady diet of anti-Western invectives and calls for jihad, the only question is, Why didn't the attacks in London or Madrid happen sooner?

Detailing the jihad's diabolical consequences, Lorenzo reveals how the terrorists in Europe have exploited the very freedoms that made Europe so alluring. But now, with ticking time bombs ready to go off every day, there is not a wide range of options left to European governments. How did Europe find itself in this mess today?

Lorenzo's book traces the rise and growth of radical Islamists in Europe and explains how they operated with virtual impunity for years. In some respects, European governments *legitimized* the radical networks and leaders by granting Islamic radicals fleeing the Middle East political asylum, by officially recognizing their newly implanted mosques and militant organizations as "mainstream," and by allowing fund-raising for Islamic terrorist groups without any interruption or restrictions. Adding to that combustible mix a radicalized Islamic environment—through schools, mosques, imams, electronic broadcasts, textbooks, videos, and the Internet—in which the West, Americans, and Jews were portrayed as the "enemy of Islam," it is not difficult to see why second generations of Muslims in Europe, who had all the economic opportunities available to them as other generations, would turn to violence.

From terrorist cells in Stockholm to recruiting stations in Milan, from ricin plots in France to train bombings in London and Madrid, Lorenzo's book tells a story that comprehensively reveals the extent of the terror network that operates worldwide—but is ironically stationed from the safety of Europe.

By 2005 Europe had woken up to a series of lethal bombings, interdicted plots, terrorist cells, and body bags. The Empire was finally poised to strike back. But whom would it strike? And would it be enough? And what would be the implications for the United States?

To find out the answers to these questions and to the larger one of how extensive the jihad network has become in Europe, this book will tell you. It's a remarkable piece of investigation and analysis.

Steven Emerson

INTRODUCTION

In the American collective imaginary the terrorist who will try to carry out the dreaded follow-up to the 9/11 attacks fits a certain stereotype. He is a young Arab male, barely speaks English, and may have a long beard. Perhaps he will try to cross the US border hidden in a container sent from a remote Middle Eastern country, or sneak into the country through a tunnel built by Mexican drug smugglers.

While such an attempt cannot be ruled out entirely, authorities and analysts consider a different scenario much more likely. The next Mohammed Atta will probably come to the United States on a direct flight from London or Paris, landing at JFK or LAX. He will be wearing trendy sneakers and expensive sunglasses, with his iPod dangling from the back pocket of his Gucci jeans. On the plane he might even sip a glass of chardonnay. Following the medieval Islamic doctrine of "necessity permits the forbidden," formulated by Sheik Ibn Taymiyah seven centuries ago, he will justify the consumption of alcohol by his need to fool the infidels into believing he is not a Muslim, or at least an observant one.

Then, at customs, while immigration officials scrutinize the visas of Ukrainian nannies and Indian computer workers, he will breeze by after showing his British (or German, Belgian, French, Danish . . .) passport. Since citizens of Western European countries do not need a visa to enter the country, he will be subjected to an examination that lasts, according to data released by US immigration authorities, less than a minute.

With this picture in mind, in the spring of 2005 some members of Congress began to question whether the Visa Waiver Program, which allows citizens of Western European countries to enter the United States without a visa, had to be revised. Yes, European countries are our friends, and the vast majority of their citizens come to the States for business or to see America's beauties, conceded the legislators. Nevertheless, we cannot ignore the disturbing new reality.

Let's consider Great Britain, America's foremost ally. In 2001 a British-born convert to Islam, Richard Reid, attempted to blow up a transatlantic flight by igniting explosives he had hidden in his shoes. Omar Sheikh, born in London and a former student at the London School of Economics, has been sentenced to death for his role in the gruesome assassination of *Wall Street Journal* reporter Daniel Pearl. All four suicide bombers that attacked London on July 7, 2005, were British citizens, three of them by birth. And British authorities estimate that no fewer than three thousand British-born or British-based individuals have passed through al Qaeda training camps in Afghanistan. Any one of them could enter the United States with no visa and no security check.

Every other European country finds itself in the same predicament, as each confronts the new face of Islamic terrorism. The 2004 Madrid train bombings and the 2005 attacks in London represented the first massive strikes of Islamist terrorists on European soil. Nevertheless, the attacks are simply the most visible sign of a much larger problem. Over the past twenty years, Europe has become a major base of operations for al Qaeda and other Islamist terrorist groups, a fact that has major consequences for security around the world—including in the United States.

Almost every terrorist attack carried out by al Qaeda before 9/11 has some link to the Continent. In 1992 Ahmed Ajaj, one of the planners of the 1993 bombing of the World Trade Center, landed at JFK with a fake Swedish passport. The documents for the bombers of the American embassies in Kenya and Tanzania were supplied by a charity that was a Dublin-based front. And when, two days before 9/11, al Qaeda wanted to kill Ahmed Shah Massoud, the leader of the Afghan Northern Alliance—for years a determined opponent of the Taliban—it resorted to two suicide bombers who came from Belgium.

The attacks of 9/11 revealed Europe's centrality in al Qaeda's operations. While the devastating attacks were conceived in the dusty caves of Afghanistan, their operational details were perfected in Hamburg and in a resort on the Spanish coast. The key perpetrators of the worst terrorist assault the world has ever seen met in a mosque, a school, and an apartment of the affluent German city. More troublingly, most of these men were not extremists when they left their homes in North Africa or the Middle East—they discovered radical Islam in the modern and secularized West.

After 9/11, following al Qaeda's loss of its central base in Afghanistan, Europe gained even greater importance. Cells operating in Europe play a crucial role in raising and laundering money, running Web sites, planning attacks, and procuring weapons and false documents for the global jihadi network. Militants recruit new adepts in the mosques, schools, prisons, gyms, and coffeehouses of every large European city. While some of the terrorists operating on the Continent are immigrants from Muslim countries, a growing number of them were born in Europe, a by-product of the inability of European countries to integrate their burgeoning native Muslim communities (currently estimated to number around 20 million) into civil society.

The foundations of this security disaster were laid in the 1980s, when many European countries either granted political asylum to, or simply allowed the entrance of, hundreds of Islamic fundamentalists, a large proportion of whom were veterans of the war in Afghanistan against the Soviets. Europeans naively thought that, once in Europe, these committed fighters would stop their violent activities. To the contrary, as soon as they settled on European soil, most Islamic radicals exploited the Continent's freedoms to continue their efforts to overthrow Middle Eastern governments.

And it was in Europe that Islamic radicals from different countries forged strategic alliances. Originally intending only to fight the secular regimes of their own countries, top members of various terrorist groups joined forces in Europe's radical mosques, where bin Laden's vision of a "global jihad" came to life. Moreover, the mosques and networks established by radicals who had been given asylum have been key in helping to create what can be considered Europe's biggest social and security problem: the radicalization of its growing Muslim population.

This book was conceived after lengthy discussions with US officials worried about the situation in Europe and its repercussions for the United States. Drawing on material collected over years and on numerous trips throughout Europe, it aims to show the extent of the penetration of Islamist terrorism on the Continent. From original government documents (intelligence reports, indictments, transcripts of intercepted conversations) gathered from various European countries and the United States we gain a portrait of an extremely determined and highly organized network that is now bent on attacking its hosts, as the events in Madrid and London have shown.

The first of the book's four parts analyzes who the terrorists operating in Europe are, categorizing them according to where and when their radicalization took place. It shows that while the seed of hate was planted by the "imported threat" (those radicals that obtained asylum in Europe), the most serious danger is now posed by the "homegrown" (European-born Muslims and converts) and the "home-brewed" (immigrants who radicalized in Europe). It tells the story of how their lives of deceit are spent hiding in plain sight in the Muslim neighborhoods of cities such as Rotterdam, Lyon, and Barcelona, exploiting Western freedoms while striving to destroy them. It concludes by examining the difficulties experienced by European authorities as they seek to shut down Islamist networks.

The remaining parts describe, by detailing failed and successful operations, the inner workings of three of the most important networks operating on the Continent. Part 2 examines the Algerians, a network that served as bin Laden's main franchise in Europe in the 1990s. Part 3 depicts how al Qaeda is conducting a massive recruitment campaign throughout Europe to fill its ranks in Iraq. Finally, part 4 considers the Moroccans, the network behind the Madrid bombings and the assassination of the Dutch filmmaker Theo van Gogh.

Ample anecdotal evidence throughout the book shows what, aside from their religious fanaticism, binds these three networks together: all took advantage of Europe's lax attitude toward radical Islam. Asylum is generously provided, irrespective of past crimes. Immigration laws are seldom enforced. Governments provide generous benefits. Self-styled clerics are free to preach their vicious and hate-filled ideology. In many cases recruitment for a foreign terrorist organization is not considered a crime. And authorities do not have the means or the legislative authority to aggressively pursue terrorist networks. Europe is the ideal place for a terrorist to operate.

Things cannot stay as they are. The attacks of 9/11, the bombings in Madrid and London, the assassination of Theo van Gogh, and the tensions with its Muslim population that, to varying degrees, every European country is facing are making Europeans rethink their policies. "The rules of the game are changing," said a determined Tony Blair in the wake of the London bombings. It will take a long time, it will not be easy, but we will change the rules. First, we must understand how we got to this point.

PART I

A DAGGER
IN THE SOFT HEART

CHAPTER 1

PROFILING AL QAEDA IN EUROPE

God loves us because our wish was to come to Europe and go back to our country with money, but God loves us because now Europe is in our hands because God showed us the way and we understood that we are mujahideen in His name. Now we are mujahideen muhajireen [immigrant fighters], this is the goal we always have to accomplish with honor.
—Ben Heni Lased, German-based Libyan militant (Milan, March 2001)

David Courtailler, Christian Ganczarski, Thomas Fischer. These aren't the types of names one expects to see when reviewing a list of those charged with participation in Islamic terrorism in Europe. Nevertheless, the three men, all Christian converts to Islam, are part of the extremely varied community formed by al Qaeda on the Old Continent. Members of the network include middle-aged Pakistani mothers, European-born teenagers, and experienced Arab mujahideen who have fought in Afghanistan against the Soviets. While many of them are born in Europe, of parents either Muslim or Christian, others come from places such as Uzbekistan, Venezuela, or the United States. Many are poor, but some of them represent the cream of the upper classes of their countries of origin.

Some live at the margins of society, bouncing from one odd job to another or dealing drugs, while others appear to represent success stories of Muslim integration into European societies.

What binds all of them together is their strict adherence to al Qaeda's message. Homegrown or new immigrants, rich or poor, experienced jihadis or fresh converts, they all believe they are living in the "land of the infidels," that a war is being waged by the West against Islam and that only a violent jihad will bring about their dream of making the word of Allah the only religion in the world. Their different profiles, elusive nature, and swelling numbers make the work of European intelligence agencies a true nightmare.

Given all the different types of individuals who have been involved with Islamic fundamentalism in Europe, to precisely catalog them is an extremely difficult task. But they can be divided into different groups and subgroups according to their relationship to the Continent and to fundamentalism. Indeed, it is very useful to categorize European Islamic terrorists by how and when they entered Europe and embraced radical Islam. This kind of analysis both reveals the astonishing diversity of the Islamist movement on the Continent and provides chilling insights into the enormous mistakes made by Europe over the past thirty years in its relationship with radical Islam.

THE HOMEGROWN THREAT

"You look at your average church priest, and what does he do? Who would he go to war with? No one. So how can Christianity claim to be a religion when its followers don't believe in spreading the word? The fact that Western politicians like Bush and Blair are scared of Islam means that it is a great religion."[1] These are the words of a twenty-year-old Englishman who converted to Islam, changed his name to Salim Yunus, and joined al Muhajiroun, a radical London-based group that openly seeks to turn Britain into an Islamic country following a Taliban-style interpretation of Islamic law.

Yunus is one of the hundreds of thousands of Europeans who have abandoned the Continent's traditional religions and chosen to convert to Islam. Researchers estimate that, in France alone, one hundred thousand Christians have turned to Allah's faith. Because most European countries do not poll their citizens' religious affiliation, exact numbers are difficult to obtain; but the phenomenon has been on the rise for the past twenty years and the events of 9/11 only increased the Europeans' interest in Islam.

But Yunus, unlike most European converts, has chosen to embrace a radical and militant form of Islam. He is one of the disturbing number of converts whose search for direction in their lives has led them to militancy. Over the last ten years, European security officials have noticed that dozens of European converts have joined terrorist groups. Some of them have played minor roles in terrorist cells, exploiting their appearance to go undetected by law enforcement agents. Others died fighting in places such as Chechnya and Afghanistan. A few have even reached the highest ranks of al Qaeda, masterminding attacks throughout the world.

Disillusioned with mainstream society, these disaffected young men are attracted by the sense of community that Islam offers. While those who adopt mainstream Islam find solace in its teachings, the result can be quite different when converts turn to fundamentalism. What often happens is that these men find in militant Islam an alternative to better-known antisocial outlets such as neo-Nazi or anarchist groups. Radical Islam enables them to channel their anger into a structured movement that is, in their view, fulfilling God's will. Militant Islamists, in turn, have been actively exploiting their longings in an all-out recruitment drive.

In an interview with the British newspaper the *Observer*, Paul Weller, a professor of interreligious studies at Derby University, tried to explain the phenomenon: "There is a clear rise in the politics of identity. Young white men who join Islam might be feeling out of place from modern life. So you find that when they join a religion like Islam they have an unbending view. Their views on jihad, for example, might be less compromising than the views of people who were born Muslims."[2]

The men make this choice for various reasons. Some convert because Islam fills their spiritual void, answering questions that they feel Christianity cannot answer. Alan, a twenty-four-year-old Englishman who changed his name to Mohammed Khan and joined the radical al Muhajiroun, told the *Observer* reporter of his sense of disillusionment with Christianity: "It didn't give me any sense of respect. No one goes to church any more. At least the mosques are full, so Islam obviously has something."[3]

It is that "something" that has attracted so many malleable Westerners to the jihadi cause. Almost all think that something is missing in their lives—they feel disconnected from their families, from their jobs, or from society as a whole. Many are attracted by Islam's strict rules. Young men with no direction find in radical Islam a guide for their daily life; they believe that by following precise orders they can avoid going astray. They are the living confirmation of the validity of Dean Kelley's theory that the more liberal and ecumenical denominations and religions are declining in membership and losing members to those that are more conservative and fundamentalist.[4] For disoriented young men in search of discipline, Christianity's liberal practices are not as attractive as Islam's stringent requirements.

Another reason often cited for the conversion of Westerners to radical Islam is the sense of belonging and community that some young men gain from their first contacts with the Muslim community. Philibert Lepy, the lawyer for the French terrorist David Courtailler, explained the reasons for his client's conversion: "He told me that the first time he went to a mosque, it was luminously lit and the atmosphere was convivial. That's the opposite of what you'll find in our Catholic churches these days." Lepy added his own analysis of the phenomenon: "The rise of Islam in France is a reflection of the spiritual emptiness of so much French life. When there's a vacuum, nature abhors a vacuum. Something else fills its place. We can't go on the way we've been living, cheerfully buying refrigerators."[5]

Lepy's client, David Courtailler, together with his brother Jerome, provides a case study of a convert turned al Qaeda member. Raised in a small town in the French Alps, David and Jerome spent their teens helping in their father's butcher shop. When the shop failed and their parents divorced, the Courtaillers began using drugs and drinking heavily. They moved to a poor neighborhood of London; there the brothers converted to radical Islam and attended the same mosques as a number of notorious terrorists, including the would-be 9/11 hijacker Zacarias Moussaoui. After months of indoctrination by radical preachers, the brothers accepted the offer of a local al Qaeda recruiter to attend training camps in Afghanistan; they also received $2,000 and a visa to Pakistan. Following months of instruction in Afghanistan, the brothers made their way back to Europe undisturbed, taking advantage of their French passports and Western looks.[6]

Once in Europe, the Courtaillers began plotting terrorist attacks, drawing on the network of contacts they had made in Afghanistan. Jerome became involved in a cell that was planning to bomb the US Embassy in Paris in September 2001. Investigators also believe he had a role in supplying the documents to the two al Qaeda suicide bombers who killed the Northern Alliance commander Ahmed Shah Massoud in northern Afghanistan two days before 9/11.[7] David, who met with some of the perpetrators of the Madrid train bombings and with other terrorists throughout Europe, was sentenced by a French court in May 2004 to four years in prison for "conspiring with criminals engaged in a terrorist enterprise,"[8] a formula often used by French authorities to charge individuals who have not carried out any attack but have consorted with other terrorists.

The Courtaillers are not the only Frenchmen who turned to radical Islam in their search for direction in their lives. Lionel Dumont grew up in a family with a solid Christian background and wanted to become a journalist. In 1992, surprising his family, he dropped out of college and joined the French army, volunteering for a peacekeeping mission in Somalia. His experience in the war-ravaged and poverty-stricken African country shocked Dumont, who was unable to fit back in once he returned to France.[9]

Dumont then converted to Islam, changing his name to Abu Hamza. He traveled to Bosnia to join the foreign mujahideen that were battling Serb and Croat forces in defense of local Muslims. After the end of the conflict in the Balkans, Dumont returned to France, where he became a member of the infamous Roubaix Gang, a group of North African Islamic fundamentalists that turned quiet areas of northern France into the Wild West, carrying out a string of armed robberies and engaging the police in bloody shootouts. In March 1996 the group placed a car laden with explosives near the site of the Group of Seven meeting in the French city of Lille. French police fortunately discovered the car and defused the bomb hours before the leaders of the world's major industrial democracies were supposed to meet.[10]

Dumont was just one of the many European and American converts who took up arms in Bosnia. Another Frenchman, Christophe Caze, fought in the Balkans and then headed the Roubaix Gang on his return to France.[11] A British convert, David Sinclair, was killed by Croat forces while fighting with the foreign mujahideen in Bosnia.[12] Dozens more reportedly trained in Afghanistan. Some, like the "American Taliban," John Walker Lindh, battled alongside Taliban forces. Thomas Fischer, a young German convert to Islam, was killed by Russian forces while fighting beside Chechen rebels in November 2003.[13]

Thomas Fischer represents another kind of convert to radical Islam: the shy, reclusive teenager who does not fit into Western society. Born Catholic in the rural German town of Blaubeuren, Fischer was a lonely child with a speech impediment and no friends. At fourteen he found his first friends at the local mosque. The imam and other worshipers taught the young Thomas about Islam, and, at age twenty, he converted. After wandering from mosque to mosque and establishing an Islamic cultural center that is today under close surveillance by German authorities, the impressionable Fischer traveled to Chechnya, where he found his death.[14]

Young men interested in Islam receive a warm welcome from European Muslim communities, as it is a duty for every Muslim to introduce the religion of the Prophet to all nonbelievers. But recruiters for terrorist organizations also put a particular effort into finding such seekers, as they know how valuable young converts can be for their cause. Thomas Fischer was a weak youth who could be easily turned into a fundamentalist. A French intelligence report published in 2004 makes clear that "the conversion to Islam of fragile individuals undoubtedly leads to the risk of diversion to terrorism."[15]

Converts are extremely valuable because they do not fit the traditional profile of the Islamic terrorists and therefore attract little attention.

Men with names like Dumont, Fischer, or Sinclair can cross borders, board planes, rent cars, and apply for visas without drawing the scrutiny given to Middle Eastern males. In May 2001, Italian authorities intercepted a conversation between Abdelhalim Remadna, a top al Qaeda recruiter based in Milan, and his contact in Saudi Arabia. It dealt in part with a young Italian man who was interested in going to Saudi Arabia. "He is a brother, but he is of Italian nationality," said Remadna to overcome doubts about the Italian's loyalty, "He is the most enthusiastic of them all and even has a doctorate in chemistry and is twenty-seven. . . . If you give him the order, he reaches you the same day." When Remadna mentioned that the man was married, his associate's reply revealed al Qaeda's interest in converts and their Western documents: "That is not a problem. This is the second phase. We don't care about that, we care about that paper."[16]

Though generally converts have been al Qaeda's foot soldiers, recent instances have come to light of Europeans climbing the ranks of the organization to reach positions that have traditionally been occupied by men of Middle Eastern descent. Particularly telling are the cases of Pierre Robert and Christian Ganczarski, two European converts who had direct contacts with the top al Qaeda leadership and guided attacks throughout the world.

Robert was a young Frenchman who enjoyed beer and bikes before his conversion to Islam. He spent time in al Qaeda camps in Afghanistan and then settled in the Moroccan city of Tangier, where he began recruiting and training local youngsters.[17] In the wake of the deadly May 2003 Casablanca bombings, Robert was arrested by Moroccan authorities, who accused him of planning similar suicide attacks in Tangier. In September 2003, Robert, dubbed the "blue-eyed emir" by the Moroccan media, was sentenced to life in prison.[18]

Ganczarski was a Polish-born German citizen who dropped out of high school and found a job as a metalworker. He was introduced to Islam by some Muslim coworkers; shortly after converting, he traveled to Saudi Arabia to take up a scholarship at the University of Medina, a school known for its fundamentalist teachings. Ganczarski then traveled to

Afghanistan, where he reportedly met with Osama bin Laden. After leaving, Ganczarski became a key player in al Qaeda's European network. He is currently being detained by French authorities, who accuse him of having plotted the deadly April 2002 suicide bombing directed against a synagogue in Djerba, Tunisia.[19]

While individuals such as Robert and Ganczarski are European security officials' nightmare, another type of convert, the lone wolves who lack ties to organized networks but adhere to al Qaeda's ideology and harbor a deep hatred for the West, could also represent a serious threat to Europe's security. Officials fear that new converts, driven by the desire to prove to other Muslims that their conversion is "true," might attempt on their own to carry out spectacular acts of terror. That they are unaffiliated with any known group makes them particularly dangerous, as individual agents are more difficult to track down and monitor.

Italian authorities suspected they were dealing with a lone wolf when they witnessed a series of amateurish bombing attacks after 9/11. Between the fall of 2001 and May 2002, several rudimentary explosive devices were found in a downtown station of the Milan subway system and in Agrigento, Sicily, near a famous Greek temple and in front of a church and a penitentiary in the modern city. The attacks had no victims, and present at all of them were bed sheets marked with writings praising "the Afghan brothers" and "the only true God, Allah."[20]

While these attacks were clearly in some way motivated by post–9/11 tensions, the crudeness of the devices and the manner in which responsibility was claimed led profilers to immediately rule out the hypothesis that an organized group was behind them. A lengthy investigation confirmed the authorities' theory. The perpetrator was Domenico Quaranta, a young Sicilian man who had converted to Islam in jail a few years earlier. Investigators collected evidence of Quaranta's ties to North African men in Sicily and near Milan, where he had lived for a few months, but they believe that he acted alone out of a desire to avenge the lives of Muslims killed in Afghanistan.

Quaranta is one of the many young Europeans who converted to radical Islam in jail. One Frenchman accused of being a member of a group of Algerian terrorists operating in the Paris area told investigators: "Islam made me abandon crime and gave me a healthy way of life."[21] Ruddy Terranova, a tall and imposing young man from the suburbs of Marseilles, never met his real father, his stepfather died in a street fight, and his mother committed suicide when he was young. At seventeen he joined the French Foreign Legion. While still in his twenties, between 1994 and 1997, Terranova collected an impressive number of convictions for attempted robbery, assault, and attempted murder.[22]

Like many other converts, Terranova discovered Islam in prison. French prisons, where the majority of the inmates are Muslims, have become fertile recruiting pool for radicals. There, many young Muslim criminals "rediscover" their roots and become more religious, and some native Frenchmen find a new sense of direction in Islam. Karim Bourti, an Algerian militant who was arrested with Terranova, testified to French judges about his associate: "He told me that he had been very turbulent, violent and that, once he embraced Islam, he became humble and serene."[23]

Though some inmates who convert in jail find a positive new direction, as they manage to get their lives on the right track, Terranova was among those who chose instead to follow a radical interpretation of Islam. Once released from jail, he married a Senegalese woman and attended a radical Quranic school in Sudan. In the process of learning combat skills, he received injuries to his arm and body. Terranova then returned to Europe and settled in London, where he attended the radical mosques in which preachers such as Abu Hamza and Abu Qatada spread their vicious interpretation of Islam. Once back in France, the "humble and serene" Terranova teamed up with a group of Algerian terrorists and reportedly attacked Abderrahmane Dahmane, the president of a French Muslim organization that the group deemed too moderate.[24]

But while some turn to Islam for guidance and direction, others convert as a form of protest against the system, the West, society as a whole. The French scholar Olivier Roy, who calls their acts "protest conversions," claims that young men "convert to stick it to their parents, to their principal. . . . They convert in the same way people in the 1970s went to Bolivia or Vietnam."[25] A few take their rebellion to the next level and engage in terrorist activities. According to another French scholar, Antoine Sfeir, Islamic terrorism for these young Europeans is "a kind of combat against the rich, powerful, by the poor men of the planet."[26]

An Italian intelligence report released in 2005 confirms that many native Europeans view their conversion as a form of political protest, as "Islamic ultrafundamentalism" offers them "an ideological frame into which they transferred their preceding militant anti-imperialist and anti-Semitic views."[27] According to the report, militants who convert to Islam come from both the right and the left, as both extremes are attracted to radical Islam's revolutionary message.

Those on the far left admire fundamentalist Islam's strong opposition to bastions of capitalism like the United States. Radical Islamic organizations are well aware of such affinities and try to use them to their advantage. Anjem Choudray, chairman of the radical al Muhajiroun movement, has spoken openly of appealing to radical leftists:

> Al-Muhajiroun has one goal. We would like to see the implementation of the sharia law in the UK. Under our rule this country would be known as the Islamic Republic of Great Britain. To do that, attracting young Asians is not enough. So we are making a conscious effort to recruit large numbers of non-Muslims. Whites, Chinese, Japanese and Indians in this country are all bored with the capitalist system. It's a bankrupt ideal. We have found that young non-Muslims, like our Asian followers, want something new. You can tell that from the anti-globalisation movement. So we're offering them something pure: a religious mission, the values of sharia law and jihad.[28]

On the opposite side of the political spectrum, radical right-wingers are also fascinated with fundamentalist Islam's opposition to capitalism, its martial discipline, and its profound hatred of Jews. Several members of European fascist and Nazi organizations expressed their support for the 9/11 attacks, and there have been reports of contacts between their groups and radical Islamic organizations. Though their numbers are still small, some of these extremists have converted to Islam and embraced the religion's most vicious interpretation.

One of them is Steven Smyrek, a German neo-Nazi who converted to Islam, trained in an al Qaeda camp in Afghanistan, and reportedly traveled to Israel with the intention of carrying out a suicide attack.[29] Israeli security services arrested him in 1997 and released him in 2004, after he signed a document renouncing violence. Back in Europe, Smyrek was interviewed by a documentary filmmaker: "It's an honor to die for Islam and for Allah," he said. "When the order comes you have to carry it out and there's no time to ask if there is a God or not, or to think what will happen after you're dead, without feeling you simply have to lay down your life as Allah decreed."[30]

A significant subgroup of those who turned to radical Islam are children born into a mixed marriage—one parent a native of a Muslim country, the other a European. Such children often struggle to find their identity and while some ultimately find their diverse background enriching, others remain conflicted. In some cases, during their struggles to bridge the two cultures, they fall under the influence of extremists who draw them to radical Islam.

One well-known example is Said Bahaji, the son of a Moroccan immigrant and a German mother who was the only German citizen in the infamous Hamburg cell of the 9/11 plot. Bahaji spent his childhood and teens traveling between Morocco and Germany. Bahaji's mother described her son's uneasiness with both cultures: "In the eyes of the Moroccans he was obviously a foreigner, just as he'd been in Germany."[31] Bahaji settled in Germany to study electrical engineering at the Technical University of Hamburg-Harburg. "What a shame Hamburg students are so boring. They can't open their mouths unless they're drunk," wrote a lonely Bahaji on his home page after a few months of school.[32] At the university, Bahaji met Mohammed Atta and others who attended the radical al Quds mosque, the center of Hamburg's Islamist scene. Bahaji, whom the 9/11 Commission described as "an insecure follower with no personality and with limited knowledge of Islam," easily bought into the radical rhetoric of Atta and the other members of the Hamburg cell.[33] Within a few months, he had moved in with Atta and Ramzi Binalshibh, two of the masterminds of 9/11, and he allegedly helped them prepare for the attacks. After providing logistical support for months, and knowing that the attacks were imminent, Bahaji left Hamburg for Pakistan just a few days before September 11 in order to escape arrest.[34]

Children of mixed marriages, like converts, often know little about Islam and its teachings. Cunning preachers can therefore easily persuade them to accept a distorted interpretation of the religion, one in which a violent jihad against all non-Muslims is presented as a direct command from Allah. "The problem is that the less you know about Islam when you come into it, the easier it is for someone to present you with the 'forgotten obligation' of jihad," explains Steven Simon, a former top US counter-terrorism official.[35]

But Muslims born in the West can be equally vulnerable. Indeed, young European Muslims are the fundamentalists' easiest prey. Many of these teenagers or young men are confused by the two worlds they have to straddle. At home, they find a conservative and pious environment, as most of the families that have moved to Europe as workers over the past four decades have emigrated from rural and backward areas of North Africa or Southeast Asia. The larger European society in which they find themselves is secular, and often crassly sexualized. Their economic possibilities are scant, as unemployment rates for young Muslims throughout Europe are two to five times those of native Europeans. Most live in grimy immigrant neighborhoods where crime is rampant and violence is everywhere.

Thus dangerously high percentages of second- and third-generation Muslim immigrants live at the margins of European societies, trapped between unemployment and petty crime. Although they hold French, Dutch, or British passports, they have no attachment to their country, where they feel like foreigners. Whether this troubling situation is rooted in Europe's reluctance to fully accept newcomers or in some Muslims' inflexibility when faced with new circumstances is hard to say. Nevertheless, given the burgeoning numbers of Muslims now being born and still immigrating to Europe, the social repercussions of this lack of integration are potentially explosive.

"After things didn't work out with work, I decided to devote myself to the Koran," explained a militant interviewed by the German magazine *Der Spiegel*.[36] As they see no economic future for themselves and search for acceptance and identity, many young European Muslims turn to their ancestral religion. Some of them take comfort in the peaceful teachings of their rediscovered faith, but others adopt the most belligerent interpretation of Islam and embark in a holy war against their own country.

Particularly telling is the story of Khaled Kelkal. Born in Algeria in 1971, at age two Kelkal came to France with his family, as part of a wave of North Africans looking for menial jobs in the industries based in the country's urban areas.[37] The Kelkals settled in a depressing slum at the doors of Lyon, France's second-largest city. Vaulx-en-Velin was the quintessential French immigrant suburb: ugly, poor, and ridden with violence —and Kelkal grew up as its typical product.

When he was nineteen, he told German sociologist Dietmar Loch that he "didn't stay the course" in high school. "I had the ability to succeed, but I could not fit in because I told myself it would be impossible to become totally integrated. As for them, they had never seen an Arab in their class. I started to skip lessons. That is where the trouble started."[38] Loch, who in 1992 interviewed young French Muslims for a study on immigration, could not have imagined that, three years later, one of his subjects would become France's public enemy number one.

After leaving school, Kelkal became involved with petty crime. His largely Muslim neighborhood, as he described it to Loch, was dominated by anarchy, not the state's law: "Here 70 percent of people are into stealing because their parents cannot afford to buy them things when there are six children. When you steal, you feel free. It's a game, which either you win or lose."[39] In the mid-1990s, almost half of Vaulx-en-Velin was under twenty-four years old, vividly exemplifying the demographic revolution still sweeping Europe; 24 percent of those between eighteen and twenty-four were unemployed.[40]

Kelkal's conduct soon landed him in prison. And, like many other young European Muslims, it was in prison that Kelkal changed his life, turning to radical Islam. Embracing the religion gave Kelkal, who had always felt out of place in French society, a sense of belonging to a big family, a group of trusted brothers. He told Loch: "I'm neither Arab nor French. I'm Muslim. . . . When I walk into a mosque, I'm at ease. They shake your hand, they treat you like an old friend. No suspicion, no prejudices. . . . When I see another Muslim in the street, he smiles, and we stop and talk. We recognize each other as brothers, even if we never met before."[41]

Kelkal, once released from jail, combined his newfound faith with his past as a hoodlum, recruiting a few of his childhood friends and creating a full-fledged terrorist cell. According to French authorities, in the spring of 1995 Kelkal met with Boualem Bensaid,[42] a representative of the Algerian Armed Islamic Group (GIA), a terrorist organization then battling the Algerian government in a bloody civil war. He was on a mission to recruit operatives to carry out attacks against France, as the GIA wanted to punish the French government for its support of the Algerian regime. Bensaid could not have found better candidates than Kelkal and his crew.

In the summer of 1995, the streets of France were bloodied by an unprecedented string of attacks. At the end of July, a bomb exploded in a Paris metro station, killing seven people. In the following weeks, other devices either blew up or were defused by French bomb experts throughout the country.[43] On August 26, French investigators found Kelkal's fingerprints on an unexploded device that had been placed along the tracks of the TGV (Train a Grande Vitesse), the high-speed train that is the pride of France.[44] The frantic manhunt that followed ended on September 29, when, before the cameras of French national television, French gendarmes killed Kelkal after a spectacular gunfight.[45] The images shocked the French public, as policemen were heard shouting to each other, "Finish him, finish him!" and were shown kicking Kelkal's body to make sure he was dead.[46]

Kelkal's dramatic killing triggered riots in Vaulx-en-Velin, where hundreds of cars and trash cans were burned by groups of angry French Muslims.[47] The riots quickly spread to the immigrant suburbs of other French cities, including Mulhouse, Strasbourg, and Paris.[48] Elements of the country's First Infantry Division had to be brought in to quell the protests.[49] Such riots, which were not new to France, demonstrate the social and racial tensions afflicting the country. In his interview with

Loch, Kelkal himself had commented on the race riots that erupted in Vaulx-en-Velin in 1990: "This is just the beginning. It's going to heat up, and then it will be too late."[50]

Clearly, Kelkal had become some kind of folk hero for the disillusioned young Muslims of the suburbs. Some young Muslim men were reportedly aware of Kelkal's activities but did not report them to the police.[51] Their sense of anger toward French society made them sympathize with a man who was, in his brutal way, fighting the system. According to a French intelligence report, radical Islam represents for some French Muslims "a vehicle of protest against . . . problems of access to employment and housing, discrimination of various sorts, the very negative image of Islam in public opinion."[52]

Jean Louis Bruguière, a senior French counterterrorism judge, explains how easily young French-born Muslims are lured to radical Islam: "They have no job. They have no information, no hope for the future. One day they meet a guy who is interesting, who has good knowledge of Islam. They tell him: 'I can give you something, a task for you, for the future.' They explain Islam. They bring a global conception of their life, teach them a skill and they say: 'We have a goal for you in the future.' They say, 'you can continue to deceive, continue to forge papers, but now you do it as a sign of the measure of God, for Allah.'"[53]

European security officials are painfully aware that the suburbs of the Continent's big cities are the breeding grounds for thousands of jihad candidates. And while this radicalization often takes place in mosques and Islamic centers, officials recognize that European prisons are another main place of recruitment. An official at the French Ministry of Interiors worries, "Prison is a good indoctrination center for the Islamic radicals, much better than the outside. There are about 300 Islamic radicals in prisons in Paris, and they spend a lot of time converting the criminals to Islam."[54]

Though no official statistics are provided by the government, most reports put Muslims at between 50 and 70 percent of France's prison population. These thousands of angry and alienated young men constitute the ideal raw material for creating terrorists. Khaled Kelkal spoke for many European Muslims when he described the process to Loch: "After prison

I realized I was a 100 percent loser but I told myself I didn't regret it. I know that in prison I learned a lot of things. I even learned my own language. I shared a cell with a Muslim. It was there that I learned Arabic and my religion, Islam. I learned a great opening of the mind by discovering Islam. The freedom to be yourself, the freedom to be with a good friend, getting on well, a group, a tight-knit group. That was the most important thing."[55]

France, with its six million Muslims and its astonishingly high percentage of Muslim inmates, is the country that is most intently monitoring its penitentiary system, but its neighbors have similar problems. In Spain, where one in ten inmates is of Moroccan or Algerian descent, Islamic radicals have been actively recruiting in jail for the past ten years. In October 2004, Spanish authorities dismantled a cell that was planning a bloody sequel to the March 11 Madrid bombings—an attack on the Audiencia Nacional, Spain's national criminal court. Most of the men, who called themselves the Martyrs of Morocco, had been recruited in jail, where they were being detained for credit card fraud and other common crimes.[56]

Baltasar Garzon, the Spanish judge conducting the investigation, explains how Muslim inmates are lured into fundamentalist views: "They are initially exposed to the extremist vision of Islam as a means of atonement for their previous sins."[57] Recruiters play on their disillusionment and offer radical Islam to them as a means of purification, a way to wash away their earlier misdeeds in the world of the "infidels." Young men who have grown up in Muslim families with only a very superficial knowledge of Islam are taught the basics about the religion and then, as soon as they are seen to be responsive, its extremist interpretation.

Recruiters also prey on the bitterness that young Muslim prisoners often feel about life in a Western country. Non-Muslims are portrayed as enemies; Europeans as racists who hate Islam. Radicals know that their vitriolic rhetoric will be welcome in prisons, and, reportedly, some recruiters even deliberately try to get arrested to gain access to this matchless pool of potential recruits.[58] Once the re-Islamization behind bars is complete, the new recruit is given contacts of other radicals in the outside world. The men are ready to complete their "purification" by working for the cause and, in some cases, by sacrificing their life for it. Such was the intention of Richard Reid, the Englishman who converted to radical Islam in jail and then attempted to blow up a jet flying from Paris to Miami by igniting the explosives hidden in his tennis shoes.

Critics of European integration policies use stories like those of Kelkal and hundreds of other radicals from the immigrant neighborhoods of cities from Madrid to Copenhagen to link Islamic fundamentalism and terrorism to poverty and segregation. Intelligent young men, feeling unjustly excluded from society and often victimized by racism, are radicalized only because they see no future. Many claim that offering these youths a genuine possibility of getting out of their slums and gaining economic success would have kept them from taking the path of fundamentalism. Though such analysts point to real problems experienced by immigrants in Europe, their equation of militancy with poverty is simplistic and, indeed, disproved by the evidence. Many European-born Muslim extremists that have been involved with terrorism came from solid families, were financially stable, and were completely immersed in the mainstream of European society. At least on the surface, they seemed to epitomize full integration.

Ahmed Omar Saeed Sheikh, for example, the British-born son of a wealthy Pakistani clothes merchant, grew up in the affluent London suburb of Wanstead.[59] Sheikh attended the Forest School in East London, a prestigious private institution where he was well liked by the other mostly white and native English pupils. A spokesman at Forest described him as a model student, "a good all-round, solid and very supportive pupil."[60] After three years in Pakistan, where he attended Aitchison College, a school favored by the Pakistani elite, Sheikh returned to Forest. His peers admired him for his good humor and strength—he had become a member of the British arm-wrestling squad, and he was always ready to show off against other students.[61]

In October 1992, after graduating from Forest with excellent grades, Sheikh began studying statistics at the London School of Economics, one of Europe's top universities.[62] But after a year he left school and traveled to Bosnia, where war was raging among Croats, Serbs, and Bosnian Muslims. It was the beginning of Sheikh's adventurous life as a world-famous Islamic terrorist. Sheikh subsequently traveled to Kashmir, where he allegedly fought alongside Muslim rebels against the Indian Army.[63] In 1994 Indian police arrested him for his crucial role in the kidnapping of several British and American tourists; his reassuring British accent had tricked them into trusting him. In 1999 he was one of the three men freed from Indian prisons in exchange for the release of the hostages on an Indian Airlines flight that had been hijacked by terrorists.[64] Sheikh's name resurfaced in 2002, when he was sentenced to death by a Pakistani court for his involvement in the gruesome beheading of *Wall Street Journal* reporter Daniel Pearl.[65] The son of a prosperous tradesman, the recipient of an excellent and expensive education, Sheikh had become, for no apparent reason, one of the world's best-known terrorists.

And Omar Sheikh is hardly unique. In March 2004, Scotland Yard broke up a cell of nine men who were allegedly plotting attacks inside England. Police discovered that the men were holding nearly 500 kilograms of ammonium nitrate fertilizer in a self-storage facility in West London.[66] Just half that amount had been enough to kill two hundred Western tourists in the October 2002 bombing of a Bali night club.[67] The British public was shocked to learn that all the men were British-born young Muslims of Pakistani descent. Three in the cell were teenagers, all of whom were described as coming from respectable families and as living contentedly in the middle-class suburbs of Crawley.[68] One of them, Omar Khyam, was a computer student who had captained the Sussex Under-18 cricket team and was seen as likely to play for the English national team.[69] Others were said to be regular students and big Manchester United fans. But in 2000, the eighteen-year-old Omar, after telling his parents he was going to France for study, traveled instead to Pakistan and then Afghanistan, the primary destination for terrorist wannabes.[70] From that time on, the group of young Muslims kept in contact with militants in Pakistan and, while enjoying fish and chips, cricket, and cheering for their soccer heroes, made plans to strike their native country.

Such cases of European-born Muslims who choose to embrace radical Islam despite their enviable success at economic and social integration into the larger society show that terrorism cannot be attributed to poverty and segregation alone. To be sure, Europe must change how it deals with the masses of immigrants that it has attracted over the past thirty years, but it is not solely responsible for the rise of Islamist terrorism on its soil: terrorism is the by-product of a vicious ideology that can appeal to rich and poor alike. Nevertheless, Europe needs to find solutions rapidly, as the rise in the number of its sons who are choosing to espouse radical Islam could be fatal to its security and its social fabric.

THE HOME-BREWED THREAT

"When I arrived in Germany in 1992, I was a man who loved the joys of life and was very happy . . . I had no relationship to religion and lived in the European style: alcohol, women and hashish."[71] So an Algerian man convicted of terrorism in Germany described his life before his conversion to radical Islam. After some years of indulgence in "the European style," he was shocked into a transformation when a fellow Algerian showed him images of civilians killed by the Algerian army: "I was very shaken and decided to change my life, which had previously been devoted on my own well-being, to focus on my own country. . . . I began praying and seeking the truth."[72] A few months later, the man left Europe, first attending a Taliban-run religious school and then an al Qaeda training camp in Afghanistan; he returned to the Continent to plan an attack on French territory.

As challenging to Europe's security as the sizable proportion of its young native Muslim population that is turning to militant Islam are the discontented among its immigrant population. Each year, Europe receives hundreds of thousands of young Muslim men seeking their fortunes in the West. Most of them simply experience the typical life of an immigrant, with its struggles, problems, and its occasional successes. But many of them lose their way, unable to adapt to a new culture or to win financial security.

The story of Shadi Abdallah, a Jordanian who moved to Germany as a teenager, provides a telling example. He explained to German authorities: "My family is very poor. I wanted to come to Germany to start a new life. Another reason was the opportunity to live a freer life in Germany. This involves my sexual tendencies toward men. I had expected problems and disadvantages in relation to this in Jordan. So I traveled with Abu Ali to Germany."[73] But Germany was not the paradise Abdallah was expecting: "My life became very empty. I was entangled in drugs and spent all my money. For this reason I accepted the offer of food from a mosque. It was cheap and I could pay at the end of the month. The condition was that I would have to engage myself in Islam."[74] In the mosque, the young and confused Abdallah met radicals who began teaching him their interpretation of Islam. Within months he was in Saudi Arabia, where he accepted the offer of an al Qaeda recruiter to go to Afghanistan.

By his own account, in Afghanistan Abdallah met with Abu Musab al Zarqawi and even briefly served as a bodyguard for Osama bin Laden.[75] Once back in Germany, Abdallah became part of a cell of Jordanians and Palestinians who, at al Zarqawi's direction, were planning to attack Jewish and Israeli targets inside Germany.[76] The stories of other members of the cell were similar. The leader of the group, a Palestinian named Ashraf al Dagma, had spent years in Berlin selling cocaine and heroin near the city's zoo. Arrested and jailed, he rediscovered his Islamic roots: "I have decided to stop what I have been doing up to now," al Dagma explained to German authorities.[77]

Why should young Muslim men come to embrace views in the Christian and secular West for which they have shown little interest or sympathy while living in their home countries? In many cases, radical Islam provides disillusioned individuals with guidance, strict rules that take them away from their lives of drugs and crime. It offers them a much-needed sense of finally being part of something meaningful, comforting them with the camaraderie among religious brothers. But it would be a mistake to think that only poor and marginalized Muslim immigrants convert to Islamism while in Europe and to attribute the troubling phenomenon to Europe's failure to economically integrate its large foreign population. Just like European-born Muslims, immigrants from every level of society have turned to fundamentalism.

In fact, European sociologists who study immigration and integration were shocked, in the wake of the attacks of 9/11, to learn that some of the perpetrators were young Muslim students from the upper classes of their countries of origin who had discovered radical Islam while in Germany. These ambitious and gifted Middle Eastern students had come to the West to further their educations and careers. Most of them came from stable families with wealthy parents who paid for their expenses. Religion was not part of their life in their home countries, and, initially, they conducted themselves much like Westerners. On their way to success, something happened.

Perhaps the most striking transformation was displayed by Ziad Jarrah, the only son of a wealthy Lebanese family that owned a condominium in Beirut and a second house in the countryside.[78] His parents were secularized Sunni Muslims, and they sent him to a private Christian school.[79] Reportedly, Jarrah lived the life of a playboy, cruising up and down Beirut's trendy seafront in his parents' Mercedes looking for girls. Jarrah knew all the hip clubs in town and nobody remembers seeing him in the mosque. Pictures of his days in Lebanon show a handsome young man sporting sunglasses and fancy shirts. In 1996, after graduating from high school (with difficulty), Jarrah traveled to the small German city of Greifswald, where his cousin was enrolled in college. There the partying continued. "Once we drank so much beer we couldn't ride straight on a bike," Jarrah's cousin recalled.[80] Relying on the generous allowance his parents were sending him from Lebanon, the carefree Jarrah smoked marijuana and dated a university student.

But, in Greifswald, Jarrah also met Abulrahman Makhadi, an encounter that changed his life. Makhadi, a Yemeni in his forties who had been trying to earn a degree in dentistry in Greifswald for more than ten years, was the imam of the local mosque, which served as a meeting point for the small community of Muslim students attending the university.[81] Makhadi aided Muslim students as they settled in Greifswald, finding them an apartment or helping them to obtain a residency permit. But Makhadi was also a religious fundamentalist, monitored by authorities because of his fiery sermons and his contacts with known terrorists operating in Germany.[82] After a few months under Makhadi's influence, Jarrah was changing his view of the world and of his life; by the end of 1996, he was a different man. Though he continued to date his girlfriend, Jarrah reportedly began reading religious books and radical Islamist publications. A friend of his girlfriend's told investigators that Jarrah had said that he was "dissatisfied with his life up to till now" and "didn't want to leave Earth in a natural way."[83] In the spring of 1997, Jarrah moved to Hamburg, where he enrolled at the University of Applied Sciences. It was in Hamburg that Jarrah's transformation became complete, as he began to befriend a group of Moroccan students that worshiped at the city's radical al Quds mosque.[84] At the mosque, Jarrah met other extremists—among them, Mohammed Atta and Marwan al Shehhi. Three years later, Jarrah, Atta, and al Shehhi would pilot three of the four planes hijacked on September 11.

The reasons that young immigrants turn to fundamentalist Islam while in Europe are many. In most cases, radical mosques played a key role in their conversion. Some, like Shadi Abdallah, turned to the mosque simply because it offered the cheapest meals. Once there, they become fascinated with radical sermons and caught up in terrorist activities. Others begin going to the mosque out of homesickness. Even secular Muslims living in European cities are drawn to the mosque as it is often the only place where they can speak their native language and eat food that reminds them of home. Many consider it more a social center than a place of worship. Nevertheless, after hearing the fiery words of local radicals, some change. And recruiters seek out young Muslims wherever they congregate—coffeehouses, restaurants, falafel shops, gyms, soccer fields—to persuade them to go to the mosque. Khaled Kalkel remembered: "The only meeting place we heard about was the mosque. They came from the mosque into our neighborhood and said: 'Instead of staying here, come to the mosque. It will only be good for you.'"[85] Attending the mosque is often the first step in the radicalization process.

In these mosques, which may be little more than garages or basements turned into places of worship, imams preach about the evils of the West and the need for the faithful to defend fellow Muslims who are under attack throughout the world. Playing on the sympathy that most Muslims have for the plight of Palestinians, Chechens, or, most recently, Iraqis, skilled preachers convince young worshipers that the West is at war against Islam and that Muslims have a sacred duty to defend it. Itinerant imams, self-proclaimed religious authorities who come from the most remote and backwards areas of Egypt, Morocco, or Pakistan, tour from mosque to mosque like rock stars and spread their message of hate across the Continent. Local imams often promote an even more virulent strain of Islam.

Italian authorities received a stunning firsthand account of the metamorphosis undergone by young Muslim immigrants once they fall under the spell of radical imams from X, a former low-level al Qaeda operative who decided to cooperate with authorities. "When I first moved to Italy, I lived in an apartment in Buccinasco with other North African immigrants," he said. His roommates' strange behavior—they ordered him to stay inside, told him to keep the windows closed, and regularly woke up late and left the apartment dressed very elegantly—led X to believe that they were probably small-scale drug dealers and therefore X moved out.[86] But when, after a few months, X revisited his former roommates, he was shocked:

> We thought we went to the wrong apartment. There were no more pictures, photos, Western movies, tapes with music, but only prayer rugs, the Quran, books for the interpretation of the Quran, and other books bought at the mosque. And the clothes were only white. Sami, with a long beard, serious, told us that he had to go to the other room for the Asr prayer and told us that, from that moment on, nobody could smoke in the apartment, nobody could smoke or drink alcohol and then visit the apartment, and that when we were with him we could not greet any Italian. Then he took a tape shot in Afghanistan and told us about these people that had left everything behind and had reached this country to pursue the goal that we should all have: to die as martyrs and fight these pigs.[87]

A few months later, X began his own journey into Islamic fundamentalism. He started attending Friday worships at the mosque of the infamous Islamic Cultural Institute in Milan, where he found the fiery sermons of the local imam, Abu Imad, "very convincing." And there, X also became involved with a terrorist cell. To test his loyalty, the leaders of the cell assigned him simple tasks, but he was ready for more. "For a short time," he confessed to Italian authorities, "about two months, I would have accepted to be a kamikaze. I was not well psychologically, I wanted to die. . . . I was convinced that the only way to go to Paradise without being questioned was martyrdom. It was the opportunity to be genuinely happy."[88]

X was arrested before he could carry out any attack, but he is just one of the many weak, disillusioned, and lost Muslim immigrants who have found their identity in radical Islam. According to a Dutch intelligence report released in 2002, new adherents to fundamentalism find in it "a sense of self-respect, involvement, brotherhood and identity. They feel that they are involved in a fight between good and bad, which guides them into a certain direction and provides answers to existential questions they are dealing with."[89] Europeans are astonished to learn of these secular Muslim immigrants who become radicalized while living on the Continent. Their growing numbers present an enormous potential security threat. Immediate steps are possible and necessary. European countries must crack down on radical preachers, shut down fundamentalist mosques, and promote more moderate interpretations of Islam. But the task is monumental. Laws that protect free speech and religious rights complicate the authorities' work. And when mosques are closed or imams deported, the extremists go underground, meeting in basements and listening to radical sermons circulated on tape. One European extremist commented sarcastically, "If the Beatles cannot go on any tours any more, then their records can go on trips."[90] Europe needs to stop both the Beatles and their tapes.

THE IMPORTED THREAT

"I live here but I still think America and Britain are enemies of the Afghanistan people and Muslim people." With these words, published by the *Telegraph* in February 2003, Wali Khan Ahmadzai expressed his gratitude to Great Britain for granting him political asylum. But the twenty-three-year-old Afghan was no ordinary refugee: he was a member of the

Taliban who had admitted to battling American and British forces in Afghanistan before fleeing in a convoy paid for by bin Laden. Ahmadzai was only one of the beneficiaries of the generous British asylum system. In January 2002, while British forces were still engaged with Taliban and al Qaeda remnants on the ground in Afghanistan, British immigration authorities shocked the public by announcing that political asylum had been granted to some Taliban fighters. Ahmadzai openly told his story: "When I came to Britain 13 months ago I didn't have any documentation at all to show who I was. I told them the truth, that I fought for the Taliban and was scared of what the new government would do to me. The Home Office gave me exceptional leave to remain here for four years." Ahmadzai also admitted knowing of at least one former comrade who had been granted asylum in the United Kingdom and was "potentially dangerous."[91]

Paradoxical as it might look, Wali Khan Ahmadzai's was not an isolated case; over the past forty years, European countries have knowingly and voluntarily hosted hundreds of Islamic fundamentalists. Acting on humanitarian motives, for decades countries such as Britain, Sweden, Holland, and Germany have made it their official policy to welcome political refugees from all over the world. But, blinded by their laudable intentions of protecting all individuals suffering political persecutions, most European countries rarely distinguished between democracy-supporting opponents of autocratic regimes and Islamic fundamentalists who had bloodied their hands in their home countries with heinous terrorist acts. As a consequence, some of the world's most radical Islamists with a legitimate fear of prosecutions in the Middle East found a new, convenient base of operation in Europe.

The influx began in the 1950s, when the regimes in Egypt and Syria began a crackdown on members of the Muslim Brotherhood, an international Islamist movement seeking to replace existing Middle Eastern governments with an Islamic theocracy. Hundreds of young members of the Muslim Brotherhood fled the Middle East and took refuge in Europe. The exodus reached its peak between the end of the 1980s and the first years of the 1990s, as the war in Afghanistan ended. Thousands of Arab mujahideen who had fought against the Soviets in Afghanistan realized they could not return to their home countries, where they were generally perceived as a threat to political stability and would have been killed or imprisoned. Many of them were allowed to settle in Europe, as European governments viewed them simply as freedom fighters suffering unjust persecution by dictatorial regimes.

What the European governments failed to understand was that they were inviting a monster into their own backyard. Many thought that once in peaceful, secular Europe, these committed Islamic fundamentalists would stop their violent activities and live a quiet life. Europeans also naively believed that by giving the mujahideen asylum, they would spare themselves the radicals' murderous wrath. These assumptions were completely false. Most of the relocated Islamic radicals continued their efforts to fight Middle Eastern regimes, by raising money, supplying weapons and false documents, and forging new alliances with Islamic terrorist groups already operating in Europe. And within a few years, as bin Laden's message of "global jihad" took hold, they turned on their hosts.

Less than a month after 9/11, Egyptian president Hosni Mubarak assailed the West's naive policies: "Political asylum should be granted to a person who faces political injustice. But to give political asylum to a killer, or leave him alone and say 'human rights.' What human rights? Human rights should be for the weak and innocent who is killed together with members of his family. But a criminal killer? What human rights? This means that terrorism is encouraged and then a terrorist operation is committed against these countries (which grant killers asylum). This happened in England and in America also."[92] Mubarak has good reasons to be angry with European governments, which Egypt has long been fighting in order to obtain the extraditions of dozens of Egyptian Islamic fundamentalists who have been given political asylum.

Among the most intense of these diplomatic battles has been that waged over the granting of political asylum to several high-ranking members of one of Egypt's most radical and violent terrorist organizations. In the early 1990s, while the Gamaa Islamiya was carrying out a brutal terrorist campaign against the Egyptian regime and targeting Western tourists vacationing in the country, many of the group's leaders fled to

Europe, where they obtained political asylum in various countries. There they continued their operations undisturbed, planning new attacks in Europe as well as Egypt.

In 1993 Denmark granted political asylum to Abu Talal al Qassimi, the Gamaa's spokesman. After being repeatedly imprisoned in Egypt for his involvement in the 1981 assassination of President Anwar Sadat and his role as the Gamaa's official representative in the city of Minya, al Qassimi traveled to Afghanistan in the mid-1980s to join the jihad against the Soviets.[93] While directly participating in military activities, al Qassimi also teamed up with an Egyptian senior aide to Osama bin Laden and began publishing the Gamaa's official magazine, *Al Murabitun*. As the war against the Soviets ended and civil war engulfed Afghanistan, al Qassimi decided to leave the country. Realizing that he undoubtedly would have been imprisoned on his return to Egypt, al Qassimi decided to go to Europe and seek political asylum, which was generously granted by Danish authorities.[94]

Once in Denmark, al Qassimi intensified his efforts to spread the Gamaa's propaganda. Along with other Gamaa operatives who had found refuge there, he continued to publish *Al Murabitun*. Ayman al Zawahiri, currently al Qaeda's number-two man, reportedly also became involved with the publication while living in Copenhagen in the mid-1990s.[95] Though Danish authorities admit that al Zawahiri spent time in Copenhagen, they do not confirm reports that in 1991 Denmark offered asylum to one of the world's most-wanted terrorists.[96]

Al Qassimi did not limit his activities to Denmark but kept in close contact with other Egyptian radicals spread throughout Europe. As a political refugee, he was free to travel and continue his propaganda and fund-raising efforts for the Gamaa throughout Europe. For example, al Qassimi frequently visited Milan's Islamic Cultural Institute, another Gamaa bastion in Europe. In 2001 the Lebanese journalist Camille Eid managed to purchase a tape containing a 1994 speech that he gave at its mosque. His words ominously signal the willingness of al Qassimi, like the other radicals welcomed in Europe, to attack whoever did not share his radical interpretation of Islam, wherever they were: "Islam is the religion of strength and the Muslim has the duty to be a terrorist, in the sense that he has to terrorize the enemies of Allah to represent peace and security to the faithful. Terrorism against the enemies of God is a duty in our religion. Whoever leaves jihad lives in humiliation."[97]

Milan was an unsurprising venue for al Qassimi's speech as it was home to another charismatic leader of the Gamaa, Anwar Shabaan. Once he was given asylum by the Italian authorities, Shabaan immediately became imam at Milan's Islamic Cultural Institute, which he began using as a launching pad for the operations of mujahideen in the Balkans. As the conflict began in 1991, hundreds of Arab volunteers, mostly veterans of the Afghan war, answered the call to arms and traveled to Bosnia. Shabaan, a charismatic leader and a skilled orator, became the leader of the Foreign Mujahideen Battalion fighting against the "infidel" Croatian and Serbian troops. Milan, Copenhagen, and Vienna, where another senior Gamaa leader had taken over a large mosque, became the main centers for the Gamaa Islamiya in Europe and played a crucial role in finding recruits for the war in Bosnia.

The network established by Gamaa leaders who had found refuge in Europe became so sophisticated that the Egyptian government lodged formal complaints with authorities in Italy, Denmark, and Austria. Egyptian militants in Europe were raising significant amounts of money for their "brothers" operating inside Egypt, and even the 1995 attempt to assassinate Hosni Mubarak in Ethiopia was partially conceived on the Continent. Documents seized by Italian police during a 1995 raid of Milan's Islamic Cultural Institute indicate that in 1993 the Gamaa Islamiya's European cohorts met in Copenhagen and created the "Shura Council of the European Union," a pan-European entity whose purpose, according to official transcripts of the meeting translated by Italian authorities, was to deliberate on such issues as "how to support groups in North Africa," "how to use humanitarian organizations and charities for the cause of the Gamaa," and, more interestingly, "how to cut people's throats."[98]

For years the Egyptians warned European governments that the individuals who had been given asylum were extremely dangerous. Cairo repeatedly suggested that regimes in the Middle East were not the radicals' only targets and that eventually they would turn against their hosts. Another document found in Milan's Islamic Cultural Institute by Italian authorities, titled "Charter of Islamic Labor," lends support to that warning:

> We as Muslims have been given the task of realizing the supremacy of the law of God on earth and of not allowing any group on earth to rule without the law of God. We fight whoever refuses obedience. The goal of the fight for Islam is that there is no temptation and religion is only that of God.
>
> The fight is imposed on us to remove the apostate rulers from the land of Islam, to fight those who support them and their laws, to impose the caliphate, to avenge Palestine, Spain, the Balkans, the Islamic republics in Russia, and to free the Muslim prisoners. Our enemies are: Christians, Jews, apostates, those who adore the cow and fire, our secular rulers that replace the laws of Islam, and the hypocrites.
>
> Jihad has been introduced to spread God's religion and to destroy any ruler that is not subject to the adoration of God. Islam is not local *dawaa* [religious propaganda] referring only to Arabs, but for all of humanity and we must spread the word; jihad has the purpose of making God's word the highest. Fighting the infidels has the purpose of exalting the revelation of God.[99]

Here the agenda of the Gamaa Islamiya in Europe is fully revealed. Though the secular Egyptian regime is the initial target, Europe is second on the list. As the charter ominously declares, "Jihad has been introduced to spread God's religion and to destroy *any* ruler that is not subject to the adoration of God" (italics added). Other extremist groups based throughout the Muslim world that have been allowed to operate in Europe took the same position. Ignoring these alarming statements of purpose, Europe opened its doors to murderers who openly declared their intention of fighting any regime that was not based on Islamic law.

Though a few European countries—most notably, France—understood the danger of welcoming known radicals, others maintained their ultraliberal policies that offered asylum to any person facing persecution in a foreign country, whatever the circumstances. An interesting conversation taped in 2000 by a bug placed by Italian intelligence inside the car of Mahmoud Abdelkader Es Sayed, a high-ranking Egyptian al Qaeda member operating in Italy, recorded a conversation that reveals how easily Islamic fundamentalists exploited Europe's asylum system. Es Sayed, who had in fact disclosed to Italian immigration authorities his affiliation with the Egyptian terrorist group Islamic Jihad, is explaining to his unidentified passenger how he had gained asylum:

> Man: Did you get political asylum?
>
> Es Sayed: Yes, when I got here I went to Rome, I came to Milan only after obtaining the asylum. Anyway, when I came here I shaved my beard and I "shaped up. "
>
> Man: Yes [laughing], of course they never got to know anything about your extremism. . . .
>
> Es Sayed: I filed my claim in Rome . . . [laughing] . . . naturally I told them I have three brothers in jail . . . I also told them I had been in jail. . . .
>
> Man: Even with the brothers from the Aden Army?[100]
>
> Es Sayed: This is a thing . . . I left Egypt a long time ago . . . I told them I was a wanted man . . . I told them I was unjustly persecuted . . . that my wife had a car accident . . . bad luck . . . but I told them that the accident had been caused by the Egyptian secret service.
>
> Man: Very nice!
>
> Es Sayed: All this seemed like persecution and, as a consequence, they gave me the asylum in the month of November . . . December.[101]

Later, Es Sayed complains about changes in the policy:

> Es Sayed: Now there is a law in Italy that requires that asylum claims, even those that have already been approved, have to be reviewed every three months to see if the initial conditions are still in place . . . this is a very strange thing . . . by doing so a person can suffer oppression . . .
>
> Man: This is a form of terrorism.
>
> Es Sayed: Of course it is terrorism . . . Italy is a terrorist country . . . it is a criminal country . . . all this shows you that in Italy you cannot obtain a real political asylum . . . the intent of the government is to take advantage of the Muslims living in this country.

With remarkable temerity, Es Sayed both brags about lying to win asylum and calls Italy a "terrorist" and "criminal country" just because it dared to pass a law requiring a periodic review of asylum claims in order to verify their validity.

In his deception and ingratitude, Es Sayed is typical of Islamic radicals who have obtained asylum in Europe. Europeans dreamed that these fundamentalists would integrate easily into their societies, but reality has been quite different. Not only have the refugees continued their terrorist activities, but they have also recruited European Muslims and new immigrants to their cause, establishing radical mosques and Islamic centers throughout the Continent. Just as the Gamaa Islamiya leaders who received asylum in Denmark, Italy, and Austria created a sophisticated fund-raising and recruiting network, so, too, did members of other Islamist groups. The Syrian Muslim Brotherhood, for example, settled in the German city of Aachen, where Issam El Attar, one of its leaders, had received political asylum, and turned the former Carolingian capital into a hotbed of fundamentalism.[102] Members of the Algerian Armed Islamic Group who were welcomed in England established their headquarters at London's Finsbury Park mosque, which soon became one of the beacons of Islamic radicalism in Europe.[103]

Similar examples of undeserved and pernicious generosity abound. In the 1980s, Germany granted asylum to Metin Kaplan, a known Turkish Islamic fundamentalist who had fled the death penalty in his home country.[104] Once in Germany, Kaplan settled in Cologne, where he and his father ran an ultraradical Islamist organization, Caliphate State; it aimed at violently replacing the Turkish republic with an Islamic state. Followers of the "Caliph of Cologne" were involved in a plot to crash an aircraft into the Ataturk Mausoleum in Ankara on the seventy-fifth anniversary of the creation of the secular Turkish Republic.[105] But Kaplan did not limit his activities to Turkey; he proselytized among Germany's vast Turkish community, and his followers reportedly killed a rival imam in Berlin in 1997.[106] His contempt for secularism and Western society influenced many Turks living in Germany, and German authorities estimate that in the late 1990s, Kaplan's organization had about thirteen hundred members and an even larger number of sympathizers.[107]

Some of the most important terrorist leaders of the last decade have successfully won asylum in Europe. Abu Qatada, the man who is commonly described as bin Laden's ambassador to Europe, was granted asylum in Great Britain in 1994 after claiming he was persecuted because of his religious beliefs.[108] Abu Qatada is believed to have been the spiritual leader of most of the key terrorists who have set foot on European soil, including the 9/11 hijackers and the Madrid train bombers. Mullah Krekar, the founder and spiritual leader of Ansar al Islam, a terrorist group that has been sending scores of suicide bombers to attack US and civilian targets since the beginning of the war in Iraq, is also one of Europe's imported threats, as he was given asylum by the Norwegian government in 1991.[109] Authorities have proved that Krekar spent more than a decade fund-raising across Europe for Kurdish terrorist groups, and they suspect that from his Oslo apartment he has also directed attacks against US targets in Iraq.[110]

Europe is now paying the price for its naïveté and shortsightedness, as the radicals it has welcomed for years are now turning against it. Imported fundamentalists thrived in Europe's free and open environment, establishing their headquarters and attracting new adherents. European authorities ignored the explosive potential of mixing seasoned radicals and young, disillusioned Muslim men: the perfect candidates for jihad were already present on its territory, and Europe opened its doors to professional recruiters. The cost to its security has been extremely high.

Moreover, the high-profile terrorists that have entered have further tarnished the image of Islam in the eyes of many Europeans, perpetrating a vicious circle of mistrust. That 80 percent of native Norwegians say that the case of Mullah Krekar has made them more skeptical toward "immigrants" (a euphemism for Muslims) underscores the decades-long mistake of the European political class. To some extent, 9/11 was a wake-up call. But while some countries changed their policies (Germany, for example, deported Kaplan to Turkey in October 2004),[111] the case of Wali Khan Ahmadzai, the Taliban member welcomed to England after he fought against British forces in Afghanistan, shows that Europe is still not united in stopping the entry of terrorists.

FAMILIES, WOMEN, LONE WOLVES

In 2003 Italian authorities intercepted a phone call between a Tunisian man living in Milan and his family members at home.[112] In the lengthy conversation, the man and his family talked about the death of Said, the man's brother who had died a few days earlier in a suicide attack against US forces in Iraq.

> Man: My brother Said became a martyr the day before yesterday.
> Second man, in Tunisia: We heard he is a martyr.
> [The second man than passes the phone to a woman.]
> Man: Mom, congratulations for Said.
> Mother: Great news!
> [They recite verses from the Quran together.]
> Man: Mom, did you have a dream about him?
> Mother: He is OK, he is fine. Do not have fear, my son. God is everywhere. God shows the right path. Do not have fear, you have to fear only God.
> Man: Mom, are you happy?
> Mother: Yes!
> Man: Tell me the truth, did you have a dream about Said?
> Mother: Yes, he is fine. Everything is open for him.
> Man: Here everybody loves admire and envy him. They all say they had a dream about him and came to tell me.
> Mother: He is in good, in good.
> Man: Do you always see him?
> Mother: He is fine.
> Man: Here there are people who are complimenting me
> Mother: God is great. Thank God.

At the end of the call, the man tells his mother that a man who used to pray with Said at the same Milan mosque from which he is calling has decided to send eight thousand euros to Said's family in Tunisia. He politely asks if he can keep half of the money to "fix the house."

Though it is hard for Westerners to understand how a mother can celebrate the death of her twenty-three-year-old son, this conversation is representative of a troubling tendency among the families of Islamic terrorists. Traditionally, terrorists have been rebels, lone wolves who turn against their past and former environment to pursue their revolutionary goals. Europe experienced domestic terrorism in the 1970s, when communist and fascist extremist groups shed blood in the streets of Germany, Italy, and France. Those involved were largely young men and women who broke away from their families and friends to embrace a radical ideology that brought them to the margins of society. While many Islamic terrorists operating in Europe today still fit this profile, other jihadis stay close to their families and acquaintances, who provide moral or material support for their activities.

Militants' families often do not accept their decision to join the jihad. Strong resistance comes not just from the families of converts, who generally have no understanding of or sympathy for Islam, but also from Muslim parents, who frequently fight their sons' fundamentalist positions and try to convince them that they have embraced a false interpretation of Islam. Young men who become extremists often cut all ties to their families, contacting them only sporadically and hiding their real whereabouts. The image of the moderate Muslim father going from mosque to mosque, looking for his young son who has become prey to the extremists, is now commonplace in the European Muslim world.

Nevertheless, Said's mother and family are far from unique. Evidence from various parts of the world suggests that many terrorists operate with the support of their relatives, who feel a sense of pride in the actions of their next of kin. In many Middle Eastern countries, the families of suicide bombers celebrate the martyrdom, with mothers and fathers publicly declaring their joy and pride over their son's actions. Some Palestinian mothers have shocked the public by declaring that they wished they had more children so that they could provide more suicide bombers to the cause. Parents of "martyrs" are generally revered by the whole community, which brings sweets to the hero's house to honor him at festive celebrations.

The situation is different in Europe, where if such emotions are felt they cannot be openly displayed. The public reaction of families of suicide bombers or other Islamic terrorists is always one of disbelief and defense of their next of kin. Parents invariably describe their sons as normal young men, as moderates who enjoyed a quiet life and were loved by everybody. In most cases they deny all the charges, blaming the accusations either on a mistake or on the authorities' prejudices toward Muslims and Islam. While in many cases this reaction is genuine, authorities sometimes strongly suspect that families knew more about the terrorist acts than they admitted.

Over the past few years, several European countries have prosecuted or investigated family members of terrorists, believing that they had information on their relative's activities. In April 2004, for example, British authorities brought to trial the wife and two relatives of Omar Sharif, a British Muslim who participated in a suicide operation that killed four people at a popular café on the seafront of Tel Aviv.[113] Prosecutors believed that Sharif had communicated his murderous intentions to them via both e-mail and telephone.[114] Indeed, European authorities have recently seen cases of entire families actively involved in jihad, dispelling the myth of the jihadi as the lone warrior estranged from his family.

Amel Benchellali, a twenty-six-year-old resident of Venissieux, a poor immigrant neighborhood on the southern outskirts of Lyon, protested in 2004, "I don't know why they have picked on my family."[115] Her complaint rings hollow in the ears of French magistrates and intelligence officials, who are well aware that the Benchellalis are a textbook case of a jihadi family: two generations of radicals working together to kill infidels.

Amel's father, Chellali Benchellali, was born in Algeria in 1944.[116] After immigrating to France in the 1960s, he settled in Venissieux—a low-income suburb of Lyon that, with its violence and high levels of unemployment, epitomizes the problems of France's *banlieux*. Benchellali, a man known for his religious fervor and radical views, proclaimed himself imam of the Abu Bakr mosque, a small prayer room located on the ground floor of his building. Benchellali has repeatedly attracted the media's attention. In 1991 he sparked a national debate by requiring his daughters to wear their veils at school, clashing with school authorities and starting a controversy that continues to rage in France.[117] In 1996 he openly defied French law again, this time by taking a second wife.[118]

In 1994 Benchellali made two trips to war-torn Bosnia, allegedly to transport humanitarian aid to local Muslims fighting Serbian and Croatian forces. He, along with two other men from Venissieux, was reportedly arrested by Croatian police and tortured while in detention.[119] Upon his return to France, he was arrested by French authorities when he was found to be in possession of a weapon.[120] These incidents made Benchellali even more radical and popular in the neighborhood, and his fiery sermons began to draw more worshipers. Benchellali was known to preach against the infidel governments of Israel, America, Russia, and also France, where Muslim women could not wear the veil in public offices and schools. In addition, Benchellali began to openly collect money for militants in several parts of the Muslim world, focusing his efforts on Russia's breakaway republic of Chechnya.

While Chellali Benchellali became one of the religious leaders of Venissieux, his three sons slowly embraced his radical worldviews. The eldest, Menad, was very popular in the neighborhood, a strong character who always flirted with extremes. According to childhood friends, Menad used to organize long soccer games and often wore Hugo Boss and other trendy clothes. He bragged about his intentions of marrying a Westernized Turkish girl in the neighborhood and frequented the most transgressive bars of Paris. But when he reached his mid-twenties, Menad completely changed, declaring that now he "possessed the truth" and denouncing France for not being an Islamic country. Menad began to travel to places such as Sudan, Syria, and England, always shrouding his activities in mystery.[121] Between 1998 and 1999, Menad completed his formation as a fundamentalist by attending an al Qaeda training camp in Afghanistan.[122]

Menad had clearly entered the world of radical Islam and began introducing other young Muslims from the neighborhood to it. "He knew how to entangle others and managed to win over the younger kids with his talk," recalled one Venissieux native.[123] One of Menad's first recruits was his twenty-year-old brother, Mourad. In June 2001, Mourad, along with his childhood friend Nizar Sassi, left Venissieux for Afghanistan's training camps, traveling with false documents provided by other men from the neighborhood linked to Menad.[124] The adventure of the two ended a few months later, as they were both captured by US forces in Afghanistan and detained for more than three years in Guantanamo Bay.

Shortly after his brother's departure, Menad also left France and traveled to Afghanistan, arriving at al Qaeda's training camps once again. Menad became particularly skilled in the use of chemical substances, which he tested on animals.[125] After the fall of the Taliban and the destruction of the training camps, Menad left Afghanistan and found refuge in the Pankisi Gorge, a mountainous and remote area of Georgia bordering Chechnya. His traveling partner was Mourad Merabet, an Algerian chemist who served as imam in another radical mosque of Venissieux.[126] In the gorge, they continued their training in chemical warfare with Arab militants linked to Abu Musab al Zarqawi who had settled in the area. After a few months, they made their way back to Europe.[127]

Once back in France, Menad returned to his parents' apartment in Venissieux. There he continued his experiments with chemical substances, storing the results in Nivea Cream jars and small bottles. Allegedly, Menad wanted to produce botulin and ricin, deadly toxins he would have used in attacks in France and other European countries. In December 2002, after he had told some acquaintances he was ready to go to action, Menad Benchellali was arrested on the outskirts of Paris during a series of raids that netted a dozen Chechen-trained terrorists who were planning attacks in France. No chemical substances were found, but Menad did not hide his calling. "Chemistry," he said proudly to French interrogators, "is one of the components that each combatant needs to master as part of their paramilitary training."[128]

What seems particularly shocking to the public is the claim of French authorities that his entire family helped him in his endeavors. Menad's father Chellali, the imam, acknowledged that he was aware of his son's experiments. His mother admitted to giving him her kitchen utensils and allowing him to turn her sewing room into a makeshift laboratory. "I knew well that it was to make chemical bombs or something like that," she confessed to French magistrates, "but I didn't know the details."[129]

One of his sisters made shopping trips for him, buying castor oil and other products.[130] In January 2004, after a yearlong investigation, Menad's father, mother, and younger brother Hafed were charged with terrorist conspiracy, along with Mourad Merabet and other minor figures in the plot.[131] His parents are accused not only of sheltering Menad while he was conducting his deadly experiments but also of financing his trip to the Pankisi Gorge. In fact, Menad's mother admitted that her husband had wired thousands of euros to Menad when he was in Georgia.[132]

Clearly the Benchellalis are an extreme case, as few other Muslim families are likely to tolerate a makeshift laboratory in their home. Nevertheless, they illustrate a dramatic trend in most Muslim communities in Europe. Islamic fundamentalism is attracting more and more supporters, and one avenue of its spread is within families, as fathers teach it to their sons. The Benchellali children learned hatred for the infidels from their father, and so do thousands of other European-born Muslims.

But the case of the Benchellalis also makes clear another troubling development. The network established by the family could count on dozens of supporters in the town of Venissieux. And after the arrests of the Benchellalis, hundreds of young men took to the streets of the neighborhood in protest. "We are treated like animals," some shouted. "We are in the basement of France."[133] That same anger was displayed after the death of Khaled Kelkal by those who rioted in Vaulx-en-Velin (located, like Venissieux, on the southeastern outskirts of Lyon) and is shown by thousands of young, disillusioned Muslims in the suburbs of Madrid, Rotterdam, Munich, or Zurich. Neighborhoods where unemployment is skyrocketing and the police are absent are the breeding grounds for terrorists. In the degraded Muslim ghettos of Europe, as the example of Menad Benchellali shows, one young man with charisma can attract dozens of his friends to radicalism, creating an almost impenetrable network based on childhood friendships, family ties, and religious fanaticism.

Finally, the story of the Benchellali family also sheds light on the role played by women in jihad. In the world of Islamic fundamentalism, women generally have only the ancillary function of pleasing and supporting the endeavors of jihadi men. Women, especially in Europe, might seem to have no reason to embrace the path of jihad, but for most of them it is not a choice. Many wives of Islamic fundamentalists living in Europe were given to their husbands in arranged marriages in which they had little or no say. Secluded at home, most are prevented by a mix of fear, ignorance, and respect for the family from rebelling and leaving. Aside from a few European women converts, almost no Muslim woman has found the courage to come forward and denounce her husband as a terrorist.

In some other cases, women are willingly supportive of their husbands' terrorist activities, sharing their militant views. Most Westerners view radical Islam as a strongly misogynistic ideology, yet some Muslim women strongly adhere to it and have joined the ranks of al Qaeda. And al Qaeda, always looking for new and diverse recruits, is happy to accept them. In the summer of 2004, for example, a Saudi-based group linked to al Qaeda launched a new online magazine only for women, *al Khansa*, with the intention of providing guidelines and suggestions for those whose husbands and sons are involved in jihad. The magazine proudly declared, "The blood of our husbands and the body parts of our children are our sacrificial offering," and it advised women on how to bring up their sons in the path of jihad and how to provide first aid.[134] But *al Khansa* also provided information on what kind of training women should undergo in order to prepare themselves for fighting in jihad. And in fact, women have directly participated in terrorist acts throughout the world. Chechen women, the infamous "black widows," have carried out a string of deadly suicide attacks inside Russia, including the simultaneous downing of two Russian jetliners in August 2004. Palestinian women, sometimes mothers, have repeatedly been used by various terrorist groups for suicide operations in Israel. And two fourteen-year-old female twins were recruited by a Moroccan terrorist group to carry out suicide attacks in a Rabat supermarket.[135]

In March of 2003, al Qaeda publicly declared its interest in directly employing women in its operations: a self-described female mujahid claiming to be training female volunteers for al Qaeda declared in an interview with an Arab newspaper that the organization was "building a women's structure that will carry out operations that will make the U.S. forget its own name."[136] The FBI believes that several women have been recruited and trained to carry out attacks worldwide. One of them is Aafia Siddiqui, a Pakistani national and US-educated microbiologist; currently wanted by US authorities, she is believed to be a high-level al Qaeda operative.[137]

Female bombers could be targeting Europe soon. Because women rarely attract the attention of immigration and law enforcement authorities, they are ideal for carrying out attacks. In May 2004, Italian authorities intercepted a conversation between Rabei Osman El Sayed Ahmed, a high-ranking al Qaeda member operating in Europe and the purported mastermind of the March 11 Madrid train bombings, and his young roommate. Ahmed's words provide a chilling insight into al Qaeda's activities and future plans:

> Do you remember the woman who I told you about, do you remember? Her name is Hotaf. I have bad news, she was discovered, but there will be the victory of Islam. I am sorry, there are other women, but I am sorry for Hotaf. Do you know how Mouattaf trained her? She already trained her with many medical products. If they throw a stick it blows away an American neighborhood . . . [inaudible] May peace be upon him [Mouattaf], may his soul rest in peace, but she [Hotaf] is not the first nor will she be the last, there is Fatiha, there is Amal, there is Palestine, Chechnya, Afghanistan, Indonesia, Kashmir, Pakistan, and Malaysia . . . *you just have to warn them and they come*. There is Amal, Hanan, you just have to warn them; I am sorry the tactic of the first one did not work, she was discovered; now we have Amal, she is ready. . . . God is great.[138]

European authorities are faced with enormous challenges. As shown above, the profile of the Islamic radical operating on the Continent varies widely, ranging from the Muslim teenager from the suburbs to blue-eyed converts to a middle-aged woman microbiologist. To make their job more difficult, the Muslim communities are becoming ever more radicalized and hostile toward the native European populations; cooperation with authorities is therefore increasingly rare. Only a combination of aggressive law enforcement actions and improvements in socially and financially integrating its burgeoning Muslim population will enable Europe to make progress in its uphill battle against Islamic terrorism.

NOTES

1. Burhan Wazir, "Essex Boys Sign up for 'Holy War,'" *Observer*, February 24, 2002.

2. Ibid.

3. Ibid.

4. Dean M. Kelley, *Why Conservative Churches Are Growing: A Study in Sociology of Religion* (New York: Harper & Row, 1972).

5. Paul Wells, "Joining the Enemy," *National Post*, December 10, 2001.

6. Sebastian Rotella and David Zucchino, "Response to Terror," *Los Angeles Times*, October 21, 2001.

7. Craig S. Smith, "Europe Fears Islamic Converts May Give Cover for Extremism," *New York Times*, July 19, 2004.

8. "Frenchman Jailed for Terror Ties," BBC, May 25, 2004.

9. Evan F. Kohlmann, *Al-Qaida's Jihad in Europe; The Afghan-Bosnian Network* (Oxford: Berg, 2004), pp. 188–89.

10. Hal Bernton, Mike Carter, David Heath, and James Neff, *The Terrorist Within*, monograph of the *Seattle Times,* June 23–July 7, 2002, chap. 5. http://seattletimes.nwsource.com/news/nation-world/terroristwithin/chapter5.html

11. Ibid.

12. Kohlmann, *Al-Qaida's Jihad in Europe*, p. 95.

13. Press conference with presidential aide Sergei Yastrzhembsky, Official Kremlin International News Broadcast, December 24, 2003.

14. David Crawford, "German's Path to Death in Chechen Rebel Camp Puzzles Investigators," *Wall Street Journal*, October 14, 2004.

15. Craig S. Smith, "Europe Fears Islamic Converts May Give Cover."

16. Official DIGOS (Divisioni Investigazioni Generali e Operazioni Speciali, Divisions for General Investigations and Special Operations), report al Mohajiroun 3, November 21, 2001, Milan, pp. 35–36.

17. Sebastian Rotella, "Al Qaeda's Stealth Weapons," *Los Angeles Times*, September 20, 2003.

18. "Three Get Life in Morocco Trial," BBC, September 19, 2003.

19. Rotella, "Al Qaeda's Stealth Weapons."

20. Alberto Samona', "Preso l'attentatore di Allah, e' un Italiano convertito," *Libero*, July 18, 2002.

21. Piotr Smolar, "Ruddy Terranova, orphelin, delinquant, bagarreur et amoreux, a decouvert le Coran en prison," *Le Monde*, May 4, 2004.

22. Ibid.

23. Ibid.

24. Ibid.

25. Rotella, "Al Qaeda's Stealth Weapons."

26. Smith, "Europe Fears Islamic Converts May Give Cover."

27. "Cellule Islamiche attive in Italia," *Corriere della Sera*, March 3, 2005.

28. Wazir, "Essex Boys Sign up for 'Holy War.'"

29. Peter Finn, "Unlikely Allies Bound by a Common Hatred," *Washington Post*, April 29, 2002.

30. Justin Sparks, "Freed Terrorist Vows He'll Fulfill Suicide Mission," *Times*, February 8, 2004.

31. *Inside 9-11: What Really Happened*, by the reporters, writers, and editors of *Der Spiegel* magazine, trans. Paul De Angelis and Elisabeth Kaestner (New York: St. Martin's Press, 2002), p. 198.

32. Ibid., p. 199.

33. *9/11 Commission Report*, p. 164.

34. *Inside 9-11: What Really Happened*, p. 199.

35. Smith, "Europe Fears Islamic Converts May Give Cover."

36. Dominik Cziesche, Georg Mascolo, Sven Roebel, Heiner Schimmoeller, Holger Stark, "As If You Were at War," *Der Spiegel*, March 22, 2004. Accessed via FBIS.

37. Dietmar Loch, "Boyhood of a Terror Suspect," *Guardian*, October 11, 1995.

38. Ibid.

39. Ibid.

40. Frank Viviano, "Killing Exposes France's Racial Divide," *San Francisco Chronicle*, October 27, 1995.

41. Milton Viorst, "The Muslims of France," *Foreign Affairs*, September/October 1996, p. 78.

42. Erich Inciyan, "Un Terrorisme d'un Nouveau Genre," *Le Monde*, September 29, 1995.

43. Viviano, "Killing Exposes France's Racial Divide."

44. "Bomb Explodes, Vehicles Torched in Unrest over Terrorist's Death," AP, October 4, 1995.

45. "La Mort en direct de Khaled Kelkal," *Le Monde*, September 30, 1995.

46. Amy Barrett, "Youth Riots Spread, Police Probe Bombing Suspect's Killing," AP, October 3, 1995.

47. "Bomb Explodes, Vehicles Torched in Unrest over Terrorist's Death."

48. Barrett, "Youth Riots Spread."

49. Viviano, "Killing Exposes France's Racial Divide."

50. Ibid.

51. Robert S. Leiken, *Bearers of Global Jihad? Immigration and National Security after 9/11* (Washington, DC: Nixon Center, 2004), p. 48.

52. Testimony of Robert S. Leiken before the US House of Representatives, International Relations Committee, Subcommittee on International Terrorism, Nonproliferation and Human Rights, June 16, 2004, http://wwwc.house.gov/international_relations/108/lei061604.htm.

53. Steven Erlanger and Chris Hedges, "Terror Cells Slip through Europe's Grasp," *New York Times*, December 28, 2001.

54. Ibid.

55. Loch, "Boyhood of a Terror Suspect."

56. Spanish Ministry of Interiors, Summary of Anti-Terrorist Activities, 2004.

57. Renwick McLean, "Spanish Prisons Provide Pool of Recruits for Radical Islam," *New York Times*, October 31, 2004, p. 18.

58. Dutch intelligence official, interview with author, The Hague, June 2003.

59. "Profile: Omar Saeed Sheikh," BBC, July 16, 2002.

60. Alex Hannaford, "The Toughest Boy in School," *Guardian*, February 23, 2005.

61. Ibid.

62. "Profile: Omar Saeed Sheikh," BBC, July 16, 2002.

63. Ibid.

64. Ibid.

65. Hannaford, "The Toughest Boy in School."

66. "Explosives Find in UK Terror Raid," CNN, March 30, 2004.

67. Selcan Hacaoglu, "Fertilizer Bombs Favorite Terrorist Weapon, but U.S. Not Joining EU, Turkey in Restricting Sales," *Time*, April 14, 2004.

68. Crawley, a commuter town in West Sussex, was home to Yasir Khan, one of the British men killed in the fall of 2001 while fighting alongside the Taliban in Afghanistan. Khan was also raised in a middle-class Pakistani family and played cricket.

69. William Tinning, "He Was Not Political. He Wanted to Play Cricket for England," *Herald*, April 1, 2004.

70. Ibid.

71. Erik Schelzig and Peter Finn, "Repentant Algerian Tells of Bomb Plot," *Washington Post*, April 24, 2002.

72. Ibid.

73. Desmond Butler and Don Van Natta Jr., "Threats and Responses; Terror Network; Al Qaeda Informer Helps Investigators Trace Group's Trail," *New York Times*, February 15, 2003.

74. Ibid.

75. Federal Court of Karlsruhe, Interrogation of Shadi Abdallah, April 24, 2002.

76. Ibid.

77. Cziesche et al., "As If You Were at War."

78. Dirk Laabs and Terry McDermott, "The World; Column One: Prelude to 9/11," *Los Angeles Times*, January 27, 2003.

79. *9/11 Commission Report*, p. 163.

80. *Inside 9-11: What Really Happened*, p. 199.

81. Ibid.

82. Ibid.

83. Dirk Laabs and Terry McDermott, "Prelude to 9/11," *Los Angeles Times*, January 27, 2003.

84. Ibid.

85. Loch, "Boyhood of a Terror Suspect."

86. Stefano Dambruoso, *Milano Bagdad: Diario di un magistrato in prima linea nella lotta al terrorismo islamico in Italia* (Milan: Mondadori, 2004), pp. 94–98.

87. Ibid.

88. Ibid.

89. AIVD (Algemene Inlichtingen- en Veiligheidsdienst, or General Intelligence and Security Service), "Recruitment for the Jihad in the Netherlands; from Incident to Trend," December 2002.

90. Cziesche et al., "As If You Were at War."

91. John Downing, "Taliban Refugee Still Sees the UK as His Enemy," *Telegraph*, February 16, 2003.

92. President Hosni Mubarak, dialogue with army officers on October 4, 2001, Egyptian State Information Service Web site, http://www.sis.gov.eg/online/html5/m041021y.htm.

93. Kohlmann, *Al-Qaida's Jihad in Europe*, pp. 26–27.

94. Analysis of the June 26, 1995, searches of the Viale Jenner mosque, DIGOS, September 15, 1997.

95. Kohlmann, *Al-Qaida's Jihad in Europe*, pp. 26–27.

96. Giles Foden, "The Hunt for 'Public Enemy No 2,'" *Guardian*, September 24, 2001.

97. Camille Eid, "Arringa ai Musulmani: Terrorizzare e' un Dovere," *Avvenire*, November 30, 2001.

98. DIGOS, analysis of the June 26, 1995, searches of the Viale Jenner mosque, September 15, 1997.

99. Ibid.

100. That is Islamic Army of Aden, a Yemeni terrorist group closely linked to al Qaeda; Es Sayed had established close ties with it during his stay in Yemen (before he went to Italy).

101. DIGOS report, "Al Muhajiroun 3," November 21, 2001.

102. Report on the Islamic Center of Aachen by the Innenministerium, Nordrhein-Westfalen, http://www.im.nrw.de/sch/581.htm.

103. The Algerian network and the Finsbury Park mosque will be discussed in depth in part 2.

104. "Profile: the Caliph of Cologne," BBC, May 27, 2004.

105. Federal Office for the Protection of the Constitution, "Islamic Extremist Activities in the Federal Republic of Germany," December 1998.

106. Ibid.

107. Ibid.

108. "Britain 'Sheltering al Qaeda Leader,'" BBC, July 8, 2002.

109. Tribunal of Milan, Indictment of Muhamad Majid and others, November 25, 2003.

110. Krekar will be further discussed in chap. 10.

111. "Deported Militant Flown to Turkey," BBC, October 12, 2004. In June 2005, Kaplan was sentenced to life in prison by a Turkish court for planning the attack against the Ataturk Mausoleum in Ankara.

112. Paolo Biondani, "Festeggio il Martirio di mio Figlio," *Corriere della Sera*, December 3, 2003.

113. Sue Clough, "Suicide Bomber 'Told Wife He Was Not Coming Back,'" *Telegraph*, April 30, 2004.

114. Vikram Dodd and Press Association, "Suicide Bomber's Family 'Kept Plan Secret,'" *Guardian*, April 27, 2004.

115. "Inside France's Hotbeds of Discontent," *Telegraph*, August 6, 2004.

116. Piotr Smolar, "Quatre Islamistes Interpelles en Seine-Saint-Denis dans l'Enquete sur les 'fileres tchetchenes,'" *Le Monde*, December 27, 2002.

117. "Ramifications of French Terror Network Examined," *Le Figaro*, January 17, 2004. Accessed via FBIS.

118. Craig S. Smith, "Web of Jihad Draws in an Immigrant Family in France," *New York Times*, July 31, 2004.

119. "Ramifications of French Terror Network Examined."

120. Smith, "Web of Jihad"; "Ramifications of French Terror Network Examined."

121. "French Report Profiles Venissieux Network Suspect," *Le Figaro*, January 12, 2004. Accessed via FBIS.

122. Smith, "Web of Jihad."

123. "French Report Profiles Venissieux Network Suspect."

124. "French Imam's Wife, Daughter Questioned in Ongoing Inquiry into Suspected Terrorist Network," *Liberation*, January 10, 2004. Accessed via FBIS.

125. "French Authorities Investigate Possible Plans for Chemical Attack in Europe," *Le Monde*, January 11, 2004. Accessed via FBIS.

126. "Ramifications of French Terror Network Examined."

127. Smith, "Web of Jihad."

128. "Son of French Muslim Cleric Held in Terror Probe Admits Knowing How to Make Bombs," AFP, January 13, 2004. Accessed via FBIS.

129. Smith, "Web of Jihad."

130. "French Authorities Investigate Possible Plans for Chemical Attack in Europe," *Le Monde*, January 11, 2004. Accessed via FBIS.

131. Ibid.

132. "French Imam's Wife, Daughter Questioned in Ongoing Inquiry into Suspected Terrorist Network," *Liberation*, January 10, 2004. Accessed via FBIS.

133. Jean-Baptiste Labeur, "Father of Guantanamo Bay Detainee Held," AP, January 6, 2004.

134. Sebastian Usher, "Jihad Magazine for Women on Web," BBC, August 24, 2004.

135. "Rabat Bomb Plot Twins Are 14-Year-Old Girls," AFP, September 5, 2003.

136. "FBI Warns of Al Qaeda Women," CBS News, April 1, 2003.

137. Michael Isikoff and Mark Hosenball, "Tangled Ties," *Newsweek*, April 7, 2004.

138. Tribunal of Milan, indictment of Rabei Osman Ahmed El Sayed and others, June 5, 2004.

CHAPTER 2

LIFE AMONG THE INFIDELS

*If a Muslim is in a combat or godless area, he is not obligated to have
a different appearance from (those around him). The (Muslim) man may
prefer or even be obligated to look like them, provided his action brings
a religious benefit of preaching to them, learning their secrets and informing Muslims, preventing their harm, or some other beneficial goal.*
                                 —Sheik Ibn Taymiyah, Islamic scholar (1263–1328),
                                          quoted in an al Qaeda training manual

RECRUITMENT

Today, hundreds of thousands of Muslims residing in Europe embrace, to
varying degrees, a militant interpretation of Islam, favoring the introduction of sharia law and despising Western values and principles. "Islam
will return to Europe as a conqueror and victor, after being expelled from
it twice," is the dream expressed by one of the world's most respected
Islamic scholars, Sheikh Yusuf al Qaradawi, and shared by thousands of
European Muslims. But al Qaradawi points out that though in the past
Islam repeatedly tried to conquer Europe with force, "the conquest this
time will not be by the sword but by preaching and ideology."[1]

That so many Muslims reject the values that rule the countries in which they live clearly threatens the harmony of Europe's future, but it does not necessarily mean that they directly threaten its security. Radicalization is just the first step on the road toward terrorism. In fact, only a minority of those who support radical Islam become terrorists and decide to resort to violence to pursue their political goals. Generally, before an Islamist turns into a terrorist, he (or she) needs to be recruited by a terrorist organization. And the recruiter—the individual who is somehow connected to a terrorist organization and is looking for new militants—often finds it unnecessary to present jihad propaganda, as candidates have already been indoctrinated. As the Dutch General Intelligence and Security Service (Algemene Inlichtingen- en Veiligheidsdienst, or AIVD) noted in a 2002 dossier on recruitment for jihad in the Netherlands, "before a recruiter approaches a potential recruit . . . this young person is probably already acquainted with or even sympathises with Islamic fundamentalism."[2] The AIVD reiterated the point in 2004: "The complex of interrelated sentiments like (a lack of) self-respect, commitment to the Islamic ideal, solidarity with the oppressed Muslims and identity problems is a major point of departure for recruiters. In some cases, these sentiments are fuelled by recruiters, but in other cases they develop independently."[3]

Radicalization can take place anywhere. As chapter 1 showed, young Muslims are introduced to militant Islam in prison, in private groups with friends, or on the Internet. Nevertheless, most young European Muslims convert to radical Islam in the mosque. Such radicalization can occur one of two ways, depending on the role played by the mosque's leadership. In some cases, the radicalism is institutionalized: that is, the imams and other leaders directly promote fundamentalist views. In many other cases, however, radicals and recruiters attend the mosque but oppose the more moderate views of its imam, thereby often creating conflicts among the congregation.

Though mosques where radicalism is institutionalized are in the minority, there are many of them in Europe. In mosques such as Finsbury Park in London, the Islamic Cultural Institute in Milan, or al Quds in Hamburg, places of worship have been turned into hotbeds of fundamentalism, with the chief imams directly urging the believers to fight jihad and recruiters operating with the full knowledge and support of the mosque's leadership. Donations for the mujahideen fighting throughout the world are openly collected and videotapes recording their gruesome endeavors are publicly shown. Recruiters operate freely inside the mosque and frequently even hold an official position.

But many young Muslims are introduced to radical Islam in small groups within mosques that do not directly support terrorist activities, though they espouse a conservative brand of Islam. Often these groups are composed of young men who have grown up in the same neighborhood and been friends since childhood. Spontaneously, they form small clusters that share a radical interpretation of Islam, creating a subgroup inside the mosque.[4] The AIVD describes the process: "Several youths visiting the orthodox mosque which is also frequented by their families, often share the same fascination for the Islamistic war. They watch jihad videos together and attend lectures, conventions and summer camps organized for them."[5]

These clusters of young extremists provide ideal pools for the recruiters. The 2002 Dutch intelligence dossier reveals how easily recruiters can find potential recruits: "All they have to do is join in the prayers, conversations and activities to get in touch with these youths."[6] While the radicalization is the first phase of the recruiting process, the second, which the AIVD calls "spotting," takes place quite publicly.[7] A French intelligence official observes gloomily, "The influence of the extremist networks grows stronger every day. . . . What the recruiters do is not illegal at first. Neither the republic nor the families of the recruits have found a way to stop them."[8] Recruiters lurk in mosques, Islamic bookstores, and the cafés of Arab neighborhoods, waiting for the right moment to strike up a conversation. They often operate at the margins of the mosque, and often mosque officials try to force them out. "He imposed himself in the mosques," commented an Algerian journalist on the activities of one recruiter, Karim Bourti (the journalist had gone undercover to investigate the recruiting networks operating in the Arab neighborhoods of Paris). "The imam spoke upstairs. But downstairs,

Karim and the fundamentalists were in control. That's a metaphor for what is going on."[9]

Recruiters' strong character, jihad experience, and religious knowledge draw many young men to them. Most of them have a mujahid background, having fought in Afghanistan against the Soviets or in Bosnia or Chechnya. They recount glorious stories of jihad, praising the endeavors of fallen mujahideen and urging the young potential recruits to imitate their heroic example. The clusters of young radicalized men view these veterans of jihad as heroes themselves, for having fulfilled the highest duty of a good Muslim. The recruiters also generally exert influence through their superior knowledge of Islam. Though most have only a limited grasp of Islamic doctrine, their expertise is superior to that of most second- or third-generation Muslims living in Europe. The recruiter, who is usually older than his recruits, uses his experience and knowledge of Islamic theology to put himself in a leadership position over the small clusters of fundamentalists. In short order, he will have created a small following of young jihadi wannabes who look to him for guidance and direction.

Once the clusters are co-opted by the recruiter, they normally break away from their original environment, thus arriving at the third phase of the recruiting process: isolation from society.[10] The radicalized clusters often clash with mosque officials, accusing them of being too moderate and failing to defend Muslims. In some cases, mosques officials ask recruiters to depart from the mosque because of their militant views, and their clusters leave with them. Those who leave the mosque also leave mainstream society, entering completely the self-segregated world of militant Islam. At this point, the clusters withdraw into a separate existence, meeting in private apartments or garages. Every aspect of their life becomes secretive, as they begin to make contacts with more individuals who have been involved with terrorist acts and are under surveillance. In some cases the recruit is assigned to a "buddy," an experienced militant who shadows the potential new holy warrior every step of the way.[11] Recruits spend their days listening to cassettes of radical Islamic scholars and watching tapes of the mujahideen fighting in Bosnia, Chechnya, or Afghanistan. The tapes are interrupted only for speeches given by experienced jihadis, authoritative figures who teach the recruits the importance of jihad and beauty of martyrdom. When they are alone, they spend hours on the Internet, browsing the thousands of radical Islamist Web sites.

It is at this stage that the role of the recruiter becomes crucial. Though his involvement in the candidate's initial radicalization was probably marginal, he has complete power over the destiny of the "complete" radical—the recruit who has undergone a total transformation and is now willing to fully commit himself to jihad. Now the recruiter exercises his discretionary powers and decides what the new jihadi will do. This is in fact his core task. The studies on recruitment for jihad undertaken by Marc Sageman, a former CIA official and an adjunct professor of psychology at the University of Pennsylvania, have revealed that al Qaeda carries out no top-down recruitment; instead, spontaneously formed clusters of young radicals naturally team up with recruiters, who select those who have skills and dedication that can be useful to the cause.[12] "It's actually very much like applying to Harvard," says Sageman, pointing out that al Qaeda's problem is selection, not recruitment.[13]

Recruiters are better described as experienced jihadis who travel around Europe and operate as gatekeepers of terror, selecting the best candidates for terrorism. The recruiters have contacts with terror masterminds around the world who can open the doors of organized terrorism to young motivated individuals. Before the training camps were destroyed in 2001, the young militants were sent to Afghanistan. Today, they either go to other fields of jihad, such as Iraq or Chechnya, or simply are used to create cells inside Europe. The recruiter evaluates the recruit, analyzes his weaknesses and strengths, and decides where he can best serve the organization.

In December 2000, Italian authorities taped a conversation between Mahmoud Abdelkader Es Sayed, a high-ranking al Qaeda operative then living in Milan, and Adel Ben Soltane, a young Tunisian radical who met Es Sayed at the city's Islamic Cultural Institute.[14] It is an excellent illustration of the interplay between an al Qaeda recruiter and his young recruit.

> Es Sayed: It is not that I don't trust you, it's not up to me . . . I have only analyzed you . . . you are ready to eat the stones of the desert . . .

but you have to understand the meaning of it . . . in your mind do you think that I would stop a young man like you who wants to go to jihad? Of course not . . . to the contrary, I encourage him . . . I take him with me and I consider him like he was part of my family . . . I even give him my pants . . . you have to know that it is not up to me and every thing has its time . . . you see that you did not understand my words when I told you that you are a street fighter? Jihad is not the weapon . . . even this is jihad.

Ben Soltane: Sheikh, you confuse me, there are many plans, but then . . .

Es Sayed: Believe me, brother, I love you in the name of God and what I wish for me I wish it for you too.

Ben Soltane: God bless you, but I made a promise to God and I have a goal and in this sense no human can stop me . . . I don't like playing around . . . but, honestly, sheikh, you have many things and problems, but you did not base it on one thing.

Es Sayed: You are giving me too many faults . . . it is not like that . . . I am just checking you . . . I observe you . . . I need proofs.

Ben Soltane: Why? My proofs are not enough?

Es Sayed: This is not the reason, at the moment I have nothing and after that what God brings is welcome . . . I can tell you one thing . . . you have a lot of confidence in yourself and a lot of faith. A lot of people who lived in Europe have this enthusiasm, but then they go back . . . I am telling you, it is very difficult, extremely difficult, it's hard.[15]

Anxious to leave Italy and fight jihad, Ben Soltane is complaining that Es Sayed, whom he respectfully addresses as "sheikh," is delaying him. But Es Sayed is acting as the perfect selector. He spends entire days with Ben Soltane, analyzing his characteristics to see if he could be a good jihadi: "I observe you . . . I need proofs." Before sending him to Afghanistan, Es Sayed has to be sure that Ben Soltane could make it in the harsh Afghan camps, where trainees endure arduous conditions. "A lot of people who lived in Europe have this enthusiasm, but then they go back . . . I am telling you, it is very difficult, extremely difficult, it's hard." Thanks to his charisma and authority, Es Sayed convinces Ben Soltane that even a logistic role in Europe is important to the cause:

Es Sayed: So now everything is clear . . . and it's not everything. . . . If you want to work with me this is the job . . . if the brothers want to hide, we hide them, if the brothers want documents, we take care of their documents, if the brothers want to move, we move them . . . if they need a weapon, you give them a weapon. . . . One thing. . . . Adel, you should not tell anybody what I am telling you. If you feel under surveillance or observed or you have a doubt, delete everything and stay away from me . . . but I need one like you . . . I am sorry that you think I don't trust you . . . this is not trust.

Ben Soltane: God bless you![16]

Finally, at the end of the conversation, Es Sayed asks Ben Soltane about his motivations. The response provides further proof that radicalism does not result only from social or economic segregation:

Es Sayed: So, this is al Qaeda . . . but I am curious about one thing . . . don't you like this good life? You want to die?

Ben Soltane: Listen, sheikh, if I liked this life . . . I would have gone to my cousin who is waiting for me in Germany and wants to marry me, in five years I would have the German passport and I would live in peace.

Es Sayed: God willing, I am the first person to wish you to die as a martyr . . . do you see this way? You need to know how to enter and exit, right? . . . These are the basics of al Qaeda.[17]

LIFE

Once the militants have been recruited, they need to have proper training. The recruiter uses his extensive international network to send his new "pupil" to the right place.[18] The recruit is often provided with money, false documents, and an airline ticket. Even more important, the recruiter tells him how to contact a trusted accomplice at his destination. A letter of recommendation signed by the recruiter is sometimes needed to open the doors of organized terror to the budding new jihadi. A man at the other side of the world, seeing the letter from a trusted jihad veteran he knows, will welcome the new brother coming from Europe.

Before 9/11, training took place mainly in Afghanistan, where al Qaeda operated several facilities that graduated thousands of future terrorists. After the fall of the Taliban and the destruction of the camps, the jihadis have had more difficulty finding locations for their bases. There are reports of training facilities being operated in remote, lawless areas of Pakistan, Algeria, and Somalia that are controlled by terrorist groups. Militants also gain direct experience in jihad in places such as Chechnya and Iraq, where Islamic fundamentalists can train in camps and participate in combat at the same time.

But European jihadis do not necessarily have to leave the Continent to undergo terrorist training. Much as the terrorists who bombed the World Trade Center in 1993 practiced with guns in the woods of Connecticut, so for years European militants have been operating training camps in mountainous regions of France, Italy, and Spain. Willie Brigitte, a French terrorist accused of heading a Sydney-based terrorist cell planning to blow up Australia's only nuclear reactor,[19] told French authorities that Islamic radicals had been training potential recruits in at least seven locations throughout France. The sessions, which were held in rugged areas near the Alps and in a forest near Paris, included physical training and religious indoctrination. They were intended to determine which recruits were ready to fight in Afghanistan or on other battlefields of jihad.[20] Reportedly, weekend weapon practices are still held throughout Europe in backwoods locations, where experienced jihadis share their knowledge with eager recruits.[21]

To supplement the actual training, jihadis have also created a virtual library of their murderous knowledge—thousands of pages on which their terrorist skills are condensed into a form easily learned by new recruits. In 2000, while searching the residence of a suspected al Qaeda operative, British police discovered a computer file containing an Arabic book titled "Declaration of Jihad against the Country's Tyrants—Military Series."[22] The one-hundred-eighty-page volume, dubbed "Al Qaeda Training Manual" by US authorities, is a compendium of the organization's knowledge. Its twelve chapters teach operatives all the tricks of the trade, from how to communicate undetected to how to gather intelligence.

Other manuals, circulating both in paper editions and on CD-ROM, provide instructions on how to build bombs out of everyday components and how to carry out urban warfare. More recently, al Qaeda has invaded the Internet, setting up hundreds of Web sites that provide propaganda and training to the mujahideen. In 2003 the Saudi branch of al Qaeda created *Al Battar*, an online magazine that covers subjects ranging from target selection to how to handle an Uzi submachine gun. "Oh Mujahid brother," the first issue declares enthusiastically, "in order to join the great training camps you don't have to travel to other lands. Alone, in your home or with a group of your brothers, you too can begin to execute the training program. You can all join the Al-Battar Training Camp. "[23]

Once he is properly educated, the terrorist is assigned to a cell, created perhaps to provide logistical support to the network or for the sole purpose of carrying out a specific attack. The cells' operational independence varies significantly. Some of them follow strict orders from al Qaeda's leadership, striking at preassigned targets as instructed by the masterminds in Afghanistan. Thus, in the 9/11 attacks the targets and the weapons were chosen by Khalid Sheikh Mohammed and Osama bin Laden in Afghanistan. In the post–9/11 era, as al Qaeda's leadership finds it increasingly difficult to communicate with its operatives, this micromanagement is less common; analysts believe that al Qaeda cells now simply receive the green light for an attack whose specifics—the targets and specific operational details—remain under their control. The March 11 Madrid train bombings are thought to have followed this model. In other cases, cells operate independently of any organization, though their members may have received their training in al Qaeda camps. Cells of "nonaligned mujahideen" are spread throughout Europe and represent a nightmare for intelligence officials. While these cells share al Qaeda's ideology and global goals, they see bin Laden only as an inspirational figure, not as their commander. Their independence makes them more difficult to detect, as their contacts with monitored terrorists are sporadic at best.

The greatest number of militants operating in Europe are assigned to logistical cells, which provide the network with all the tools it needs to operate. Sometimes they operate directly and knowingly in support of a cell that is carrying out an operation. For example, attacks often are carried out by terrorists who come to the targeted city just a few days or weeks before they intend to act. The logistical cells must provide the newly arrived operatives with safe houses, money, cars, explosives, and the false documents they might need to leave the city after their work is done. In some cases logistical cells also undertake target surveillance, necessary preparatory work done with extreme dedication and patience. Potential targets such as bridges, government buildings, landmarks, and transportation systems are surveilled for months and their vulnerabilities are analyzed. To gain additional intelligence, operatives try to get inside facilities to which access is restricted—for example, seeking work as airport workers or cleaners. Operatives reportedly have even deliberately committed a crime in order to have the opportunity to assess the vulnerabilities of the inside of a police station.[24]

In many cases, cells operate without even knowing whom they are helping. A cell in Spain might simply be ordered to provide one hundred blank passports to an operative in Belgium, with no further details supplied. An operative in a port city could be asked to host a couple of individuals who are wanted by law enforcement agents without being told why. Cells often raise funds that go to the network's collectors, but only few know what exactly the collectors will do with the money. Bound together by their common faith in jihad, cells operate without asking too many questions about the rest of the network's activities.

Europe, a place where terrorists can operate with relative freedom, is the logistical cells' ideal environment. False documents are easily available on the black market, the transportation system is first-rate, money is abundant, and European intelligence agencies are not as repressive as their Middle Eastern counterparts. It is therefore not surprising that almost every attack carried out by al Qaeda throughout the world has had some link to Europe. A Dublin-based charity provided material support to some of the terrorists who attacked the US embassies in Kenya and Tanzania in 1998.[25] False documents provided by a cell operating between

Belgium and France enabled two al Qaeda operatives to portray themselves as journalists and assassinate Ahmed Shah Massoud, the commander of the Afghan Northern Alliance, just two days before 9/11.[26] And the attacks of 9/11 themselves were partially planned in Hamburg, where three of the four pilots of the hijacked planes received extensive financial and logistical support.

After 9/11, as the al Qaeda network became less dependent on its leadership in Afghanistan and more decentralized, the cells operating in Europe took on even greater importance. Most of the planning for the April 2002 bombing of a synagogue in the Tunisian resort town of Djerba was done in Germany and France.[27] According to Moroccan authorities, the funds for the May 2003 Casablanca bombings came from Moroccan cells in Spain, France, Italy, and Belgium. Cells operating in Europe have also directly targeted the Continent and attacks have been either planned or executed in Madrid, Paris, London (in at least four different instances), Milan, Berlin, Amsterdam, Rome, and Porto. In all these cases, investigations revealed the involvement of various European cells.

The importance of a logistical cell cannot be overestimated, as no operation can be carried out if the terrorists do not have the documents required to enter the country, the money with which to buy explosives, and the safe houses in which to hide. Islamist cells operating in Europe are impressively skilled in supplying most of these necessities, but they particularly excel in acquiring forged documents. Al Qaeda has always placed great emphasis on obtaining high-quality false papers for its operatives. Documents from Western countries are considered the most valuable, as they allow the bearer unrestricted travel to most countries and they draw less attention from immigration officials throughout the world.

For this reason, al Qaeda cells operating in Europe have specialized in creating state-of-the-art false European documents, which have been supplied to operatives throughout the Continent and overseas. Usually militants doctor stolen documents they have bought on the black market, simply replacing the picture. In some cases, cells print their own documents, teaming up with gangs of document forgers and human smugglers. In other cases, they manage to obtain batches of blank documents stolen from diplomatic facilities or other government offices. Ideally, cells try to create a complete set of documents, providing the operative with a passport, identity card, and driver's license reflecting the same false identity. As the al Qaeda manual recommends, the photos on the document generally show the operative clean-shaven, in order to attract less attention.[28] If his Arab or Middle Eastern features are not too strong, he is given a European-sounding name, as a Thomas or a Christopher is less likely to be stopped than a Mohammed.

The various cells scattered throughout Europe are independent, insofar as they tend to finance their own activities and carry out their operations autonomously. But they are also part of a network, and they work constantly with other cells on the Continent and in other parts of the world. Generally, only the leader of the cell keeps contacts with other cells. Occasionally a high-ranking member of the network travels around Europe, visiting the various cells and coordinating their efforts. Worries about security limit communication between cells to what is strictly necessary, but operational needs force operatives into frequent contact.

The telephone is a terrorist's most treacherous friend. Though human couriers are their ideal means of communication, it is often impractical, if not impossible, to use messengers to quickly send information to a cell operating hundreds of miles away. Therefore, the telephone is a necessary companion of the terrorist. But as the terrorists well know, the telephone is easily monitored by intelligence agencies. An outburst by a Munich-based al Qaeda operative visiting an Italian cell that had been monitored for months by Italian authorities gave them an interesting insider's perspective on terrorist cells' use of telephones. The man, who clearly is holding up a cell phone for emphasis, lectures his associates:

> Do you see this? This was created by an enemy of God. You can't imagine how many operations this has made fail and how many arrests it has caused. How do you think the brothers in Germany got arrested? Thanks to this they found out many important things! Because when they spoke, the others [i.e., the police] were already listening. Several operations were prevented. It is nice, you can use it to communicate. It's

fast. But it causes you huge problems. They created it and they know how to intercept it.[29]

Terrorists do not trust telephones, the invention of the "enemies of God," but they are forced to use them. Few operatives install a landline in their apartment, as they know that landlines are easy to trace and bug. When they do, they periodically check it for listening devices. Cell members often use public phones, but since they fear that those close to their apartment or mosque may be monitored as well, they may travel for miles just to use what they think is a "clean" telephone. Phone booths in the many phone shops that have sprung up in the immigrant neighborhoods of most European cities are also used. Operatives are instructed to memorize telephone numbers, not to write them down.[30] If they do have to commit them to paper they use codes, substituting a number with another. or omitting parts of the number.

Terrorists favor cell phones, which are more difficult to monitor. In a constant race against European intelligence fueled by their paranoia, operatives repeatedly change cell phones, often using more than one at a time, switching the prepaid cards after every phone call or even stealing a cell phone for just one call. Operatives frequently communicate using cryptic phone text messages, which are more difficult to detect and understand. In some cases, they use cell phones bought in another country, knowing that, for example, French authorities will have more difficulties monitoring a Danish or a Portuguese cell phone. Terrorists around the world have relied on European cell phones. Satellite phones purchased in Europe have been used by al Qaeda leaders in Afghanistan and, more recently, by Abu Musab al Zarqawi's operatives in Iraq.

Swiss mobile phones have been particularly attractive for terrorists, as Swiss regulations formerly did not require buyers to disclose their names. Authorities believe that terrorists bought hundreds of Swisscom's SIM cards: prepaid telephone cards that allow phones to connect to cellular networks in more than a hundred countries. In 2004, fearing that terrorists were taking advantage of Swiss laxity, Bern finally passed a law requiring users of prepaid phones to register their names and addresses.[31] Nonetheless, the terrorists' passion for Swiss prepaid phone cards ended up being a blessing for Western intelligence agencies. The terrorists' confidence in the anonymity provided by the SIM cards was false: A joint operation conducted by intelligence agencies of the United States, Switzerland, and more than dozen other countries that focused on the monitoring of Swiss cell phones led to the arrest of Khalid Sheikh Mohammed, the mastermind of the 9/11 attacks, and several other important al Qaeda operatives.[32] After discovering that Mohammed used a Swisscom SIM card, authorities began tracing his movements inside Pakistan until he was finally arrested in Rawalpindi in March 2003. Other operatives were later tracked down through their Swisscom prepaid card. "They'd switch phones but use the same cards," one intelligence official remarked. "The people were stupid enough to use the same cards all of the time."[33]

After 9/11, realizing that their telephone conversations were under closer surveillance, al Qaeda operatives increasingly began to find other ways to communicate. As noted, couriers are ideal but impractical for all but the most important and secret information. In some cases militants have fallen back on other traditional methods—letters, for example, whose real meanings are carefully hidden in innocent-sounding words. The militants' imagination has sometimes led them to decidedly low-tech solutions, such as placing messages inside jars of food or bottles of soda. But technology has been enormously helpful to them, offering an abundance of tools for communicating with minimum risk of detection. E-mail messages are widely used by terrorists in Europe and elsewhere, even though they can be intercepted by intelligence agencies without much difficulty. Al Qaeda is known to encrypt messages on Web sites, using technology that is quite complicated and not very widespread. In some cases, militants hide their messages on Web sites that require a password to be accessed. The password is either known to the operatives or can be easily determined only by them (for example, the instructions might be "enter the name of Abdullah's cousin, the one living near the butcher").

In order to prevent agencies like the National Security Agency (NSA) from intercepting messages sent online, operatives have adopted a cunning e-mail method dubbed the "dead drop box."[34] It was used by Mohammed

Momin Khawaja, a Canadian man arrested in March 2004, and by a cell of Pakistani militants in London accused of planning to bomb unspecified targets in Britain.[35] A message is written and simply saved in the "draft" box of an e-mail account. Various people in different parts of the world who have the password of the account can read the message without it ever being sent, thereby avoiding the risk of interception.

Since most online chat services allow registration under aliases, terrorists often use these to communicate. In some cases, militants use chat rooms of known radical Islamic Web sites; in others, they simply insert their murderous conversations into chat rooms focused on gardening, pet care, or anything else. Using a pseudonym such as Ahmed23 or JohnnyK, an operative sitting in an Internet café in Rotterdam or Barcelona can anonymously communicate in real time with an associate at the other end of the world with no fear of being traced.

However they communicate, militants tend to use coded language. To be sure, operatives sometimes forget their instructions and openly talk on the phone about false documents or planned attacks (often leading to an angry rebuke from the listener), but in general, they are extremely careful about what they say. All the important terms are changed; therefore, Rachid might become Mohammed and false documents could be referred to as "the books." After years of experience listening to terrorists speaking in codes, Italian authorities have learned how to decode the conversations of terrorists; thus in 2002 they moved quickly to arrest the militant who was heard saying, "Now the field where we have to play football is ready. The people went to play football . . . think carefully. . . . Everything is ready, the game is ready, we have to play."[36] They knew that an attack was imminent.

Information gained from arrests carried out across Europe after 9/11 significantly improved authorities' understanding of the codes used by terrorists. In September 2001, British authorities arrested a North African militant named Kamel Daoudi, who was reportedly found in possession of a codebook. With its help, investigators could interpret the criminal messages that North African terrorists operating in Europe were disguising in seemingly innocent conversations.[37] According to the manual, the secret services are called "the snakes," an armed group is "the family," and a man under surveillance is "a sick man." Weapons are identified by their country of production; thus a Kalashnikov is referred to as "the Russian," and an Israeli-made Uzi submachine gun is called "the Jew." A lawyer is "a doctor," and an operative who was killed in action "got married."[38]

Fear of detection keeps operatives perpetually on edge and drives them to maniacally organize every aspect of their everyday routine. They worry that not just their telephones but also their apartments and cars are bugged, and they therefore periodically check them for listening devices. In some cases, distrusting the privacy of their own apartments, they go to public parks and sit on a bench to conduct an important conversation.[39] Militants agree to knock on apartment doors in special ways so that potentially undesired outsiders can be immediately recognized. Al Qaeda even advises its operatives to devise special signals to indicate that an apartment is not currently under surveillance, such as "hanging out a towel, opening a curtain, placing a cushion in a special way, etc."[40]

Operatives also are instructed in how to detect surveillance by intelligence agents. Militants should walk down dead-end streets or stop suddenly to observe if someone is following them. They should drop something out of their pockets and see who picks it up.[41] Militants occasionally walk in pairs, with one trailing some fifty yards behind the other to see if he is being followed. Sometimes they enter a metro station and let a train go by, knowing that anyone else who does the same is probably an agent. If they take a bus, they get off with a quick jump to force into sight any individual who might be following.

European cities often become the settings of extensive games of cat and mouse between terrorists and intelligence agents. Generally, at least three to four highly trained agents are needed to follow a single terrorist in an urban environment.[42] If he travels by car, at least two cars are required to track his movements, since operatives often stop to check for tails. Sometimes the militants deliberately slow down when coming to a traffic light, only to speed through as soon as it turns red. They know that any car that follows them through the red light is likely tailing them.

Nobody can predict how long the day of a surveillance agent tracking a militant will be. The target of the operation can spend weeks secluded in his apartment and then, without warning, leave for another European city. After quickly communicating to his or her supervisor that the target has taken a train, the agent must follow, often without knowing where the mission will go. If the militant travels to another country, as it frequently happens in Europe now that borders are effectively open to other EU members, the authorities of that country have to be contacted and asked to monitor the suspect. Of course, cooperation among countries, with their independent bureaucracies and different languages, is not always easy.

Knowing that their telephones are tapped, militants sometimes feed agents false information.[43] A militant living in Cologne, for example, can discuss his plans to leave the following day for Paris at noon from the city's main train station. German authorities then contact their French counterparts, informing them of the suspects' plans and asking them to wait for the terrorists at the station. But the next day, the militants take some different action—for example, they travel by car, leaving at five in the morning. And perhaps their true destination is Vienna. In that case, Austrian authorities have only a few hours to be ready with a team to follow them.

And these problems that intelligence agencies experience while tracking known militants look small beside their difficulties in profiling potential terrorists. As chapter 1 made clear, Islamist terrorists operating in Europe are drawn from almost every social type, from educated Westerners to illiterate North African women. Some have rewarding jobs or are pursuing graduate studies. Others have menial jobs as a cover for their real activities and a means to raise petty cash for jihad. Many are unemployed or involved in crime, committing burglaries and drug-related offenses. Some dress in traditional Arab garb and wear long beards, while others wear trendy Western clothes and sport expensive sunglasses. Many go to mosques, still a key meeting point for militants despite their increased scrutiny by European intelligence agencies after 9/11. Some terrorists even hold official positions at a mosque and sleep inside it. Others never visit a place of worship, carefully avoiding any location where "the snakes" would be likely to look for Islamic fundamentalists.

Life among the "infidels" can be hard for Islamic militants. Some of them strictly avoid any contact with native Europeans, shopping and eating only at places run by fellow Muslims. The large immigrant neighborhoods of many European cities constitute de facto parallel societies— small islands of Arab culture where a Muslim man can get by without speaking the local language or interacting with non-Muslims. Still others mingle easily with the enemy, hiding their deep hatred for the West behind the façade of the simple immigrant who wants nothing more than to integrate into his or her adoptive country. Many of them make a point of looking like a Westernized Muslim rather than an Islamic fundamentalist to avoid raising suspicion. Several Islamic scholars have provided support for such actions, issuing religious decrees that justify a jihadi's behaving like an infidel while living in the enemy's land. Sheik Ibn Taymiyah, one of the most eminent religious authorities among Islamic fundamentalists, declared seven centuries ago: "If a Muslim is in a combat or godless area, he is not obligated to have a different appearance from (those around him)."[44]

The idea that "necessity permits the forbidden"[45] has been wholeheartedly embraced by a number of Islamic fundamentalists operating in Europe. The Western appearance of its operatives is the particular trademark of and, at the same time, the particular danger posed by one ultra-fundamentalist sect, Takfir wa'l Hijra (Exile and Excommunication). The movement was born in Egypt in the 1970s, composed of extremely violent radicals who believed that anybody that did not follow their interpretation of Islam was not true a Muslim and should therefore be excommunicated.[46] According to Takfir wa'l Hijra's ideology, the punishment for excommunication was death. The movement has found new strength in Europe, with thousands of loosely connected but committed adherents throughout the Continent. Takfiris not only look like Westerners but even indulge in European decadence, drinking alcohol in large quantities, dating women, and smoking marijuana. And Takfiris do not hesitate to commit crimes to finance their activities, convinced that any method used to carry out their jihad is lawful.

THE MONEY

Youssef Nada, seventy-four years old, rarely leaves his lakefront mansion in Campione d'Italia, a posh Italian enclave in Swiss territory. When he does, he enjoys a quick breakfast in one of the elegant bars of Lugano and a chat with local bankers. The seventy-six-year-old Ahmed Idris Nasreddin spends his days in the quiet of his Tangiers villa; near the mansion of the king of Morocco, it sits on the edge of a hill overlooking the Mediterranean. He dedicates most of his time to reading Islamic scholars and taking care of his businesses, located from Nigeria to Switzerland. Nada and Nasreddin are the very picture of successful Muslim businessmen who have retired and now tend to their small empires from home.

But according to the intelligence agencies of a dozen countries, Nada and Nasreddin have also been the masterminds of a sophisticated terrorism-financing network that spanned four continents and funneled millions of dollars to various Islamist groups. The US Treasury Department, which designated both men as terrorist financiers in the months following 9/11, claims that Nada and Nasreddin ran an array of banks and "shell companies lacking a physical presence" whose sole purpose was to finance terrorism. It points in particular to Al Taqwa, a bank headed by both men and incorporated in the Bahamas, which since its foundation in 1988 has financed terrorist groups such as Hamas, the Algerian Armed Islamic Group, and al Nahda in Tunisia. Moreover, the Treasury Department claims that Al Taqwa "provid[ed] a clandestine line of credit to a close associate of Usama Bin Laden" and that al Qaeda itself received funding from the bank until September 2001.[47]

Although Al Taqwa was based in the Bahamas to take advantage of the country's strict privacy laws, the bank formed part of a sophisticated network of more than twenty companies headquartered in Italy, Switzerland, and the tiny principality of Liechtenstein. Both Nasreddin and Nada had spent most of their lives in Europe, creating their fortunes in Italy, Switzerland, and Germany. The Ethiopian-born Nasreddin is an Italian citizen who briefly held the title of honorary consul of Kuwait in Milan and paid the rent of the city's infamous Islamic Cultural Institute, which the Treasury Department has called "al Qaeda's main stationhouse in Europe."[48] Nada, an Egyptian-born naturalized Italian businessman and son of an adviser to the late Palestinian leader Yassir Arafat, masterminded the financial activities of the Muslim Brotherhood in Europe for more than thirty years.[49] It is safe to say that, in all likelihood, Nada and Nasreddin have been the two largest financiers of terrorism to have operated in Europe over the past twenty years.

But Nada and Nasreddin also exemplify the difficulties faced by European (and American) authorities seeking to adequately punish terrorist financiers. Despite the serious accusations leveled against them by US and European counterterrorism agencies, Nada and Nasreddin have never served a single day in jail and are still managing their fortunes from the comfort of their mansions. Though they have been subjected to official designations and sanctions by the United Nations, United States, and European Union, the two businessmen have not been charged with any crime and have suffered little from the freezing of some of their assets.

In fact, since the various resolutions that target terrorism financing allow authorities only to freeze the bank accounts of the suspected financiers, the businesses and residential and commercial properties belonging to Nada and Nasreddin have remained untouched. Both men, financial experts with decades of experience, have also devised a system of front companies and secret off-shore bank accounts that enables them to circumvent resolutions and shelter their wealth and enterprises from any actions by the authorities. Nada still maintains business interests in Switzerland and Liechtenstein; Nasreddin still owns a luxurious hotel in downtown Milan.[50]

The cases of Nada and Nasreddin illustrate how ill-designed European legislation is to tackle terrorism financing; entities and individuals that have raised funds for terrorism have generally been punished merely with a "designation," an administrative decision of little practical value if detailed investigations and repressive measures do not follow. But European authorities have not paid enough attention to this issue. Whereas in 2002 the US Treasury had more than a hundred trained analysts in its terrorism-financing unit, the Bank of England had only seven, the German Bundesbank one, and the French Ministry of Finance two—working part-time.[51]

Lax laws on financial transactions, poor enforcement, and the vast amounts of money in circulation make Europe the terrorists' ideal place for raising money. If Nada and Nasreddin, who moved millions of dollars for decades, can go substantially unpunished, terrorists who raise small amounts know that they can operate in Europe with almost complete freedom. Therefore, terrorist organizations have set up hundreds of front charities, humanitarian organizations, companies, and businesses across the Continent with the primary purpose of raising or laundering money.

Legal businesses have traditionally been an important source of funding for terrorist groups. Wealthy charities closely linked to royal families in the Arab Gulf countries have operated in Europe and funneled money to known militants for years. Terrorist financiers have managed real estate firms in Spain, import/export businesses in Germany, and restaurants in England. In 2001 Italian authorities shut down an association of cooperatives run by North African men that in fact did nothing more than launder money and sponsor militants for visas to enter the country.[52] Syrian businessmen closely linked to the Muslim Brotherhood ran a complicated network of companies in Spain and Germany that allegedly financed al Qaeda activities in Europe and even employed some of the 9/11 hijackers.[53]

At the same time, militants have often resorted to crime for a significant portion of their funds. Many Islamic fundamentalists are former street thugs who have found a new direction in Islam. Some of these experienced criminals simply keep on doing what they were doing before their conversion to radical Islam—though now, they are told, they are acting "for the cause of Allah" and are, therefore, doing a good and necessary deed. Justifying the commission of crimes with the religious formula mentioned in the previous section, "necessity permits the forbidden," terrorists have raised money by carrying out credit card fraud, forging documents, using counterfeit banknotes, and stealing. Reportedly, Islamic fundamentalists have sometimes relied on Mafia-style techniques, threatening fellow Muslim shopkeepers to extort money for jihad in exchange for protection.[54]

Militants have often financed their activities with robberies, since stealing the money of the infidels for jihad is considered permissible. An investigation conducted by a Russian television station revealed that Parisian street gangs composed of young Muslim men from the city's slums were robbing jewelry stores and sending part of the profits to Islamic fighters in Chechnya. Ahmed, a young French Muslim interviewed in the program, described how the robbers ride up to jewelry shops in motorcycles, smash the windows with a sledgehammer, and take all they can in less than a minute. The jewels are sold few hours later on the city's black market or quickly carried to stores in Antwerp, Europe's main market for precious metals and diamonds. According to Ahmed, couriers, often accompanied by women in order to appear less suspicious, then transport the profits of the robberies to Chechnya, traveling with bags packed with cash along a carefully planned route that goes through Italy, Slovenia, the Balkans, Turkey, and Georgia. At every stop along the way, members of the network facilitate the couriers' passage.[55]

Paris-based members of the Moroccan Islamic Combatant Group, the terrorist organization behind the Casablanca bombings, devised a particularly cunning robbery. As a spokesman for the French Interior Ministry described it, "Hassan Baouchi organized his own kidnapping and the theft of the money for the cash machines. The stolen money was destined to finance terrorist activities in France and abroad."[56] In March 2004, Baouchi, a twenty-three-year-old technician with a security company whose job was to fill ATMs with cash, claimed to have been forced by three masked robbers to open the machines in six different locations in the northern suburbs of Paris. It appeared that the thieves had managed to steal more than a million euros.[57]

French authorities immediately doubted Baouchi's story. Their check into his background raised additional suspicions, as Baouchi's brother had been arrested in April 2004 for his role in the Madrid train bombings. Mustapha Baouchi, a skilled mujahid who had visited Afghanistan at least twice, was the leader of the Paris cell of the Moroccan Islamic Combatant Group, a group of French-born Islamists who had raised funds for the Madrid train bombers and for other operations carried out by the Moroccan group.[58] A thorough investigation of the "robbery" revealed that Hassan

Baouchi had staged the whole incident and that the group had used the money, which was never found, for terrorist purposes. An alleged accomplice of the Baouchis, a man with close ties to the Chechen mujahideen, was detained in Algeria in October 2004 with forty thousand euros in cash.[59] Hassan Baouchi was arrested by French authorities one month later.[60]

The Paris ATM case is just one example of the frauds planned by Islamic fundamentalists to raise money. In January 2005, German authorities in the western city of Mainz arrested Mohammed Khalil, a twenty-nine-year-old Iraqi, and Yasser Abu Shaweesh, a thirty-one-year-old Palestinian, on the charge that they had planned suicide attacks in Iraq.[61] Khalil, a high-ranking al Qaeda operative who had direct contacts with Osama bin Laden and had spent years in Afghanistan, had done more than recruit Shaweesh for a suicide operation: he had devised an elaborate scheme to benefit financially from Shaweesh's death. His plan was to purchase life insurance for Shaweesh and to subsequently stage his death in a car accident in Egypt, complete with a purchased dead body to add to its realism. The money from the life insurance was to be collected by Shaweesh's wife, who would have kept part of it for herself and given the rest to Khalil to finance additional operations. After his staged death, Shaweesh intended to travel to Iraq and die in a suicide attack against US forces. Since insurance companies do not share data, Shaweesh reportedly had planned to buy life insurance from at least ten companies in order to maximize the organization's financial gains from his death.[62]

Though robberies, frauds, and thefts are crimes that target infidels and are, therefore, easily justifiable by more militant interpreters of Islamic law, many radicals consider the sale of drugs to be *haram* (prohibited). Mainstream Islam strictly prohibits involvement with any substance that impairs the mind and a person's judgment, making any drug-related activity a sin. Nevertheless, other radicals believe that any method of raising money is permissible if the profits are used for jihad. The most extreme sects of fundamentalist Islam, like Takfir wa'l Hijra, condone trafficking in drugs, and some adherents have sold heroin, cocaine, and hashish in small amounts on street corners and have even organized large-scale smuggling.

Already in 1993, French intelligence was warning that the sale of drugs in the slums outside the country's large cities was in the control of North African gangs led by veterans of the Afghan war against the Soviets and linked to terrorist groups operating in Algeria. There were reports that some drug dealers operating in the southern outskirts of Paris were enforcing a brutal version of Islamic law, chopping off the hands of drug addicts who did not pay their debts.[63] As part 4 will show, some of the key terrorists behind the Madrid train bombings, most of whom adhered to Takfir wa'l Hijra's ideology, financed their operations with drug trafficking between Spain and Morocco. According to Spanish authorities, the two hundred twenty pounds of dynamite that the terrorists used in the attacks were acquired in exchange for sixty-six pounds of hashish.[64]

Over the past few years, Islamic terrorists have also engaged in one of Europe's most profitable illegal activities: human smuggling. The GSPC (Groupe Salafiste pour la Predication et le Combat, or Salafist Group for Preaching and Combat), a radical Algerian Islamist group operating in the desert areas of North Africa, is actively involved in smuggling large groups of sub-Saharan migrants across the desert and then to Europe. There the GSPC can count on an extensive network of cells that provides the illegal immigrants with false documents and safe houses. In 2003 German authorities dismantled a network of Kurdish militants linked to Ansar al Islam, the terrorist group led by Abu Musab al Zarqawi that is battling US forces in Iraq. The Kurdish cells had organized a sophisticated and profitable scheme to smuggle hundreds of illegal Kurdish immigrants into Europe and thereby raise hundreds of thousands of dollars.[65] Given that each migrant pays, on average, about $4,000 to his smugglers and that around half a million illegal immigrants reach Europe every year,[66] terrorist groups have every reason to get into the business.

A report published by the Italian secret service in the summer of 2003 made an alarming claim: "There is the fear, too, that the same routes used for illegal immigration are being used by militants to help form Islamic groups."[67] European authorities worry that terrorist organizations have created a dangerous strategic alliance with groups of human traffickers, pooling their logistical and financial resources. Such an alliance might offer terrorist groups not just a share of the profits but also a means of smuggling operatives. European intelligence agencies believe, in fact, that dozens of terrorists have slipped into the Continent among the masses of illegal immigrants that regularly reach through land and sea. For example, a cell dismantled by Swiss authorities in 2004 attempted to facilitate the entrance in Switzerland of Abdallah ar-Rimi, an important member of al Qaeda in Saudi Arabia. The cell, made up of Yemenis and East Africans had established a well-oiled mechanism to smuggle hundreds of Middle Eastern immigrants into Europe, supplying them with false documents. The cell, which was also engaged in illegal gold trading, sent the profits of its business to a Yemeni charitable organization linked to al Qaeda.[68]

In other instances al Qaeda has tried to smuggle operatives inside containers. In October 2001, Italian authorities, inspecting the *Ipex Empedor*, a cargo ship transiting through the port town of Gioia Tauro on its way to Canada from Egypt, heard noises coming from one of the ship's containers. The inspectors were not surprised to find a man, as hiding inside such containers is a standard ploy of illegal immigrants. But they were shocked to discover that he had with him a laptop computer, two satellite phones, and badges granting access to restricted areas of airports of three different countries. The Egyptian, who had attended a course for airplane mechanics in Canada, was detained on suspicion of links to terrorism.[69]

Containers are also used to smuggle counterfeit goods in and out of Europe's commercial harbors, as well as operatives and weapons. Islamic extremists are reported to be behind complex plans to smuggle counterfeit fashion products, CDs, video games, and leather purses from Asia and Africa to Europe. In 2002, for example, Danish authorities seized a boat full of counterfeit perfume and shampoo coming from Dubai and later established that they had been sent by an al Qaeda operative. According to Interpol officials, the counterfeiting trade is already an important source of revenue for terrorist organizations and has the potential to become "the preferred source of funding for terrorists."[70] Trading in the opposite direction, terrorists are believed to be exporting stolen cars from Europe to the Middle East via ships.

There are even indications that al Qaeda owns its own fleet. US intelligence officials estimate that directly or indirectly, al Qaeda controls at least fifteen ships, which can be used as sea taxis to transport operatives around the world.[71] Substantial numbers of suspicious boats have been seen in Europe's southern sea, the Mediterranean, and the US Navy, working closely with European allies, has been monitoring its waters since the months after 9/11. In the summer of 2002, American maritime intelligence became particularly interested in the *Sara*, a ship registered in the tiny Pacific island of Tonga. Reliable sources indicated that the owners of the ship had murky connections and suggested that the vessel could have been used by terrorist groups to smuggle operatives into Europe. In July, while the ship was docked in the Moroccan port of Casablanca, its Romanian captain, Adrian Pop Sorin, received a phone call from its owner telling him that fourteen new Pakistani sailors had been hired who would be joining the other Pakistani man already on board. As soon as the ship began making its way toward the Mediterranean, Sorin realized that the men had absolutely no experience as sailors; indeed, many of them exhibited extreme seasickness. After Sorin complained about the incompetent sailors to his employer, he received specific orders to keep them on board and to stay in international waters. He nevertheless tried to get rid of the Pakistanis in Malta, but the authorities did not authorize the *Sara*'s docking. Sorin finally docked in the Sicilian port of Gela in August, after pretending to have engine troubles.[72] There the Pakistani sailors were found to be in possession of false passports and detained.

The captain of the ship, who had not received his salary in months and clearly had little love for his employer, revealed that the *Sara* had changed its name repeatedly—from *Nador* to *Palona* to *Ryno*—over the few months before its docking in Gela. This information proved to be very important, as Italian and American maritime intelligence agents had information indicating that a ship named *Ryno* had been used by Islamic fundamentalists from South Asia to enter Europe. After a short investigation, Italian authorities charged the fifteen Pakistanis with being members of Lashkar-e-Jhangvi, a Pakistani terrorist group with close ties to al Qaeda; the men were suspected of having been sent to Europe to carry out attacks. The information provided by Sorin and the Romanian crewmen was crucial in the investigation. The Romanians claimed that the Pakistani sailors, besides often feeling seasick, were completely unwilling and unable to do any work on the ship. Allegedly, one of them bragged about being a Taliban and the men proudly showed the Romanian sailors a cellular phone that displayed a picture of Osama bin Laden. The suspicions of the Italian authorities grew when they learned that the men had paid more than $1,200 to reach Casablanca from Pakistan, using a three-month open airplane ticket. The indictment noted that these tickets cost more than the men would have earned in the three months they were supposed to work on the boat before returning to Pakistan.[73]

The story of the *Sara* reminded Italian authorities of an incident that had occurred a few months earlier in Trieste, a harbor in the north of the country. In February 2002, Trieste port authorities stopped another Tongan boat, the *Twillinger*, which was carrying eight Pakistani sailors with false documents. The men were from the same mountainous region of Pakistan as the fifteen sailors of the *Sara*, and they, too, were described by the Romanian crew as uncooperative and often seasick. One of them was a graduate of the Lahore Business School, an unusual credential for a sailor. Italian authorities found out that the men had open airplane tickets to Pakistan, $30,000 in cash, several magazines containing reports on 9/11, and a map of Rome with a circle around Vatican City. Even though the case raised suspicions, no specific terrorist connection could be proved and the men were deported to Pakistan.[74] The connection between the *Sara* and the *Twillinger* was deeper than these numerous similarities. As Dimiciu Enaiche, the Romanian cook who worked on both, confirmed, the two ships had the same owners.[75]

Those owners, a Greek businessman living in Romania and a Pakistani with American citizenship, are behind several companies that control the *Sara*, the *Twillinger*, and other boats suspected of ferrying terrorists around the world. Their operations exemplify the intertwining of legal and illegal activities that makes the authorities' work very difficult. How can authorities prove that the shipowners knew their ships were transporting terrorists? And, by the same token, how can they prove that an individual who sent money to a terrorist knew that it would be used for a terrorist attack? Can the worshipers of a mosque that raises money later funneled to terrorists be accused of funding terrorism? All these unanswered questions prevent European (and American) authorities from effectively tackling terrorism financing.

Perhaps the millions of dollars that went into building al Qaeda's global network before 9/11 are no longer flowing so freely, but today's fight against the financing of terrorism is even more difficult. Cells have become more independent and they rely on simple mechanisms to sustain themselves, financing their activities through petty crime or legal activities. Moreover, the sums needed to carry out an attack are often risibly small. For example, authorities estimate that the Madrid train bombings cost no more than $10,000 and the May 2003 attacks in Casablanca only $4,000.[76] Though Europe definitely needs to step up its efforts, authorities have to accept that complete success is almost impossible. As the 9/11 Commission observed, "Trying to starve the terrorists of money is like trying to catch one kind of fish by draining the ocean."[77]

NOTES

1. "Leading Sunni Sheikh Yousef al-Qaradhawi and Other Sheikhs Herald the Coming Conquest of Rome," Middle East Media and Research Institute (MEMRI), Special Dispatch #447, December 6, 2002.

2. AIVD (Algemene Inlichtingen- en Veiligheidsdienst, General Intelligence and Security Service), "Recruitment for the Jihad in the Netherlands; from Incident to Trend," December 2002.

3. AIVD, "Background of Jihad Recruits in the Netherlands," March 10, 2004, p. 3.

4. Michael Taarnby, "Recruitment of Islamist Terrorists in Europe," Centre for Cultural Research, University of Aarhus, Denmark, January 2005.

5. AIVD, "Recruitment for the Jihad in the Netherlands."

6. Ibid.

7. Ibid.

8. Sebastian Rotella, "The Hunt for al Qaeda, Sunday Report; Extremists Find Fertile Soil in Europe," *Los Angeles Times*, March 2, 2003.

9. Ibid.

10. Taarnby, "Recruitment of Islamist Terrorists in Europe."

11. AIVD, "Recruitment for the Jihad in the Netherlands."

12. Marc Sageman, *Understanding Terror Networks* (Philadelphia: University of Pennsylvania Press, 2004).

13. Sageman, quoted in Marlena Telvick, "Al Qaeda Today: The New Face of the Global Jihad," PBS Frontline Special, January 2005, http://www.pbs.org/wgbh/pages/frontline/shows/front/etc/today.html.

14. Es Sayed is believed to have died while fighting US forces in Tora Bora, Afghanistan, in December of 2001. In 2004 a Milan court sentenced him in absentia to eight years and four months. Ben Soltane was sentenced in 2003 by the Milan Court of Appeals to four years and six months.

15. DIGOS report, "Al Muhajiroun 1," Milan, April 2, 2001.

16. Ibid.

17. Ibid.

18. AIVD, "Recruitment for the Jihad in the Netherlands."

19. "Brigitte 'Plotted to Blow up Reactor,'" *Age*, November 12, 2003.

20. "Report: Islamic Militants Ran 7 Recruitment camps in France," AP, December 10, 2003.

21. Rotella, "The Hunt for al Qaeda, Sunday Report."

22. "Al Qaeda Training Manual," available in part on the US Department of Justice Web site, http://www.usdoj.gov/ag/trainingmanual.htm.

23. "The Al Battar Training Camp: The First Issue of Al-Qa'ida's Online Military Magazine," MEMRI, Special Dispatch #637, January 6, 2004.

24. Stefano Dambruoso, *Milano Bagdad: Diario di un magistrato in prima linea nella lotta al terrorismo islamico in Italia* (Milan: Mondadori, 2004), pp. 94–97.

25. Judith Miller, "Some Charities Suspected of Terrorism," *New York Times*, February 19, 2000.

26. "Ex-Wife Massoud-Killer Arrested in Switzerland," AFP, March 31, 2005.

27. Bruce Crumley, "The Alliance Lives!" *Time*, June 15, 2003.

28. "Al Qaeda Training Manual."

29. DIGOS report, "Al Muhajiroun 1," Milan, April 2, 2001.

30. "Al Qaeda Training Manual."

31. Ginny Parker, "Prepaid Phones Get a Bad Rap from Crime Use," *Wall Street Journal*, February 17, 2005.

32. Don Van Natta Jr. and Desmond Butler, "How Tiny Swiss Cellphone Chips Helped Track Global Terror Web," *New York Times*, March 4, 2004.

33. Ibid.

34. Ontario Court of Justice, Her Majesty the Queen v. Mohammed Momin Khawaja, Ottawa, Ontario, Canada, May 3, 2004.

35. Jason Bennetto and Kim Sengupta, "Terror Arrests: Bomb Plot Linked to Canada Suspect," *Independent*, April 1, 2004.

36. Fabrizio Gatti and Guido Olimpio, "Presi Quattro di Al Qaeda: 'l'Italia e' un Nemico," *Corriere della Sera*, October 11, 2002.

37. "France Terror Code 'Breakthrough,'" BBC, October 5, 2001.

38. Guido Olimpio, *La Rete del Terrore* (Milan: Sperling & Kupfer, 2002), pp. 73–75.

39. Dambruoso, *Milano Bagdad*, pp. 53–55.

40. "Al Qaeda Training Manual."

41. Ibid.

42. Dambruoso, *Milano Bagdad*, pp. 53–55.

43. Ibid., pp. 58–59.

44. "Al Qaeda Training Manual."

45. Ibid.

46. Gilles Kepel, "*Jihad; The Trail of Political Islam*," trans. Anthony F. Roberts (Cambridge, MA: Harvard University Press, 2002), pp. 254 ff.

47. US Treasury Department press release, "The United States and Italy Designate Twenty-Five New Financiers of Terror," August 29, 2002, http://www.ustreas.gov/press/releases/po3380.htm.

48. Tom Hundley, "European Loopholes Too Inviting," *Chicago Tribune,* November 11, 2001.

49. Servizio per le Informazioni e la Sicurezza Democratica (SISDE, the Intelligence and Democratic Security Service), official dossier on Ahmed Nasreddin, April 6, 1996.

50. Marco Cobianchi, "L'FBI Sbaglia Indirizzo," *Panorama*, December 5, 2003.

51. William F. Wechsler, Lee S. Wolosky, and Maurice R. Greenberg, *Terrorist Financing; Report of an Independent Task Force* (New York: Council on Foreign Relations, 2002).

52. Indictment of Essid Sami Ben Khemais and others, Tribunal of Busto Arsizio, April 6, 2001.

53. John Crewdson and Laurie Cohen, "Charity Founders Tied to Hamburg Terror Suspect," *Chicago Tribune*, November 3, 2002.

54. Magdi Allam, "I Soldi delle Moschee per i Fanatici di Allah," *Corriere della Sera*, September 24, 2003.

55. "Russian TV Looks at European Supply Routes for Mercenaries in Chechnya," RTR Russia TV, December 21, 2003. Excerpts provided by BBC Monitoring International Reports.

56. Emmanuel Jarry, "French Nab Suspect in Robbery for Islamic Militants," Reuters, November 21, 2004.

57. Piotr Smolar, "Faux Braquage de six Banques pour Financer le Terrorisme," *Le Monde*, November 21, 2004.

58. Ibid.

59. Jarry, "French Nab Suspect in Robbery for Islamic Militants."

60. Smolar, "Faux Braquage de six Banques pour Financer le Terrorisme."

61. "Al-Qaida-Verdaechtiger bekam Auftrag direkt von Bin Laden," *Der Spiegel*, January 25, 2005.

62. David Crawford, "German Terror Cell Shifts Focus to Iraq," *Wall Street Journal*, February 23, 2005.

63. "Le Spectre de Reseaux Islamistes Algeriens," *La Depeche Internationale des Drogues*, no. 26, December 1993.

64. Sebastian Rotella, "Jihad's Unlikely Alliance," *Los Angeles Times*, May 23, 2005.

65. Tribunal of Milan, Indictment of Muhamad Majid and others, November 25, 2003.

66. Luke Baker, "Italy Study Sees Al Qaeda Link to Human Smuggling," Reuters, September 7, 2003.

67. Ibid.

68. Swiss Federal Police Office, "2004 Report on Switzerland's Internal Security," Bern, May 2005, p. 29.

69. "Uomo Arrestato in Calabria; Forse Legami con Terrorismo," *Repubblica*, October 24, 2001.

70. Jon Ungoed-Thomas, "Designer Fakes 'Are Funding Al-Qaeda,'" *Sunday Times*, March 20, 2005.

71. John Mintz, "15 Freighters Believed to be Linked to al Qaeda," *Washington Post*, December 31, 2002.

72. "Arrestati a Gela 15 Pakistani Legati ad al Qaeda," *Avvenire*, September 13, 2002.

73. Tribunal of Caltanissetta, Indictment of Zahid Mehmood and others, September 25, 2002.

74. Carlo Barbacini, "Uomini di Al Qaeda sulla Tvillinger," *Il Piccolo*, October 22, 2002.

75. Ibid.

76. Mark Chediak, "Following the Money: Tracking Down al Qaeda's Fund Raisers in Europe," PBS *Frontline* Special, January 25, 2005, http://www.pbs .org/wgbh/pages/frontline/shows/front/special/finance.html; *Los Angeles Times*, September 26, 2004.

77. *The 9/11 Commission Report: Final Report of the National Commission on Terrorist Attacks upon the United States* (New York: Norton, 2004), p. 382.

CHAPTER 3

EUROPE'S TIED HANDS

There has to be a balance between individual liberty on one hand and the efficiency of the system to protect the public on the other. In an ideal world, I would choose the first, but this is not an ideal world, and when dealing with Islamic extremists we have to be brutal sometimes.

—Alain Marsaud, member of the French parliament (2005)

"These guys are smart. They are using our laws and the rights we have given them when we welcomed them into Europe against us. They are taking advantage of the very same liberties they want to destroy."[1] A German intelligence official speaks for many Europeans in expressing his frustration over the inability of his country and others to fashion effective legal tools against Islamic terrorism. Throughout Europe, judges and security officials often find themselves unable to detain known terrorists under current laws.

That terrorism is a crime not easily defined in law makes it extremely difficult to prevent. If an attack is carried out, the authorities have many effective tools available to prosecute the perpetrators. But more difficult questions arise when they must deal with the accessories to the crime. Is the person who provides a false passport to a suicide bomber a member of a terrorist organization? Can he be charged with a role in the attack? If so, then in order to prove his guilt, prosecutors have the difficult task of proving mens rea, his criminal intent—that is, that the individual provided the document knowing that it would be used by a terrorist in an attack. Otherwise his act constitutes not terrorism but a common crime, generally punished with a few days in jail. And what if the document is provided and the attack does not take place? Or if it does take place, but in a country other than the one where the provider of the false passport operated? And what about people who adhere to the jihadi ideology, praise Osama bin Laden, and declare their willingness to die and kill for jihad? Experience shows that these characteristics are displayed by the people who have committed the most heinous terrorist acts. Can those who voice such views be prosecuted even if there is no information that they are actually planning any specific terrorist act? If not, must we just sit and wait until they strap explosives to themselves and kill dozens of innocents?

Many countries in the world, particularly in the Middle East and Africa, do not bother answering such questions. Such regimes, using emergency laws passed decades ago and never repealed, simply incarcerate whoever is somehow, even peripherally, involved with a terrorist act or a terrorist organization. Most of those who are arrested never see a judge, and the trials that do take place are often a farce. A defendant's basic rights are commonly violated and punishments are harsh. Western countries, by contrast, generally respect constitutional guarantees such as the right to a lawyer and to a fair trial. The West rightly prides itself on these rights and freedoms, which should be cherished by men and women throughout the world.

Nevertheless, the West, and Europe in particular, finds itself in a difficult position. The rights granted by most European legal systems are currently exploited by terrorists who are seeking to destroy the very societies whose freedoms make their operations possible. The response to this new threat has to be firm, but what if the needed methods undercut centuries of liberalism and respect for civil rights? Europe is struggling to find the right balance between fighting for its survival and maintaining its essential identity.

In most European countries, laws prevent intelligence agents from sharing information with prosecutors or law enforcement agencies unless they follow a lengthy and complicated procedure. With few exceptions, the monitoring of individuals has to be authorized by a judge who has been presented with convincing evidence of the suspect's guilt. These safeguards, the product of a democratic legal tradition, are meant to forestall the creation of a police state. They epitomize Europe's success in creating a civil society in which the government cannot unduly interfere with its citizens' lives. But, at the same time, they create an ideal shelter for the terrorists. Europe needs to adapt to the new threat that it is facing.

Jean-Louis Bruguière, France's most famous antiterrorism magistrate, has spoken loudly and authoritatively in support of introducing harsher measures in the fight against terrorism: "Terrorism is a very new and unprecedented belligerence, a new form of war and we should be flexible in how we fight it. When you have your enemy in your own territory, whether in Europe or in North America, you can't use military forces because it would be inappropriate and contrary to the law. So you have to use new forces, new weapons."[2]

The enemy that has declared war on the West hides among the civilian population and does not wear a uniform. And this is what makes it so lethal. Authorities cannot do much if they just know that certain individuals are talking about jihad and about killing themselves in suicide operations. Action can be taken only when there is specific information that an attack is pending—but such information is rarely available. What was Mohammed Atta guilty of on the morning of 9/11? Had the CIA or the FBI intercepted the cryptic e-mail in which Atta announced to his accomplice Ramzi Binalshibh that September 11 was the "big day," could US authorities have arrested him? Technically, until the moment he seized control of American Airlines Flight 11 over the skies of Massachusetts, Atta had committed no crime except planning the attack. But it is quite difficult to prove that an attack is being planned, especially when the planners are skilled murderers who have been trained to cover their tracks.

Had they known the details of Mohammed Atta's life, authorities might have suspected that the future 9/11 leader was a person of interest.

His training in al Qaeda camps in Afghanistan, his role as a leader of a group of radical Muslims frequenting Hamburg's most extremist mosque, and his travel patterns should have raised red flags. If, hypothetically, this information had been put together with the e-mail declaring September 11 "the day," authorities in all likelihood would have stopped Atta and his accomplices at the gates of Logan Airport in Boston before they could board their flight on the morning of September 11. A terrible crime would have been at least partially prevented, but it is nonetheless unlikely that a solid case could have been brought against Atta, who probably would have walked free out of Logan after a few hours of questioning.

The aftermath of 9/11 showed that Western legal systems are ill-prepared to deal with the new legal issues that the war on Islamic terrorism has brought to the fore. The excellent work done by European intelligence and law enforcement agencies has often been squandered by the courts, which are governed by laws that are designed to punish individuals who form associations for terrorist purposes only when an attack is carried out—and even then, they may be inadequate to the purpose. The trials in Germany of Abdelghani Mzoudi and Mounir El Motassadeq, two of the accomplices of Atta and the other hijackers in Hamburg, have revealed Europe's legal impotence against terrorism.

Mzoudi and Motassadeq, the only two men to be tried in Germany in connection with the 9/11 attacks, have been waging a complicated legal battle against German prosecutors for more than three years and are currently free men. According to prosecutors, Mzoudi's Hamburg apartment served as the meeting place of a group of Islamic radicals who, bound by their common hatred for the United States and Jews, planned an attack that would shock the world. After gathering countless times at Mzoudi's apartment, some members of the Hamburg cell went to the United States to attend flight schools and carry out the lethal 9/11 plan; others remained in Hamburg to provide logistical support. Prosecutors assert that while the men who worked from Germany may not have known every detail of the plot, they were well aware of the fatal intentions of their US-based associates. For instance, Mounir Motassadeq allegedly told a friend that they "want to do something big. The Jews will burn and we will dance on their graves."[3]

Mzoudi helped facilitate this murderous scheme by allowing Mohammed Atta and Marwan al Shehhi, pilots of the planes that hit the Twin Towers, to use his Hamburg apartment address.[4] This arrangement enabled Atta and al Shehhi to conceal their real whereabouts while they traveled to Afghanistan and applied to flight schools in the United States. Al Shehhi also used Mzoudi's address on a new passport issued to him by the United Arab Emirates after he claimed to have lost the one he had.[5] Terrorists wishing to conceal their visits to Afghanistan frequently claim such "losses" so that they can acquire clean passports.

Mzoudi had an integral role in managing the finances of Hamburg cell members. For example, Mzoudi sent money to al Shehhi while al Shehhi was attending flight schools in the United States. He also took care of the finances of another Hamburg cell member, Zakariya Essabar, as Essabar trained in an al Qaeda camp in Afghanistan (Mzoudi himself attended an al Qaeda training camp near Kandahar in 2000).[6] Motassadeq, too, was involved in the finances of the operatives in Florida, as Marwan al Shehhi had granted him power of attorney and thus access to his bank account. That Motassadeq also was a witness to Mohammed Atta's will provides further evidence of his close relationship with the hijackers.[7]

Motassadeq and Mzoudi were charged in Hamburg with being accessories to the murder of more than three thousand people and being members of a terrorist organization. Motassadeq was initially found guilty and sentenced to fifteen years in prison. Mzoudi's trial was more complicated, as it began after the September 2002 arrest in Pakistan of Ramzi Binalshibh, one of the key members of the Hamburg cell. Mzoudi's lawyers demanded that they could examine Binalshibh, claiming that his testimony was essential to demonstrate Mzoudi's real role in the plot. Because the US government, which has detained Binalshibh since his arrest, refused to disclose even his location, the German judges reluctantly released Mzoudi. "Mr. Mzoudi, you are acquitted, but this is no reason to celebrate," said the presiding judge, adding that the court was not convinced he was innocent and that he had been acquitted only because the prosecution had failed to prove its case.[8] A month after Mzoudi's acquittal, an appeals court ordered a retrial for Motassadeq, on the grounds that the US refusal to allow Binalshibh to testify had denied him a fair trial.[9] In August 2005 a Hamburg court convicted Motassadeq again. Nevertheless, the Moroccan was found guilty only of belonging to a terrorist group and was acquitted on charges of accessory to murder in the 9/11 attacks. He was sentenced to just seven years, a sentence that he immediately appealed.

The difficulty for German prosecutors was that both Mzoudi and Motassadeq were facilitators, sending money and providing apartments to terrorists but not actually carrying out terrorist acts themselves. Indeed, the lawyers for both men have argued that their clients believed they were simply helping fellow Muslims. When asked why he wired money to al Shehhi, Motassadeq explained: "I'm a nice person, that's the way I am." Mzoudi also claims he knew members of the Hamburg cell only casually and had no knowledge of their violent intentions.

Similar frustration in the courtroom occurred following a 2003 Dutch intelligence investigation of twelve Muslim men accused of selling and smuggling large quantities of drugs, then using the profits to provide support to fellow members of the GSPC (Groupe Salafiste pour la Predication et le Combat, or Salafist Group for Preaching and Combat), an Algerian terrorist group closely linked to al Qaeda. According to the indictment, the men also provided safe haven and false documents to other extremists and recruited and indoctrinated young Muslims in the Netherlands, preparing them for jihad against the West.[10] Nevertheless, in May 2003 a Rotterdam court acquitted all twelve of the charge of providing material support to an international terrorist organization. The judge ruled that most of the evidence presented against the men was inadmissible, as Dutch law requires that the police conduct their own investigation. Information gathered by intelligence agencies can be used as a basis for this investigation, but not as evidence in a trial, and in this case the evidence presented by the prosecution was not enough to win a conviction.

Yet the Dutch investigation had demonstrated that the men were potentially quite dangerous and clearly constituted a cell. Prior to their arrest, the twelve men used to congregate at Eindhoven's al Furqan mosque,[11] a recognized base of radical activities. For years, the al Furqan mosque hosted seminars on Islamic law organized by the al Waqf al Islami Foundation, a well-funded Saudi organization. These courses, which invariably expressed extreme anti-Western views, were attended by hundreds of Islamic radicals from across Europe, including some of the planners of the 9/11 attacks.[12]

The purported leader of the cell was Kassim al Ali, a twenty-eight-year-old Iraqi Shiite married to a Dutch convert. Al Ali arrived in Holland in 1997 and immediately asked for political asylum. But after discovering that al Ali had previously made an unsuccessful asylum application in Germany using the pseudonym "Talal Ala," Dutch police arrested him for carrying a false Iraqi ID. During their subsequent search of his Arnhem apartment, police found a scuba diving license.[13] This seemingly insignificant discovery took on vital importance when investigators discovered that al Ali had once attended a diving school in Eindhoven called Safe Diving. Though Eindhoven is a relatively small town, miles from the sea, more than fifty Muslims were enrolled there. Safe Diving's owner, Bill Megens, told the Dutch newspaper *Rotterdams Dagblad* that most of the Muslim students wore traditional Arabic garments and had long beards.[14] Several were familiar to Dutch intelligence because of their radical ties. Investigators nicknamed them the "al Qaeda Diving Team."

Possible terrorist attacks launched either under or on the surface of the water seriously concern law enforcement and intelligence authorities worldwide. In May 2002, the FBI issued a bulletin warning that "various terrorist elements have sought to develop an offensive scuba diver capability."[15] Manuals about scuba diving have been discovered in an al Qaeda safe house in landlocked Afghanistan, and al Qaeda has already carried out a deadly high-seas attack—against the USS *Cole* in 2000. In addition, in 2002 Moroccan authorities thwarted a strike on British and US ships in Gibraltar, arresting three Saudis. In the phone book of one of them, Abdullah M'Sfer Ali al Ghamdi, investigators found al Ali's number—though at his trial, al Ali denied knowing al Ghamdi.[16] He also denied knowing the other Muslims attending the Safe Diving school, flippantly remarking, "It is difficult to introduce yourself underwater."[17] Yet Megens told reporters that al Ali appeared to be the leader of the group;

he recalled that on the day the men took pictures together, everybody wanted to be in a snapshot with Al Ali.[18]

Others among the twelve defendants also have ties that merit further investigation. The Eindhoven mosque came to the public's attention in January 2002 when two young Moroccans who regularly worshiped there were killed in Kashmir while fighting the Indian Army. Intelligence gathered shows that some in the cell knew these two Moroccans intimately. One of them, Anwar al Masrati, owned a photograph of one of Moroccans and admitted having taught him Arabic and the Quran.[19] Another, Zouhair Tetouani, was taped while telling a friend some unpublished details about their deaths. Tetouani's two e-mail addresses include the phrases "Preparing for Jihad" and "Dreamer of Paradise."[20] Tetouani, like many of the twelve, made no attempt to hide his allegiance to the jihadist cause.

Despite the men's radical views, terrorist ties, and declared intentions to kill themselves in suicide operations, Dutch authorities could do nothing more than keep them under surveillance, as the country's laws provided no grounds for detaining them. Sadly Holland is not the exception but the rule in this regard; the legal systems throughout Europe rarely pay sufficient attention to activities that do no direct harming but are instrumental to the execution of a terrorist attack. Though supplying a terrorist with the false documents that enable him to enter the country is as crucial to his mission as providing him with explosives, few countries punish the two crimes with equal severity. Before 9/11, most European countries permitted the recruitment of individuals for a terrorist organization, as long as that organization operated outside their own borders. With laws like these, it is no wonder that Europe has become one of al Qaeda's favorite bases of operations.

Italy experimented with a potential solution to this problem in the fall of 2003. For more than three years, Italian intelligence (Divisioni Investigazioni Generali e Operazioni Speciali, or DIGOS) monitored a cell, primarily made up of Moroccans, in the northern Italian city of Turin. Tipped off by the CIA, who had found telephone numbers of some of its members in a raid of a Peshawar office used by al Qaeda operatives, DIGOS discovered that the cell was active in recruiting youths within the wide local Muslim population, who were then sent to train and fight in Afghanistan, Algeria, and Chechnya.[21] Among the most notorious of these recruits were two "Italian" detainees in Guantanamo Bay, Mohamed Aouzar and Mohamed Ben Salah Sassi.[22] In addition, the leader of the cell had been involved in smuggling weapons to the Algerian Armed Islamic Group (Groupes Islamiques Armés, or GIA) since the mid-1990s and was in close contact with extremists throughout Europe and North Africa.

Despite the substantial amount of evidence that was collected, no action was taken against the members of the cell for more than three years, a delay that frustrated Italian and American intelligence agents. Although the magistrates in Turin agreed that the men posed a threat and that something should be done to disrupt the cell, they could find no legal means to do so. The men had committed no crime, and there was no intelligence indicating that the cell was planning a specific attack. Prosecutors could have charged them only with providing material support to a terrorist organization—but they realized they had little chance of winning that case. Most of the evidence pertaining to the cell comes from Aouzar and Sassi, the two recruits whose confessions were made at Guantanamo Bay; and like most Western legal systems, Italy's generally does not allow testimony from a witness whom the defense is unable to cross-examine. Even if the judge should rule that the two confessions were admissible, the defense could easily claim that they were false, made under physical and psychological pressure. Italian authorities were therefore stuck: they knew that a cell was operating out of Turin, but they could do nothing about it.

The situation became even more complicated after Moroccan authorities became interested in the cell. Moroccan intelligence agents investigating the deadly Casablanca bombings of May 2003 uncovered several European links to the attacks, which brought them, among other places, to Turin. Working closely with DIGOS, they discovered that members of the Turin cell had prior knowledge of the operation. In fact, the men had been collecting money for the families of the suicide bombers before the attacks took place. Moroccan and Italian authorities informally explored the possibility of extraditing the men. Nevertheless, no formal request was made, since both sides knew that it would have been pointless—the Italian constitution forbids the extradition of suspects to countries where they might face the death penalty. Although the evidence on the cell was piling up, Italian authorities still could take no action.

Then came the November 12, 2003, suicide attack in Nassaryia, which killed nineteen Italian soldiers deployed in Iraq. The attack, which was carried out by Islamic fundamentalists, understandably left emotions in Italy running high; in this changed political climate, the public was ready to accept measures of unprecedented harshness. The minister of the interior, Antonio Pisanu, decided to crack down on the cell and realized that the best method was to deport the members. Using powers granted him by a rarely used law, Pisanu decreed the expulsion of the men for "security reasons."[23] By simply deporting them to their home countries, he solved all the legal problems. Prosecutors could drop their fruitless search for statutes under which to charge them; and because the men were not extradited to Morocco and Algeria to face charges, no constitutional issues arose. As cunning as the legal device was in this case, deportation cannot provide a permanent answer. Valid concerns about the human rights of the deported will likely prevent governments from using it regularly. Clearly, better legislative solutions must be found.

Many believe that France has the legal system that is best suited to this problem. Based on the Napoleonic tradition of vesting ample powers in magistrates and strengthened by tough antiterrorism legislation during the 1980s, the French penal code provides investigating judges with legal tools beyond those available in any other Western country. The wave of terrorist attacks carried out throughout France by the Algerian Armed Islamic Group in 1995 motivated the French government to find better ways to fight Islamic terrorism. In their wake, Interior Minister Jean-Louis Debré solemnly declared: "We are at war. It is the war of modern times, and I will tell you that the government is determined to win that war and will make no concessions."[24]

In France individuals can be detained for up to ninety-two hours before charges are filed, a practice that appalls civil rights advocates. When French magistrates suspect that an individual is linked to terrorism but do not have enough evidence to go to trial, they can jail him for up to three and a half years using a catchall and intentionally vague charge, "association with terrorists." The long detention, which has no parallel in other European countries, is intended to give the magistrate the time to obtain evidence needed to prosecute the suspect. Moreover, it can be based simply on intelligence and not necessarily on evidence admissible in court.

These harsh provisions are just part of France's aggressive attitude toward Islamic terrorism. Taking advantage of the strict laicism of the French constitution, authorities have no qualms in scrutinizing places of worship—something that other European countries and the United States are reluctant to do. Authorities closely monitor more than forty mosques nationwide,[25] sending undercover agents to tape Friday sermons and to mingle with known radicals. Using a network of informants established over more than twenty years, the French keep close tabs on the country's large Muslim community. And while most European countries desperately need more qualified Arabic translators, France boasts specialists skilled even in the various Algerian and Moroccan dialects. In addition, France is quick to expel imams who have preached violence or racial hatred, and authorities often detain suspected terrorists for common crimes. Giles Leclair, the director of France's domestic intelligence, makes no secret of his agency's determination to use every trick to stop terrorists: "Sometimes, of course, we can bring some trouble in the personal life, but I think it's better to make trouble for some people for one day and avoid 200–300 people from dying in a blast."[26]

Ironically, the French, who have been among the loudest critics of the methods used by the United States in its war on terror, employ counterterrorism measures that make the US PATRIOT Act look soft. Yet they have set off scant public outcry. Most of the criticism comes from the lawyers of those charged with "association with terrorists." The lawyer of David Courtailler, a French convert sentenced to four years in prison on that charge, expressed their shared complaint: "He has really been convicted for what he may have been able to do, not for what he has done."[27] Alain Marsaud, a former magistrate and a member of France's parliament, has an answer for the critics of France's terror laws: "This is considered by some to be an attack on the liberty of individuals and I agree totally. But it stops the bombs. There has to be a balance between individual liberty on one hand and the efficiency of the system to protect the public on the other. In an ideal world, I would choose the first, but this is not an ideal world, and when dealing with Islamic extremists we have to be brutal sometimes."[28]

However one views France's attitude toward Islamic terrorism, it is anomalous on a continent where respect for civil rights still takes precedence over achieving more security. Consider the different treatments received by the European detainees released from Guantanamo Bay. In most countries, the men were immediately released on their return home, and often they became media darlings. In Sweden, the local government is even helping a former detainee sue the US government for his detention.[29] In France, in contrast, they were detained under the usual charge—association with terrorists—as soon as they set foot on French soil.[30] In effect, the French government, despite its public criticism of the Guantanamo Bay detention camp, took precisely the same action as the Americans: they held the French suspects without accusing them of a specific crime.

Adding to the paradox, the United States' closest ally in its war on terror, Great Britain, is known to take an extremely soft line toward the Islamic terrorists operating on its soil; indeed, on occasion its levels of tolerance border on masochism. The United Kingdom has always taken pride in its tradition of tolerance and respect of free speech—commendable characteristics that have long attracted thousands of refugees, dissidents, and activists who were unjustly persecuted in their countries of origin. But over the past twenty years, the country has also attracted hundreds of radical Islamists, who have exploited Britain's freedoms to continue their jihad against the secular governments in their home countries and, in a second phase, against the West. Even when radicals began preaching and plotting attacks against the United Kingdom, the British government decided not to change its policies.

It should therefore come as no surprise that Britain, unlike France, welcomed home the four Muslim men who were released from Guantanamo Bay in January 2005. One of them, Moazzem Begg, has since frequently appeared on television talk shows and is reportedly working on a memoir.[31] Similarly, the British government's consistent refusal to extradite terror suspects, not only to Middle Eastern countries that have the death penalty but also to other European countries, is predictable. France, for example, has been unsuccessfully fighting with London for almost a decade over the extradition of Rachid Ramda, whom the French accuse of masterminding the deadly 1995 bombings of the Paris metro system.

The problems that Britain faces in combating terrorism on its soil are epitomized by the chaos that characterized the government's attempts to draft more effective antiterrorism legislation in the wake of 9/11. In December 2001, Britain passed the Anti-Terrorism Crime and Security Act, which allowed the government to indefinitely detain foreign terror suspects without charge or trial. The law, which de facto suspended the right to fair trial guaranteed by the charter of the European Union, was harshly criticized by human rights advocates and members of Prime Minister Tony Blair's own party.[32] The British government was extremely careful not to abuse its enormous new powers; only ten foreign terrorists, deemed the most dangerous in the country, were held under the act's provisions in Belmarsh, the country's maximum-security prison. Among them were Abu Qatada, a Palestinian described by Spanish authorities as "al Qaeda's ideologue in Europe," and a handful of Algerian terrorists involved in plots to carry out attacks in France and England.

Because the law could be applied only to foreign nationals, many British citizens who were involved in terrorist organizations faced no legal barriers to continuing their activities even after 9/11. The British public was outraged at the case of Hassan Butt, a twenty-two-year-old British Muslim born in the grimy town of Luton. Butt publicly bragged about his endeavors as terrorist recruiter, claiming that he had persuaded hundreds of British Muslims to fight alongside bin Laden and the Taliban in Afghanistan after 9/11: "I have helped to bring in at least 600 young British men. These men are here to engage in jihad against America and its allies. . . . That there are so many should serve as a warning to the British government. All of them are prepared to die for the cause of Islam." In December 2002, the *Mirror*, a wide-circulation British tabloid, published pictures of Butt brandishing a loudspeaker and inciting a crowd of young men waving the black flag of the Taliban during a rally in Lahore, Pakistan.[33] Despite his activities and his not-so-veiled threats against the British government, Butt was allowed to return to England undisturbed. There he was contacted by a reporter from the *Mirror* and agreed to be interviewed for the price of £100,000. When the reporter informed British counterterrorism officials of the meeting and asked them if they wanted to interview Butt themselves, their response was shocking: "I know this sounds ridiculous," said a detective from the antiterrorist squad. "But we can't get involved. All our checks, all our intelligence, show that he is not wanted for any offences in the UK."[34] Since recruiting for a terrorist organization operating outside of Britain—even an organization that was battling British troops in Afghanistan—was not a crime and the new law applied only to foreigners, Butt was free to roam the streets of Luton.

But the harshest attacks on the Anti-Terrorism Crime and Security Act came from those who deemed it inhuman, not from critics of its loopholes. On December 16, 2004, after two years of legal controversy and political debates, the Law Lords, the country's highest legal body, ruled that the law was incompatible with the European Convention on Human Rights. They set a ninety-day deadline for the release of the ten men detained at Belmarsh under the law's provisions, allowing the government three months to devise new legal measures to deal with them.[35] In January 2005, the Blair government introduced the Prevention of Terrorism Bill, new legislation that attempted to correct the legal flaws of the earlier act while maintaining its substance. For the next two months, a fiery debate raged over the proper balance between Britain's traditionally unconditional respect of civil rights and the new need for security.

Opponents of the bill, most of whom were members of Blair's Labour Party, argued that the legislation was "un-British,"[36] stressing that in barring prisoners' access to a judge it went against eight hundred years of legal tradition. Supporters of the bill pointed to the unprecedented threat that Islamic terrorism posed to the country: "The main opposition to the bill is from people who simply haven't understood the true horror of the terrorism we face," said Sir John Stevens, former commissioner of London's Metropolitan Police. "For the safety of the vast majority, occasionally we will have to accept the infringement of the human rights of high-risk individuals."[37] But by February, sixty-two Labour members of Parliament had staked out positions against the bill, heightening the battle.[38] As the days went by, the embarrassing prospect that the ten men detained in Belmarsh could be the beneficiaries of this political infighting drew nearer. On March 11, the first anniversary of the Madrid train bombings, the front pages of British newspapers lambasted their politicians for failing to reach a compromise that would keep Abu Qatada, who was considered the spiritual leader of the men who carried out the Madrid attacks, securely in prison.[39]

On March 11, after a thirty-hour session—one of the longest in British parliamentary history—the new antiterror legislation was passed. The law allows authorities to monitor the movements of suspected terrorists, who can be required to wear electronic tags, to stay at home for twelve hours a day, to refrain from using computers or cellular phones, and to have only preapproved meetings.[40] As the exhausted members of Parliament headed home, eight of the ten Belmarsh detainees were released on bail and put under the new "control orders" created by the new legislation. Had the agreement been reached just a few hours later, some of Europe's most dangerous terrorists would have walked out of prison free.

Less than four months later, London was hit by terrorism. According to British authorities, on the morning of July 7, 2005, four suicide bombers almost simultaneously detonated four rucksacks full of explosives on three Tube trains and a double-decker bus, killing more than fifty people. Exactly two weeks later, in a clumsy attempt to copy the July 7 attacks, four individuals attempted to detonate more bombs on other trains and buses but were unable to cause a proper explosion. The investigation revealed that the July 7 suicide bombers, the first ever to strike on European soil, were three British-born Muslims of Pakistani origin, while the fourth was a Jamaican-born naturalized British citizen. The second group of attackers was made up of successful asylum-seekers from various East African countries who had lived in the UK for more than a decade. Britain was under attack from within, as all men had radicalized and, in all likelihood, conceived the plot, inside their very own country.

After the July attacks the country and, finally, its elite, realized the seriousness of the threat the Blair government and top security officials had been warning of for years. On August 5, a month after the first bombings, Tony Blair unveiled his government's renewed agenda to tackle Islamic extremism in Britain. Blair began his speech with a not-so-veiled attack against its critics: "The anti-terrorism legislation of course passed in 2002 after September 11th was declared partially invalid, the successor legislation hotly contested. But for obvious reasons, the mood now is different, people do not talk of scare-mongering."[41] Downing Street's new proposals are harsh and signal a strong break with the past: "Let no one be in doubt," said a determinate Blair, "the rules of the game are changing." Under the new proposed measures, individuals linked to terrorism or "fostering hatred, advocating violence to further a person's beliefs, or justifying or validating such violence" will be sent back to their countries of origin. If that country does not have the death penalty and guarantees that the alleged terrorist's rights will be respected, deportation will be very quick. "Cases such as [above-mentioned] Rashid Ramda," said Blair, "wanted for the Paris Metro bombings ten years ago, and who is still in the UK whilst France seeks extradition are completely unacceptable." But the new measures proposed by Blair also include deportation to countries with the death penalty: "The circumstances of our national security have self evidently changed, and we believe we can get the necessary assurances from the countries to which we will return the deportees, against their being subject to torture or ill treatment contrary to Article 3 [of the European Convention on Human Rights]. We have now concluded a Memorandum of Understanding with Jordan [home country of Abu Qatada], and we are close to getting necessary assurances from other relevant countries."[42]

Blair's proposals include also the closure of radical mosques and bookshops, banning extremist groups such as al Muhajiroun and Hizb ut Tahrir, and making justifying or glorifying terrorism a criminal offence.

Known foreign extremists will be either deported or denied entry. British radicals will be stripped of their citizenship, if naturalized, or put under stringent control orders if British-born. The Blair government is also thinking of using another legal tool to punish British nationals who engage in extremist activities. In the aftermath of the London attacks some well-known radical figures made outrageous statements. Omar Bakri, the leader of the al Muhajiroun movement, was taped by an undercover journalist from the *London Times* while allegedly referring to the July 7 suicide bombers as "the fantastic four" and declared his joy over the attacks.[43] Hassan Butt, the above-mentioned Briton and former al Muhajiroun member whom British police could not even interview, said in an interview to *Prospect* magazine that only Muslims who have sought refuge in Britain are bound by an Islamic covenant not to attack country. As for British-born Muslims, Butt said: "Most of our people, especially the youth, are British citizens. They owe nothing to the government. They did not ask to be born here; neither did they ask to be protected by Britain."[44] Signaling the end of Britain's patience with this kind of rhetoric, authorities are examining the possibility of charging radical Muslim preachers who hold British passports with treason under existing legislation.

Blair's proposals, if accepted, would impress a major change to Britain's attitude toward Islamic radicalism. While opposition is not as stiff as it was in previous occasions, various forces immediately criticized the new proposed measures. Several Muslim organizations claimed that they would alienate large parts of the Muslim community. Members of the Left and human rights organizations accused them of limiting basic rights such as free speech. And Amnesty International derided Blair's announcement that his government was making agreements with several Middle Eastern countries like Jordan on the respect of human rights of individuals to be deported, describing this kind of conventions with such countries as "not worth the paper they are written on."[45]

But while political opposition is inevitable but could be overcome, the biggest challenges to Blair's measures might come from the law. According to most legal analysts, some of the key provisions are severely incompatible with both the British Human Rights Act and the European

Convention on Human Rights. And while the British government can obviate to its incompatibility with the former by amending it (something Blair has already vowed to do if necessary[46]), the problems with the European Convention appear almost insurmountable, as the only possible way to derogate from it is to deratify the whole convention, de facto withdrawing the country's membership in the Council of Europe, a move no European government is even remotely likely to make.[47] Moreover, even if the measures are passed, prosecutors will find significant difficulties in making their cases in court, especially in free speech cases.

The struggle Britain is facing to set definitive rules illustrates the difficulties that most European countries are experiencing in balancing security and individual rights. The debate over how best to fight terrorism will likely last for years to come. Even though politicians may have different views from country to country about precisely what measures should be taken, there is widespread awareness that something has to be done. Other European countries besides Britain have also changed their laws after 9/11 to better address the new problem. One area on which the new laws are focusing is excessive bureaucracy, which all the European countries agree is one of the biggest obstacles to effectively fighting terrorism. Intelligence officials often must wait for weeks to receive a judge's authorization to tap the phone of a suspect, delays that may prevent them from obtaining valuable information. International terrorism, by its nature, operates fast. In some cases, terrorists enter the country they have targeted only a few days before carrying out their attack, and the inability to take swift action against them could be fatal.

In addition, European authorities, like their American counterparts, are scrambling to find competent translators. The vast majority of the conversations and documents pertaining to Islamic terrorism are in Arabic, and tribunals and law enforcement agencies lack skilled and trusted linguists. Even when they rely on nonnative speakers, they find few available. And these translators are a poor substitute for native Arabic speakers, who are familiar with not only the language but also the terrorists' culture. Militants often use a jargon rich in references to religion and to popular Middle Eastern traditions, which is extremely difficult for outsiders to comprehend. Moreover, terrorists operating in Europe generally use minor dialects of North Africa, not classical Arabic.

But the difficulties in finding and retaining reliable translators who are native Arabic speakers are immense. On the one hand, on several occasions translators in different countries have been threatened by militants, who accuse them of being "traitors" because they are working for the "infidels" against "the brothers." Often these translators, after enduring years of fear, have been forced to quit their jobs and take their families to a new location. Low salaries do not help authorities as they try to persuade the translators to ignore the threats. On the other hand, they worry that the native Arabic speakers they recruit may be infiltrators. Several translators have been either fired or reassigned on suspicion of sympathizing with the individuals being investigated. At times, translators have intentionally failed to translate incriminating words or phrases, potentially jeopardizing a case. Recently a Dutch-born Muslim translator for the Netherlands' internal intelligence agency, AIVD (Algemene Inlichtingen- en Veiligheidsdienst, or the General Intelligence and Security Service), was discovered passing classified information to the targets of an ongoing investigation. One of the men who received the leaked documents was the roommate of Mohammed Bouyeri, the killer of Theo van Gogh.[48]

As daunting as the problems faced by individual countries can be, the need for cooperation among countries creates even greater difficulties. Stefano Dambruoso, a leading Italian counterterrorism magistrate, has called the bureaucracy involved in a transnational investigation "depressing."[49] According to Dambruoso, if an Italian magistrate wants to contact a counterpart outside of Italy, he or she has to fill out, in the language of the recipient country, a document that is at least four pages long. If the form is being sent outside the Schengen countries—Austria, Belgium, Denmark, Finland, France, Germany, Iceland, Italy, Greece, Luxembourg, the Netherlands, Norway, Portugal, Spain, and Sweden—it must first pass through the Ministry of Justice in Rome. Most European countries have similar procedures.

Though several conventions have been signed and public promises of collaboration have been made, antiterrorism cooperation across Europe is still inadequate. Bureaucratic delays can make the effort pointless, for the information sought is often useless by the time it is received. It is common knowledge among magistrates and security officials that some European countries simply do not respond to official interrogatories or even informal requests for help. They frequently have to rely on personal contacts within other countries to speed up an otherwise endless process. Internal bureaucratic problems, language barriers, and centuries of diffidence and outright rivalry among European countries all tend to thwart effective joint counterterrorism efforts.

In response to such problems, various institutions have been created. The largest and best-funded is Europol, which was founded in 1992 to facilitate legal cooperation among European countries on numerous issues, including terrorism. But as currently constituted, it cannot efficiently aid Europe's fight against terrorism. By law, every member country must provide Europol with up-to-date information on terrorist activities on its soil, which Europol will give to any member upon request. In theory, Europol should serve as a clearinghouse for intelligence. But, inexplicably, the law requires that the country from which the information originated be notified of the request and give its consent before the information can be passed to the inquiring country. Thus Europol does little more than add another layer of bureaucracy: it collects massive amounts of information that cannot be directly shared with European law enforcement agencies. Such restrictions led a frustrated senior German intelligence official to fume, "Muslim activities are more globalist—more pan-European—than Europeans are."[50] A terrorist cell can easily be based in Germany, raise money in Holland, obtain weapons in Belgium, and simultaneously plan an attack in France. European investigators trying to prevent such an attack would find it almost impossible to coordinate their efforts. The terrorists have taken full advantage of the new Europe, paying no attention as they cross the Continent's now-invisible borders. "We drag ourselves and they run,"[51] says Dambruoso, highlighting how terrorists stay several steps ahead of European authorities.

Such obstacles and difficulties make Europe even more appealing to al Qaeda operatives and other terrorists as a base of operations. They fear

not the Continent's authorities but the foreign intelligence agencies operating inside Europe. Dambruoso offers a particularly telling anecdote in
his book on Islamic terrorism. One night a group of Italian counterterrorism agents raided the apartment of a group of North Africans. The
agents were in plain clothes and had their faces covered with balaclavas.
Since all the occupants of the apartment were North African, one of the
agents barked a couple of words in Arabic, his Italian accent muffled by
the mask he was wearing. The men panicked, thinking that the Italians
were from the *mukhabarat*, the intelligence agencies of their home
country (the name is used throughout the Arab-speaking world). When
the officers identified themselves as Italian police, the militants were so
relieved they almost burst into tears.[52] They knew that agents in Italy, like
those in all European countries, would follow the rule of law. The men
might be arrested, charged, and detained, but all would be able to see a
lawyer in a few hours and all would be charged with a specific crime.
Most important, they knew they would not be tortured, a guarantee by no
means enjoyed by those whom the *mukhabarat* of an Arab country detain.

Middle Eastern intelligence agencies have been operating in Europe
for decades, monitoring the activities of known radicals who have left
their native countries and joined the Arab diaspora in Europe. Their
agents have infiltrated mosques and Islamic organizations, often operating without the knowledge of European authorities. Typically, Middle
Eastern regimes dispatch a few intelligence agents to keep tabs on radicals who have been convicted for their terrorist activities in their home
countries but have managed to flee to Europe, where they take advantage
of liberal asylum policies. Since most European countries refuse to extradite individuals to countries where they could be punished with the death
penalty, Arab regimes have occasionally decided to take the law into their
own hands after long and unsuccessful political and legal battles. In some
cases, the *mukhabarat* have gone beyond mere monitoring and have "disappeared" some important radicals. Such disappearances occur domesti-
cally in several Middle Eastern countries: Individuals are seized off the
street and taken to a secret jail, where they are often tortured, and sometimes they never return. Evidence of this practice in Europe is strong. For

example, it is widely believed that Cairo's *mukhabarat* "disappeared" a known militant, Abu Talal al Qassimi in 1995, while he was in Croatia (Egyptian authorities deny any involvement). Al Qassimi, who was the European spokesman for the Gamaa Islamiya, was reportedly arrested by Croatian police and handed over to the Egyptians, who have detained him ever since.[53]

After 9/11, European countries began to change their attitudes, and the total ban on extradition was occasionally relaxed. In December 2001, Sweden, traditionally one of the staunchest defenders of human rights and a country that has welcomed thousands of political refugees, extradited two Egyptian militants, Mohammed al Zery and Ahmed Agiza, less than a day after seizing them. A high-ranking Swedish official justified his country's new position: "We had very clear indications that these individuals had leadership positions in organizations involved with terrorist acts. . . . And the seriousness of these cases was underlined by the events of the 11th of September."[54]

Stockholm's action came at a delicate moment and after strong pressure from outside. The events of 9/11 shocked countries around the world into realizing what might happen on their own soil, but the change in US attitudes was understandably most dramatic. While Islamists and other unconfirmed sources allege that the United States played a role in several "disappearances" or other forms of extradition of questionable legality even before 9/11, the United States has since embraced a much more aggressive stance toward Islamic terrorists, spearheading efforts to see militants living in Europe put behind bars at any cost. A month after 9/11, President Bush wrote a letter to Romano Prodi, at the time president of the European Commission; among his requests was that the European Union explore "alternatives to extradition including expulsion and deportation, where legally available and more efficient."[55] America was clearly pushing Europe to relax its standards, inviting it to get rid of the known terrorists living on its soil by any means possible.

Since 9/11, America has been directly involved in several cases of disappearances or "lightening-extradition": suspected Islamic terrorists have been kidnapped from the streets of Europe, hurled onto a plane, and sent to undisclosed locations, often to some secret jail in the Middle East. The CIA refers to these operations as "renditions"; while they are necessary and useful in the war on terror, they have caused embarrassing diplomatic rows between Washington and some European countries. Indeed, months after the two Egyptian militants were extradited from Sweden to Egypt, evidence emerged that the CIA had been behind the entire operation. After Swedish police arrested them, "America security agents just took over," according to a former Swedish diplomat who led the efforts for a Swedish parliamentary investigation into the incident. Alleged CIA operatives shackled and sedated the two men before putting them on an American plane. The men were then flown to Egypt, where they have been reportedly tortured while in detention.[56] As allegations of their torture in Egypt surfaced in Swedish newspapers, human rights advocates began lambasting their government's actions. Public opinion and the political elite class expressed their disappointment in the whole incident, declaring their reluctance to participate again in any similar operation.

While the CIA never comments on such matters, journalists who have tracked the movements of the American plane that flew al Zery and Agiza from Stockholm to Cairo have uncovered sufficient information to affirm that the same aircraft is often used by the CIA for renditions. Registered to a front company in Massachusetts, since 9/11 the aircraft has touched down in all the hot spots of the war on terror, reportedly flying on several occasions to Jordan, Afghanistan, Morocco, Iraq, Egypt, Libya, and Guantanamo Bay.[57] The plane, in all likelihood, acts as a shuttle between countries where the Americans first detain suspected terrorists and places where the individuals are subsequently held. Of course, when the individual is held in a country such as Egypt, it is very probable that he will be subjected to torture.

A more serious diplomatic incident caused by the CIA's renditions took place in Italy, where nineteen CIA operatives have been indicted in the summer of 2005 for their role in the kidnapping of Nasr Osama Mustafa Hassan, better known as Abu Omar, the imam of a radical Milan mosque and a known Gamaa Islamiya operative with experience in the Balkans and Afghanistan. According to a witness, Abu Omar was pushed into a car by two Italian-speaking men on the morning of February 17, 2003, while he was walking on a street in Milan. For more than a year nobody heard from the cleric. Then, in April 2004, Abu Omar called his wife from Egypt, telling her he had been kidnapped by the Italian and American secret services and detained in Egypt ever since. Abu Omar, who had been temporarily released without explanation by Egyptian authorities, also claimed to have been beaten and tortured with electric shocks, leaving him with permanent injuries.[58]

The investigation opened by the Tribunal of Milan uncovered evidence that a CIA team had carried out the kidnapping of Abu Omar. Italian magistrates identified more than 20 CIA operatives who, divided in different teams, had seized him in Milan, driven him to the US military base in Aviano (in northern Italy), and flown him to two other US military bases (one in Germany and one on the Red Sea) and then to Cairo, where he was reportedly brought to the infamous al Tora prison, the high-security facility where most Egyptian political prisoners are detained. Reportedly, the CIA operatives left several obvious clues behind them, renting cars under their real names and using regular Italian cellular phones.[59] Italian investigators, who treated the kidnapping as a common criminal case, put together compelling evidence against the men involved in the operation and, between June and July of 2005, nineteen alleged CIA operatives were charged in relation to Abu Omar's kidnapping.

The day after the indictments were made public, the names of the operatives were splashed on front pages of most Italian and American newspapers. The men and women involved in the operation risk more than 10 years in jail if they are caught in Italy. While it is unlikely the operatives will ever set foot in Italy again, the cover of those who have been identified by their real names has been blown.

More importantly, what has been seriously put in jeopardy is the relationship between the United States and Italy, one of its key allies in Europe. Milan magistrates accuse the United States of "having severely violated Italy's sovereignty."[60] Technically, they are right. Moreover, they allege that, by kidnapping Abu Omar, the CIA prevented Italian authorities from fully investigating the imam's contacts in Milan, as the man was already under surveillance at the time of his "disappearance." Immediately after the indictments came out, members of Italy's center-left opposition began to publicly attack the US operation and accused the center-right Berlusconi government of not being able to defend Italy's sovereignty. Italian Prime Minister Silvio Berlusconi, whose close relationship with President Bush and support for the Iraq war have already been under fire, was accused of knowingly allowing agents of a foreign country to operate on Italian soil and violate Italian law. Former intelligence agents on both sides of the ocean agreed that the Italian government must have been aware that the CIA was behind Abu Omar's kidnapping, a man that was closely monitored by security services, at least after the action took place, if not earlier. Obviously, the Italian government denied any knowledge of the fact and, on July 1, it summoned the US ambassador to Italy, Mel Sembler, a necessary act under the circumstances. Italy still remains one of America's strongest allies, but, thanks to the CIA's clumsiness, it is very unlikely that will allow this kind of operation on its soil again.

The Italian and the Swedish cases are just two examples that rebuke the US government's official claim that it is not involved in renditions. In fact, there is substantial evidence to the contrary. In March 2005, the *New York Times* reported that in the days immediately following 9/11, the White House issued a classified directive authorizing the CIA to "transfer suspected terrorists to foreign countries for interrogation."[61] Unconfirmed but reliable reports indicate that at least 100 renditions have taken place since 9/11.[62] The Egyptian prime minister Ahmed Nazif revealed that at least sixty individuals have been flown to his country by the United States since 9/11 under the rendition program.[63] Critics of the practice allege that the individuals who are shipped by the United States to prisons in Jordan or Egypt are often tortured. The common accusation is that the United States, while not itself torturing alleged terrorists, is "outsourcing torture."[64] The official position of the US government, expressed by President Bush in a January 2005 interview, is that "Torture is never acceptable, nor do we hand over people to countries that do torture."[65]

In reality, America is indeed handing over suspects to countries that use torture. But in some cases it is difficult to blame the United States.

"The option of not doing something is extraordinarily dangerous to the American people," notes Michael Scheuer, a former senior CIA official and the author of the book *Imperial Hubris*.[66] America, unlike most European countries, perceives itself to be at war. The common sentiment among US officials is that in times of war, every weapon available should be used. The argument takes on added force in this conflict, as the enemy has decided to engage the West in an asymmetric war.

Renditions are probably not the best solution to the terrorist threat, as they undoubtedly raise strong legal and moral issues. They are troubling not just because of the likelihood that intelligence agencies occasionally make mistakes and "disappear" the wrong person but also because respect for the law and human rights is part of what the West is fighting to preserve. Nevertheless, the West now finds itself involuntarily engaged in the first years of a long war that it is not yet prepared to fight. The price of defeat in this war would be the loss of all freedoms. While the civil rights of any individual are sacrosanct, every political leader should keep in mind that the survival of the country should be his or her paramount aim. In the balance between the respect of the civil liberties of a few and the survival of the many, the guiding principle should be *ubi maior minor cessat* (in the presence of the greater, the lesser loses importance).

NOTES

1. German intelligence official, interview with author, Frankfurt, February 2004.

2. Craig Whitlock, "French Push Limits in Fight on Terrorism," *Washington Post*, November 2, 2004.

3. Federal Court of Karlsruhe, Indictment of Mounir El Motassadeq, August 30, 2002.

4. Federal Court of Karlsruhe, Indictment of Abdelghani Mzoudi, October 9, 2002.

5. Ibid.

6. Ibid.

7. Federal Court of Karlsruhe, Indictment of Mounir El Motassadeq.

8. "Sept. 11 Terror Suspect Acquitted," *Deutsche Welle*, February 6, 2004.

9. Desmond Butler, "German Judges Order a Retrial for 9/11 Figure," *New York Times*, March 5, 2004.

10. Tribunal of Rotterdam, Indictment of Mohammed Ramzi and others, May 20, 2003.

11. Ibid.

12. Ian Johnson and David Crawford, "A Saudi Group Spreads Extremism," *Wall Street Journal*, April 15, 2003.

13. Notes taken by a source of the author at the Rotterdam trial.

14. "Het raadsel van de al Qaeda-duikers," *Rotterdams Dagblad*, June 5, 2003.

15. "Wide-Ranging New Terror Alerts," CBS News, May 25, 2002.

16. "Het raadsel van de al Qaeda-duikers." Notes taken by a source of the author at the Rotterdam trial.

17. "Grote leider en oprichter criminale Jihad-organisatie ontbreekt in Rotterdam," *Rotterdams Dagblad*, May 15, 2003.

18. "Ha, daar heb je het al Qaeda Diving Team," *Rotterdams Dagblad*, May 12, 2003.

19. "Grote leider en oprichter criminale Jihad-organisatie ontbreekt in Rotterdam."

20. Tribunal of Rotterdam, Indictment of Mohammed Ramzi and others.

21. DIGOS, Report 24640/01, Turin. Date unspecified.

22. Alberto Custodero and Carlo Bonini, "Cellula di Al Qaeda a Torino. La Procura: 'Arresti impossibili," *La Repubblica*, January 31, 2003.

23. "Terrorismo, a Torino decise altre sette espulsioni," *La Repubblica*, November 18, 2003.

24. Frank Viviano, "Killing Exposes France's Racial Divide," *San Francisco Chronicle*, October 27, 1995.

25. Scheherezade Faramazi, "France, a Past Victim of Terrorism, Doesn't Pull Punches in Fighting Back," AP, December 11, 2004.

26. Ibid.

27. "Frenchman Jailed for Terror Ties," BBC, May 25, 2004.

28. "We French Don't Understand Your Way of Fighting Terrorism," *Telegraph*, February 27, 2005.

29. Whitlock, "French Push Limits in Fight on Terrorism."

30. "We French Don't Understand Your Way of Fighting Terrorism."

31. Ibid.

32. Richard Ford, Philip Webster, and Stewart Tendler, "Terror Laws in Disarray as Suspect Is Let out of Prison," *Times*, March 11, 2005.

33. Jeff Edwards, "Beyond the Law," *Mirror*, December 17, 2001.

34. Ibid.

35. Ford, Webster, and Tendler, "Terror Laws in Disarray."

36. "We French Don't Understand Your Way of Fighting Terrorism."

37. Brendan Bourne, "Up to 200 Al-Qaeda Terrorists in Britain," *Sunday Times*, March 6, 2005.

38. Ford, Webster, and Tendler, "Terror Laws in Disarray."

39. Ibid.

40. "UK Anti-terrorism Law Approved," *Reuters*, March 11, 2005.

41. Prime Minister Tony Blair's Press Conference, August 5, 2005, http://www.number-10.gov.uk/output/page8041.asp.

42. Ibid.

43. "Undercover in the Academy of Hatred," *Times*, August 7, 2005.

44. Aatish Taseer, "A British Jihadist," *Prospect* magazine, no. 113, August 2005.

45. Amnesty International, Press Release, July 20, 2005. Despite opposition, on August 10, 2005, the British government announced it had signed the agreement with Jordan. Under the agreement, Jordan is bound to guarantee that a deportee would not be tortured or otherwise mistreated and would not face the death penalty.

46. Prime Minister Tony Blair's Press Conference.

47. "Blair's Extremism Proposals Attacked as the Hunt Continues for Terror's New Breed," *Times*, August 7, 2005.

48. Stephen Castle, "Secret Service Link to Film-maker's Killing," *Independant*, January 11, 2005.

49. Stefano Dambruoso, *Milano Bagdad; Diario di un magistrato in prima linea nella lotta al terrorismo islamico in Italia* (Milan: Mondadori, 2004), p. 23.

50. David Rising, "Terror Groups Said Working in Europe," AP, March 5, 2005.

51. Dambruoso, *Milano Bagdad*, p. 23.

52. Ibid., pp. 54–55.

53. Many believe that al Qassimi was actually handed over by the Croatians to the United States, which brought him to Egypt on a US Navy vessel.

54. Peter Finn, "Europeans Tossing Terror Suspects out the Doors," *Washington Post*, January 29, 2002.

55. Ibid.

56. "CIA Flying Suspects to Torture," CBS News, March 6, 2005.

57. Ibid.

58. Indictment of Nasr Osama Mustafa Hassan, Tribunal of Milan, June 23, 2005.

59. Paolo Biondani, "I pm di Milano: arrestate gli agenti della CIA," *Corriere della Sera*, June 24, 2005.

60. Indictment of Nasr Osama Mustafa Hassan.

61. Douglas Jehl and David Johnston, "Rule Change Lets C.I.A. Freely Send Suspects Abroad," *New York Times*, March 6, 2005.

62. "CIA Flying Suspects to Torture."

63. Shaun Waterman, "Egypt Admits US Hands over Terror Suspects," UPI, May 18, 2005.

64. The phrase was introduced into the official language of US politics by Rep. Edward J. Markey (D-Mass), who, in February 2005, introduced a bill to eliminate the practice of renditions.

65. Elisabeth Bumiller, David E. Sanger, and Richard W. Stevenson, "Bush Says Iraqis Will Want G.I.'s to Stay to Help," *New York Times*, January 28, 2005.

66. "CIA Flying Suspects to Torture," CBS News, March 6, 2005.

PART II

THE ALGERIAN NETWORK

CHAPTER 4

THE ALGERIAN NETWORK AND ITS ORIGINS

We must destroy Rome. The destruction must be carried out by sword.
Those who will destroy Rome are already preparing the swords. Rome
will not be conquered with the word but with the force of arms. Rome is
a cross. The West is a cross and Romans are the owners of the cross.
Muslims' target is the West. We will split Rome open.
—Sheik Abu Qatada, "spiritual leader" of al Qaeda in Europe

When, on a cold day of January 2003, Greater Manchester police agents entered a run-down red-brick house in the city's northern suburbs looking for an Algerian asylum seeker, they did not expect to encounter any particular problems. Even though they knew that the man might be connected to terrorists, the police carried out the raid unarmed, as used to be tradition in Britain. After detaining the young Algerian, police found, to their surprise, that the man had two roommates, also from North Africa, who were staying in the house.[1] For more than an hour police quietly searched the apartment while waiting for the results of the background checks on the other men. But suddenly, one of the two roommates grabbed a kitchen knife and engaged the unarmed cops in a violent struggle. The fight lasted several minutes; when it was over, Detective Constable Stephen Oake, a forty-year-old father of three who had occasionally served on Queen Elizabeth's and Prime Minister Tony Blair's detail, was fatally wounded, with multiple stab wounds to the chest.

Stephen Oake's killing represented the dramatic conclusion of a plot hatched by a group of terrorists trained in the Caucasus to carry out attacks in Europe. But it also represented the last act of an extremely well-organized network of Algerians that had established a massive presence in Europe and had been behind the vast majority of terrorist activities in Europe throughout the 1990s.

The roots of this network are to be found in the Algerian civil war. The former French colony had supported a fervent Islamist scene in the 1980s, when thousands of young volunteers traveled to Afghanistan to fight the Soviets and then came back to Algeria more radicalized and eager to fight for the establishment of an Islamic state. A homegrown movement, the Armed Islamic Movement—led by Mustafa Bouyali, a veteran of the war of independence against France—had also been actively advocating the violent overthrow of the secular Algerian government and the introduction of Islamic law. These and more moderate forces came together in 1989, forming the Islamic Salvation Front (Front Islamique du Salut, or FIS), an Islamist party. By the end of 1991, FIS had become Algeria's largest party and was poised to win the national elections. Alarmed by the real possibility that an Islamist party could rule the country, the Algerian military, which has a strong tradition of secularism, canceled the elections scheduled for January 1992, preventing the likely shift of power. The reaction of the Islamists to what was in effect a coup d'état was extremely violent, and the country plunged into a brutal civil war, which according to conservative estimates has caused at least a hundred thousand deaths over more than ten years. Soon after the beginning of the conflict, a new, more radical group, the Armed Islamic Group (Groupes Islamiques Armés, or GIA), was created. FIS members never completely closed the door to a peaceful solution with the government, but the GIA was against any compromise and embarked on a campaign of terror.[2] Within a few months, the GIA had supplanted the FIS as the main Islamist group fighting the Algerian government.

While fighting a brutal war at home, the GIA also established a solid presence in Europe. The first wave of GIA supporters settled in France, joining the hundreds of thousands Algerians who were living in the suburbs of the country's main cities. GIA members created an extensive network that supplied the "brothers" fighting in Algeria with weapons, money, and false documents. But when the GIA targeted French interests and citizens in Algeria, Paris decided to crack down on the network. At that point some of the key members of the GIA left France for London. Even though the United Kingdom did not have a large Algerian community, its tradition of tolerance toward refugees and its extremely liberal attitudes toward Islamic radicals made London a perfect choice.

When, in September 1994, Jamal Zitouni became emir (military leader) of the GIA, the conflict with France escalated, as he decided to take the battle inside France.[3] On December 24, 1994, four members of the GIA hijacked an Air France jet in Algiers. The plane landed in Marseilles; a French antiterrorist unit stormed the plane and killed the four terrorists, who had killed three hostages.[4] Reportedly, in what could have been a gruesome anticipation of 9/11, the hijackers had planned to crash the plane into the Eiffel Tower.[5] For the first time, Islamist extremists took their jihad to Europe.

The summer of 1995 witnessed a bombing campaign that bloodied French streets. Eight bombs, detonated throughout the summer in metro stations, markets, and other public places chosen "to maximize civilian casualties," claimed the lives of twelve people and injured hundreds. Fingerprints left on unexploded devices led investigators to Khaled Kelkal, the alleged leader of a group of French-born Algerian militants who acted on behalf of the GIA.[6] The subsequent investigation revealed a wide network that encompassed not just the French cities of Paris, Lyon, and Lille but also London.

That radicals living in the British capital were involved did not surprise French authorities, who had been paying close attention to the activities of GIA operatives in London. As early as 1994, French authorities had found several fax numbers linked to London addresses when they raided the residences of suspected Algerian terrorists in Paris. Some of them were connected with the Finsbury Park mosque, located in a northern London neighborhood with a large Muslim immigrant population.[7] The importance of this mosque, which became the unofficial headquarters for Algerian terrorists in Europe, will be analyzed in more depth in chapter 6. One of the Algerians in London being monitored by French authorities was Rachid Ramda; Paris has been unsuccessfully seeking his extradition from the United Kingdom for his involvement in the 1995 bombings since 1997.

As early as the beginning of 1996, British newspapers speculated about a link between the Algerian network and a little-known Saudi millionaire, Osama bin Laden. There were unconfirmed reports that Ramda was receiving cash from bin Laden.[8] Ramda, who the French believe is one of the financial brains of the GIA's European network, was actively involved in the publication of *Al Ansar*, a weekly newsletter that reproduced GIA's communiqués and thus was the organization's official mouthpiece in Europe. Originally published in France, the magazine was moved to London, in a country that "allowed more freedom of speech," after its publishers came under pressure from the French authorities.[9]

Most of the radicals who became involved in the *Al Ansar* newsletter were regulars at the Finsbury Park mosque. The newsletter became a magnet for terrorists, drawing not just Algerians but also Islamic extremists and activists of other nationalities who worshiped at the London mosque. In fact, the newsletter's two editors were a Palestinian, Omar Mahmoud Othman, and a Syrian with Spanish citizenship, Mustafa Setmariam Nasar.[10] In the following years both men would gain importance in the Islamist network, becoming two of al Qaeda's most important ideologues and leaders in Europe. Othman, who is better known as Abu Qatada, has been called al Qaeda's "spiritual ambassador to Europe" and "the spiritual leader of European Salafists"[11] and has been detained by British authorities since 2002. Nasar, who is better known by his nom de guerre Abu Musab al Suri, became a trainer in an al Qaeda camp in Afghanistan and is suspected to be one of the masterminds of the bombings of four commuter trains in Madrid in March 2004.[12] He is also considered one of the chief ideologues behind Abu Musab al Zarqawi's campaign in Iraq, providing him with religious guidance and justifications for his attacks. Other individuals that participated in the publication of the newsletter also later became involved in terrorist plots.

By 1997 the savagery of Algeria's civil war had escalated: GIA militants were massacring entire villages, including women and children. Their indiscriminate and senseless tactics had completely lost the GIA the support of the vast majority of Algerians. The militants in London were also deeply concerned about the GIA's brutal actions. When, in August 1997, the GIA issued a communiqué accusing the Algerian people of being infidels and apostates, its London supporters decided to distance themselves from the organization.[13] Such a statement was a declaration of war against the entire Algerian population, as the punishment for apostasy, under the strict interpretation of Islamic law embraced by the GIA, was death. It was thus a religious justification for the indiscriminate killing of civilians.

Most of GIA's European supporters decided not to follow the group's line. They had no problem with the killing of "infidels" (Christians and Jews) or of Muslims who worked for the "apostate" Algerian government, but they viewed the latest declaration as a huge strategic mistake. Qatada and al Suri, along with two terrorist organizations, the Egyptian Gamaa Islamiya and the Libyan Armed Group, withdrew their support from the GIA because it was guilty of "deviations in the implementation of jihad."[14] The leaders in Finsbury Park understood that it was impossible for a movement that had embraced such a destructive philosophy to one day rule the country. As Abu Hamza, the one-eyed imam of Finsbury Park, wrote in his book *The Khawaarij and Jihad*, the GIA had been "one of the most terrifying groups to the kuffars [infidels] this century," but it ended up "being Genghis Khan versus the Muslims."[15]

After their formal denunciation of the GIA, members of the Ansar group and worshipers at the Finsbury Park mosque were threatened by militants loyal to the GIA.[16] But their threats were hollow, as the GIA was losing support both in Algeria and in Europe. The time was ripe for the creation of a new group, and in 1998 a former GIA commander, Hassan Hattab, decided to form the Salafist Group for Preaching and Combat (Groupe Salafiste pour la Predication et le Combat, or GSPC).[17] In his first communiqué, Hattab condemned the wholesale slaughter of civilians by the GIA and pledged to continue the armed jihad against the "infidel" Algerian government without harming civilians.[18]

By creating a group that had an ideology very similar to the GIA's, but at the same time condemning the GIA's indiscriminately gruesome tactics, Hattab immediately gained the sympathies of the Finsbury Park radicals and their followers throughout Europe.[19] The recruiting and fund-raising network that for years had helped the GIA gave its full support to Hattab instead. In a very short time, the GSPC eclipsed the GIA and became "the most effective armed group inside Algeria."[20] Moreover, the GSPC managed to avoid the internal disputes that had plagued the GIA. The GSPC has not strictly kept its pledge not to harm innocent civilians, and there are frequent reports of GSPC operatives setting up road blocks and shaking down bystanders for money, though it is a vast improvement over the GIA.[21]

The GSPC completely replaced the GIA in Europe, where it had the opportunity to interact with other networks of radicals—particularly al Qaeda. According to several sources, bin Laden had a role even in the creation of the GSPC. Information gathered by an Italian court in 2004 revealed that the GSPC "was constituted with the approval and cooperation of Bin Laden."[22] A former GSPC leader, Mohamed Berrached, testified that in the summer of 1998, Osama bin Laden had contacted Hassan Hattab, then a member of GIA. Bin Laden urged Hattab to form GSPC in order to give a better image of jihad.[23] Others dispute the claim that bin Laden was involved in the group's formation.[24]

What, in any case, is undeniable is that al Qaeda and GSPC have cooperated extensively for years. Hundreds of GSPC militants have trained in al Qaeda camps in Afghanistan, and, in return, the Algerian group has put its far-reaching European network at bin Laden's service. Over time, the GSPC, while not losing focus on its main enemy, the Algerian government, has increasingly embraced al Qaeda's global jihad. The commonality of the organizations' intentions and goals was made more public after 9/11. On September 15, 2001, the GSPC issued a communiqué in which it threatened to strike, especially in Algeria, "the interests of European countries and of the US."[25] In addition, in late 2003 it officially proclaimed its allegiance to a number of jihadist causes and movements, including al Qaeda.[26] Such announcements are hardly necessary, as the activities and the plots to which the Algerians have been linked from the late 1990s until today prove their close interaction and cooperation with other terrorist groups.

Various events led the members of the GSPC to expand their focus from a regional struggle to a global jihad. Of particular importance was the return of hundreds of volunteers from the wars in Bosnia and Chechnya. In those two jihads, mujahideen from different countries met and built important alliances. As they fought together in defense of fellow Muslims, they realized that the struggle of one group was that of the entire Muslim Ummah (religious community). Algerians went to battle in such places as the Philippines, Kashmir, and Sudan, teaming up with like-minded militants.

Another event that spurred this globalization of jihad was the formal creation in 1998 of the International Islamic Front for Jihad against the Jews and the Crusaders. This organization established and led by bin Laden brought together militants from throughout the world. As the Taliban, which had welcomed bin Laden in 1996, extended its power over much of Afghanistan, bin Laden found himself in indirect control of a country where his organization could flourish undisturbed. The Algerians and the GSPC, with their years of experience in jihad and their extensive European network, played a key role in bin Laden's project. Indeed, according to European intelligence officials, by the end of the 1990s bin Laden's global jihad had become more important than the Algerian conflict to many Algerian militants based in Europe.[27] Their network cooperated so closely with his organization that the distinction between GSPC and al Qaeda, at least in Europe, became blurred.

The Afghan camps run by al Qaeda were crucial in the formation of new alliances between groups that shared similar ideologies, as representatives from different terrorist organizations trained alongside one another. A revealing account of life in the Afghan camps and the role of the Algerians in them has been provided by Ahmed Ressam, the Algerian terrorist who was arrested in December 1999 while trying to cross the

Canadian border into Washington state with explosives hidden in his car's spare tire well.[28] Ressam, who trained in Afghanistan from March 1998 to early 1999, described how militants in the Pakistani city of Peshawar, the gateway to Afghanistan, were gathered by nationality. Groups of six to fourteen militants from the same country would form a cell, and the cell would be assigned to the same Afghan training camp. Ressam and his Algerian cell, for example, were assigned by al Qaeda's gatekeeper Abu Zubaydah to the Khaldan camp, where they received extensive training in subjects that included the positioning of explosives at strategic points, military operations in urban settings, and countersurveillance techniques. According to Ressam, every cell trained during the week and met every Friday to discuss various issues, such as the best ways to establish contacts in Algeria, how to create new cells in Europe, how to raise money for jihad, and possible future operations.[29]

But despite their division by nationality, volunteers from different countries interacted regularly. Ressam revealed that members of the same cell, though in the same camp, did not always live together and that fighters from different countries would often share a tent. Moreover, when every morning the volunteers were sent to the daily training sessions in different specialties, members of the same cell would not necessarily be assigned to the same "class." Ressam painted a picture of constant interaction with members of other groups. He spoke of meeting and fraternizing with members of Hamas, the GIA, the GSPC, Hezbollah, al Qaeda, and other groups.[30]

It was in these camps that the Algerians built solid relations with other groups. The undisputed architect of this new strategy was Abu Doha, a senior member of the GSPC and a prominent figure in the London Islamist scene. Abu Doha, who is also known as Doctor Haidar or "the Doctor," was the brains behind the extensive structure through which hundreds of volunteers were recruited to train in al Qaeda camps in Afghanistan and to fight alongside al Qaeda–linked Islamic forces in Chechnya.[31] By the end of the 1990s, Abu Doha devised the Algerian network's "delocalization" and the redefinition of its targets, so that it focused less on the Algerian government and more on al Qaeda's goals.

In fact, according to US authorities, Abu Doha met bin Laden in Afghanistan in 1998 "to discuss cooperation and coordination between al Qaeda and a group of Algerian terrorists whose activities Abu Doha coordinated and oversaw."[32]

And it was in Afghanistan that Abu Doha conceived a plot that would have proven the Algerians' commitment to bin Laden's cause. In the spring of 1998, while an emir in an al Qaeda training camp, Abu Doha formed a cell of Algerians and began exploring the possibility of attacking US interests both at home and overseas. One of the men that made up Abu Doha's cell was the "millennium bomber," Ahmed Ressam. Ressam told US authorities that members of the cell had agreed to travel to Canada to carry out attacks inside the United States. Abu Doha oversaw the whole operation and also agreed to help Ressam return to Algeria after he had carried out the attack.[33] His time spent in Afghanistan had clearly led Abu Doha to embrace bin Laden's anti-American agenda, and Ressam's attack inside the United States was intended to signal the Algerian network's full support of al Qaeda's plans.

Crucial coalitions were being formed as well in the suburbs and run-down mosques of London, where various terrorist groups had set up their headquarters. One of Abu Doha's most important strategic alliances—with the Tunisians—was established there. Though spared the violence that has racked neighboring Algeria, Tunisia also contains militant Islamist groups that want to overthrow the secular government. Tunisian authorities have always harshly repressed Islamist forces, often using tactics that meet with Western disapproval. Several prominent members of various Tunisian Islamist groups had found refuge in Italy, Switzerland, France, and, of course, England, building a network similar to the Algerians' (though not as extensive). Around 1998 Abu Doha and the emir of the Tunisians, Seifallah Ben Hassine, started to cooperate closely.[34] Sharing a similar ideology, they began combining their recruiting and fund-raising efforts. These two leaders had similar experiences: both had been emirs in training camps in Afghanistan and both were living in London. The alliance between their networks marked the success of bin Laden's pan-Islamic vision and portended things to come.

NOTES

1. Helen Gobson, "The Algerian Factor," *Time*, January 27, 2003.

2. Gilles Kepel, *Jihad: The Trail of Political Islam*, trans. Anthony F. Roberts (Cambridge, MA: Harvard University Press, 2002), pp. 254 ff.

3. Tribunal of Naples, Indictment of Yacine Gasry and others, January 24, 2004.

4. US Department of State, *Patterns of Global Terrorism, 1994* (Washington, DC: GPO, 1995).

5. *The 9/11 Commission Report: Final Report of the National Commission on Terrorist Attacks upon the United States* (New York: Norton, 2004), p. 344.

6. US Department of State, *Patterns of Global Terrorism, 1995*.

7. Ian Burrel, John Lichfield, and Robert Verkaik, "Manchester Police Killing: Islamists—Warning Signs of Algerian Terror Cells as Early as 1994," *Independent*, January 16, 2003.

8. Ibid.

9. Sheikh Abu Hamza al Masri, *The Khawaarij and Jihad*.

10. Ibid.

11. Central Court of Madrid, Proceeding 35/2001, September 17, 2003; Tribunal of Milan, Indictment of Merai and others, March 31, 2003.

12. "Report: FBI Finds Link between 9/11, Madrid Bombers," *Reuters*, November 11, 2004.

13. Sheikh Abu Hamza al Masri, *The Khawaarij and Jihad*.

14. Kepel, *Jihad*, pp. 254 ff.

15. Sheikh Abu Hamza al Masri, *The Khawaarij and Jihad*.

16. Ibid.

17. Tribunal of Naples, Indictment of Yacine Gasry and others. The GSPC has been designated as a terrorist organization by the United Nations, the United States, and the European Union.

18. Tribunal of Naples, Indictment of Yacine Gasry and others.

19. Ibid.

20. US Department of State, *Patterns of Global Terrorism, 2003*, http://www.state.gov/s/ct/rls/pgtrpt/2003/.

21. Tribunal of Naples, Indictment of Yacine Gasry and others.

22. Ibid.

23. "Bin Laden Held to Be behind an Armed Algerian Islamic Movement, AFP, February 15, 1999.

24. Nesser Petter, "Jihad in Europe. Exploring the Sources of Motivations for Salafi-Jihadi Terrorism in Europe Post-Millennium," Norwegian Defense Research Establishment (FFI), January 15, 2004, pp. 53–54.

25. Tribunal of Naples, Indictment of Yacine Gasry and others.

26. US Department of State, *Patterns of Global Terrorism, 2003*.

27. Tribunal of Milan, Indictment of Essid Sami Ben Khemais and others, April 2, 2001.

28. *9/11 Commission Report*, pp. 178–79.

29. FBI dossier on Ressam, July 24, 2001.

30. Ibid.

31. *USA v. Abu Doha*, 01 MJ 1242, Southern District of New York, July 2, 2001.

32. *USA v. Abu Doha*, 01-CR-00832, Southern District of New York, August 21, 2001.

33. *USA v. Abu Doha*, 01 MJ 1242.

34. Tribunal of Milan, Indictment of Essid Sami Ben Khemais and others, April 2, 2001.

CHAPTER 5

THE STRASBOURG PLOT

You are all Jews. I don't need the court. Allah is my defender. Our only judge is Allah. We'll get out of prison soon and go to heaven.
—Lamine Maroni, Frankfurt courthouse (April 2002)

THE CELL

In the summer of 2000, activity among Islamic fundamentalists in Europe was unusually intense. Hundreds of North African recruits who had trained in al Qaeda's camps in Afghanistan streamed into Europe, ready to put their newly acquired skills to good use. At the same time, the ties between the Tunisians and the Algerians had grown significantly closer; Ben Hassine had even sent several Tunisian militants to fight in Algeria in the ranks of the GSPC (Groupe Salafiste pour la Predication et le Combat, or Salafist Group for Preaching and Combat).[1] But intelligence gathered by various European law enforcement agencies indicated that Abu Doha's network also had plans for the Continent.

Their evidence indicated that a cell connected to the Algerian network was active in the German city of Frankfurt, the country's financial capital.[2]

Over the past thirty years Frankfurt has become home to a large number of ethnic groups; in several of its neighborhoods, Germans are a minority. Its large Muslim community, location in the heart of Europe, and superlative communication system make it an ideal place for terrorist operations. The BKA (Bundeskriminalamt), Germany's internal intelligence agency, had received information from its French counterparts that the leader of the Algerian network's cell in Frankfurt was a certain "Meliani."[3] This information was corroborated in December by Italian authorities. While searching a Milan apartment used by two known terrorists, DIGOS (Divisioni Investigazioni Generali e Operazioni Speciali) had found a Post-it note on which was handwritten "Meliani al Ansari al Germi" (Meliani the supporter from Germany) and a German cell phone number.[4]

With the help of the leads coming from France, Great Britain, and Italy, German federal investigators identified five militants who made up the Frankfurt cell and began monitoring their activities.[5] On the night of December 20, 2000, a team of specialists from the German police clandestinely entered an apartment used by the cell. German authorities had learned that the group had received some weapons sent from Belgium in a bag and they decided to place a tracking device in it. To their surprise, the agents found not one but two bags filled with weapons in the apartment.[6] Not knowing if the apartment's occupants would be out long enough for them to procure a second tracking device from their central offices, they decided to take a chance and simply choose one bag to trace, hoping that it would take them to the rest of the cell.

On the afternoon before Christmas, an ominous phone call was intercepted by Scotland Yard. One of the members of the Frankfurt cell, Hicham El Haddad, told Abu Doha in London that an attack was planned for the days around New Year's Eve and that he intended to personally carry it out. Haddad also informed "the Doctor" that the group needed more German marks—the expenses for the attack had been higher than expected, as the cell found it necessary to rent two rooms.[7] The Germans' worries grew when one of the two bags was moved on Christmas Day. The apartment was under round-the-clock surveillance; so even though the bag contained no tracking device, the man carrying it was followed to another Frankfurt apartment.[8] Fearing that the group was no longer a sleeper cell, the Germans acted. A few hours after the bag was moved, armed policemen stormed the two apartments and arrested four of the five members of the cell. "Meliani," the group's leader, managed to avoid arrest, as he had left Frankfurt a few days earlier.

The search of one of the flats confirmed that the cell was ready to carry out an attack. Police found several chemical substances and electronic components commonly used in making bombs, nails, a pressure cooker, detailed instructions for fabricating and using explosives, and various toxic substances. Moreover, the men had already begun mixing them. The members of the cell, who were subsequently all charged with being members of a terrorist organization and planning an attack with explosives, also were in possession of two machine guns, seven pistols, three rifles, silencers, and large quantities of ammunition.[9]

The four men arrested in Frankfurt offer a kind of cross-section of the Islamic militants operating in Europe. Two of them had very similar backgrounds: both were young Algerian immigrants who came to Europe looking for political asylum and ended up becoming involved in crime and terrorism, though they apparently had no ties with radical groups in their homeland. Hicham El Haddad, whose phone conversation with Abu Doha had tipped off investigators, had tried to claim political asylum in the United Kingdom, but his application was denied because he had entered the country illegally in 1992. Nevertheless, he never left Britain. While living in the Greater London area, he committed petty crimes and was arrested for theft under the name Salim Boukhari. Lamine Maroni had also been denied asylum in the United Kingdom. Fingerprint analysis revealed that Maroni, like El Haddad, had been convicted of theft in the United Kingdom under a false name.[10] While living in England, both men fell under the spell of extremists and found a new direction in radical Islam. Between 1998 and 2000, El Haddad and Maroni, like hundreds of other young Muslims, were recruited by Abu Doha and traveled to Afghanistan, where they received their training in al Qaeda's camps.[11]

While learning their deadly skills in the Afghanistan, Maroni and El Haddad met another like-minded Algerian, Fouhad Sabour. Sabour was a different kind of radical and, to European law enforcement officials, a more troubling one. The radicalization of his immigrant peers followed their alienation from and rejection by a society where they had sought asylum; but Sabour was born in the quaint town of Romans-sur-Isère, a typical charming French village at the foot of the Alps. Sabour, who holds dual French and Algerian citizenship,[12] exemplifies the growing threat posed by homegrown radicals who decide to turn to radical Islam and follow the path of jihad.

Sabour was well known to French counterterrorism officials before his arrest in Frankfurt. In September 1999, he had been sentenced in absentia to three years in prison by the Fourteenth Criminal Section of the Paris Court of Grand Instance for being a member of a terrorist organization. Sabour had been active in the Islamist underworld since 1995, when he helped distribute *Al Ansar*, the newsletter published by GIA (Groupes Islamiques Armés, or the Armed Islamic Group) inside France. On June 4, 1996, he was arrested for his involvement in the bombings of the Paris metro carried out by the GIA in the summer of 1995. Freed in December of the same year, he ignored the conditions set by the judge for his release and traveled to Bosnia and Afghanistan.[13]

After receiving their training in Afghanistan, Maroni, El Haddad, and Sabour were sent by the leadership of the Algerian network back to Europe. Despite Sabour's known convictions and Maroni's and El Haddad's illegal status, the three had no trouble entering the United Kingdom in the summer of 2000. The men spent the fall raising the money needed for the operation they had been tasked to carry out. As they contacted al Qaeda leaders in London in order to get funding, the men also sold drugs to raise petty cash. Maroni, who had moved to Sheffield in August 2000, sold hashish to supplement the benefits given to him by the British government because he was an asylum seeker. He spent three months in Sheffield in lodgings provided by a British charitable organization without attracting the attention of British authorities, keeping in contact with Sabour and El Haddad as well as other extremists in Europe.[14]

In October, Sabour moved to Frankfurt. According to a report published by the London newspaper the *Guardian*, just a month later Maroni told his roommates in Sheffield that he was going to London to see "a doctor." Maroni never came back; instead he went to Frankfurt under a false British passport. It is possible that Maroni was making a joke that his roommates could not possibly understand and that the "doctor" in London was none other than Abu Doha, who was respectfully known in Islamist circles as "the Doctor." El Haddad, also using false British documents, traveled with Maroni. In Germany, the two reunited with Sabour, their companion from the Afghan camps, and joined the other members of the cell who had converged in Frankfurt.[15]

Waiting for them there was another Algerian man they had met in Afghanistan, Aeurobui Beandali. Beandali represents a different kind of militant roaming the streets of Europe, the imported threat. Because Sabour was born in France and had French citizenship, authorities lacked any legal tool to prevent him from operating inside Europe. Maroni and El Haddad showed no signs of links to terrorism. But Beandali disclosed his ties to a terrorist organization when he entered Europe, and lax security and immigration laws allowed him to stay for almost ten years. Beandali applied for political asylum in Germany in 1992, openly admitting to having been a member of the Algerian Islamic Salvation Front (Front Islamique du Salut, or FIS) since 1990 and having procured ammunitions and explosive materials for the organization. His application was rejected because of his affiliation, and German immigration authorities notified him of the expulsion order. But Beandali, like thousands of other illegal immigrants, simply ignored the order and continued to live in Germany. During that time, Beandali was repeatedly arrested for several different common crimes (mostly theft).[16] Despite his convictions, German authorities never bothered to enforce his pending deportation order and Beandali continued to commit crimes. More important, Beandali maintained his ties to Algerian militants and his involvement in radical activities. Like the other cell members, he traveled to Afghanistan and then returned to Europe, passing easily through immigration.[17] Beandali is living proof that the failure of most European countries to enforce immigration laws has dangerous consequences for the security of the Continent.

By the beginning of December, the Frankfurt cell was complete and ready to prepare the attack. One of the first tasks it attended to was acquiring the explosives. In one of the apartments the police found large quantities of potassium permanganate, an oxidant that can be used in making bombs. But it is also used to treat severe eczema, especially in children, and is sold to private citizens in Germany in tiny amounts (five to ten grams) when a valid prescription is presented. Although larger amounts are sold only to hospitals, the men had managed to accumulate more than thirty kilograms of the substance[18]—gained, as the German investigators later discovered, through an elaborate and very successful scam. Dressed in business suits bought for this purpose, the men visited forty-eight different pharmacies near large German airports.[19] They would tell the pharmacists that they were about to board their flights for third world countries, where they worked in pediatric hospitals. After gaining their listeners' sympathy, they would ask for help, saying that they needed potassium permanganate for the children but lacked the time to get a prescription. The pharmacists, convinced they were doing a good deed, usually sold the substance to the men, never dreaming that they were actually helping terrorists to build bombs. Nor did the scam end with this story: the investigators found that usually the cell members used false credit cards to pay.[20]

At the same time, the cell also began their surveillance of the target. The evidence gathered in the Frankfurt apartments clearly indicated that a strike was about to be launched—but against what? And why did El Haddad tell Abu Doha that he had to rent two more apartments to carry out the operation? A twenty-minute videotape found in one of the two apartments partially answered these questions. The tape, which is dated December 23, 2000, starts by showing German billboards along the freeway, then the crossing into France, and finally downtown Strasbourg. The cameraman, strolling like a tourist, paused in front of the famous Strasbourg Cathedral, focusing on its gothic façade; he then moved around the stalls of the Christmas market in the pedestrian-only Place Kleber. Occasionally there is an Arabic voiceover: In the market square, "These are the enemies of God taking a stroll"; outside a large store, "These are the enemies of God. You will go to hell, God willing."[21] The investigation revealed that the film had been shot by El Haddad and Sabour (who were careful to never appear in it) and that the voice was El Haddad's. Using false documents, the two men had rented two apartments in the German town of Baden Baden for the days between December 25 and January 2.[22] Their target was clearly Strasbourg, and Baden Baden, near the French border but out of the French authorities' jurisdiction, would be their base of operations.

El Haddad had told Abu Doha that the attack was to take place right before New Year's Eve, a time when the streets of the town's historic center would be busy with holiday shoppers. Authorities believed that the group intended to place the explosives in pressure cookers (one was found during the searches) and then explode them either in the cathedral's square or at the nearby Christmas market. In fact, Beandali admitted that just hours before his arrest, he had called another member of the Algerian network in London, Slimane Khalfaoui, to ask him to send a pressure cooker to Germany, where the kind of pressure cooker he intended to use for the attack was not available on the market. He also confessed to their plan to use pressure cookers in making bombs, a technique they had learned in al Qaeda's camps in Afghanistan.[23]

But even after two long trials (one in Germany and one in France), doubts still remain about the Frankfurt group's precise target. During the trial in Frankfurt, El Haddad and Sabour denied any intent to kill, insisting that the group had planned to target an empty synagogue.[24] Beandali initially confirmed that the group intended to attack a synagogue to "send a message to France and Israel" and told the court that the cathedral appeared in the video only because his accomplices had mistakenly thought it was a synagogue.[25] He also insisted that the men had planned the attack to take place after prayers, so that nobody would be harmed.[26] Beandali told the judge: "At no point did I think about killing one German or French citizen, as I cannot reconcile this with my beliefs." But confronted with the evidence of the tape, which wished death on innocent French bystanders, Beandali changed his story. By the end of the trial he admitted that the group intended to carry out the bombing outside the cathedral.[27]

To be sure, all of Beandali's testimony is questionable, as he lied through the entire trial. Despite his previous admission of a link to FIS, Beandali claimed before the court that he had held no radical views before his arrival in Germany. Beandali also testified that no group recruited him, that he had paid all the expenses of his trip to Afghanistan with his own savings, and that the camp he attended in Afghanistan was "a privately financed school that had nothing to do with al Qaeda or Osama Bin Laden."[28] Beandali had every reason to distance himself from bin Laden and any organized group that was involved in jihad. Though the plot had been thwarted before 9/11, the trial took place in 2002, months after bin Laden had become a household name, and Beandali realized that any link to the Saudi millionaire would not play well in court. Attempting to win the judges' sympathies, Beandali vehemently condemned the attacks of 9/11: "September 11 was a black day in history, especially for the entire Islamic world. I am horrified about such a terrible crime, particularly since it is allegedly justified through our religion. . . . I would never again participate in explosives attacks and the like, since after September 11 it is no longer possible to use such acts to call attention to political grievances in a meaningful way, since they are automatically associated with al Qaeda and Osama Bin Laden."[29] Perhaps his feeling of repentance was sincere—but probably Beandali was just practicing *takiya*, the art of double-speaking that is taught to Islamic fundamentalists in order to trick the infidels.

Conflicting information on the target also came from Ahmed Ressam, who has been helping US authorities since his arrest in Washington state in December 1999. Ressam, who had deep knowledge of the inner workings of the Algerian network, said that the Frankfurt cell meant to target "U.S., Israeli, and French interests outside Germany." In pronouncing the sentence, the Frankfurt court stated that the use of a pressure cooker full of explosives was better suited to an attack in the air rather than in a square; it concluded that the group's target could not be definitively determined.[30] That lack of certitude did not prevent the judges from imposing punishments that were quite harsh. El Haddad, whose voice was heard on the tape wishing death on the "unbelievers," received the longest sentence—twelve years in prison—while his companion on the reconnais-

MAP 5.1. THE ALGERIAN NETWORK

sance mission, Sabour, was sentenced to eleven and a half years.[31] Bean-dali, despite his public professions of remorse, received ten years. Lamine Maroni, who refused to testify or make any statement during the trial, was sentenced to eleven years. Maroni broke his silence only to spit and curse at the public and the police officers in the court. In an outburst, he shouted at the court: "You are all Jews. I don't need the court. Allah is my defender. Our only judge is Allah. We'll get out of prison soon and go to heaven."[32]

THE SUPPORT NETWORK

Whatever the intended target, the Germans—thanks largely to international cooperation—had clearly prevented an attack. The arrests had consequences in other countries as well, as leads developed in the Frankfurt investigation helped uncover cells throughout Europe that were linked to the Algerian network. The repercussions were first felt in the United Kingdom, as British authorities decided to aggressively pursue the cells that were located on their territory. Scotland Yard, investigating jointly with the German BKA, found that the members of the Frankfurt cell had ties to Britain that went far beyond a single intercepted phone call between El Haddad and Abu Doha. At the time of their arrest, El Haddad and Lamine Maroni, who had long lived in the United Kingdom, were holding British Airways tickets from London to Frankfurt. They had flown together to Germany on December 5 and were supposed to fly back to London on January 5, after the job was done.[33] Moreover, wiretaps revealed that the members of the Frankfurt cell had been in constant contact with Algerians in London, filling them in on the latest developments. It was clear that the men had been deployed to Frankfurt just for the attack: their support network was in Britain. An analysis of the chemical substances found in the Frankfurt apartments also uncovered an alarming link between the Meliani cell and England. One of the chemicals found in Frankfurt was triacetone triperoxide (TATP), a rare and highly unstable explosive.[34] During a raid carried out by British authorities, TATP was also found in the Sheffield apartment formerly occupied by Maroni.[35]

Having found explosives on British soil and realizing that London Islamists were bent on carrying out attacks in Europe, Scotland Yard decided to act. Breaking the unspoken nonaggression agreement the British government and Islamic radicals living in Britain had maintained for years, on February 13, 2001, police searched several apartments in London and arrested nine militants connected to the Algerian network. The searches produced a large assortment of blank and forged documents, counterfeit credit cards, tools to forge documents, and more than two hundred tapes of fighting by the mujahideen in the Russian breakaway republic of Chechnya. One of the men arrested, Kouidri Ilies, was found in possession of notes on chemical substances and electronic devices commonly used to fabricate bombs.[36] Another was a thirty-year-old Algerian, Mustafa Labsi, who had also been involved in the failed millennium plot with Ahmed Ressam. Together with Abu Doha, Labsi had been in charge of daily communications with the Frankfurt cell from London. Labsi had traveled to Germany repeatedly and was arrested in Berlin in February 2000 while using a false credit card. At the moment of his arrest he was carrying a picture of El Haddad in his wallet, and a letter addressed to El Haddad was found in his apartment.[37] As the investigation progressed, it became clear that the whole plot had been conceived, directed, and funded in England.

British authorities applauded the operation, which also netted Abu Qatada, the former editor of the *Ansar* newsletter and the spiritual leader of the network.[38] However, one of its main targets, Abu Doha, managed to avoid arrest. Whether directly or indirectly, virtually all the operatives involved in the Strasbourg plot had been in contact with him,[39] but authorities could not locate him on the day of the raids. But his escape from the law was brief; he was arrested just two weeks later at Heathrow Airport while trying to flee to Saudi Arabia using false documents.[40]

Abu Doha's arrest represented a massive blow to the Algerian network. The head of the DST (Direction de la Surveillance du Territoire, France's internal intelligence agency), Pierre de Bosquet de Florian, who had described Abu Doha as "the principal catalyst" behind the London network, commented that it came "a little too late."[41] The DST had been warning Scotland Yard for years about Abu Doha and his network, and the satisfaction felt on the other side of the English Channel at his arrest was understandably bittersweet. Abu Doha's arrest also immediately created legal complications, as authorities from four countries inquired into the possibility of extraditing him from Britain. While France and Germany wanted him in connection with the Strasbourg plot, Italy was interested in him because of his alleged role in a plot to attack the US Embassy in Rome. The strongest pressure for his extradition came from the United States, which had indicted Abu Doha in July 2001 for his role in the thwarted millennium plot. Abu Doha is currently sitting in London's Belmarsh prison, fighting the motions filed by the US government.

Two men traveling with Abu Doha, Rabah Kadre and Abdul Samir Nuri, were also arrested at Heathrow airport. Detained only for violating British immigration laws, they were soon let go.[42] But as the investigation progressed, authorities realized that Rabah Kadre's release had been a mistake. Kadre had been Abu Doha's right-hand man for years, and it was to him that the members of the Algerian network looked for directions after Abu Doha's arrest.[43] In the months following his brief detention, Kadre, using different identities and passports, traveled extensively to Germany, Italy, and the Netherlands to reorganize the network after the wave of arrests. He also spent time in his wife's native country, Slovenia. Later on, authorities also discovered that Kadre had been directly involved with the Strasbourg plot; German police found his fingerprint in one of the Frankfurt apartments. At the end of November 2002, French authorities issued an international warrant for his arrest.[44] By that time, Kadre was sitting in a British jail, suspected of masterminding a cyanide attack against the London underground. Even though British authorities did not extradite him to France, Kadre was tried in absentia in Paris for his involvement in the Strasbourg plot and sentenced to six years.[45]

The thwarted Strasbourg attack was not the only operation planned by Abu Doha after his return to Europe. In early January 2001, Italian authorities received information that a group of Afghan-trained militants had been dispatched by both Abu Doha and Seifallah Ben Hassine to attack the US Embassy in Rome. The threat was deemed very serious and the embassy was temporarily closed. The plot was never carried out, but investigators learned that the operatives had been instructed to contact the group of "Umar al Muhajer" on their arrival in Italy.[46]

At the time, Italy had been monitoring the activities of a group of Tunisians that was directly linked to the Algerians and Tunisians in London. It operated in the Milan area and had ties to the city's infamous Islamic Cultural Institute. The head of the cell was Essid Sami Ben Khemais, a Tunisian veteran of Afghanistan with extensive contacts throughout Europe. Other militants often called him Abu al Muhajer. It was clear that the Ben Khemais cell was involved in something big, and DIGOS, the Italian internal intelligence agency, began monitoring it around the clock. Thousands of hours of intercepted conversations shed a great deal of light on a group that was deeply plugged into the Tunisian-Algerian network. While the Italian cell never directly took part in attacks, it played a crucial role by helping militants who needed to hide from authorities, providing them with safe houses and false documents.[47]

The militants' reaction to the arrests of their associates in Frankfurt and London underscores the extent of the Italian cell's involvement with the Tunisians and Algerians. In a phone call of January 13, 2001, Ben Khemais's nervousness after the Frankfurt arrests is obvious:

Ben Khemais: I warn you, half of the group in Germany has been caught.

Man: No!

Ben Khemais: Yes, do you understand me? They arrested the brothers from Germany and they found the weapons storage in Germany, in Frankfurt.

Man: Today?

Ben Khemais: No, no, it's almost . . . [asking people in the room] Mohammed, it has been three weeks, right? Yes, more or less three weeks ago.

Man: Well . . . the important is . . . what did I want to say?

Ben Khemais: At this point you need cover.[48]

The man that Ben Khemais urged to go into hiding was Tarek Maaroufi, another Tunisian and the ringleader of a cell in Brussels.[49] Maaroufi was the quintessential example of a militant who built alliances with Islamic radicals across countries of origin in Europe. Maaroufi confessed to Belgian authorities that as early as 1991, he had been in contact with Rachid Ramda and other Algerian leaders in London. Maaroufi also wrote articles for the *Ansar* newsletter and helped bring together Tunisian and Algerian militants.[50] He is currently serving a six-year sentence in Belgium, where he was convicted for recruiting European Muslims for training in al Qaeda's camps in Afghanistan.[51]

A conversation between Ben Khemais and other men at his apartment, recorded by Italian intelligence in March 2001, reveals that the London arrests caused even more panic within the Milan cell. Similar alarm is displayed in a phone call between Ben Khemais and one of his confederates, Bouchoucha Moktar, on March 6:

> Moktar: Listen . . . Rashid . . . without me saying anything more . . . the one in Britain.
>
> Ben Khemais: Rashid . . . yes . . . London?
>
> Moktar: The one I don't want to mention.
>
> Ben Khemais: Hey!
>
> Moktar: They got them, him and another brother, at the airport.
>
> Ben Khemais: At the airport?
>
> Moktar: Yes.
>
> Ben Khemais: What were they doing at the airport? Where were they going?
>
> Moktar: They were fleeing. They were wanted.
>
> Ben Khemais [agitated]: No! What a problem! They are getting all of them!
>
> Moktar: Yes. Abdelhakim, do you know him? Yeah, you know him.
>
> Ben Khemais: Abdelhakim . . . I understand. Abdelhakim the Slim.
>
> Moktar: Yes. They arrested him as well.
>
> Ben Khemais: Abdallah, the same?
>
> Moktar: I haven't heard from him.
>
> Ben Khemais: No.
>
> Moktar: I swear. I haven't heard from him.
>
> Ben Khemais: Try to call him.
>
> Moktar: Yes. And should I try calling the other one as well? I'll call the other one and I'll tell him we'll go in the afternoon.
>
> Ben Khemais: Call him. But be careful, call him from a pay phone.

Hundreds of monitored phone calls exposed the shape of a triangle linking Milan, London, and Frankfurt. Though the operatives in Italy often took precautionary measures, frequently changing the prepaid cards in their mobile phones and using public phones, Italian investigators managed to collect an impressive amount of evidence on them; in April, Italian magistrates charged the members of the cell with being members of a terrorist organization. According to the indictment, the group operated from the northern Italian region of Lombardy, "using it as a staging post for terror attacks in other countries." In February 2002, Ben Khemais, the leader of the group, was sentenced to six years in prison; three other members of the cell each received four and a half years.[52]

In intercepted conversations, the cell demonstrated the great deal of attention it paid to new types of explosives and chemical weapons. Here, too, as a conversation of March 2001 reveals, the Algerians in London played an important role:

> Ben Khemais: The thing that the Algerian there [in London] does is "plastic" [explosive] and nowadays is old stuff. I tried to do it too, you can make it with electric wires and one day we tested it with a light switch and we had a positive result.
>
> Man: It's true, they are specialists.
>
> Ben Khemais: No, it's old stuff. I would like to learn how to use the medicine and see what effect it has when it is inhaled . . . but the Libyan has the formula . . . a professor of chemistry . . . because they have found a way to mix the fumes [of the medicine] with the explosive. . . . It's easy, but I don't know how to do it. There are many ways to use explosives with this product, it's not the same kind that was made in Germany. This is the method: you have to add hot water, then you have to divide the whole thing in four parts and after you have prepared this you add the product and you put a wire every two pieces.
>
> Third man: This is used by very smart people in Great Britain and America.[53]

Another member of the network also demonstrated keen interest in chemical substances. Ben Heni Lased, a Munich-based Libyan veteran of Afghanistan linked to the Frankfurt cell, was planning to carry out an attack in Strasbourg and thus finish the job started by the Frankfurt cell. Authorities believe that he intended to open a barrel containing some toxic material (probably a gas) at one of the two locations the cell had videotaped— Place Kleber or the city's cathedral. Returning to a previously chosen target is a common modus operandi of Islamic radicals. For example, after failing to damage the navy destroyer USS *The Sullivans* because the boat they had packed with explosives sank, al Qaeda operatives in Yemen decided to try again, and successfully hit the USS *Cole*. Even 9/11 could be considered a follow-up on a failed operation, as the 1993 bombing of the World Trade Center had been intended to topple the Twin Towers. Lased wanted to execute the operation thwarted by the Christmas raids.

Lased's plan was overheard by Italian authorities at the beginning of March 2001, when he stayed for a few days in Ben Khemais's thoroughly bugged apartment. In an emotional and long conversation, Lased expressed to Ben Khemais his frustration with the group's leadership: "I have made a decision, to fight them [the infidels], but unfortunately when you belong to a group you can't carry out operations by yourself, at least until you decide to sacrifice yourself [die as martyr], in that case the sheikhs think about it. . . . A decision must be made, I want to die as a mujahid, there is too much planning; I only ask to fight them, so that I don't have to answer to anybody."[54]

Lased's impatience reaches new heights as he comments on the sloppiness of the Meliani cell in Frankfurt in leaving the surveillance tape of the Strasbourg targets inside their apartment. By the end of the conversation, Lased is begging Ben Khemais to intercede for him with the leaders of the group:

> Talk to the sheiks, talk to them, and then I'll think about the rest. I don't need an army, but just two people, as long as they have brain and training, especially in the language [i.e., they know how to talk in code], the training must be based on this. They have to be committed and to go ahead without having anything to lose or to gain. Let me complete the operation. . . . I'll do it like the group in Germany, so at this point all I need is one person and a 10-liter barrel.[55]

Lased was arrested in Germany in October 2001 on an Italian warrant. His words were a sign of things to come, as the Algerian network's interest in nonconventional weapons would grow in the following months.

THE FRENCH TRIAL

Because the bombing was supposed to take place in French territory and the Frankfurt cell had several links to France, in February 2001 Paris decided to start its own investigation. Even though no French official would admit it on the record, another reason for opening an independent case was the lack of trust in Germany's counterterrorism agencies and laws. Both European officials and the terrorists are well aware that Germany's laws on terrorism are among the most liberal in Europe. The trials (discussed in chapter 3) of Mounir El Motassadeq and Abdelghani Mzoudi, the two Moroccans who provided logistical support to Mohammed Atta and other 9/11 hijackers, clearly demonstrate that the German legal system currently cannot adequately deal with terrorism.

After 9/11, Germany's counterterrorism officials beseeched the parliament to reform the nation's security laws, but with little success. Frustrated by the legislators' failure to understand the problem, German law enforcement officials have sometimes resorted to inventive techniques against individuals who are known to be terrorists but cannot be seized under German laws. For example, in June 2003 German counterterrorism authorities were instrumental in the arrest—outside Germany—of a top al Qaeda operative, Christian Ganczarski. Ganczarski, a German citizen of Polish descent who had converted to Islam in his teens, spent several years in Germany and was even arrested in April 2003, though he was released soon thereafter. Ganczarski had fought in Afghanistan and he was believed to be in direct contact with Osama bin Laden; he was also suspected of having played a significant role in the April 2002 attack on a synagogue in Tunisia that killed twenty-one people, including twelve Germans. Ganczarski was the last person called by the suicide attacker, Nizar Nawar, before he drove a truck bomb into the synagogue.[56]

Nevertheless, high standards of proof and legal technicalities prevented German authorities from holding Ganczarski. After his release, the German militant traveled to Saudi Arabia, where he was briefly detained for an expired pilgrim visa and then, once again, released. On June 3, Ganczarski began his journey back to Duisburg, his hometown, and Saudi authorities informed their German counterparts they had put the thirty-seven-year-old convert, his wife Nicola (a German convert as well), and the couple's four children, on an Air France flight to Paris. Authorities in Berlin recognized that this was a perfect opportunity to catch Ganczarski and to end an embarrassing situation. They informed the French police of his movements and asked for their help. Upon his arrival at Paris Charles de Gaulle airport, Ganczarski was separated him from his family and arrested.[57] He has been in French custody ever since. The Germans, knowing they could not detain Ganczarski but aware of his dangerousness, decided in effect to subcontract his arrest to French magistrates, whom they knew were in possession of far better legal tools to detain him.

Thanks to severe laws and a sophisticated intelligence apparatus that is widely considered the most effective in Europe at fighting Islamic terrorism, the French have been at the forefront of the war against al Qaeda on the Continent. It should therefore come as no surprise that the most comprehensive case against the Frankfurt cell was built by antiterrorism magistrates in Paris and not by German or British authorities. The investigative judges Jean-Louis Bruguière and Jean-François Ricard opened an investigation into the thwarted Strasbourg attack in February 2001.[58] Their patient and comprehensive work bore fruit in December 2004, when ten Islamic radicals were convicted in Paris for their supporting roles in the plot. These Algerians or French-Algerians, netted by the French in separate operations or extradited from other European countries, constituted almost all the participants in the plot.

The most important man on trial in Paris was Mohammed Bensakhria, who was described by European security officials as one of bin Laden's chiefs of operations in Europe.[59] The investigation of the Frankfurt cell revealed not only that Bensakhria had paid several visits to the apartments occupied by the members of the cell, as fingerprints proved, but that he was the group's leader and mastermind—in fact, he was the mysterious "Meliani" whom authorities in Germany were seeking. Bensakhria, who had learned the use of explosive devices in al Qaeda training camps around 1997, had left Frankfurt for Berlin shortly before the Christmas Day raids and made his way to the port town of Alicante, in southeastern Spain.[60] In order to avoid the attention of Spanish authorities, Bensakhria lived in a van in a North African immigrant neighborhood of Alicante, maintaining an appearance of being extremely poor.[61] Nevertheless, on June 22, 2001, Mohammed Bensakhria and an accomplice were arrested by Spanish police. According to intelligence sources, Bensakhria, who was found with a street map of Strasbourg when he was arrested, was in Alicante waiting for a courier to bring him false French documents.[62]

Spanish Interior Minister Mariano Rajoy touted the work of Spanish authorities and described Bensakhria as "one of the most wanted men pursued by western security services in recent months."[63] But once again, the efforts of French counterterrorism officials were crucial, as the DST provided key information on Bensakhria to the Spaniards. Shortly after his arrest, Bensakhria was extradited to France.[64] At the trial in Paris he was sentenced to ten years in prison.[65] He, like the others, was accused of being a member of a "criminal association in connection with a terrorist act,"[66] the usual catchall charge used by French magistrates.

Another of the men on trial was Slimane Khalfaoui, the man whom Beandali had asked to supply pressure cookers. Khalfaoui, described as an important member of al Qaeda in Europe who had been wanted by authorities since 1996, had also trained in Qaeda's camps in Afghanistan with Ahmed Ressam, the millennium bomber, and was a veteran of the Bosnian war.[67] Prosecutors called him one of the leaders of the group, and he was sentenced to ten years. Khalfaoui's lawyer, Isabelle Coutant-Peyre, said the convictions and sentences showed that French institutions were "racist, anti-Arab and Islamophobic."[68] Another member of the cell tried in Paris was Yacine Aknouche, who was arrested in September 2000. Aknouche, like many involved in the Strasbourg plot, had undergone military training at a camp in the tribal area between Pakistan and Afghanistan, thanks to connections established by Abu Doha in London, and was an established member of the Algerian network. Aknouche, in fact, admitted knowing several men who made headlines in the months after 9/11. He told French authorities that while in London, he befriended the shoe-bomber Richard Reid and Zacharias Moussaoui, the alleged twentieth hijacker.[69] Even though he denied any knowledge of the Strasbourg plot, Aknouche was sentenced to eight years.[70]

Six other suspects, who were alleged to have given logistical support to the plot by supplying false papers to other members of the group, were given lesser terms.[71] The story of Meroine Berrahal, one of the six, demonstrates the centrality of the Algerian network in al Qaeda's activities in Europe. When he was arrested in February 2002, the veteran of Chechnya and Afghanistan was found with the mobile phone number of Nathalie Ben Mustafa, wife of Khaled Ben Mustafa, one of the French detainees in Guantanamo. Berrahal also had been in contact with Brahim Yadel, another French detainee in Gitmo, and with Djamel Loiseau, a Frenchman who was killed fighting US forces in Afghanistan. Berrahal, Loiseau, and Yadel had all been detained earlier in sweeps carried out by French authorities against members of the GIA that were suspected of planning an attack against the 1998 World Cup, the soccer championship held in France that year.

The tenth Algerian who received a prison term (of six years) was Rabah Kadre. As mentioned above, at the time of the trial Kadre was in a British jail, having been arrested by Scotland Yard in November 2002 on suspicion of planning an attack in London. Kadre, along with two other men, was charged by British authorities with possessing "articles for the preparation, instigation and commission of terrorism acts." Reporters speculated that the three intended to carry out a chemical strike against the London underground system, possibly by releasing cyanide during rush hour.[72] Cyanide is a substance that has attracted al Qaeda's interest, and camps in Afghanistan trained militants in how to disperse it as a poisonous gas in the air-conditioning system of a building with minimum risk to themselves. Ahmed Ressam, who was an associate of Kadre, admitted having learned this technique while at the Khaldun camp. [73] British authorities denied that the London underground system had been targeted by the group and stressed that the police had found no evidence that the men possessed any form of cyanide.[74]

The story about the alleged plot, which surfaced almost a year after the second wave of arrests related to the Frankfurt cell, was the first sign that the Algerian network had managed to survive the crackdown that hit it across Europe. After years spent behind the scenes as a recruiter and organizer, Kadre had decided to take direct action. That the plan might involve a chemical substance was an ominous sign of things to come. Following Bensakhria's arrest, a senior US counterterrorism official warned that the network "remains a threat even though we have arrested some of the ringleaders."[75] The truth of his analysis was demonstrated first by Kadre's plan and then by the events of the months following his arrest, which proved to authorities throughout Europe that the Algerian network was far from dismantled.

NOTES

1. Tribunal of Milan, Indictment of Essid Sami Ben Khemais and others, April 2, 2001.

2. DIGOS (Divisioni Investigazioni Generali e Operazioni Speciali) report, "Al Muhajiroun 1," Milan, April 2, 2001.

3. The Frankfurt cell's leader took the name "Meliani" to honor a former commander in Mustafa Bouyali's Armed Islamic Movement who had been killed by the Algerian government.

4. DIGOS report, "Al Muhajiroun 1."

5. Ibid.

6. "A Jihad Warrior in London," *Guardian*, February 9, 2004.

7. DIGOS report, "Al Muhajiroun 1."

8. "A Jihad Warrior in London."

9. DIGOS report, "Al Muhajiroun 1."

10. Ibid.

11. Paul Harris, Burhan Wazir, and Kate Connolly, "Al-Qaeda's Bombers Used Britain to Plot Slaughter," *Guardian*, April 21, 2002.

12. DIGOS report, "Al Muhajiroun 1."

13. Ibid.

14. Harris, Wazir, and Connolly, "Al-Qaeda's Bombers Used Britain to Plot Slaughter."

15. Ibid.

16. DIGOS report, "Al Muhajiroun 1."

17. "Militant Admits French Bomb Plot," BBC, April 23, 2002.

18. DIGOS report, "Al Muhajiroun 1."

19. Harris, Wazir, and Connolly, "Al-Qaeda's Bombers Used Britain to Plot Slaughter."

20. DIGOS report, "Al Muhajiroun 1."

21. Verena von Derschau, "'They Will Burn in Hell'; Alleged Bomb Plotters Go on Trial in France," AP, October 6, 2004.

22. DIGOS report, "Al Muhajiroun 1."

23. "France Sentences 10 for Millennium Plot," AP, December 16, 2004.

24. "Four Convicted of Strasbourg Bomb Plot," *Guardian*, October 3, 2003.

25. "Militant Admits French Bomb Plot."

26. Erik Schelzig and Peter Finn, "Repentant Algerian Tells of Bomb Plot; Muslim Militant, 'Horrified' by Sept. 11, Says His Target Was French Synagogue," *Washington Post*, April 24, 2002.

27. "Four Convicted of Strasbourg Bomb Plot."

28. "A Jihad Warrior in London."

29. Schelzig and Finn, "Repentant Algerian Tells of Bomb Plot."

30. Piotr Smolar, "Dix Islamistes Seront Juges a l'Automne puor un Projet d'Attentat a Strasbourg," *Le Monde*, July 7, 2004.

31. "Four Convicted of Strasbourg Bomb Plot."

32. Harris, Wazir, and Connolly, "Al-Qaeda's Bombers Used Britain to Plot Slaughter."

33. DIGOS report, "Al Muhajiroun 1."

34. Ibid. TATP was also used by shoe bomber Richard Reid in his attempt to blow up the Paris-to-Miami flight. Richard Reid had close ties to the Algerian network, and it is likely that the people who supplied him with TATP had learned how to use it in the same al Qaeda camps where the members of the Frankfurt cell did.

35. Interview with Italian intelligence official, Rome, February 2004.

36. DIGOS report, "Al Muhajiroun 1."

37. Ibid.

38. Abu Qatada was released after a few days of detention, only to be arrested again in October 2002.

39. "3 Accused of Plot to Make Bioweapon," *Chicago Tribune*, February 27, 2003.

40. DIGOS report, "Al Muhajiroun 1."

41. Ian Burrel, John Lichfield, and Robert Verkaik, "Manchester Police

Killing: Islamists—Warning Signs of Algerian Terror Cells as Early as 1994," *Independent*, January 16, 2003.

42. DIGOS report, "Al Muhajiroun 1"; "France Seeks Arrest of a Man Detained in Suspected British Subway Plot," AFP, November 30, 2002.

43. Maryann Bird, "A Poisonous Plot," *Time*, January 20, 2003.

44. "France Seeks Arrest."

45. "French Court Convicts Group in Strasbourg Christmas Market Bomb Trial," AP, December 16, 2004.

46. Indictment of Sami Essid Ben Khemais and others, Tribunal of Milan, April 2, 2001.

47. Ibid.

48. Ibid.

49. Maaroufi wrote an article for the March 2001 issue of the Al Nahda publication *L'Audace* in which he claimed that the information on the attack against the US Embassy in Rome was false and had been fabricated by the Tunisian government in order to discredit its opponents in the eyes of the US government.

50. Belgian intelligence report, January 15, 2002.

51. Raphael Minder, "Al-Qaeda Network Highlighted as Belgian Terror Trial Ends," *Financial Times*, October 1, 2003.

52. Sentence against Sami Essid Ben Khemais and others, Tribunal of Milan, February 22, 2002.

53. Indictment of Sami Essid Ben Khemais and others, Tribunal of Milan, April 2, 2001.

54. DIGOS, "Investigation Al Muhajirun 2," October 5, 2001.

55. Ibid.

56. Giles Tremlett, Rory McCarthy, Luke Harding, Julian Borger, John Aglionby, Michael Howard, and John Hooper, "One Year On; The Hunt for al-Qaida," *Guardian*, September 4, 2002.

57. Uli Rauss and Oliver Schroem, "Osamas Deutscher General," *Stern*, August 4, 2005.

58. Smolar, "Dix Islamistes Seront Juges a l'Automne puor un Projet d'Attentat a Strasbourg."

59. James Graff, "Safety in Numbers; the Attack on America Had Forced the E.U. to Pool Intelligence Resources and Bolster Security," *Telegraph*, June 24, 2001.

60. Smolar, "Dix Islamistes Seront Juges a l'Automne puor un Projet d'Attentat a Strasbourg."

61. "Spain Arrests Bin Laden Associate," AP, June 22, 2001.

62. Ahmed Rashid, "Hunt for Algerians to Foil Bin Laden Attack on G8 meeting," *Telegraph*, July 13, 2001.

63. Alan Fram, "Bush Wants 18,4B More for Defense," AP, June 22, 2001.

64. "Four Convicted of Strasbourg Bomb Plot."

65. "French Court Convicts Group."

66. Smolar, "Dix Islamistes Seront Juges a l'Automne puor un Projet d'Attentat a Strasbourg."

67. "France Seeks Arrest."

68. "French Court Convicts Group."

69. Smolar, "Dix Islamistes Seront Juges a l'Automne puor un Projet d'Attentat a Strasbourg."

70. "French Court Convicts Group."

71. Ibid.

72. Sean O'Neill, "Three on Terror Charges but Tube Plot Ruled Out," *Telegraph*, November 18, 2002.

73. *The 9/11 Commission Report: Final Report of the National Commission on Terrorist Attacks upon the United States* (New York: Norton, 2004), p. 177.

74. O'Neill, "Three on Terror Charges but Tube Plot Ruled Out."

75. Ahmed Rashid, "Hunt for Algerians to Foil Bin Laden Attack on G8 Meeting," *Telegraph*, July 13, 2001.

CHAPTER 6

THE RICIN PLOT

One day the black flag of Islam will be flying over Downing Street. Lands will not be liberated by individuals, but by an army. Eventually there'll have to be a Muslim army. It's just a matter of time before it happens.

—Anjem Choudray, leader of the London-based
radical organization al Muhajiroun (June 2003)

I would like to see the Mujaheddin coming into London and killing thousands, whether with nuclear weapons or germ warfare. And if they need a safehouse, they can stay in mine.

—Abu Yusuf, British-born member of al Muhajiroun (Luton, April 2004)

FROM PARIS TO CHECHNYA AND BACK

As they progressed in their investigation, the French counterterrorism magistrates Jean-Louis Bruguière and Jean-François Ricard, two veterans of France's fight against Islamic terrorism, realized that key militants linked to the Frankfurt cell had managed to escape the Christmas raid in the German city and the subsequent arrests in London and Milan. Some of them, like Mohammed Bensakhria and Yacine Aknouche, were caught in other European countries and put on trial in Paris, as we saw in chapter 6. But others had left the European scene. Bruguière and Ricard became particularly interested in two Algerian men who had managed to flee Germany and—according to information gleaned from arrested members of the network—had gone to Chechnya.

The struggle in Chechnya, which will be further analyzed in chapter 7, has attracted hundreds of Islamic fundamentalists from Europe; they have joined local fighters and Arab volunteers struggling to gain independence from Russia. Fundamentalists have frequently referred to the plight of the Chechen people and their stubborn resistance to draw young Muslims to the Islamist cause. The Algerian network formed strong ties with the group of Arab fighters who began to establish a presence in the Caucasus in the early 1990s, and its leaders raised funds and recruited volunteers to support the militants fighting against Russian forces.

As they were monitoring every step made by members of the Algerian network throughout Europe, French authorities discovered that at least one French volunteer, Xavier Djaffo, had been killed by Russian forces while fighting in Chechnya. Djaffo was a French citizen who had been recruited at London's Finsbury Park mosque, and his death in 2000 made French authorities pay close attention to the volunteers streaming to Chechnya. The French were concerned not so much about the militants' engagement with Russian forces as about what might happen once battle-hardened jihadists returned to France. Paris worried that Chechnya could become a new Afghanistan, a place where militants could gain experience in warfare and terrorist tactics. The events of the 1990s showed that the terrorists used the knowledge acquired in Afghanistan and Bosnia for attacks against the West, and the authorities did not want to have to deal on French soil with veterans of Chechnya.

The DST (Direction de la Surveillance du Territoire, France's internal intelligence agency) saw a disturbing surge in the number of militants going to the Caucasus in the early spring of 2001, right after the arrests in Frankfurt and London. The Algerian network was, in fact, using Chechnya as it had once used Afghanistan. The French militants were joining other Arab fighters who had set up their base in the Pankisi Gorge, a mountainous area just a few miles from the Chechen border that was not patrolled by the Georgian authorities. The gorge is a congenial refuge for guerrillas, who can retreat and hide in its many caves after carrying out attacks in Chechnya. Groups of Chechen rebels and foreign terrorists had established a presence there after the Russians reinvaded Chechnya in 1999.[1]

In particular, the DST received information that two Algerians who had lived in Germany and were linked to the Frankfurt cell were among those who had traveled to the Caucasus. Said Arif and Mabrouk Echiker were both veterans of Afghanistan and members first of the GIA (Groupes Islamiques Armés, or the Armed Islamic Group) and then of the GSPC (Groupe Salafiste pour la Predication et le Combat, or the Salafist Group for Preaching and Combat), and they were wanted by European authorities because of their involvement in the Strasbourg plot. Despite all the arrests it had suffered, the Algerian network could still count on hundreds of operatives and a web of cells that was able to provide funds, safe houses, and false documents. Rabah Kadre replaced Abu Doha at its top, and in March 2001 the entire organization worked to get Arif and Echiker out of Europe.

Laurent Mourad, a member of the network living in London, was dispatched to Germany specifically to help them.[2] Before reaching Arif and Echiker, Mourad traveled to Paris, where he declared that he had lost his French passport; he was promptly issued another one. The old passport, which he had never lost, was given to Arif as a "clean" document. This was an old trick, used by Mourad both in France and in the United Kingdom, as he had declared his passport stolen five times.[3] After he joined them in Germany and supplied them with cash, Arif and Echiker decided to travel separately to lessen the chances of the police finding them. Arif journeyed directly to Italy, while Echiker went to Paris first, staying in a safe house supplied by the network in a multiethnic area near boulevard Magenta.[4] In Italy, Mourad bought them airline tickets for Tbilisi, Georgia.[5] After traveling to Georgia, Arif and Echiker settled in the Gorge, where they met other al Qaeda operatives.[6]

But Arif and Echiker were just the tip of the iceberg. After months of thorough investigation, the DST identified a group of about twenty militants who had left France for Chechnya.[7] Some of them were pious Muslims who did not belong to any group but were moved by the suffering of the Chechen people and had decided to fight alongside Chechen forces. For example, one of them, Khaled Ouldali, an Algerian who grew up in the Bordeaux region and had briefly been a member of the FIS (Front Islamique du Salut, or the Islamic Salvation Front), traveled twice to Chechnya and, according to the DST, fought in the battalion of the Arab commander Ibn ul-Khattab against Russian forces. Ouldali was arrested by Georgian forces in the Pankisi Gorge in August 2002,[8] but he has never been proved to have a connection with any network. Most men who traveled to the Caucasus, however, were Algerians or French citizens of Algerian descent who belonged to the Algerian network headed by Abu Doha in London.[9]

A steady movement of militants toward the Pankisi Gorge began in the first months of 2001, but the importance of the region grew significantly after 9/11 and the subsequent US invasion of Afghanistan. In the first months of 2002, after US and allied Afghan forces destroyed bin Laden's training camps in Afghanistan, al Qaeda operatives scattered throughout the world. Hunted by American forces and wanted by authorities in most countries, the terrorists sought new places where they could establish their presence. Abu Musab al Zarqawi, the notorious Jordanian terrorist who is believed to be behind most of the current attacks in Iraq, played a key role in the redeployment of al Qaeda operatives.[10] Reportedly, al Zarqawi moved to Iran and, subsequently, to Northern Iraq, where he teamed up with members of Ansar al Islam, a small Kurdish Islamist group with training camps in the area. Al Zarqawi also directed the departure of his closest lieutenants from the training camp he used to run on the outskirts of the western Afghan city of Herat. While some of them traveled with him and joined Ansar al Islam in Kurdistan, others settled in the Pankisi Gorge.[11]

According to Georgian officials, in early 2002 a group of about sixty Arab computer, communications, and financial specialists, military trainers, chemists, and bombers established themselves in the area. Using sophisticated satellite-based and encrypted communications, the group worked to support both Arab fighters in Chechnya and terrorists throughout the world planning attacks against US interests. Reportedly, in

2002 the "Pankisi Arabs" tried to buy a large amount of explosives that Georgian security officials believe was intended for a major bomb attack on US or other Western targets in Russia. The plan was disrupted by Georgian officials working with their US counterparts.[12]

According to US military intelligence, the man dispatched by al Zarqawi to be his representative in the Caucasus was Abu Atiya (also known as Adnan Muhammad Sadik), a former instructor at the Herat camp. In the Pankisi Gorge, Abu Atiya, a Palestinian who had lost a leg during the Chechen war, trained militants in the use of toxic gases, with the aid of what Georgian authorities described as "Middle Eastern chemists skilled in poisons." In the summer of 2002, Abu Atiya plotted to ship toxic substances from the camps in Georgia to Turkey.[13] The scheme was discovered in July 2002 by the CIA, which warned Turkish authorities that a man (at the time misidentified as a Georgian) named Abu Atiya had sent a poisonous biological or chemical substance to a man in Turkey. The CIA believed that the substance was to be used against American and Russian targets in Turkey.[14]

After the operation in Turkey was thwarted, Abu Atiya's attention switched from the Middle East and Russia to Europe. It is then that the Algerians came into play: with their unparalleled knowledge of the Continent, they were the ideal operatives to carry out the operation. During the fall of 2002, the DST received information that several French/Algerian militants who had been trained in the Pankisi Gorge were making their way back to Europe. Worried about their intentions, the DST placed several known members of the Algerian network under close watch to see if they were in contact with the returnees. On November 9, British authorities arrested Rabah Kadre, the man who had become the Algerian network's leader after Abu Doha's arrest, amid reports that he was planning an attack using chemical weapons. On the other side of the English Channel, tension was growing, as Kadre's arrest was further indication that the Algerian network was trying to go into action once again. In early November, the DST passed a secret dossier on the movements of radicals to and from the Caucasus to the counterterrorism magistrates Bruguière and Ricard. It warned of an "organized attempt by al Qaeda-linked radical Islamists to manufacture or acquire chemical or biological weapons to be used in attacks," and it also stated that the men behind the effort were "veterans of Afghanistan with chemical and biological expertise who have recently returned from fighting Russian forces in Chechnya."[15] On November 13, relying on the long preparatory work done by the DST, Bruguière and Ricard formally opened an investigation on the "Chechen network."[16]

The investigation bore fruit very soon. On December 16, 2002, the DST raided an apartment in the Paris suburb of La Corneuve and arrested four individuals—three Algerians and a Moroccan.[17] According to French authorities, in the apartment police found two canisters of butane gas, $5,000 in cash, Islamist propaganda, false documents, and "electronic materials."[18] The "electronic materials" seized were devices that would have enabled the terrorists to detonate a bomb using a mobile phone.[19] Other items found in the rundown apartment concerned French authorities even more: the DST also discovered a protective suit for use against chemical and biological weapons and several products that are commonly used to manipulate toxic substances. The substances found in the apartment were analyzed, and one of them was cyanide. The raid yielded important evidence proving that the DST's fears were well founded—the network was indeed pursuing weapons of mass destruction.

One of the individuals arrested, Merouane Benahmed, was very well known to French authorities, as he had been an emir of the GIA.[20] Benahmed, a twenty-nine-year-old with joint French-Algerian nationality, was a specialist in making bombs using electronic devices who had received his training in al Qaeda camps in Afghanistan; his wife, Saliahlebik, was also arrested.[21] Benahmed had left Afghanistan before the US invasion of the country and had traveled to Georgia and Chechnya for further training in the summer of 2001.[22] At the beginning of 2002, Benahmed made his way back to France after a short stay in Barcelona. Despite having been on the country's most wanted list for almost two years, Benahmed managed to return to Paris, where he rejoined the other members of the network.[23] The Algerians coming back from the Caucasus apparently favored the route through Spain, a country where the GSPC has established a strong presence: On December 21, another North African, Noureddine Merabet, was arrested at the French-Spanish border while trying to return to France. Merabet confessed to French authorities that he was linked to the individuals arrested at La Corneuve and that he, like Benahmed, had trained in the camps located in the Pankisi Gorge.[24]

Much was made of the arrests by French authorities, who described those apprehended as "people ready for everything, ready to die."[25] But the threat was far from being over. Just a few days after the operation at La Corneuve, the DST raided two other apartments in another Paris suburb, Romainville. French authorities had received information that Menad Benchellali, a known al Qaeda recruiter, had returned to Romainville; fearing he might be linked to the La Corneuve cell, they decided to arrest him. Benchellali, who had a formal education as a chemist, was known to have trained in Afghanistan and had spent time in the Pankisi Gorge in 2001.[26] When on Christmas Eve, French authorities carried out a raid in Romainville, Benchellali and other three Algerian men were arrested.[27] In the apartments, the DST found cash, several tapes about the jihad in Chechnya, false documents, and a handwritten list of chemical substances that could be used to produce toxic gases such as cyanide, along with the required quantity and their prices.[28] Police also found methylene blue, a substance commonly used as an antidote to cyanide poisoning.[29]

The most important figure arrested in Romainville, Menad Benchellali, told French investigators that he wrote the list of chemical substances in order to "fabricate explosives to kill Russians in Chechnya and Israelis in Palestine," but he did not rule out the possibility of attacks inside France.[30] As chapter 1 noted, Benchellali had attempted to produce ricin and botulin in his parents' Lyon apartment with the help of his entire family. Another of the arrested militants, Belmehel Beddaidj, confirmed that the Romainville cell was directly linked to the one in La Corneuve and that the two groups, under the leadership of Merouane Benahmed, were planning to strike Russian targets. The series of arrests showed that the investigators' suspicions were right. As the director of DST, Giles Leclair, told a CNN interviewer, "They are coming from the same region, most of them are Algerian, trained [in] the same place, in some camps in Afghanistan, and at the same time in Georgia in the Pankisi Gorge. They have the same trainers. And it seems, if we can recognize what we found in the searches, that they wanted to start chemical attacks."[31]

In a matter of days, the French had dismantled two dangerous cells of militants who had trained in the Caucasus. Though they were not yet certain that these cells were planning attacks in France, the French attitude toward terrorism was proactive: "it was better to arrest them before rather than wait until after,"[32] as Interior Minister Nicolas Sarkozy put it. As the investigation progressed, French authorities discovered more about the group's intentions. The police learned that the group was ready to carry out a strike against the Russian Embassy in Paris. The men chose this target to avenge the death of several militants killed by Russian forces over the preceding months. Primarily, they wished to punish the Russians for the death of Ibn ul-Khattab, a Saudi fighter who had led the foreign mujahideen in Chechnya since 1997 and was revered as a hero by Islamists throughout the world; his stature only grew after Russian intelligence killed him with a poisoned letter in 2001. The group also wanted to avenge the killing of the members of the Chechen commando unit that had seized the Dubrovka Theater in Moscow on October 23, 2002.[33] Three days later, Russian Special Forces pumped an undisclosed narcotic gas into the theater to incapacitate the terrorists and then stormed it, killing all forty-five commandos but also leaving more than one hundred twenty theatergoers dead.

In using the death of Khattab and the extermination of the Chechen commandos to justify their planned attack against the Russian Embassy, the Algerian militants were clearly showing support of and gratitude to their hosts in the Caucasus.[34] But the men also named a more personal reason for choosing a Russian target: to avenge the death of one of their Algerian "brothers" who was killed while fighting in Chechnya, a man they identified only as "Al Moutana."[35] French authorities deduced from the information collected that "Al Moutana" was none other than Mabrouk Echiker, the man who had managed to leave Europe with Said Arif after the thwarted Strasbourg attack and who had led the way to the Caucasus for other members of the Algerian network.[36]

That Echiker's death was a motivation underscores the close relationship between the members of the Paris cells and the Algerian network that suffered numerous arrests in Frankfurt, London, and Milan in the first months of 2001. Other connections emerged as the investigation went forward. French Interior Minister Sarkozy declared that Benahmed, the expert in electronic devices arrested at La Corneuve, was "linked" to the group in Frankfurt. French authorities added that Benahmed had direct ties to Abu Doha and Rabah Kadre, the Algerian network's leaders in London.[37] In particular, Kadre and Benahmed had reportedly shared an apartment in Paris in the summer of 2001.[38] The magnitude of the mistake made by British authorities—who failed to hold Kadre after they arrested him in March 2001 when he was trying to fly to Saudi Arabia with Abu Doha—became more obvious with each piece of evidence. After his release, Kadre traveled around Europe and reorganized the network. Benahmed was one of the French operatives he sent to Georgia. Kadre also made sure that once the Algerian militants returned from the Caucasus, they were sheltered and supported by his operatives, who provided them with safe houses, false documents, and money. Even though he was already in jail when the raids in La Corneuve and Romainville took place, Kadre played an important role in planning the intended attacks in Paris.

Proving the thoroughness of French magistrates, the French investigation on the "Chechen cells" continued long after the Paris arrests. After months of work, Bruguière and Ricard concluded that the network dismantled in December 2002 had more targets in sight than had previously been thought. New information on what could have been the actual target of the group came in January 2005, when French authorities arrested three Algerians in the suburbs of Paris. One of the men, Maamar Ouazane, confessed that fellow Algerian militants had told him that the group was aiming to strike not just the Russian Embassy but also some Paris landmarks—specifically, the Eiffel Tower, a large department store in the city's center, and a police station.[39] According to Bruguière, the intervention of the DST (Direction de la Surveillance du Territoire, France's internal intelligence agency) had thwarted a "major terrorist act that was probably going to target the Paris metro and other targets with a chemical weapon."[40]

THE ALGERIAN NETWORK'S LAST STAND

As had happened in the past, an investigation into Algerian extremists was leading French authorities to London, for it became apparent that leaders of the network there were responsible for the decision to establish a presence in the Pankisi Gorge. But the network did more than send volunteers from France to the Caucasus: some of the London-based militants had taken the trip themselves. Particularly telling is the story of "K," an Algerian asylum seeker and an important member of the Abu Doha network who is currently being detained by British authorities.[41] K, whose real name is withheld by British authorities, who describe him only as "a key UK-based contact and provider of financial and logistical support to extreme Islamists in the UK and overseas," was arrested by Georgian authorities while trying to enter the Pankisi Gorge using a false French passport in July 2001. He was carrying the telephone numbers of Kadre and another senior GSPC leader involved in fund-raising for the Chechen mujahideen. K later told British authorities that he was trying to reach Chechnya but denied that he wanted to join the foreign mujahideen led by Khattab; his intention, he said, was only to work as a medic there. Though he himself never managed to reach Chechnya, K over the years had facilitated the passage of several other members of Abu Doha's network to the war-torn country.[42]

K's immigration history illustrates how the United Kingdom's lax and irrational immigration policies threaten its national security. After Georgian authorities deported K to the United Kingdom, where he had applied for asylum in 1998, British authorities denied his claim. His links to terrorism and his extensive travels to the United Arab Emirates under a false French passport were cited as the reasons. K applied again for asylum; after interviewing him, British authorities temporarily admitted him into the country. But when his second asylum application was also denied in August 2001, K could not be notified—he had already disappeared, thereby violating the terms of his temporary admission. K was arrested again in October of the same year, as he showed police another false French document (this time a driver's license). But once again

British authorities did not deport him; he was instead held at the Yarl's Wood Detention Centre, an expensive facility built by the British government in 2001 to temporarily house asylum seekers. In February 2002, just four months after it opened, the Detention Centre was burned down by the asylum seekers during a riot. At least twenty detainees managed to overpower the few guards and escape, K among them.

During that same month, the inefficiency of the British immigration system benefited another key member of the Algerian network, as Rabah Kadre was set free. According to British authorities, after escaping from Yarl's Wood, K "re-involved himself in extremist activity, providing support to the network of North African extreme Islamists."[43] And so did Kadre, who was now leading the network, after Abu Doha's arrest. Both men were soon back in custody: K was arrested in September, Kadre in November. Nevertheless, in their few months of freedom, K and Kadre conceived a plan that sent shockwaves throughout Europe.

French investigators interrogating the suspects arrested in La Corneuve and Romainville learned that the two cells dismantled in Paris were only a part of a larger group of Chechnya-trained militants that was planning attacks in Europe. Benhamed, one of the key figures captured, allegedly provided particularly detailed information on militants who had moved to Britain and were ready to become operational. Paris quickly passed the information to London, where authorities were already aware that the Algerian network was plotting a strike on British soil. Not only had they arrested Kadre and two other men in November for planning an attack, but in the same month they began closely monitoring other suspected members of the network, after finding suspicious documents in an East London flat. Moreover, in the preceding weeks, British authorities had received a dossier from their Algerian counterparts, who had been gleaning information from Mohammed Meguerba, a former London resident who was incarcerated in Algeria. Meguerba detailed the activities of the Algerian network in London, providing names and addresses of key operatives.[44]

Scotland Yard and the MI5 at first simply watched the suspects in an attempt to uncover the whole network, but when they realized that the operatives might be ready to attack, they acted. In the early hours of

Sunday, January 5, 2003, British police raided five apartments in North and East London, arresting six men and one woman (she was later released). One of the apartments was located in Wood Green, a racially diverse neighborhood of London whose high concentration of Algerian immigrants has earned it the nickname "Little Algiers." It was probably no coincidence that this one-bedroom apartment on the top floor of a run-down Victorian house was located just a few yards from the flat of Mustafa Labsi, one of the key planners of the Strasbourg attack.[45] Before the raid, the MI5 warned Scotland Yard that agents might find in the apartment a "kitchen sink" laboratory and, possibly, toxic substances. And in fact, agents recovered residues of a mysterious substance that was promptly sent to military laboratories for analysis.[46]

The initial results shocked Britain: The mysterious substance was declared to be ricin, a natural poison that can be made from the castor bean plant. Ricin is fairly easy to produce, is six thousand times as potent as cyanide, and has no antidote. Ingesting one milligram of ricin can kill an adult, and the lethal substance can be dispersed via ventilation systems, drinking water, or food supplies. Ricin became famous in 1978, when Georgi Markov, a Bulgarian defector living in London, was allegedly killed by a ricin-filled pellet fired into his leg from an umbrella. Authorities believed that the men living in the Wood Green apartment, keeping in contact with the masterminds in the Pankisi Gorge via fax, had produced ricin in the small kitchen-turned-laboratory.

The discovery understandably caused considerable fear. Investigators speculated that the group intended to spread the substance on the handrails of the subway's escalators and on the door handles of cars belonging to prominent members of London's Jewish community. Security for high-profile public buildings and key transportation systems such as the London Tube and railways was significantly heightened. Doctors were also urged by authorities to be on the alert for potential signs of poisoning in those seeking care. The British tabloids, known for their screaming headlines, added to the public's anxiety.

Information uncovered on the men arrested in the raids confirmed their links to the French cells. Two of them had been questioned in 2002 by French authorities for suspected links to terrorism, and tickets found in the apartments showed that they had arrived to the United Kingdom from France just a few days before their arrest. They were also believed to have visited the apartment in La Corneuve that French authorities had raided in December.[47] Investigators think that after the December raids the two men had fled to London, where the network was already in place. The other men arrested were all Algerian asylum seekers who had lived in the United Kingdom for a few years. The Wood Green apartment, which was paid by the local council, was home to two teenagers (one from Algeria and one from Ethiopia) who were receiving benefits from the government.

Four of the men arrested during the raids were subsequently charged with "developing or producing chemical weapons" and "possessing articles of value to a terrorist."[48] Less than two months later, British authorities charged Rabah Kadre and the two other men arrested with him in November 2002 with the same crimes. Even though Kadre was in jail when the ricin was discovered, the evidence pointed to his key logistical role in the conspiracy to produce the substance. Kadre is the thread that ties together all the plots that the Algerian network concocted after the failed millennium bombing: he was directly involved in the Strasbourg attack, the alleged cyanide plot in London, and the ricin plot in France and Britain. K, the detainee at Belmarsh, is also believed to have provided crucial support to the "network of North African extremists directly involved in terrorist planning in the UK, including the use of toxic chemicals."[49]

The discovery of residues of ricin was far from reassuring. Where was the rest of the substance? Were there other cells spread across the country ready to use it? And what might be their intended targets? Some security officials revealed that a man believed to be the leader of the Wood Green cell had been monitored by the MI5 but had managed to avoid arrest. He was thought to be the chemist of the group, so he could well have been hiding the toxic substance.[50] Other reports indicated that at least three key players had escaped the raids and that up to twenty men, mostly Algerians, could have been involved in the plot. Following the leads obtained from the sweeps in Wood Green, authorities detained several individuals in other suburbs of London and in various British cities who were believed to be connected to the network. No further trace of ricin or of any other chemical substance was ever found. But what was about to happen would be almost as shocking to the public as a terrorist attack.

On the afternoon of January 14, twenty-four police officers, four from the Special Branch and twenty uniformed, descended on a red-brick Edwardian house in Crumpsall Lane, on the outskirts of the northern English city of Manchester. The MI5 had managed to track to this address a twenty-three-year-old Algerian man who was connected to the militants based in the Wood Green apartment, and the officers entered the house to execute a warrant for his arrest. Though the charges were connected to immigration violations, authorities were primarily interested in questioning him about the ricin plot. This Algerian's history is a familiar one: He had applied for asylum in 1998, had been turned down in 2001, and had disappeared from his declared address after filing an appeal.

When they broke down the door of the house after days of surveillance, the agents were surprised to see that the man had two roommates; they had expected to find him alone. The officers, armed only with batons, began interviewing the Algerian man, while the other two youths, both of whom looked North African, remained calm and silent. The process went on for more than an hour, and the three men were never handcuffed. When one of the Special Branch officers believed he had recognized one of the two unknown men, he sent details about the twenty-seven-year-old Algerian to Scotland Yard. Preliminary information came back revealing that the man, who was identified as Kamel Bourgass, might have been connected to the ricin cell too. At that point, police began sealing off the apartment, and Bourgass was asked to put on a forensic suit, which would have revealed if he had touched toxic substances. Suddenly all hell broke loose: Bourgass, who had been described by the agents as "quiet as a lamb" until a few seconds earlier, broke free from the agent holding him, grabbed a kitchen knife, and began attacking.[51] In the following violent struggle, four officers suffered stab injuries. Detective Constable Stephen Oake was fatally wounded as he rushed to save a colleague who was trying to restrain Bourgass. Stephen Oake was the first British policeman killed by Islamic terrorists on British soil.

A European police officer was quoted in the *Los Angeles Times*: "Bourgass is part of the Algerian movement of Rabah Kadre. . . . There was intelligence information on him in Europe. The stabbing happened after the officers . . . realized that he was a relevant person in the network." The man had kept quiet as long as he believed that the raid was concerned purely with immigration violations, confident that he was facing no worse than possible inconvenience. But as soon as he realized that authorities had found out who he really was, he panicked. Bourgass was the man the MI5 had been frantically searching for, the chemist who was believed to be behind the production of ricin in the Wood Green kitchen.[52] Authorities charged Bourgass for his role in the conspiracy to produce ricin and for the murder of Stephen Oake.

While seeking a man loosely connected to the plot, British authorities had found its most important player. But the price had been high, and the country was saddened and outraged by Oake's death. The public questioned the methods used by the police, who carried out the raid unarmed and did not handcuff men whom they suspected were connected to terrorism. British tabloids published the angry off-the-record revelations of security officers who claimed that authorities usually send unarmed agents to carry out raids in order not to "infringe the human rights of the suspects."[53] After it was reported that several of the men involved in the plot that led to Constable Oake's death were failed asylum seekers whom authorities had not deported, politicians and the media launched harsh attacks against the nation's ultragenerous asylum laws.

Bourgass's immigration history resembles that of many other Algerian radicals operating in the United Kingdom and shows the dangerous consequences of failing to strictly enforce immigration rules. He had entered England illegally in 2000, destroying his Algerian documents before reaching the country. He immediately filed for asylum, and his application was denied three times. Nevertheless, Bourgass ignored the rejections and stayed illegally in England, where he committed petty crimes and used four false identities. Ironically, Bourgass used a large brown envelope that originally contained a denial from the Immigration and Nationality Directorate to store the instructions for producing ricin and explosives.[54]

As fury over Oake's death grew, the British government decided to take advantage of the shift in public opinion to launch an action that earlier might have been widely condemned. Information obtained by the MI5 and Scotland Yard indicated that additional evidence on the activities of the ricin cells (and possibly the substance itself) was hidden inside the Finsbury Park mosque. With the threat of a chemical attack pending and with the public up in arms over Oake's death, the British government decided to carry out a night raid, "Operation Mermant." On January 21, one hundred fifty armed policemen wearing riot gear (having learned their lesson from Manchester) broke into the mosque at 2 AM with ladders and rams, while a helicopter's floodlight illuminated the scene. Inside they found a stun gun, an imitator revolver, several false documents (mostly French), credit cards, and a canister of tear gas. No chemicals were located, but agents recovered chemical warfare protection suits[55]— hardly items required for religious worship, and strong evidence that the mosque had been used as a shelter by individuals linked to the plot to produce chemical weapons. Seven men found inside the mosque were arrested and charged; one of them, once again an Algerian asylum seeker, was described as a "major player" in the network and as the financier of the poison plot.[56] Investigators believe that he recruited young Muslims at the mosque and financed militants by helping them file for benefits and by providing them with stolen or counterfeit credit cards.

With the arrests of Bourgass and the men hiding inside the Finsbury Park mosque, British authorities managed to detain the key operatives in the ricin plot. No other traces of the substance were found, and no other significant arrests were made. In the months following Bourgass's arrest, additional testing carried out on the substance found in Wood Green could not confirm that it was indeed ricin. An expert witness testified at Bourgass's April 2005 trial that "subsequent confirmatory tests on the material from the pestle and the mortar did not detect the presence of ricin." The scientist added that in his opinion, "toxins are not detectable in the pestle and mortar."[57] Doubts still remain. While authorities had to drop charges regarding mass murder, Bourgass was nevertheless found guilty of "conspiring to commit a public nuisance by the use of poisons and/or explosives to cause disruption, fear or injury."[58] Officials maintained that Bourgass and his accomplices planned on carrying out an attack with the poison and declared that the real target was the express train that runs from London to Heathrow airport. "It would have caused chaos and panic in London's public transport system," said a British official commenting on the thwarted attack. "Even if it did not kill anyone—which it could well have done—it would have achieved its purpose."[59] Bourgass was sentenced to seventeen years for the ricin plot, while he had been already sentenced in June 2004 to life in prison for the murder of Stephen Oake.[60] But the other four men tried with him were acquitted. The day after their acquittal they applied for asylum in Britain.[61]

Abu Doha, K, Kadre, and Bourgass were behind bars; was the Algerian network finished? It has planned no attacks since the winter of 2003, and its activities are reported to be at extremely low levels. The sweep of the Finsbury Park mosque, aside from netting seven militants, sent a strong message to the network, signaling that the British government's patience had ended. And it is a kind of poetic justice that the Algerian network's last stand took place in Finsbury Park, which for almost a decade had been its unofficial headquarters. Inside and around that mosque, a small group of charismatic preachers and leaders recruited, indoctrinated, and radicalized hundreds of young Muslims who then spread havoc through Europe and beyond.

The idea of building a mosque in the poor, largely Muslim neighborhood in North London was conceived in the early 1980s by Prince Charles, who asked for the support of wealthy businessmen and heads of state from Muslim countries. King Fahd of Saudi Arabia donated most of the funds needed for constructing the mosque, which was completed in 1990. Initially, the worshipers were mostly immigrants from Bangladesh who tried to establish a center for religious studies inside the mosque and who followed a moderate interpretation of Islam. But within a few years after its opening, groups of militants began to worship at the mosque and sought to make it their headquarters. Reportedly, the extremists, most of whom were from North Africa or the Middle East, threatened and in some cases physically attacked those who tried to resist them, eventually forcing the moderates out of the mosque. By the mid-1990s groups of radicals were sleeping in the basement of the mosque and preventing all but sympathizers from coming in.[62] Many of these militants were Algerians who had fled to London to escape Paris's crackdown on GIA members.

London, and Finsbury Park in particular, became the center of a thriving Islamist scene, earning itself the nicknames of "Londonistan" and "Beirut-on-Thames." The Algerians began to publish the *Al Ansar* newsletter, which attracted some of the most important figures in the European jihadi underworld, such as Abu Qatada, Abu Musab al Suri, and Rachid Ramda, discussed in chapter 4. But London also became the home of important Islamist leaders from Egypt, Saudi Arabia, Morocco, Syria, and many other Muslim countries. It was in London that all these dissidents met and interacted, benefiting from the traditional tolerance of the British government. Despite repeated warnings from moderate Arab governments and from French intelligence that some of these individuals were extremely dangerous, Britain let them operate undisturbed for years. Finsbury Park became the meeting point for all of Europe's Islamic radicals.

In 1996 it became clear that the takeover of the Finsbury Park mosque was complete. After the board of trustees of the mosque allowed a radical Egyptian engineering student, Abu Hamza al Masri, to give sermons during Friday prayers, the one-eyed, hooked-handed veteran of Afghanistan and Bosnia immediately began preaching his radical views. Displeased with the cleric's poisonous rhetoric, the board asked him to step down, but it found itself powerless to enforce its demand. A trustee recalled that "when we met him again to ask him to go, he had several heavily built minders with him who told us that we had to leave." Even an injunction from the High Court could not stop Abu Hamza, who used his thugs to prevent it from taking effect. Some of the more vocal trustees were ambushed outside their homes and beaten. With British authorities reluctant to interfere in something they perceived as an internal affair of the Muslim community, the Egyptian turned the mosque into something more closely resembling the guest houses for the mujahideen in Peshawar and Jalalabad than a place of worship in a European capital. Reportedly, its basement was used to plan attacks, forge documents, and practice the use of weapons. More thorough training in guerrilla warfare was provided in the English countryside on weekends organized by militants. A worshiper at the mosque told the London *Times* that by 1998, groups of young men were living inside the mosque. "They were strangers. We asked them what they were doing but they warned us not to interfere. Many of them were Algerian as many Algerian families were moving into this area."[63]

It was at that time that Abu Doha, a senior GSPC member who had spent a great deal of time in the Afghan training camps, began building his network. Splitting his time between the mosque and his apartment, located in the same neighborhood, Abu Doha recruited hundreds of young men for the training camps in Afghanistan or for the battlefield in Chechnya. His efforts were bolstered by the fiery sermons of Abu Hamza, the religious teachings of Abu Qatada (whom Spanish authorities call "al Qaeda's ideologue in Europe"), and the tales about the glory of jihad told by the many veterans of the Afghan or Bosnian war living in London. Hundreds of videotapes of jihad from various parts of the world were shown and literature from different militant groups was distributed under the eyes of British authorities. Large numbers of young, impressionable Muslim men were lured into the clerics' vision of the world, a paranoid world where Jews and Christians continuously plot against Islam and where the only solution for Muslims is to wage jihad against them.

The list of militants who traveled from places throughout the world to London and spent time in or around Finsbury Park reads like a who's who of terrorism. Almost all members of the Algerian network walked through the mosque's wooden doors. K, the unnamed detainee in Belmarsh prison who played a key role in the ricin plot, lived in the basement of the mosque for more than a year between 1999 and 2000. Yacine Aknouche, one of the militants sentenced in Paris for the Strasbourg plot, moved to London in 1996; he said that after hearing Abu Qatada's sermons and mingling with the worshipers in Finsbury Park, he was recruited by Abu Doha to go to Afghanistan. Another of the militants convicted in Paris, Laurent Mourad (the man who "lost" his passport five times), told investigators that it was in Abu Doha's Finsbury Park apartment that he met with other militants such as Kadre and Slimane Khalfaoui. There they frequently watched tapes of the jihad in Chechnya, after which Abu Doha often preached on the duty of all Muslims to fight jihad to defend their fellow Muslims.[64]

Young men with no direction, such as Mourad or Aknouche, believed they had found a purpose for their lives and agreed to go to Afghanistan. The network supplied them with money, contacts, documents, and, more important, a sense of belonging. Awaiting them in the Afghan city of Jalal-abad was the other end of the Algerian network. A veteran of the war against the Soviets, an Algerian called Abu Jaffar, was running the guest-house for his countrymen. Coordinating his activities with Abu Doha in London and with al Qaeda leaders in Peshawar and Kandahar, Abu Jaffar welcomed the recruits to Afghanistan and sent them to the camps.[65] Once their training was completed, the same sophisticated network decided where the operatives should be deployed. Often they were just sent back to London, where the leaders of the network decided how to better use them.

Several individuals who made headlines after 9/11 also had close ties to the Finsbury Park mosque. According to the brother of Zacarias Moussaoui, the only man charged in the United States in connection with the attacks of 9/11, his radicalization took place at the mosque. In 2002 Moussaoui's mother, a secularized Muslim woman who had immigrated to France from Morocco, sharply criticized Britain's tolerance for radical preachers. She told a reporter from the *Observer*: "These British imams are a very bad influence on young Muslims. The British government has a responsibility for allowing such people to preach hatred and extremism in public places such as mosques. It has nothing to do with real Islam. It is false."[66]

Other frequent attendees of the mosque included the shoe-bomber Richard Reid and Nizar Trabelsi, a former professional soccer player who was sentenced to ten years in prison by a Belgian court after admitting he planned to drive a car bomb into the canteen of the US air base in Kleine Brogel. Trabelsi, Reid, and Moussaoui were all acquaintances of another celebrity who used to worship in Finsbury Park, Djamel Beghal. The French-Algerian, who had moved to London in 1997, is thought to be one of bin Laden's top men in Europe and shuttled frequently between the Continent and Afghanistan.

Several individuals who worshiped at the Finsbury Park mosque ended up at Camp Delta, the detention facility set up by the US military in Guantanamo Bay, Cuba. Imad Kanuni, a French Moroccan detained for more than two years in Gitmo, spent time in both the Finsbury Park mosque and Abu Qatada's mosque after he returned from the camps in Afghanistan.[67] He was apprehended by US forces in Afghanistan after 9/11. Brahim Yadel, a Frenchman who also was apprehended in Afghanistan, had received money from Abu Doha to go there while he was living in London.[68] And it was information obtained from British detainees in Guantanamo Bay that led US authorities in April 2004 to indict Abu Hamza, the imam of the mosque, on eleven terrorism-related charges, which included attempting to establish a training camp inside the United States.[69] Following a request from Washington, British authorities arrested Abu Hamza; proceedings for his extradition are now under way. In October 2004, he was also charged by the British with sixteen offenses.

But critics say that Abu Hamza's arrest came too late, and that the British government's tolerance of his activities and rhetoric exemplified its naive leniency toward Islamic radicals. This tolerance was extended despite the authorities' knowledge of Abu Hamza's personal involvement, while in London, in two terrorist plots in Yemen that targeted Westerners. In December 1998, Abu Hamza's son and stepson, along with a French citizen and three British citizens, were arrested by Yemeni police for plotting attacks against British and American targets. A few days later, Yemeni militants kidnapped a group of Western tourists whom they intended to exchange for the detained European militants. Just a few hours after the kidnapping, according to Yemeni authorities, the leader of the group called Abu Hamza in London to tell him of the operation's success. No exchange was ever made: Yemeni police freed the hostages (four of which died in the operation) and arrested the militants, who were tried. Yemeni authorities sought Abu Hamza's extradition, claiming that he "was the main instigator" in both incidents.[70] British authorities did detain Abu Hamza, but they decided against extradition and released him, even though British blood had been spilled.[71]

Going beyond mere tolerance, the British welfare system also extended the radical cleric generous benefits. According to the British tabloid the *Sun*, for years Abu Hamza received more than a thousand pounds a week in benefits. While publicly calling for attacks against the British government, he did not disdain cashing its checks; his rent, too, was paid by British taxpayers—£2,400 a month. Even in detention, the cleric has continued to take advantage of government largess. He has received a new aluminum hook worth £5,000 from the national health system and has sued welfare officials for more money.[72]

Sadly, Abu Hamza's is not an isolated case. Many other radical clerics living in Britain have been the beneficiaries of the country's welfare system while preaching the destruction of the country itself. Abu Qatada was known to receive at least £400 a week in government benefits, £322 for housing, and £70 because he was too sick to work.[73] The leader of the ultraradical al Muhajiroun group in London, Omar Bakri, who has openly called for attacks against the United Kingdom and praised Osama bin Laden, receives more than £1,000 a month. Over the twenty years he has spent in Great Britain, Bakri is believed to have received more than 275,000 pounds (roughly 490,000 US dollars) in state benefits, and the government even helped him pay the lease of his 31,000-pound-worth Ford Galaxy.[74] Sayful Islam, a British-born leader of al Muhajiroun in Luton, who said he felt "elated" when he saw the planes hitting the towers of the World Trade Center, also lives on the public dole while he openly brags about his intentions of overthrowing the British government: "When a bomb attack happens here, I won't be against it, even if it kills my own children. I am a Muslim living in Britain, and I give my allegiance to Allah."[75] Mohammed al Gharbouzi, a Moroccan cleric living in London who is wanted by Moroccan authorities for his role in the Casablanca bombings that killed more than thirty people, is less fortunate, as he has to rely on his wife for benefits. But Mrs. Gharbouzi claims more than £1,000 a month in income and housing support.[76]

Aside from the UK's tolerance of radical rhetoric and generous welfare system, the chaotic and generous British immigration system is one of the main reasons why militants have flocked to London. The consequences for the country's security became clear during the ricin plot, as many of its key players were failed asylum seekers whom authorities had failed to deport. Security officials and some politicians had warned of the dangers of the nation's immigration policy, especially regarding Algerian asylum seekers, but their voices were ignored by the establishment. Mohammed Sekkoum, the chairman of the Algerian Refugee Council in London, had stated repeatedly and publicly that hundreds of his countrymen who were involved in terrorist activities were living in Britain. "People who are really terrorists are being allowed in and they are not going to stop killing when they get to this country," Sekkoum said in a January 2003 interview.[77]

In the days following the discovery of ricin, immigration officials disclosed alarming figures on Algerian asylum seekers: as a rule, just one in ten Algerians refused asylum in the United Kingdom leaves the country, and of the more than 2,500 individuals whose claims were turned down in 2001, only one hundred twenty-five were deported or left voluntarily.[78] Britain's generosity toward Algerian refugees is even more striking when compared to the policies adopted by other countries. According to a study published by the House of Lords, 80 percent of Algerians who apply for asylum status receive it in Britain, while in France only 5 percent do.[79] Obviously, not all Algerian asylum seekers are terrorists; nevertheless, authorities believe that at least one hundred known or suspected Algerian terrorists have entered the United Kingdom since 2000.[80]

Sadly, but predictably, Britain paid the price for all its mistakes in July 2005, when London was attacked in the span of two weeks by two groups of terrorists that managed, on July 7, or attempted, on July 21, to detonate explosive devices on Tube trains and buses. While the attackers did not belong to the Algerian network, the same factors that had made the Algerians thrive throughout the 1990s (tolerance for extremist preaching, ultragenerous asylum and welfare systems) paved the way to the July 2005 bombers.

Investigators discovered that all the London bombers began their journey into radical Islam in Britain, as all of them were either born in the UK or had moved to the country at an early age. They all prayed in mosques located throughout England that were well known to authorities for their radicalism but had been let free to indoctrinate young British

Muslims. Not surprisingly, investigators believe that one of the possible connections between the two teams of bombers is the Finsbury Park mosque, where key players of both July plots used to worship. [81] And authorities also had specific information on the radicalism of some of the men. In 2003 the trustees of the Stockwell mosque, a moderate place of worship in South London, reported to the police the radical and violent activities of Osman Hussein, the man who attempted to blow up a train near Shepherd's Bush station on July 21. The trustees complained that Hussein and his friends had "an agenda to turn this centre into another Finsbury Park mosque" and that "problems have now reached a level where police help is urgently needed."[82] No action was taken by the police, and Hussein was not monitored. Even more disturbing is the fact that British domestic intelligence, the MI5, was aware that Mohammed Siddique Khan, the alleged ringleader of the deadly July 7 commando, was a radical with dangerous connections, having gathered information about his involvement with a terrorist cell dismantled in 2004. Nevertheless, Khan was deemed "not a threat" by MI5 and not investigated.[83] Curiously, while still on an MI5 list as a person of interest, Khan received two generous grants from the European Union to open gyms for the Asian population of Beeston, the Leeds suburb where Khan worked as a teacher's aide and recruited some of the other July 7 bombers.[84]

And while the first team was made up of three British-born Muslims and a Jamaican convert, the "failed bombers" of July 21 were asylum seekers who obtained their residency permits and British passports through scams and irregularities. According to published reports, Mukhtar Said Ibrahim, the Eritrean man who allegedly placed a bomb on a double-decker bus on July 21, obtained a British passport even though he had spent several years in jail for mugging and knife possession. According to British law, a key condition for obtaining citizenship is that an applicant must be "of good character."[85] Ibrahim and his three July 21 accomplices, all immigrants from war-torn East African countries who sought refuge in Britain in the 1990s, are also accused of having used multiple identities and nationalities to fool British immigration authorities. The Bank of England's official order to freeze the assets of the men shows that Ibrahim used six aliases, Osman Hussein had five, Mohammed Ramzi six, and Omar Yassin five.[86] Naturally, once they fooled the nation's immigration laws, the men also took advantage of Britain's generous welfare system. Investigators believe that the four men collected more than £500,000 in state benefits since their arrival into the country.[87]

Apparently, after the outrage caused by the London attacks in the United Kingdom, things are about to change. "Britain . . . is a tolerant and good natured nation . . . however . . . this very tolerance and good nature should not be abused by a small but fanatical minority."[88] With these words, spoken less than a month after the first London attacks, Prime Minister Tony Blair unveiled his proposal for a new antiterrorism approach (examined also in chapter 3). Aside from introducing laws that punish those who advocate terror, the British government is planning to expedite deportations and extraditions of those involved in extremist activities. Blair announced that "anyone who has participated in terrorism, or has anything to do with it anywhere" will be automatically denied asylum, and naturalized British citizens who engage in terror activities will be stripped of their citizenship. Mosques, bookstores, and Web sites that advocate violence will be shut down. "Coming to Britain," concluded the prime minister, "is not a right, and even when people have come here, staying here carries with it a duty. That duty is to share and support the values that sustain the British way of life. Those that break that duty and try to incite hatred or engage in violence against our country and its people have no place here."[89]

NOTES

1. Alex Rodriguez, "Chechen Fighters Lose Stronghold in Georgia Gorge; U.S. Fears Militants Linked to Al Qaeda," *Chicago Tribune*, July 20, 2003.

2. For his role in the Strasbourg plot, Mourad was sentenced to six years in prison by a Paris court.

3. Frederic Chambon, "Comment Naissent et Vivent les Reseaux d'Al Qaida en Europe," *Le Monde*, January 3, 2003.

4. The safe house in boulevard Magenta belonged to Samir Korchi, a member of the Algerian network who was later sentenced by the French court to four years for his part in the Strasbourg plot. Korchi confessed that his apartment was often used by members of the network that needed a "safe" place to stay.

5. Chambon, "Comment Naissent et Vivent les Reseaux d'Al Qaida en Europe."

6. Italian authorities suspect that members of the Algerian network based in Milan helped Arif and Echiker with false documents and hosted them for a few weeks.

7. Piotr Smolar, "Quatre islamistes interpelles en Seine-Saint-Denis dans l'enquete sur les 'filieres tchetchenes,'" *Le Monde*, December 27, 2002.

8. Piotr Smolar, "Les Tribulations en Tchetchenie de Khaled Ouldali, qui Voulait 'Voir de pres la Guerre et ses Ravages,'" *Le Monde*, December 19, 2002.

9. Chambon, "Comment Naissent et Vivent les Reseaux d'Al Qaida en Europe."

10. Indictment of Mourad Trabelsi and others (Ordinanza di Applicazione della Misura Cautelare), Tribunal of Milan, Italy, April 1, 2003.

11. Deposition of Shadi Abdallah, Federal High Court, Karlsruhe, Germany, November 18, 2002; indictment of Muhamad Majid and others (Ordinanza di Applicazione della Misura della Custodia Cautelare in Carcere), Tribunal of Milan, Italy, November 25, 2003.

12. Paul Quinn-Judge, "Inside al-Qaeda's Georgia Refuge," *Time*, October 19, 2002.

13. Indictment of Muhamad Majid and others; quotation from Maryann Bird, "A Poisonous Plot," *Time International (Europe)*, January 20, 2003.

14. "CIA Warns Turkish Police on Poisonous Substance," Anatolia News Agency, July 10, 2002.

15. Jon Henley, "Al-Qaida Terror Plot Foiled, Say French Police," *Guardian*, January 12, 2004.

16. Piotr Smolar, "Les Policiers Portent un Premier Coup a la 'Filiere Tchetchene,'" *Le Monde*, December 19, 2002.

17. Official press release from the French Ministry of the Interior, "A propos de l'interpellation de plusieurs individus par la DST," December 27, 2002, http://www.interieur.gouv.fr/rubriques/c/c3_police_nationale/c3_actualites/2002_27_12_dst.

18. "A propos de l'interpellation de plusieurs individus par la DST."

19. This technology, which was taught in the Afghan camps, sadly was to

become known in Europe; this was the method used on March 11, 2004, to detonate the bombs that killed more than 200 commuters on four trains near Madrid.

20. "A propos de l'interpellation de plusieurs individus par la DST."

21. "France Says Arrested Men 'Planned Attack,'" BBC, December 20, 2002; "A propos de l'interpellation de plusieurs individus par la DST."

22. "A propos de l'interpellation de plusieurs individus par la DST."

23. Spanish parliament, *Diario de sesiones del Congreso de los Diputados*, 7th Legislature, November 5, 2003, pp. 4–5.

24. "A propos de l'interpellation de plusieurs individus par la DST."

25. "Sventato attacco chimico. Arrestati in Francia quattro islamici," *Corriere della Sera*, December 21, 2002.

26. "A propos de l'interpellation de plusieurs individus par la DST."

27. "France Foils Cell Linked to al-Qaida," AP, December 28, 2002.

28. "A propos de l'interpellation de plusieurs individus par la DST."

29. Jean-Charles Brisard, *Zarkaoui: Le nouveau visage d'al-Qaida* (Paris: Fayard, 2005), p. 233.

30. "A propos de l'interpellation de plusieurs individus par la DST."

31. Sheila MacVicar and Henry Schuster, "European Terror Suspects Got Al Qaeda Training, Sources Say," CNN.com, February 6, 2003.

32. "Paris Police Quiz 'Chemical Four' Plot," BBC, December 18, 2002.

33. "A propos de l'interpellation de plusieurs individus par la DST."

34. The Algerians, in the selection of their grievances against the Russians, were careful to appease both components of the anti-Russian forces fighting in Chechnya. In fact, Khattab was the leader of the foreign/Arab mujaheddin, while the Dubrovka commando was made up only of indigenous Chechen fighters.

35. "A propos de l'interpellation de plusieurs individus par la DST."

36. Official press release of Germany's Ministry of the Interior, "Zwei Jahre nach dem 11. September 2001: Schily sieht Erfolge bei der Bekämpfung des internationalen Terrorismus" (Two years after September 11, 2001: Schilly shows developments in the fight against international terrorism), September 11, 2003, http://www.bmi.bund.de/cln_027/nn_122778/Internet/Content/Nachrichten/Pressemitteilungen/2003/09/Zwei_Jahre_nach_dem_11_September_2001_Id_92936_de.html.

37. Smolar, "Quatre islamistes interpelles en Seine-Saint-Denis dans l'enquete sur les 'filieres tchetchenes'"; "Paris 'Plot' Chemicals Studied," CNN.com, December 18, 2002.

38. Spanish parliament, *Diario de sesiones del Congreso de los Diputados*, p. 5.

39. "Suspected Islamic Militant Says Radicals Targeted Eiffel Tower," AFP, February 16, 2005.

40. Brisard, *Zarkaoui*, p. 236.

41. After 9/11, special powers were bestowed on the British government, which could detain terrorists who did not hold British citizenship without charging them and with no limit of time, if they were considered particularly dangerous. A dozen individuals were detained under these laws (the above-mentioned Abu Qatada is one of them). Most of these detainees were identified only by a letter.

42. Special Immigration Appeal Commission, Appeal of "K," July 12, 2004.

43. Ibid.

44. Jason Burke, "Revealed: How Secret Papers Led to Ricin Raid," *Observer*, April 17, 2005.

45. Nick Parker and Michael Lea, "Poison Factory Yards from Osama Pal's Home," *Sun*, January 9, 2003.

46. Jason Bennetto and Kim Sengupta, "Ricin Arrests: How MI5 Homed in on Kitchen-Sink Lab," *Independent*, January 9, 2003.

47. Daniel McGrory, "'Poison Factory' Suspects were Freed by French," *Times*, January 10, 2003.

48. Mark Huband, "Four Men Due before Magistrates on Ricin Charges," *Financial Times*, January 13, 2003.

49. Special Immigration Appeal Commission, appeal of "K."

50. Jason Lewis and Martin Smith, "Terror Chief on the Run Plans Lone Ricin Killing," *Mail on Sunday*, January 12, 2003.

51. Helen Gibson, "The Algerian Factor," *Time*, January 27, 2003.

52. Sebastian Rotella and Janet Stobart, "The World; N. African Arraigned in British Slaying," *Los Angeles Times*, January 18, 2003.

53. En Perry, "Suspects in Police Murder, Ricin Plot, to Face British Courts," AFP, January 17, 2003.

54. Nick Allen, "Probe Showed How Immigrants Made Mockery of Asylum System," *Scotsman*, April 13, 2005.

55. Warren Hoge, "Mosque Raid in London Results in 7 Arrests in Connection with Discovery of Poison," *New York Times*, January 21, 2003.

56. "North African Arrested in Ongoing Ricin Probe," AFP, January 23, 2003.

57. Michael Isikoff and Mark Hosenball, "What Ricin?" *Newsweek*, April 13, 2005.

58. Crown Prosecution Statement on convictions of Kamel Bourgass, April 13, 2005.

59. David Bamber, "Ricin Terror Gang 'Planned to Unleash Terror on Heathrow Express,'" *Sunday Telegraph*, April 17, 2005.

60. Crown Prosecution Statement on convictions of Kamel Bourgass.

61. David Leppard and Nick Felding, "Ricin Defendants to Claim Asylum. Trial Has Made Return 'Unsafe,'" *Sunday Times*, April 17, 2005.

62. Daniel McGrory, "A Haven for Faithful Hijacked by Extremists," *Times* (London), January 21, 2003.

63. Ibid.

64. Chambon, "Comment Naissent et Vivent les Reseaux d'Al Qaida en Europe."

65. DIGOS report, "Muhajiroun 3," November 21, 2001.

66. Anthony Barnett, "Bin Laden Man's Mother Blames British Extremists," *Observer*, July 28, 2002.

67. Francoise Chirot and Piotr Smolar, "Entre Londres, Francfort et Jalalabad, les Itineraires de 'Quatre Petits Soldats du Djihad,'" *Le Monde*, July 28, 2004.

68. Chirot and Smolar, "Entre Londres."

69. *USA v. Mustafa Kamel Mustafa*, USDC, Southern District of New York, April 19, 2004.

70. Stephen J. Hedges, "Britain Has Been Radicals' Refuge," *Chicago Tribune*, October 29, 2001.

71. Great Britain has long had an unofficial but very consistent policy of not extraditing terror suspects. While understandable and in line with the European norm in the case of countries where the suspect could face the death penalty (such as Yemen), the policy is also applied to other countries that do not apply the death penalty, including other members of the European Union. For example, as we saw in chapter 1, France has been unsuccessfully seeking the extradition of Rachid Ramda for years.

72. "Hamza Is to Get a New Prosthetic Limb on the NHS, It Emerged Last Night," *Daily Mail*, October 20, 2004.

73. Daniel McGrory, Laura Peek, and Bill Bond, "Bin Laden's 'European Ambassador' in London," *Sunday Times*, October 21, 2001.

74. "Radical Imam Bakri Facing Benefits Bother When Back in Britain," AFP, August 10, 2005; Karen McVeigh and Gerri Peev, "Public Pays for Luxury Life of Cleric Who Preaches Hatred," *Scotsman*, August 11, 2005.

75. David Cohen, "Terror on the Dole," *Evening Standard*, April 20, 2004.

76. Euan Stretch, "Terror in UK Atrocity Fear; Wanted Linked by Morocco for Bomb Massacre to Slaughter of 200 in Madrid . . . Living 4 Miles from 10 Downing Street; the Cleric We Can't Kick Out," *Sunday Mirror*, April 4, 2004.

77. "Algerian Held in Britain on Terrorism Charges," AFP, January 16, 2003.

78. Padraic Flanagan and Alison Little, "Victim of Terror Outrage at Our Shambolic Asylum Laws as Man DC Oake Went to Arrest Is Revealed to Have Been a Fugitive Since His Plea to Live Here Was Scorned; Suspect Was on Run for 4 Years," *Express*, January 16, 2003.

79. Hedges, "Britain Has Been Radicals' Refuge."

80. Italian Security Official, interview, Rome, February 2004.

81. According to published reports, the Finsbury Park mosque was frequently visited by alleged July 7 planner and British national Haroon Rashid Aswat (*Times*, August 8, 2005), July 7 suicide bomber and ringleader Mohammed Siddique Khan, at least another July 7 suicide bomber from Leeds, and July 21 "failed bombers" Mukhtar Said Ibrahim and Yasin Hassan Omar (*Times*, July 27, 2005).

82. Daniel McGrory and Sean O'Neill, "Four Bomb Suspects 'Had £500,000 in Benefits,'" *Times*, August 6, 2005.

83. "MI5 Said Bomber Was Not a Threat," BBC, July 17, 2005.

84. Louise Male, "Suspected by MI5 and Subsidised by Europe," *Yorkshire Evening Post*, July 18, 2005.

85. Bird, Fresco, Ford, and Luck, "The Benefit Bombers Who Repaid Help with Hatred," *Times*, July 27, 2005; Duncan Gardham and Philip Johnston, "Terror Suspect Is a Convicted Mugger," *Telegraph*, July 27, 2005.

86. Bank of England News Release, August 5, 2005.

87. McGrory and O'Neill, "Four Bomb Suspects."

88. Prime Minister Tony Blair's Press Conference, August 5, 2005. http://www.number-10.gov.uk/output/page8041.asp.

89. Ibid.

CHAPTER 7

CHECHNYA, LAND OF THE FORGOTTEN JIHAD

*The liberation of the Caucasus would constitute a hotbed of jihad (or
fundamentalism as the United States describes it) and that region would
become the shelter of thousands of Muslim mujahidin from various
parts of the Islamic world, particularly Arab parts. . . . The fragmenta-
tion of the Russian Federation on the rock of the fundamentalist movement and at the hands of the Muslims of the Caucasus and Central Asia
will topple a basic ally of the United States in its battle against the
Islamic jihadist reawakening.*

—Ayman al Zawahiri, *Knights under the Prophet's Banner* (2001)

No other major cells involved in the ricin plot were uncovered in Europe
after the British arrests of January 2003. Even though the substance produced in the kitchen of the London apartment was never recovered,
British authorities had detained the man they believed had produced it,
Kamel Bourgass, the killer of Detective Constable Stephen Oake. Spain
also carried out a series of arrests attempting to dismantle the network

that had provided support to the militants returning to Europe from the Caucasus. In the meantime, French magistrates quietly continued their investigation on the *filière tchétchène*, as the case is known in France.

After arresting some smaller players, the counterterrorism magistrates Jean-Louis Bruguière and Jean-François Ricard got a big break in June 2004, when they managed to obtain the extradition from Syria of a key figure in the network, Said Arif. Arif was one of the two members of the Frankfurt cell who had escaped the Christmas Day's raids with the help of the entire Algerian network. He traveled to Georgia, where he found refuge in the camps in the Pankisi Gorge. Arif and some other cell members traveled back to Europe in March 2002, landing in Barcelona and then making their way to Paris.[1] Though his travel companions were arrested during the December 2002 raids in the Paris suburbs, Arif managed, once again, to avoid capture. In May 2004, Arif was arrested in Syria carrying a false Moroccan passport.[2] The French judges, who had issued an international warrant for Arif, obtained his extradition in June, adding an important piece to an investigation that had netted more than twenty individuals.

The French investigation can legitimately be considered very successful, but the ricin scare highlighted a problem long ignored by European counterterrorism officials: the existence of a lawless region, where hundreds of mujahideen can gain battlefield experience and train in poisonous materials, just a few hours from Europe by airplane. The Caucasus has attracted Islamic militants from throughout the world since the beginning of the 1990s, when several conflicts erupted in the area after the dissolution of the Soviet Union. Foreign Islamist fighters, mostly veterans of the Afghan war who could not return to their home countries for fear of persecution from the local government, chose instead to participate in regional conflicts such as those in Abkhazia and Nagorno-Karabakh, eventually settling in the area after the end of the hostilities.

But the real magnet for jihadis in the region has always been the breakaway republic of Chechnya, a tiny mountainous territory located in the heart of the Caucasus. Chechnya, which today has slightly more than 1 million inhabitants, has fought for centuries to obtain its independence, struggling against Czarist Russia, the Soviet Union, and most recently the Russian Federation. The Chechen population underwent mass deportations at the orders of Stalin in the 1940s and suffered pervasive discrimination in the following decades. Nevertheless, the Chechens, a proud people whose unity is bolstered by their Islamic identity, have never surrendered or accepted Moscow's authority over their land. In 1994, after the fall of the Soviet regime, Chechens took advantage of Moscow's weakness and proclaimed their independence. The unilateral secession of the oil-rich territory was not accepted by Russia, which sent troops to the region. Moscow's move signaled the beginning of the first of two brutal wars, the second of which is still ongoing.[3]

The first Chechen war, which ended with the Russian retreat of November 1996 and the creation of an independent Chechen government led by commander Arslan Maskhadov,[4] involved few foreign fighters. Reportedly, the first organized group came to Chechnya in the spring of 1995, led by the Saudi native Ibn ul-Khattab. Khattab, who had fought against the Soviets alongside bin Laden and other legendary Arab mujahideen in Afghanistan, saw media reports of the war in Chechnya and, with a few of his closest aides, decided to join the jihad in the Caucasus.[5] This vanguard teamed up with local Chechen fighters and had considerable success. Russian forces were surprised and repeatedly defeated by the mujahideen's guerrilla tactics. By the summer of 1996, Khattab and his fighters were taking part in the most intense fighting; along with the militias of the Chechen warlord Shamil Basayev, they had a primary role in the capture of the Chechen capital, Grozny.[6]

After Chechnya's independence was reluctantly recognized by the Russians in 1996, Khattab and his foreign mujahideen settled more permanently in the region. Khattab established several training camps where Chechen and foreign fighters were given military and religious instruction. The form of Islam that was taught in these camps was not the moderate Sufism that is traditional among Chechens but Saudi-imported Wahhabism. And as growing numbers of Chechens embraced Wahhabism, hundreds of foreigners from all over the Muslim world and the West flocked to Chechnya to train in Khattab's camp.

The mujahideen used the freedom they enjoyed in the newly independent Chechen republic to prepare for the next attack on Russian forces. In the summer of 1999, foreign and Chechen armed fighters led by Khattab and Basayev invaded Dagestan, a neighboring republic belonging to the Russian Federation. Russian troops quickly responded by entering Chechnya, and the second Chechen war began.[7] Since then the area has been plagued by ever-escalating violence. Indiscriminate attacks by the Russians are countered by guerrilla warfare and terrorist strikes. Thus far, the second Chechen war has been characterized by greater reliance on terrorist tactics previously unseen in the conflict and clearly imported by the foreign mujahideen. For example, while no suicide attack took place in Chechnya before 2000,[8] over the past four years several attacks by Chechen suicide bombers have been reported in Russian territory as well as inside Chechnya. Female suicide bombers, known as "black widows," were responsible for attacks at a Moscow rock concert in July 2003 and a subway station in Moscow in August 2004, as well as the simultaneous explosion of two Russian civilian airliners in September 2004.[9] Such tactics can be blamed not just on the growing desperation of Chechen fighters but also on their religious radicalization under the guidance of the Arabs. The training camps run by the mujahideen provide the Chechen fighters both with military skills and with a rigorous indoctrination in Wahhabi ideology. Not coincidentally, Khattab always maintained close relationships with al Qaeda–linked Saudi clerics, who often issued fatwas in his support.[10]

Khattab was killed in March 2002, probably by a poisoned letter sent by Russian intelligence.[11] After his death, Abu Walid al Ghamdi, another Saudi, became the leader of the foreign mujahideen in Chechnya.[12] Abu Walid, who had been in Chechnya since the late 1990s,[13] paid more attention to terrorist acts in Russia than to guerrilla warfare within Chechnya. The FSB (Federalnaya Slozhba Biezopasnosty, Russia's domestic security agency) claims that practically all suicide bombings in Russia during the past few years were financed from abroad and organized by Abu Walid.[14] For example, the FSB believes that Abu Walid was one of the planners of the February 2004 bombing in the Moscow subway that killed more than forty people.[15] Abu Walid was reportedly killed in April 2004; the specifics of his death are not known.[16] While it is unclear who has replaced him at the head of the mujahideen, foreign fighters are still active in the region. In April 2003, Colonel Ilya Shabalkin, a spokesman for Russian forces in Chechnya, said that Arabs made up about one-fifth of Chechnya's roughly one thousand active fighters. "The Arabs are the specialists, they are the experts in mines and communications," said Shabalkin.[17]

Many of those Arabs who have shaped the Chechen conflict over the past few years have come from Europe. Al Qaeda masterminds such as Abu Doha and Abu Qatada in London or other imams and recruiters throughout Europe continually made Chechnya into a battle cry for jihad, as one of the lands where the infidels were carrying out their crusade against Islam and butchering Muslims. By the late 1990s, no other major conflict involved Muslims, adding to Chechnya's attractiveness to hundreds of jihadis seeking the battlefield.

Aiding radical preachers and recruiters in their attempts at persuasion was the cunning of Khattab, a media genius who fully understood the importance of propaganda and released dozens of videotapes describing the plight of the Chechens and the endeavors of the mujahideen. These tapes, notable for both their image quality and their brutality, were distributed through a network of radical mosques and constituted an unparalleled recruiting tool. In addition, radical Islamists sympathizing with the Chechen cause ran several Web sites that showed images of the fighting and provided practical information on how to support the mujahideen. Two of the best-known (www.azzam.com and www.qoqaz.net) were operated out of London by a British man named Babar Ahmad; he was arrested in England in August 2004 on a criminal complaint issued in Connecticut that charged him with providing material support to a terrorist organization.[18] While qoqaz.net published detailed accounts of the deeds of the mujahideen, azzam.com provided guides in English on how to obtain military training, which the Web site described as "an obligation in Islam upon every sane, male mature Muslim . . . whether living in a Muslim or non-Muslim country."[19]

Azzam.com, though it took care to post a disclaimer declaring that the Web site was "only a news outlet" that did not "help or 'sponsor' people to go to for Jihad," was a de facto travel guide for jihadis living in the West who wanted to reach the battlefields of Chechnya. The Web site advised potential volunteers not to travel until the snow had melted in the spring months and to talk to "members of their own communities and countries who are known to have been for jihad." Azzam.com also indicated which charities should be used to making donations to the Chechen fighters. The investigation of its Web master revealed that Ahmad, operating out of London, was in close e-mail contact with a Chechen mujahideen leader who took part in the planning of the siege of the Dubrovka Theater in Moscow in October 2002.[20]

The Islamist Web sites and videos, with their detailed descriptions of fighting and of Muslim suffering, moved hundreds of young Muslims from throughout the world to join the jihad in Chechnya. Like Bosnia in the first half of the 1990s, Chechnya became one of the key battlegrounds for the jihadi movement. Several high-ranking al Qaeda operatives paid close attention to it. For example, in 1997 Ayman al Zawahiri attempted to enter Chechnya but was arrested by Russian police in Dagestan carrying false documents.[21] Not realizing who Zawahiri really was, the Russians sentenced him to six months and then let him go. According to the *9/11 Commission Report*, Khalid Sheikh Mohammed, the architect of 9/11, similarly failed to join Khattab in Chechnya in 1997; he could not cross the border from Azerbaijan.[22]

Mohammed was not the only terrorist involved in 9/11 that took an interest in Chechnya; several members of the Hamburg cell seriously considered traveling to the Caucasus to fight alongside Khattab. In 1999 four young Muslims who were studying in the German city decided to fight against the Russians after watching hundreds of hours of tapes of the fighting and listening to the tales of the jihad in Chechnya told by veterans of the conflict living in Hamburg. According to Ramzi Binalshibh, one of the four and a key 9/11 planner, a "chance meeting" on a train in Germany with an important al Qaeda operative persuaded them to travel to Afghanistan instead.[23] The man discouraged the group from traveling to Chechnya, stressing the difficulty of crossing the Russian border, and helped them organize their trip to the al Qaeda camps in Afghanistan. Binalshibh's companions were three of the four pilots of 9/11: Mohammed Atta, the Egyptian ringleader; Ziad Jarrah; and Marwan al Shehhi. Had the men gone to Chechnya, the history of 9/11 might well have been different. Zacarias Moussaoui, a French national and the "twentieth hijacker," reportedly fought in Chechnya, where his best friend and traveling companion, Xavier Djaffo (another Frenchman), died. After his experience in Chechnya, Moussaoui settled in London, where he became a recruiter for Khattab's group.

As noted above, London was one of the main recruiting centers for the Chechen jihad. Dozens of Algerians left for the Caucasus from London's Finsbury Park mosque, and some have been involved at the highest levels of the Chechen jihad. In September 2004, a few days after the gruesome massacre at the Beslan school, Russian authorities boasted of arresting a forty-six-year-old Algerian man linked to the gang that carried out the attack. Kamal Rabat Bourahla was apprehended by Russian forces while attempting to cross into Azerbaijan from Chechnya to have his wounds treated. The Russian Interior Ministry described Bourahla as "an extremely dangerous member of [Chechen commander Shamil] Basayev's gang[,] . . . a mercenary and demolition specialist nicknamed Abu Muskhab" who entered Chechnya in late 2000 or early 2001 after being recruited in Finsbury Park, where he was "persuaded by international terrorist Islamist organization agents to go to Russia to fight."[24]

But while Bourahla became a successful mujahid in Chechnya, other worshipers at the Finsbury Park mosque had a different experience. In March 2004, Russian forces killed three foreign fighters in a battle near the Chechen village of Kurchaloy.[25] The documents found on their bodies showed that one was a twenty-four-year-old British citizen of Algerian descent, Yasin Binatia. Another was Osman Larousi, an Algerian living in London who had entered Chechnya using a French passport. He was carrying a letter addressed to his sister in London; it not only revealed that the two Algerians had close ties to the Finsbury Park mosque but also provided insight into the life of foreign fighters in Chechnya.

Hello Fatima,

I intend to travel home, so we will see each other soon. I am tired and disillusioned. I miss Sara, you, and London a lot. Here in Chechnya it is very cold, nothing like in England or Algeria. I have a friend here. He is called Yasin. He will pass this letter on to you. You do not know him because we met here in Chechnya. We were in the same detachment. He has many friends in London and can help me. You must go with him to the Finsbury Park mosque. There you must find men by the name of Imad and Abdul Karim. Yasin has met with them previously. Abdul Karim must send my passport to Baku and then get it sent to me in Chechnya. I need my passport in order to return home. I had problems with my French passport in the name of Hamdawi Morad. Therefore, I left that passport with Ramzan in Georgia. I am afraid of returning home on that passport. The people we are with here are bad people. What they are doing is not jihad. They are ready to kill me at any moment. They are not Muslims but terrorists. They do not like Muslims. Therefore, you should locate Abdul Karim or Imad as quickly as possible. I will return home as soon as they send my passport here.

Thank you, sister.

Your brother, Osman Larousi[26]

Chechnya was an important battlefield for other European cells as well. Abu Dahdah, the leader of the Madrid cell that allegedly organized the July 2001 meeting in southern Spain during which Mohammed Atta and Ramzi Binalshibh finalized the details of 9/11, repeatedly traveled to London to meet with Abu Qatada and organize joint fund-raising efforts for the Chechen mujahideen.[27] Salahuddin Beniyach, a Moroccan who played a key role in forming the cell that organized the Madrid train bombings of March 11, 2004, fought in Chechnya and reached a position of leadership in Khattab's brigade. Salahuddin's brother, Abdelaziz, was arrested in the spring of 2002 by Ukrainian border guards as he was trying to reach Chechnya. Both Beniyach brothers have been arrested for their involvement in the May 2003 Casablanca bombing that killed more than forty people.

Abdelaziz Beniyach's traveling companion was a Dutch-born militant named Samir Azzouz. After returning to the Netherlands from his failed trip to Chechnya, the sixteen-year-old Azzouz became active in the so-called Hofstad group, a band of young Muslims that planned several attacks in Holland and to which the murderer of the filmmaker Theo van Gogh belonged. Authorities believe that the teenage holy warrior, who had purchased a gun, ammunition, night-vision goggles, and materials that could be used to make a bomb, was personally involved in a plan to blow up Amsterdam's international airport and a nuclear reactor.[28]

Militants operating in every European country have links to Chechnya. In Italy, the cell led by Essid Sami Ben Khemais was known to recruit and fund-raise for the Chechen mujahideen. Moreover, Italian authorities think that one man linked to the cell—Lakhdar Boughagha, also known by his nom de guerre, Abu Gharib—is currently in Chechnya.[29] Abu Gharib is known to Italian counterterrorism officials for his fanaticism; he reportedly killed a fellow trainee at an al Qaeda training camp in Afghanistan because he considered him to be too moderate. Officials fear that this human time bomb, who has pledged to die a martyr, will come back to Italy and carry out an attack, aided by knowledge acquired on the Chechen battlefield.

At least three German Muslims, including Bavarian convert Thomas Fischer, were killed by Russian forces in Chechnya between October 2002 and November 2003.[30] The Chechen jihad has attracted volunteers even from Scandinavia. Authorities believe that young Muslims from Norway and Sweden fought in Chechnya in the end of the 1990s. And upon returning to Denmark, Slimane Abderrahmane, the Danish detainee released from Guantanamo Bay in September 2004 after signing an agreement with the US government renouncing violence, immediately declared: "The document is toilet paper for the Americans if they want it. . . . I am going to Chechnya and fight for the Muslims. The Muslims are oppressed in Chechnya and the Russians are carrying out terror against them."[31]

The ricin plot, whose key planners had trained in the use of toxic substances in and near Chechnya, supplies more proof of how useful the ongoing conflict in the Caucasus is for European jihadis. Chechnya provides terrorists with the bases that they need, now that the Afghan training camps no longer exist. The senior French judge Jean-Louis Bruguière, in the wake of the arrests in the ricin plot, offered a concise analysis of the threat posed to Europe by the militants training and fighting in Chechnya: "There has been a change of sanctuary and a change of strategy. We know that some of the suspects were trained with chemicals in Georgia and Chechnya. The Chechens are experts in chemical warfare. And Chechnya is closer to Europe than Afghanistan."[32]

NOTES

1. Piotr Smolar, "La Syrie a Extradé vers la Fance un Activiste Islamiste," *Le Monde*, June 19, 2004.

2. Valerie Gas, "Un 'gros poisson' d'Al Qaida Extradé pal la Syrie," *Radio France*, June 18, 2004.

3. Matthew Evangelista, *The Chechen Wars: Will Russia Go the Way of the Soviet Union?* (Washington, DC: Brookings Institution Press, 2002).

4. Anatol Lieven, *Chechnya: Tombstone of Russian Power* (New Haven: Yale University Press, 1998), p. 144.

5. *Life and Times of Ibn ul Khattab* (London: Ansaar News Agency, 2002), video.

6. "Profile of Ibn ul Khattab, Ameer of Foreign Mujaheddin in the Caucasus," Azzam Publication, www.qoqaz.net. Accessed and saved in 2002.

7. US Department of State, "Eurasia Overview," *Patterns of Global Terrorism, 1999*, http://www.state.gov/www/global/terrorism/1999report/eurasia .html#Russia.

8. John Reuter, "Chechnya's Suicide Bombers: Desperate, Devout, or Deceived," American Committee for Peace in Chechnya, September 16, 2004, www.peaceinchechnya.org/reports/SuicideReport/SuicideReport.pdf.

9. Russia's 'Black Widows' Wreak Terror," CNN.com, September 3, 2004, http://www.cnn.com/2004/WORLD/europe/09/01/russia.widows/.

10. Russian Federal Security Service, "The Federal Security Service (FSB) of Russia has Reliable Information about the Ways and Methods of Financing Armed Formations Acting in the Territory of the Chechen Republic," report (n.d.), p. 36.

11. US Department of State, *Patterns of Global Terrorism, 2003*, http://www.state.gov/s/ct/rls/pgtrpt/2003/31759.htm; "Khattab's Brother Interviewed on Khattab's Life, Death in Chechnya," *Al Sharq al Awsat*, May 2, 2002.

12. Russian Federal Security Service, "The Federal Security Service (FSB) of Russia Has Reliable Information," p. 35.

13. Sharon LaFraniere, "How Jihad Made Its Way to Chechnya," *Washington Post*, April 26, 2003.

14. Steve Gutterman, "Russian Security Chief Says 10 al-Qaida Members in North Caucasus Region," AP, October 6, 2004.

15. "Top Guerrilla Killed in Chechnya, Saudi Who Led Fighters Was Suspect in Moscow Bombing," *Washington Post*, April 19, 2004.

16. "Top Guerrilla Killed in Chechnya."

17. Sharon LaFraniere, "How Jihad Made Its Way to Chechnya."

18. US Attorney's Office, District of Connecticut, "British Man Arrested on Several Terrorism-Related Charges," press release, August 6, 2004, http://www.usdoj.gov/usao/ct/Press2004/20040806.html. It is interesting to note that, in 2005, Babar Ahmad was a candidate for a seat in the British parliament for the Peace and Progress Party, the human rights party founded by the actors Vanessa and Corin Redgrave. At the press conference presenting Mr. Ahmad as a candidate, Mr. Redgrave said: "Electing Babar would be the most powerful message on human rights and justice that could be given. Just let the Americans try to say that an elected MP should be extradited. . . . We are living in the last remnants of democracy in this country. A vote for Babar is a vote that says 'We believe in the fundamental rights that generations have fought for in this country and all over the world and we will not accept that they will be destroyed'" (*Guardian*, April 27, 2005).

19. "How Can I Train Myself for Jihad?" online guide downloaded from www.azzam.com.

20. "British Man Arrested on Several Terrorism-Related Charges."

21. Lawrence Wright, "The Man behind Bin Laden," *New Yorker*, September 16, 2002.

22. *The 9/11 Commission Report: Final Report of the National Commission on Terrorist Attacks upon the United States* (New York: Norton, 2004), p. 149.

23. *9/11 Commission Report*, p. 165.

24. Ministry of the Interior of Russia, press release, September 19, 2004.

25. Utro, March 10, 2004. Accessed via FBIS.

26. Ibid.

27. Central Court of Madrid, Proceeding 35/2001, September 17, 2003.

28. David Crawford and Keith Johnson, "New Terror Threat in EU: Extremists with Passports," *Wall Street Journal,* December 27, 2004. More on Azzouz in chapter 12.

29. "In Italia i Capi di Al Qaeda," *Il Giornale*, September 5, 2004.

30. Press conference with presidential aide Sergei Yastrzhembsky, Official Kremlin International News Broadcast, December 24, 2003.

31. "Danish Detainee to Join Rebels," BBC, September 30, 2004.

32. Sebastian Rotella, "Extremists Find Fertile Soil in Europe," *Los Angeles Times*, March 2, 2003.

PART III

AL QAEDA'S MAIN STATION HOUSE IN EUROPE AND THE IRAQI JIHAD

CHAPTER 8

THE ISLAMIC CULTURAL INSTITUTE OF MILAN

You must remember that we are in a country of enemies of God, but we are always mujahideen. . . . We can fight any power using candles and airplanes: they will not be able to stop us with even their most powerful weapons. We must hit them. And keep your head up. . . . Remember: the danger in the airports.

—Abdulsalam Ali Ali Abdulrahman,
Yemeni intelligence agent (Bologna, August 2000)

Drivers in Milan know that every day they have to cope with the city's unnerving traffic. Most of the city center's streets were built centuries before cars were invented and consequently are very narrow and unfit to serve the needs of Italy's financial and commercial heart. In the 1930s, a four-lane loop was built around the city center as part of Milan's effort to compete with other big European cities. While traffic on it can sometimes be brutal, the *circonvallazione* ("loop," in Italian) took many cars off the city's overburdened minor streets. But many Milanese drivers have learned that on some Friday mornings they had better avoid the north-western part of the *circonvallazione*, where traffic often comes to a halt. In that section, police officers frequently either stop or divert traffic from the loop to the side streets, increasing the irritation of the notoriously short-tempered Italian drivers.

This weekly police intervention is made necessary by the behavior of some of the worshipers at the city's infamous Islamic Cultural Institute (ICI), a garage-turned-mosque located right on the *circonvallazione*. In the mid-1990s, a few years after the mosque's foundation, the only people affected were the shop owners and the residents of Viale Jenner, the boulevard that the mosque faces. Every Friday, year-round and in any kind of weather, worshipers began laying their prayer rugs on the side-walk right and left of the main entrance of the center, preventing customers from entering the adjacent shops. Although Italian law considers the occupation of public soil an offense punishable with a fine, complaints by some of the shop owners were ignored.

After a few years, as the mosque attracted more worshipers, during the most important religious holidays the rugs began to spill from the sidewalk to the edge of the street. Pedestrians who tried to walk on the sidewalk were forced to walk in one of Milan's busiest arteries. Drivers who complained were threatened and, reportedly, roughed up by some worshipers angered at any perceived interruption in the religious service. After police were repeatedly forced to break up scuffles between drivers and worshipers, city officials decided to set up a police patrol most Friday mornings. Instead of enforcing the law and keeping worshipers off the street and sidewalks, authorities preferred to slow down drivers. Those shopkeepers who have not sold their businesses have given up and close their stores for a few hours, taking an early and long lunch.

While Milanese drivers are familiar with the city's Islamic Cultural Institute for its effects on Friday's traffic, counterterrorism officials around the world know it as one of the most active centers of Islamic fundamentalism in Europe. Labeled by the US Treasury Department "the main al Qaeda station house in Europe,"[1] the ICI has been directly or indirectly involved in dozens of terrorist plots and has hosted some of the most famous terrorists who have walked the streets of the Continent. Only London's Finsbury Park mosque can claim a similar importance for Islamic radicalism in Europe.

Founded in 1989 by a group of mostly Egyptian immigrants unhappy with the more moderate views of the majority of worshipers at one of the city's other mosques, the ICI began to attract the attention of intelligence agencies during the investigation of the 1993 bombing of the World Trade Center in New York. The FBI believed that Ramzi Yousef, the mastermind of the operation, had spent time in Milan, where militants at the institute provided him with a fake passport.[2] But a more routine crime led Italian investigative magistrates to focus on the Institute in 1994: An Egyptian butcher told authorities that individuals linked to the ICI had organized a racketeering scheme against the city's halal slaughterhouses.[3] He claimed that local Islamic butchers were forced to buy the meat from a distributor linked to the institute, and that those who refused were threatened with arson. What began as a simple racketeering case involving poor immigrants became one of the first and most comprehensive investigations of Islamic fundamentalists in Europe, covering hundreds of individuals and exposing links to four continents.

Italian authorities in fact discovered, to their dismay, that the ICI was the main European headquarters of the Gamaa Islamiya,[4] an Egyptian terrorist organization that has killed hundreds of Egyptians and Westerners in its attempt to overthrow the country's secular government. From Milan, the militants kept in close contact with other Egyptian radicals in the Middle East, Europe, and even the United States, the home in exile of the Gamaa's spiritual leader, Omar Abdel Rahman (the so-called Blind Sheikh).[5] The ICI focused its activities on providing false documents, safe haven, and financing to Egyptian militants and on spreading the group's radical ideology.

When the conflict in Bosnia began in 1992, the ICI played a key role in recruiting volunteers to fight in defense of Bosnian Muslims. The imam of the center—Anwar Shabaan, one of Gamaa Islamiya's most important leaders—became the commander of the "Mujahideen Battalion," a paramilitary unit made up of Arab fighters (mostly veterans of the Afghan war against the Soviets) that fought against Serbs and Croats. Along with the Sahabah mosque in Vienna, another major bastion of the Gamaa, the ICI became the headquarters for European Muslims who wanted to fight in Bosnia.[6] Other terrorist groups began using the Institute as a meeting point, and the militant sermons preached inside the mosque radicalized those worshipers who were not already involved in jihad. The ICI was conceived as the organization's base in Europe, and its importance in spreading Gamaa's message throughout the Continent was clearly recognized by the group's leaders. In the words of Shabaan, which appear in a letter to a wealthy donor in Qatar, "Islamic projects in Europe must have absolute priority, considering how making these places stable bases for Muslims can be useful for Muslims all over the world."[7]

The investigation on the ICI, which was dubbed "Sphinx" by DIGOS (Italian intelligence, Divisioni Investigazioni Generali e Operazioni Speciali), culminated in a dramatic raid on the mosque in June 1995 and in the indictment of seventeen militants—only a fraction of those investigated.[8] Inside the center, police found hundreds of false documents, radical magazines, tools for forging documents, and letters proving its ties to extremists worldwide. The leader of the ICI and Sphinx's main target, Shabaan, could not be arrested, as he had already escaped to Bosnia. In December, Shabaan was killed in an ambush by Croatian police.[9]

Though Sphinx was the last major antiterror operation of the 1990s in Italy, the country remained a magnet for Islamic fundamentalists. By the end of the decade, when various groups were beginning to embrace Osama bin Laden's pan-Islamic project, the Center was playing an essential part in shaping the new face of terrorism in Europe. In a report written in 2001, Italian authorities described the role of the ICI in those years: The institute "because of the charisma shown by some of its most important representatives, performs the double function of putting forth the most radical Islamic views with substantial propaganda and indoctrination and, at the same time, binding together different networks, as it is the meeting point that is believed to be the safest for eluding police surveillance."[10] Much as was happening in Finsbury Park (to which the ICI had very close ties), in those years various networks mingled at the Center.

Friendships built in al Qaeda camps in Afghanistan turned into strategic alliances once the fighters were back in Europe and behind the walls of the former garage on the *circonvallazione*. Egyptians, who had founded the Center, continued to hold vital positions, but militants from Morocco, Algeria, Tunisia, Libya, and other countries became active inside the mosque. The ICI became one of the key facilities where the "delocalization of jihad" took place at the end of the 1990s.

As we saw in chapter 5, by the beginning of 2000, Italian authorities had begun monitoring a group of North African militants (mostly Tunisians) who were connected to the Algerian network led by Abu Doha in London. The group, led by the Afghan veteran Essid Sami Ben Khemais, was based in the northern outskirts of Milan and maintained close ties to the ICI, which members of the cell used as a meeting point. As described, the cell was dismantled by DIGOS in the spring of 2001, after British and German authorities had arrested associated cells in London and Frankfurt as part of the investigation of the Strasbourg plot. In addition to providing the evidence needed to arrest the core members of the group, DIGOS's activity uncovered the cell's impressive network in northern Italy, which provided Ben Khemais and his group flawless false documents. These were used by members of the Algerian-Tunisian network throughout Europe.

After the arrests, DIGOS continued to investigate individuals linked to the dismantled Ben Khemais cell; not surprisingly, it found that all roads were leading to the ICI. Specifically, the group looked inside the ICI for help when it wanted to send one of its affiliates to the training camps in Afghanistan. Two men linked to the Center attracted DIGOS's attention: Abdelhalim Remadna, the Algerian secretary of the ICI's imam, and Yassine Chekkouri, a mysterious Moroccan whom authorities quickly nicknamed "the Monk" because of his reclusive way of life. Both Remadna and Chekkouri lived inside the ICI, almost never leaving the premises. Months of investigation revealed them to be key players in a sophisticated network that was recruiting hundreds of European Muslims for al Qaeda training camps in Afghanistan.[11]

Indeed, Remadna was one of the most important recruiters and organizers in Abu Doha's network.[12] Sitting all day long inside the office of the ICI, Remadna used the center's phones to maintain unbroken contact with the network's leadership in London and in Afghanistan. His communications were especially frequent with Abu Jaffar, the keeper of the Algerians' guesthouse in Jalalabad, with whom he coordinated the moves of the small groups of volunteers who left Europe for the Afghan camps. Hundreds of hours of wiretapped conversation confirm the group's high level of organization. Remadna provided volunteers with state-of-the-art false documents, which have always been the specialty of Italian cells. The militants preferred European documents showing Arab names, but if the facial characteristics of the traveler allowed it, a European-sounding name was even better. Most of the time, the documents were purchased by Remadna from trusted forgers who worshiped at the mosque. Even visas were taken care of by Remadna, who could count on a couple of travel agencies run by worshipers at the ICI to obtain visas from the Iranian consulate.[13]

In order to minimize the likelihood of interception by intelligence agencies, the network had devised an itinerary to Afghanistan that went through Turkey and Iran instead of using the most common route, through Pakistan. By the end of the 1990s, authorities were examining passports of suspected militants for any sign of travel to Pakistan, which was taken as an indication of their affiliation with al Qaeda. Iran became a reliable alternative, owing to what one of the members of Remadna's network described as the Iranians' "complete cooperation."[14] Remadna provided the volunteers with addresses of hotels and safe houses, where members of the network would meet them and help them cross from Iran into Afghanistan. Phone traffic shows that militants from at least six European countries relied on Remadna's "travel agency" to reach the Afghan camps.

Remadna took care of the needs of the network's leaders in Afghanistan as well. In particular, he was repeatedly tasked to purchase equipment for Abu Jaffar, the gatekeeper in Jalalabad. In May 2001, Remadna, who was always very careful not to say anything compromising on the telephone, had a lengthy conversation with a lieutenant of Abu Jaffar who told him, "The brother Jaffar has opened new rooms and they need training . . . the problem is that they need trainers, machines for training, and keys." During the same conversation, the man told Remadna they could spend $17,000.[15] Remadna, as was his practice when his interlocutor began to speak too freely, hung up the phone hastily, but enough had been said to allow Italian authorities to understand Remadna's activities: Abu Jaffar was clearly asking for equipment and instructors for his camps. Another of Abu Jaffar's assistants spoke even more directly, telling Remadna: "What we need exactly is a device that gives a signal even if under the earth there is a match or something that can go 5 meters underground but with a video . . . anyway, that allows us to see everything that there is underground."[16] The request for the monitoring device was made on September 9, 2001, just two days before the devastating attacks in New York and Washington, and Abu Jaffar may well have been anticipating American retaliatory attacks on Afghanistan that would force al Qaeda and Taliban fighters to find shelter in the country's cave-filled mountains.

Not all to whom he talked were as scrupulous as Remadna on the telephone, and their slips enabled investigators to collect evidence on the Algerian recruiter. For example, though Remadna never named Iran, agents broke his code when they realized that his interlocutors sometimes mentioned Iran in contexts in which Remadna spoke of "98" (the country's international phone code, 0098). Even more careful than Remadna was his associate Yassine Chekkouri, who never left the Center and seldom used the phone. Nevertheless, DIGOS managed to gather information proving that he was a recruiter and a "travel agent" for the Moroccan and Tunisian networks, just as Remadna was for the Algerian network.[17] The two men, working together inside the mosque, had created an apparatus that was used by North African extremists living throughout Europe to reach al Qaeda's training camps in Afghanistan.

While investigating Remadna and Chekkouri, Italian authorities realized that a very high-ranking Egyptian operative had entered the country and contacted militants at the ICI just a few months earlier. Mahmoud Abdelkader Es Sayed, a close associate of al Qaeda's number-two man, Ayman al Zawahiri, had settled in Milan, following orders that came directly from al Qaeda. The Egyptians, who have always been the real brains behind al Qaeda and had played a key role in Europe during the first half of the 1990s, had lost their centrality and had been considerably weakened by internal struggles and waves of arrests in both Egypt and Europe. Es Sayed was sent to Italy to revitalize the Egyptian network in Milan and northern Italy, setting up new cells and establishing contacts with the other networks operating in the area. He thus kept close ties to the ICI even as he immediately became the undisputed leader of the other radical mosque in Milan, the Via Quaranta mosque. Opened shortly before Es Sayed's arrival, Via Quaranta was built to create a new gathering place for militants in the southern part of the city: Milan's Muslim population was burgeoning and the ICI could not satisfy the needs of all the radicals.[18]

That a man of Es Sayed's experience was sent to Milan shows the importance of the city to the Egyptians. A high-ranking member of the Egyptian Islamic Jihad, Es Sayed had led a cell of the organization in Sudan and was sentenced to ten years by an Egyptian court for terrorist activities. During his stay in Italy, Es Sayed was frequently in contact with senior militants around the world and also had encounters with government officials. In August 2000, Italian authorities recorded a conversation between Es Sayed and a Yemeni militant, Abdulaziz Mohamed al Zubairi, that took place in Es Sayed's car.[19] Es Sayed recalled his imprisonment in Syria, explaining that the jailing was something of an error:

> They did not know anything about us over there and that made them angry. Anyway they considered us heroes. That's how the Syrian government sees us, because the cause is common: striking at the Jews. After three days Mustafa Tlass came to visit us and I told him: "You have had a border with Israel for twenty-one years and you have not fired a single shot. . . . Our goal is to stop the peace process." He said that we should have told him that. . . . He wanted to know if we were backed by a Syrian organization. I told him not to worry because we are just ten, fifteen guys, but that was not true.

Mustafa Tlass was no ordinary visitor but the Syrian minister of defense. A longtime friend of the late Hafiz al-Assad, then president of Syria, and a member of the Baath Party since 1947, Tlass has been a member of the Syrian establishment for more than forty years.[20] He also owns a publishing house in Damascus and has personally written several anti-Israeli and anti-Semitic works, some of which include allegations that Jews kill non-Jews and use their blood to make pastries for religious holidays.[21]

As Es Sayed described it, Tlass's reaction was astonishing: "Then the minister said 'God willing you will be free soon.' Then he gave me the telephone numbers of Hamas and Al Jihad." According to Es Sayed, the visit was planned by Assad and led to his release. Though Es Sayed had been caught smuggling weapons out of Syria, the Syrians let him go as soon as they understood where the weapons were headed and why. According to Es Sayed, Syrian authorities also released all the other Egyptians that were detained with him. Es Sayed bragged that those Egyptians "now work with Hezbollah in Lebanon and Syria and nobody bothers them." If this account of collaboration with terrorist groups at the highest levels of government is true, it adds support to the claim that Syria is one of the biggest sponsors of international terrorism.

Tlass is not the only official from a Middle Eastern government who had dealings with Es Sayed. Another close associate was Abdulsalam Ali Ali Abdulrahman, a powerful politician with the Yemeni ruling party who was the director of a section of the Political Security Organization, Yemen's domestic intelligence agency. Despite his government position, Abdulrahman, who is also known as Al Hilal, had close ties to radical organizations and was known to have provided false documents and airline tickets to al Qaeda members to facilitate their travels to Europe. According to intelligence gathered by Italian authorities, in May 1998 Al Hilal traveled to Switzerland to purchase tools used to forge Schengen visas, which allow their holder to travel without border controls through fifteen countries of the European Union.[22]

Es Sayed had spent significant time in Yemen before seeking political asylum in Italy, and while there he and Al Hilal were involved in an extraordinary counterespionage operation. The story—discovered in the files of an al Qaeda computer in Kabul that was obtained by a *Wall Street Journal* reporter after the fall of the Taliban—began in early 1998, when an Egyptian member of al Qaeda living in Yemen decided to become an informant for the Yemeni government.[23] Ahmed Nasrallah, a hardened jihadi who had spent time in Egyptian jails in the 1970s, had gone to Yemeni intelligence willing to reveal all he knew about the organization. Nasrallah immediately provided authorities with names and locations of nearly a dozen high-ranking militants based in Yemen, including Ayman al Zawahiri. Nasrallah also volunteered to travel to Afghanistan to gather more information on bin Laden and his organization.

It clearly had never occurred to Nasrallah that the Yemeni intelligence officers would be anything but enthusiastic about damaging al Qaeda. The head of the agency, Mohammed Al Surmi, assigned the case to Al Hilal, who met with Nasrallah in a rented flat in Yemen's capital, Sana'a. The meeting was taped by a hidden camera, installed by Es Sayed on Al Hilal's instructions. Instead of acting on the priceless information provided by Nasrallah to arrest the militants based in Yemen, Al Hilal warned them. Among those who fled the country was Ayman al Zawahiri, who went to Afghanistan.[24] Al Hilal's sympathy toward Islamic radicals was typical of the attitude shown by elements in the intelligence services of some Middle Eastern countries, especially before 9/11. Italian authorities speculate that Es Sayed trained to be an expert forger under Al Hilal's supervision.[25] This skill became particularly useful once Es Sayed relocated to Italy, the European country that al Qaeda has traditionally used as its document factory.

The two men continued their friendship after Es Sayed left Yemen for Italy. In August 2000, Al Hilal traveled to Italy to attend a three-day meeting organized by the ICI in the countryside near Bologna.[26] Es Sayed picked him up at the airport of the Italian city, and once again, the conversation inside Es Sayed's car was recorded.[27]

Es Sayed: How are the camps in Yemen going?
Al Hilal: Well hidden, they are proceeding on a world scale. How is the youth over here?
Es Sayed: We have to train them. They need sheikhs like you.
Al Hilal: Are there youth at the camp?

Es Sayed: Few; eighty. How was the trip?

Al Hilal: Good, I am studying airplanes.

Es Sayed: Of which airline?

Al Hilal: God willing, I hope next time I will be able to bring you a window or a piece of the airplane. I flew Alitalia: there is no security, Sana'a's airport is more secure than Rome's.

Es Sayed: What, operation "Jihadia"?

Al Hilal: In the future listen to the news and remember these words: above the head.

Es Sayed: You make me dream . . . my dream is building an Islamic state.

Al Hilal: God willing we will, because the government in Yemen is weak, sooner or later we will dominate it. But the big blow will come from the other country: one of those blows no one can ever forget.

Es Sayed: Ah, is sheikh Ayman [possibly Ayman al Zawahiri] doing well?

Al Hilal: He is a bit tired, but doing well. Our focus is only on the air, sheikh Abdelmajid [Abdelmajid Zindani, the leader of the radical Yemeni Islamist party Islah and a personal friend of Osama bin Laden] made arrangements also with the Algerian. . . . The group should not be disturbed. . . . You will find a good plan, but don't get specific, otherwise you'll dig your own grave.

Es Sayed: One must be cautious, like in Iran; not a single photo.

Al Hilal: No, it's worse, moving from south to north, from east to west: whoever created this plan is crazy, but he's also a genius. It will leave them speechless. You know the verse: "He who touches Islam or who believes himself strong before Islam must be hit."

Es Sayed: They are dogs, they must all go to hell!

Al Hilal: We marry the Americans, so that they study the Quran. They feel like lions, the power of the world, but we will hit them and afterward love will be seen.

Es Sayed: I know brothers who went to America with the trick of the wedding publications [both laugh].

Al Hilal: Because they like Egyptians over there; President Mubarak has many interests with them, but sooner or later he will end up like

Anwar Sadat [president of Egypt, killed by Islamic fundamentalists in 1981].

Es Sayed: It was a good attack, inside the military parade.

Al Hilal: You must remember that we are in a country of enemies of God, but we are always mujahideen; we must take the youth like sheikh Abdelmajid, everyone has his task. We can fight any power using candles and airplanes: they will not be able to stop us with even their most powerful weapons. We must hit them. And keep your head up. . . . Remember: the danger in the airports.

Es Sayed: Rain, rain.

Al Hilal: Oh yes, there are big clouds in the sky, in that country the fire is already on and is only waiting for the wind.

Es Sayed: Jihad is still high.

Al Hilal: If it happens the newspapers from all over the world will write about it.

The chilling conversation alarmed officials before 9/11, but it took on a completely different resonance after the attacks had taken place. Al Hilal, who had close connections to the highest ranks of al Qaeda, likely knew about the plan in advance and had told Es Sayed about it.

Other evidence also suggests that some of the militants in Milan had prior knowledge of the attacks of September 11. DIGOS discovered that on September 4, someone had downloaded a photograph of the New York skyline at night, with the Twin Towers in the foreground, on a computer in the library of the Via Quaranta mosque[28]—not an image one expects to find in a mosque where America is commonly referred to as "an enemy of Islam." On September 6, Adel Ben Soltane, a Tunisian detained in Milan for his role in the Ben Khemais cell, received a letter from a fellow militant. Following standard procedure, prison guards opened it and found an empty chewing gum wrapper inside the envelope. The discovery was considered odd but not alarming until after the 11th, when the guards realized what they had seen and immediately contacted investigators. The wrapper was from Brooklyn gum, a popular Italian brand that features a picture of the Brooklyn Bridge. Investigators believe that militants used the wrapper to inform Ben Soltane about the upcoming attacks in the United States.[29]

After September 11, the whole network suddenly went underground. Chekkouri cut all contacts with the outside. Remadna exchanged a few phone calls with some militants on the day of the attacks. In one of them, he giggled briefly with a Tunisian man over the difficulties of using mobile phones that day, clearly showing his high spirits but making no direct comment. On September 13, he received a text message from another militant living near Venice that read "Congratulations for the USA"; almost complete silence until the middle of October followed.

Spurred by the arrests of some militants connected to the ICI on October 10, Remadna started planning his escape from Italy. He began inquiring about a visa for Turkey, thinking about reaching Afghanistan by the same Turkish-Iranian route on which he had aided so many others. On November 12, he shaved his beard and tried to catch a train to Rome, where he intended to take a flight out of Italy. Police intercepted him at Milan's Central Station and found him in possession of a false document. Knowing that Remadna's arrest would certainly have alarmed the ever-careful "Monk," the Italians also arrested Yassine Chekkouri to prevent him from attempting to leave the country. By a curious coincidence, Chekkouri's brothers, Younis and Reduoane, two important members of the Moroccan Islamic Combatant Group, were also arrested just a few days later on the other side of the world, in Afghanistan, where they had worked at a training camp as instructors specializing in explosives.[30] They were later sent to the detainee camp in Guantanamo Bay.[31]

To its dismay, DIGOS could not apprehend the main target of their investigation, Mahmoud Es Sayed, who had managed to flee to Afghanistan just a few weeks before Italian police acted. Authorities are not certain about his fate, but there are credible reports that Es Sayed was killed by US forces in Afghanistan in December 2001 during the battle of Tora Bora.[32]

After the arrests of Remadna and Chekkouri, the pressure to close the ICI mounted. With images of the smoking rubble of Ground Zero appearing nightly on television, the Italian public did not like the idea of hosting one of al Qaeda's main recruiting stations on its territory. As the newspapers and television stations put the center under a kind of media siege, the leadership of the ICI began its public defense. Day after day the president of the Center, Abdelhamid Shari, stood in front of the cameras repeating that a place of worship cannot be considered responsible for the misguided actions of some of its worshipers. Shari added that condemning the whole Institute would be like saying that the bishop of Milan is guilty because some of the people who attend churches in Milan are criminals.[33]

While some thought that the comparison had a nice ring to it, it is based on false premises. The analogy would be correct if only people who visited the mosque for services had been involved with the terrorism, but this is hardly true of the ICI. In addition to the dozens of simple worshipers who have been indicted over the years, the Center's leadership and administration have been investigated and charged by authorities. Remadna, who gave the mosque's address to immigration officials as his legal residence, was the secretary of the imam, Abu Imad. Chekkouri lived inside the mosque, where he occasionally worked as a librarian, and the wiretaps made clear that even the cook was involved in the group. The imam himself, Abu Imad, is a hardened jihadi who fought in Bosnia and Afghanistan and was the personal assistant of Anwar Shabaan, the center's first imam, who had led the foreign mujahideen in Bosnia. Abu Imad's speeches have often urged worshipers to fight jihad against the infidels. The Institute organized events at which the elite of Islamic fundamentalism spoke, and its bookstore sold hundreds of books and tapes about jihad and the deeds of the mujahideen. And, not surprisingly, the ICI's funding came from questionable sources: Since its foundation, the Center's rent had been paid by Anwar Shabaan's former employer, Ahmed Idris Nasreddin, the wealthy businessman who headed Al Taqwa (as discussed in chapter 2).

Despite the demands from a large segment of the public and some politicians, Italian authorities decided against closing the Center. As a result, the government has often been criticized for simply wishing to avoid a head-to-head confrontation with the Muslim community, especially in times delicate as the months after 9/11. But some security officials believe the decision to have been a sound one, as it allowed them to continue tracking the activities of several local radicals who might otherwise have disappeared from their radar screen. Though it is common knowledge that intelligence agencies monitor the Center, and most key players therefore now avoid it, many lower-level militants still use it as a place of worship and a meeting point, unintentionally providing authorities with new leads.

NOTES

1. David S. Hilzenrath and John Mintz, "More Assets on Hold in Anti-Terror Effort; 39 Parties Added to List of Al Qaeda Supporters," *Washington Post*, October 13, 2001.

2. Guido Olimpio, *La Rete del Terrore* (Milan: Sperling & Kupfer, 2002), pp. 87, 89.

3. *Halal* (literally, "allowed") is the Arabic term for meat slaughtered according to Islamic law, the only meat that devout Muslims are supposed to eat.

4. Divisioni Investigazioni Generali e Operazioni Speciali (DIGOS), note on ICI, November 9, 1996.

5. Paolo Biondani, "Alla Sbarra gli Estremisti Islamici," *Corriere della Sera*, December 13, 1995.

6. DIGOS, note on ICI, November 9, 1996.

7. DIGOS, report on the searches at the ICI, September 15, 1997.

8. Fabrizio Gatti, "Islamici della Sfinge, Tutti a Casa," *Corriere della Sera*, January 3, 1996.

9. DIGOS, note on ICI, November 9, 1996.

10. DIGOS, "Muhajiroun 3," November 21, 2001.

11. Ibid.

12. Italian authorities suspect that Remadna provided safe haven and false documents to Said Arif, Mabrouk Echiker, and Meroine Berrahal—members of the Meliani group who left Germany and spent a few months in Italy before fleeing to the Caucasus.

13. DIGOS, "Muhajiroun 3."

14. DIGOS, "Muhajiroun 2," October 5, 2001.

15. DIGOS, "Muhajiroun 3."

16. Ibid.

17. Ibid.

18. Milan currently has at least ten official and semi-official mosques; in addition, a number of apartments or basements have been turned into places of worship. Via Quaranta and the ICI on Viale Jenner follow a radical Salafi interpretation of Islam and have been repeatedly involved in terrorist activities, but most of the other mosques are moderate and have nothing to do with terrorism. The Muslim population in the Greater Milan area is estimated at one hundred thousand.

19. DIGOS, "Muhajiroun 3."

20. "Lt. Gen. Mustafa Tlass," *Middle East Intelligence Bulletin*, July 1, 2000.

21. Hugh Levinson, "A Dark Lie through the Ages," BBC, January 23, 2004.

22. DIGOS, official report, May 15, 2002. The Schengen countries are Austria, Belgium, Denmark, Finland, France, Germany, Iceland, Italy, Greece, Luxembourg, the Netherlands, Norway, Portugal, Spain, and Sweden.

23. Andrew Higgins and Alan Cullison, "The Story of a Traitor to al Qaeda," *Wall Street Journal*, December 20, 2002.

24. After an interesting series of events, Nasrallah reportedly managed to leave Yemen and escape the anger of his fellow al Qaeda members. The militants had decided to avoid troubles with Yemeni authorities and to kill Nasrallah not on Yemeni territory but in Afghanistan. Allegedly, they bought him a one-way ticket to Afghanistan, but Nasrallah, fearing a trap, escaped from Yemen and made his way back to his native Egypt, where he was arrested by local authorities. The destiny of Al Hilal is also particularly adventurous. In September 2002, Al Hilal flew to Egypt for business, and after contacting his family from Cairo, disappeared. His brother and informed Islamist sources believe he was kidnapped by Egyptian intelligence and, possibly, handed over to the CIA. In March 2005, Human Rights Watch reported that Al Hilal is currently detained in Guantanamo Bay.

25. DIGOS, "Muhajiroun 3."

26. The retreat attracted some of the most notorious fundamentalists operating in Europe. Aside from Es Sayed and Al Hilal, other important invitees were Mohammed Fazazi, the spiritual leader of the Moroccan group Salafia Jihadia (responsible for the Casablanca attacks) and imam at the Hamburg's al Quds mosque, and Ayub Usama Saddiq Ali, one of the closest collaborators of al Qaeda's number 2, Ayman al Zawahiri.

27. DIGOS, official report, May 15, 2002.

28. Stefano Dambruoso, *Milano Bagdad: Diario di un magistrato in prima linea nella lotta al terrorismo islamico in Italia* (Milan: Mondadori, Milan, 2004), p. 101.

29. DIGOS, "Muhajiroun 3."

30. DIGOS, official report, May 15, 2002.

31. Tim Golden and Don van Natta Jr., "U.S. Said to Overstate Value of Guantanamo Detainees," *New York Times*, June 21, 2004.

32. Es Sayed was nonetheless tried in absentia in Milan, where, in February 2004, he was sentenced to eight years and four months. At the same trial Remadna was sentenced to seven years and three months, while Chekkouri received four years. In October 2004, the Court of Appeals of Milan gave an additional six months to Remadna and three to Chekkouri.

33. Andrea Morigi, "Ma nei Centri Islamici Bin Laden Rimane un Eroe," *Libero*, October 11, 2001.

CHAPTER 9

FROM AFGHANISTAN TO IRAQ THROUGH EUROPE

Enemies of God. I am sure they will ask you about people who went to Afghanistan, they want the head [i.e., the chief]. Damned. They love life, I want to be a martyr, I live for jihad. In this life there is nothing, life is afterward, brother, the feeling that is impossible to describe is dying a martyr. God, help me to be your martyr!
      —El Ayashi Radi Abd El Samie Abou El Yazid, better known as Merai, Ansar al Islam recruiter (Milan, March 2003)

The events following the attacks of 9/11 completely destabilized al Qaeda and the worldwide network created by the group. After the US assault in Afghanistan, the group found itself without a base of operation. The training camps, which had served not only to educate volunteers in terrorist tactics but also to provide a place where members of different groups could form strategic alliances, were destroyed. Many of the chief planners of the group in Afghanistan—key figures such as al Qaeda's military chief, Mohammed Atef, and the gatekeeper Abu Zubaydah—had been either killed or captured. And the leaders who remained, including Osama bin Laden and Ayman al Zawahiri, were unable to operate effectively, as they were in continuous motion to evade American forces in the border area between Afghanistan and Pakistan.

The Islamic fundamentalist scene in Europe was also quite confused. The Algerian network, which had been dominant in the late 1990s, was already in disarray because so many members had been arrested in Germany, France, and Great Britain. Several key al Qaeda operatives had left the Continent in the months before 9/11, probably warned by the group's leadership that a major attack was imminent and would likely trigger a crackdown. Several important operatives who had remained in Europe were either arrested or put under close surveillance, as European security agencies vigorously ramped up their counterterrorism efforts.

But despite these difficulties, al Qaeda was far from being defeated, and it soon found the energy to reinvent itself. The first problem that the organization had to solve was the loss of its safe haven. With Afghanistan now off-limits, al Qaeda simply found alternative locations for its training camps. There were reports that improvised training camps sprang up in places such as Pakistan, the Philippines, Indonesia, and Somalia. Various regional terrorist groups that had received support from bin Laden's organization during the years stepped in to help al Qaeda restructure its activities.

A key figure in the group's reorganization was Abu Musab al Zarqawi, a Jordanian who had fought in Afghanistan against the Soviets in the 1980s and whose ties to al Qaeda were minimal before 9/11. He was the head of a small terrorist group called al Tawheed (Unity of God), whose headquarters were in the western Afghan city of Herat. The group attracted mostly Jordanians and Palestinians and its primary aim was to overthrow the secular Jordanian monarchy, which it viewed as un-Islamic and too friendly to Israel.[1] Though Zarqawi maintained good relations with bin Laden and reportedly received some funding from al Qaeda, he remained independent and never swore the *bayat* (the oath of allegiance) to bin Laden while he was in Afghanistan.[2]

Zarqawi's importance grew significantly in the months following 9/11, as he and his al Tawheed network, hitherto virtually unknown to the world's security officials, began expanding into those areas where bin

Laden's organization was unable to operate. In chapter 6 we saw that one of Zarqawi's key operatives, Abu Atiya, was dispatched to the Pankisi Gorge to set up training camps. But Zarqawi also began strong operational cooperation with Ansar al Islam, an Islamist group that resulted from the merger of several radical Islamist Kurdish groups operating in the parts of Iraq that were no longer under Saddam Hussein's rule after the 1991 Gulf War. After the massacres of Kurds in the north by Saddam's forces at the end of the Gulf War, American and British (and, initially, French) air patrols established indirect control of the region. Taking advantage of the de facto independence created by the no-fly zone, Kurds set up political parties and their own government. Small groups of radical Islamists such as Jund al Islam, the Islamic Movement of Kurdistan (IMK), and Hamas, determined to create an Islamic state, also took root and began to battle the secular Kurdish government.[3] These groups united in 2001 to form Ansar al Islam. While small in number, the group managed to gain control of some areas of Kurdistan and impose its strict interpretation of Islamic law on a few Kurdish villages. In the summer of 2001, representatives of Kurdish radical groups traveled to Afghanistan and met with al Qaeda's leaders in Kandahar. The Kurdish delegation received moral and financial support during the visit but had something important to offer as well, suggesting to the al Qaeda leadership that it might be possible to create an alternative base for the group in Kurdistan.[4] The proposal came at the right time, as in a few months American bombs would destroy al Qaeda's Afghan sanctuary.

The man who was put in charge of establishing al Qaeda's presence in Kurdistan was Abu Musab al Zarqawi. He moved some of his most trusted lieutenants to northern Iraq and began cooperating closely with Ansar al Islam. Zarqawi also helped hundreds of Arab fighters fleeing the Afghan scene pass into Iran, where authorities turned a blind eye. The fighters then relocated in the Ansar al Islam camps around the Iraqi city of Sulaimaniya. A camp near the town of Kurmal became the headquarters of the Arabs. There, one of Zarqawi's top aides from the training camp in Herat, Abu Taisir, reportedly began training operatives in the use of toxic substances such as cyanide and ricin.[5]

At the same time, Zarqawi was also extremely active on the European front. While most security agencies in the Continent were busy chasing al Qaeda operatives, Zarqawi was able to establish a small but effective network of graduates of his Herat camp throughout Europe. Headquartered in Germany and with cells in at least four other European countries, his network gained relevance as more and more members of the "old" al Qaeda network were being arrested. His operatives never competed with al Qaeda, however. As its importance grew, al Tawheed changed its priorities and replaced its traditional target, the Jordanian monarchy, with al Qaeda's global targets, the West and, specifically, America. But by no means was any attempt made to replace bin Laden as the leader of the international jihadi movement. Zarqawi filled an operational void, but after 9/11 he always operated as if he were part of al Qaeda.

In fact, driven by the same ideology and sharing the same enemies, the remnants of al Qaeda in Europe and the members of al Tawheed effectively became one network, and their collaboration reconfigured the face of Islamic terrorism in Europe. Though operatives had sometimes had contacts before 9/11 as well, European investigators believe that the alliance was made official in February 2002, when Zarqawi had a meeting with leaders of North African terrorist groups that have networks across Europe.[6]

Hints of what this new phase signified were provided by a lengthy conversation intercepted by a bug placed inside the Via Quaranta mosque in Milan. In June 2002, less than a year after 9/11, Italian authorities listened to a disturbing conversation between Abu Omar, the imam of the Via Quaranta mosque who was allegedly kidnapped by the CIA in February of 2003 (see chapter 3), and an unidentified man visiting from Germany; authorities believe he was a high-ranking member of the al Tawheed network. The man had just given a presentation to the congregation, and Abu Omar thanked him for his speech. As they spoke, the man disclosed the plan of the organization to Abu Omar.[7]

Abu Omar: Congratulations, you have encouraged the youth.
Man: It doesn't stop here. There are many things to change to eliminate the enemies of God, the policies of Israel, and those who follow them.

Abu Omar: It's our wish.

Man: The 16th of last month a meeting took place in Poland with the sheikhs, the final decision was to completely change the front of the Hizb ut Tahrir and to build a new organization that takes care of the national and of the international territory, but we need, at every level, a lot of educated people.

Abu Omar: It takes time.

Man: We do have time, we proceed slowly. There are people who are already inside.

Abu Omar: How?

Man: Now the sheikh Adel and the sheikh Abdelwahab have created different groups in which there are brothers who have returned from Chechnya.

Abu Omar: And sheik Adlen?

Man: He moved before I came here. I met him in 1987. But let's go back to our topic. Our project needs people who are intelligent and very educated. As for jihad, Abu Serrah has a program to create a battalion with twenty-five, twenty-six divisions, but the project has to be carefully studied.

Abu Omar: As long as the devil does not enter in it.

Man: The first thing I tell you is that we are aware that we are under surveillance. We know that half of the brothers are in jail, included those accused of raising funds, I repeat, the project needs to be studied in the details, because the thread starts in Saudi Arabia. He who takes care of this project is Abu Suleiman, who has the same blood as the emir Abdullah. No need of comments about this.

[Both men laugh. According to Italian authorities, the "emir Abdullah" in all likelihood is Osama bin Laden; the men laugh knowing that a project taken care of by a relative of bin Laden is guaranteed success.]

Man: The mosques are too visible and have to be left alone. We need new structures, we are looking for seven to nine buildings. We have recently bought a four-story building.

Abu Omar: And we don't take care of the mosques?

Man: Yes, we do. We also finance them, but the money has to bring in more money because the goal is to form an Islamic army that will have the name of "Force 9."

Abu Omar: How are things in Germany?

Man: I can't complain. We are already ten, we are interested in Belgium, Spain, Holland, Turkey and Egypt, Italy, and France but the
headquarters remain in London . . . sheikh Adlen gave a lot of
money, as I said earlier this project does not need further comments
and words.

Abu Omar: I hope this will enlighten the youth.

Man: This is our goal, each one of us has his duty; for example, if one
has at his disposal ten operatives, he is their chief and it's up to him
to decide whether to organize them in smaller groups or to keep
them the way they are. The important thing is to use the brain.

Abu Omar: Even if they are foreigners [i.e., non-Arabs]?

Man: It's not important, we need foreigners as well, we have Albanians,
Swiss, Brits . . . as long as they have a high cultural level. In Germany we have interpreters that translate books, we have them also
in telecommunications, also in Austria, the important thing is that
their faith in Islam is sincere.

Abu Omar: We have never had any problems with them, to the contrary
we have noticed that they are very enthusiastic and participate fully.

Man: Then you and I are not those who decide whether to take them or
not, those who decide are those from Hizb al Tawheed.

Abu Omar: I am really excited about this program.

Man: Never think about the money, because the money of Saudi Arabia
is your money; the important thing is not to run, because everything
is new, there is still something old, but the education is all new.
Whoever wanted to create this program is close to the emir
Abdallah [again, bin Laden] and we are grateful to the emir
Abdallah. Get ready.

Abu Omar: I am ready

Man: We are also waiting for the sheikh from Iraq

Abu Omar: Isn't he the one from Algeria?

Man: The one that was in London before.

Abu Omar: I heard there are some problems with the sheikh Wahab.

Man: I don't think so.

Abu Omar: I just heard a rumor.

Man: Beware of the Internet, it scares. These are the first instructions of the sheikh Adlen, we must ignore the Internet. If you communicate through the Internet use another language . . . the main issue is that every group protects the other group without destroying each other, and every group has to be far from the other. Chechnya takes care of the education [military training] of the youth, another group takes care of information. Even for the air we breathe a group takes care of it. There is just one condition. In each reunion one or two people of the group participate. Where they speak about their situation and listen to the others. The important thing is that these people are at the same level as the others . . . and everybody should know about everything. We all are one and God is one.

Abu Omar: We fight for the word of God, also through paper.

Man: Yes, this is also among our projects. There are different information that I can't give you until I see you next time, God willing. . . . We need businessmen, professors, engineers, doctors, instructors, but on a point . . . for this cause we have the money, but the money needs to bring more money, as I told you before I am not the one making decisions. Who fails pays according to the sharia [Islamic law] and there are exams to pass. I take care of my city in Germany. The other in Algeria takes care of his city. Every city had its disciples. It's him, the *kaid* [military chief], who chooses them. The responsibility is all his, if one fails it's the kaid who is responsible. But dear Abu Omar, it's not the quantity but the quality; even if they are ten it's enough. Because you can study them, understand them psychologically. You do like in school, there is the kindergarten, elementary school, middle and high school. At every step there is an exam. But the important things are security, prudence, intelligence, order, and communications, which have to be done through a messenger or we speak in another language [i.e., in code], so we have to study this point carefully, because every group refers to its region. For example: Italy is part of Austria, Germany is part of Holland, Holland is part of London. This is just an example because also for this we need lessons because prudence is what saves you. Take for example the case of Ismail, who has been in Holland since 1979 and nobody knows who he is . . . I repeat, the organization needs to be impeccable when it comes to secrecy.

Abu Omar: And I . . . what do I take care of?

Man: You sell, buy, print, register, then the person who is interested comes to you and talks to you personally . . . as long as you don't mix things, and it is necessary to avoid easy arrests, we know very well that you and I and the others we are all under surveillance. I know that I am followed by the police, but I fool them, the important thing is to find a way to convey the message to the others. Dear Abu Omar, to fight the enemies of God we need technology.

Abu Omar: It's true.

Man: For this reason the sheikhs insist we need to have very educated people.

Abu Omar: Yes, yes.

Man: We need to have a lot of intelligence. If there is the sheikh Abu Khalil, the sheikh Abu Qatada[8] or the sheikh Aden the Syrian that are under surveillance, there are other people in their place who run the situation. Secondly, we need to be very careful in the way we speak, you don't have to throw the words around like that, the tongue has to be controlled. Our groups are spread from Algeria throughout the world. For example, one from Poland can direct the group perfectly, like sheikh Abdulaziz, he has a group, it's called Katilea group, his organization is amazing, one can communicate even through a book.

Abu Omar: What, he wrote a book?

Man: Even more. He, in the books . . . they are books, but they are full of dollars.

Abu Omar: He sends dollars in the books?

Man: Yes, also other things.

Abu Omar: How, in the mail?

Man: Yes, also in the mail.

Abu Omar: So easily?

Man: Yes. Because that is not Europe. Now Europe is controlled in the air and on the ground, but in Poland, Bulgaria, and in countries that are not members of the European Community, everything is easy. First of all they are corrupt, you can buy them off with ten dollars. I get the substance over there and I send it here and there, those countries are less controlled, there are not too many eyes. But the country where everything starts is Austria. There I meet all the sheikhs and all our brothers are there. There it has become the country of international communications. It has become the country of the contacts, as I told you before, all the contacts come either from Austria or from Poland. The most convenient country is Austria and the countries neighboring it. If you are wanted, you have two possibilities: either you hide there in Austria or in the mountains. Especially the Sahafi mosque, the old mosque, has been a very hot mosque for a long time, very hot[9] . . . they are very close, especially after the fact that happened recently.

Abu Omar: There is only one God and Mohammed is his Prophet.

Man: I will send you the explanation with a brother, just pay attention to the union and to the Hizb al Tawheed.

Abu Omar: I only need directions.

Man: God willing you will get them. It is just a matter of days, because at this moment the sheikhs are traveling in Algeria, Morocco, and Bosnia. With calm and patience, you never have to run. Also the people who are with you, each line has its duty. The youth and jihad . . .

In these words, Italian counterterrorism analysts heard an explanation of "the birth of a new transnational terrorist structure, whose branches extend to our country, made up of members with ideological and military preparation, divided in cells and operationally subjected to the decisions of al Tawheed."[10] The al Tawheed network was joining forces with the old al Qaeda networks that had operated in Europe for a decade, creating a new and better organized apparatus.

The conversation alarmed Italian authorities, who placed Abu Omar under close watch. Abu Omar, whose real name is Nasr Osama Mustafa Hassan, was already well known to DIGOS (Italian intelligence, Divisioni Investigazioni Generali e Operazioni Speciali) as a seasoned member of the Egyptian Islamic Jihad who had fought in Afghanistan against the Soviets. When the Afghan conflict ended, Abu Omar, like many other Egyptian militants, moved to Albania, where he was arrested in 1996 for involvement in a plan to kill the Egyptian foreign minister during his visit to Tirana. Following his expulsion from Albania, Abu

Omar traveled to Germany and finally to Italy, where he received political asylum in May 1997. After living in central Italy and serving as an imam near Rome for a few years, Abu Omar moved north to Milan in the summer of 2000. His move was timed to coincide with the arrival of Mahmoud Abdelkader Es Sayed.[11]

Once in Milan, Abu Omar immediately settled in Es Sayed's apartment and the two began working together closely. They both maintained ties to the ICI, but they made the newly founded mosque on Via Quaranta their headquarters. Es Sayed, who was the leader of the Via Quaranta mosque, appointed Abu Omar as its imam. Abu Omar immediately established strong contacts with other militants operating in Milan, particularly with Abdelhalim Remadna.[12] The wave of arrests that hit Milan's Islamist community in the months following 9/11 spared Abu Omar, but the careful monitoring of his activities enabled authorities to understand the changes taking place in the network both in Milan and in Europe.

Just a few days after his conversation with the unidentified al Tawheed member from Germany, Abu Omar left the Via Quaranta mosque because of his strong disagreements with the mosque's leadership, who accused him of endangering the mosque by hosting veterans of the Chechen conflict inside the mosque and by openly fund-raising for "the mujahid brothers" and for the "families of the martyrs."[13] The director of the mosque, (rightly) convinced that these activities would attract the authorities' attention, repeatedly asked Abu Omar to stop; after his continued refusals, the cleric was asked to leave his position.

As soon as he left the mosque, Abu Omar was contacted by two Kurdish men living in the small city of Parma, one hundred sixty kilometers southeast of Milan, who had learned of his falling out with the Via Quaranta mosque. Mohammed Tahir Hammid and Mohammed Amin Mostafa were already known to Italian authorities, for they had previously been in contact with Milan operatives investigated in the past, including Remadna, Yassine Chekkouri, and Es Sayed. The two Kurds invited the cleric to Parma for Friday prayers, mentioning the possibility of hiring him as imam of their mosque. Under the watchful eyes of Italian agents, on August 9, 2002, Abu Omar took a train from Milan's Central Station;

an hour later he arrived in Parma, where the two Kurds picked him up in a red Volkswagen Golf.[14] As they monitored this apparently innocuous visit, Italian investigators uncovered a network that reached from Milan to Baghdad, from Istanbul to Hamburg.

Abu Omar's trip to Parma prompted Italian authorities to look into the activities of the two Kurds, who had been only peripheral figures in earlier investigations and had been left free to operate. The new information gathered by DIGOS suggested that the men were key members of Ansar al Islam, sent to Europe to recruit and raise funds for the group. Months of wiretapping and patient tailing revealed that they were at the center of a highly sophisticated network that was recruiting militants in Europe to train in the Ansar al Islam camps in northern Iraq in preparation for the US invasion of that country.[15] The network, coordinated by Zarqawi in Iraq, operated in several European countries and drew on the structure established by al Qaeda before 9/11. Indeed, the Kurds were simply a new element in a well-oiled machine that had worked smoothly for years. While the destination was different, the modus operandi, centers of operation, and the key recruiters (for the most part) were the same as al Qaeda had used to send militants to Afghanistan before 9/11.

Authorities discovered that the two Kurds were in frequent contact with Merai,[16] an Egyptian man living in Milan whom they knew had collaborated closely with Remadna and Chekkouri—formerly al Qaeda's top recruiters in Italy. In providing some help to Remadna and Chekkouri in their recruiting efforts, Merai gained significant knowledge in the art of facilitating travel for volunteers of jihad. Merai and the two Kurds had set up an elaborate scheme that sent volunteers from Europe to the camps in northern Iraq through Turkey or Syria, where human smugglers linked to the group helped them enter Iraq.[17]

After Remadna and Chekkouri were arrested in November of 2001, Merai, who also made the ICI his headquarters, became Italy's main recruiter. Merai had no shortage of volunteers, whose numbers were swelling as the war on terror continued, but he needed to find new places where they could train. The two Kurds from Parma provided this much-needed alternate location. The same network that had recruited for

Afghanistan began sending militants to Iraq, where they reached the Ansar al Islam camps for training by Zarqawi. Moreover, Zarqawi's European network became involved in the operation, as its German-based al Tawheed operatives cooperated with Kurdish members of Ansar al Islam in Munich. Individual affiliations often became blurred as Ansar al Islam members in Italy and Germany, together with al Qaeda and al Tawheed recruiters in Germany, Italy, and France, labored to send volunteers to Iraq's Ansar al Islam camps that now hosted al Tahweed and al Qaeda operatives. Zarqawi and Ansar al Islam provided new energy and a new destination to the old and well-established al Qaeda network in Europe. All were working together in harmony as they pursued a common goal.

The first group of militants from Europe was allegedly sent by Merai and the Kurds to Iraq in the fall of 2002, when eight Tunisians and three Iraqis left Europe from the French city of Marseilles for Damascus. The men then traveled to Iraq, using forged Moroccan passports provided by Merai and relying on a scheme conceived by Mullah Fouad, a Kurd who was the top Ansar al Islam operative in Damascus. To cross the Syrian-Iraqi border without raising the suspicions of Iraqi security guards, they declared that they were Shiite pilgrims on their way to the holy city of Karbala.[18] Their claim is ironic in light of the later bombings of Shiite mosques in Karbala, carried out by Ansar al Islam as part of the group's war against Shiite Muslims.

The first group was followed by many other volunteers from European countries, including Germany, France, Holland, Sweden, and Finland. In Damascus the network could count on Mullah Fouad, who had spent time in Italy with the two Kurds from Parma before returning to Syria in the fall of 2002. Now he worked closely with them and with Merai, coordinating the movements of the volunteers going to Syria. His long experience with Ansar al Islam made him a revered figure in the network. Italian authorities intercepted communications between the men as they exchanged phone numbers of contacts, requested money or documents, and talked about the passage of the groups of volunteers. At the same time that Mullah Fouad was giving orders to the operatives in Europe, he was in direct contact with the Ansar al Islam camps in Kur-

distan and with Abu Musab al Zarqawi, with whom he even shared a telephone card.[19]

For months the men talked about "the education of the youth," by
which they meant training in the camps, and the constant skirmishes
between those in the camps and local Kurdish forces. But the tension on
both sides of the Mediterranean grew significantly in the first months of
2003, as the likelihood of a US invasion of Iraq increased daily. As the
Bush administration was trying to build a coalition and the Pentagon was
amassing US forces in the areas surrounding Iraq, Ansar al Islam was getting ready for its most important battle. The leadership of the group
immediately realized that if a conflict should take place, Ansar al Islam
would be one of the first targets of the American forces. In his speech
before the UN Security Council, Secretary of State Colin Powell had
named the presence of Ansar al Islam as one of the main reasons for going
to war against Iraq, and US officials frequently called the organization the
missing link between Saddam's regime and al Qaeda.

Though the prospect of being pounded by American B-52s was
hardly pleasant, Ansar al Islam and Zarqawi also realized that the invasion of Iraq would provide them with an unprecedented opportunity,
allowing them to come face to face with American troops and avenge the
shameful defeat that al Qaeda had suffered in Afghanistan. Ansar al Islam
intended to transform Kurdistan and the whole of Iraq from a place of
training to a battlefield where American forces would be attacked. And
the group began to prepare itself to inflict as much damage as possible. In
March 2003, just a few days before the beginning of the war, Italian
authorities intercepted the following conversation between Merai in
Milan and Mullah Fouad in Damascus:[20]

Merai: This week some "guests" will come to you.
Fouad: I agree with you, but the guests have to be smart and prepared
Merai: No, good people who love you.
Fouad: I don't need good people, I need people who are smart and pre-
    pared in *khataf* [literally "kidnapping," "hijacking"].
Merai: OK, what do you want me to do? You want me to hit the ground
    to take out a watermelon? [an idiomatic expression]

> Fouad: No, worse. . . . We urgently need those that you know. . . . I
> want people who can hit the ground and make the iron come out of
> it. Look for those who were in Japan.
>
> Merai: I have one. He is sick, he was already sick and tired. . . . There
> are people who are ready . . . you'll be fine with them, because they
> have the good . . .

Though they used coded language, it is clear that Mullah Fouad is asking Merai to recruit suicide bombers. "Those who were in Japan" refers to kamikazes, the Japanese suicide pilots of World War II. As the conflict with the United States approached, Ansar al Islam was ratcheting up its efforts to train suicide bombers, a tactic it had never employed before Arab militants had joined the group.

The phone call alarmed Italian investigators, who were almost ready to close in on the cell. A few days later, authorities were forced to wrap up the investigation and arrest the members of the network, as the arrival of an important radical from London marked significant new developments. On March 23, they overheard an unidentified speaker from Syria giving precise instructions to Merai in Milan about the man's visit, and suspected that someone important was coming.[21]

> Merai: Are the men I sent you still there or did they leave?
> Man: Not yet, they haven't left yet.
> Merai: This week I'll send you three or four.
> Man: Don't worry, we need up to forty, but good as those from before.
> Merai: Yes, yes, no problem . . . look, they are of different nationalities.
> Man: Listen, you will be contacted by a brother from Sudan . . . sorry,
>   Somali, his name is Mohammed . . .
> Merai: Tell me, Abu Ali, Somali or Sudanese?
> Man: Somali, Somali . . . when he will contact you be at his complete dis-
>   posal. Whatever he asks you, give it to him, whatever he needs, find it.
> Merai: I am at your service, God willing.

In the following days Merai received several phone calls from the mysterious Somali man, who called as he traveled from London to Milan through Holland. The men set up a meeting at Milan's Central Station on the 24th. Once in Milan, the Somali again called Merai. Not knowing each other, both men described what they were wearing and agreed to get together at an Internet café near the station. But the agents from DIGOS, who had intercepted the conversation in real time, approached the Somali man as he was walking off the train; they staged a routine check to see who he was, then let him go.[22]

Authorities immediately realized that the Somali visitor was, indeed, an important figure in the European al Qaeda network. The man was Maxamed Cabdullah Ciise, an experienced operative who specialized in fund-raising for al Qaeda. According to information passed on by Scotland Yard, Ciise engaged in sophisticated money-laundering schemes, transferring large amounts between London and Somalia through Sweden and Dubai. Ciise, who was a member of al Ittihad, a Somali terrorist group closely linked to al Qaeda, had also been involved in financing the November 2002 terrorist attacks in Mombasa, Kenya.[23] Suicide bombers drove a jeep into the lobby of an Israeli-owned resort hotel, killing fifteen people and wounding more than eighty. Simultaneously, terrorists fired two surface-to-air missiles at an Israeli airliner taking off from the Mombasa airport but missed.

What was a big shot like Ciise doing in Milan? Merai had been ordered to help him with everything he wanted. But what did he want? The Italians had to wait only a few minutes to know the answer to these questions. Worried about having been stopped by Italian police the moment he stepped off the train, Ciise decided to call his contact as soon as he met Merai. Ciise used Merai's phone to call a man named Abderrazak, expressing his frustrations and his fears that Merai and his helpers were under surveillance, and he repeatedly asked for reassurance. Abderrazak, whom Italian authorities at the time were unable to identify, tried several times to calm Ciise, telling him that Merai was a trusted operative and that he would find him what he needed. The conversation also revealed that Ciise had come to Italy to obtain false documents that he intended to use to travel to Syria and then to Iraq.[24]

The days following Ciise's arrival were particularly hectic for both the terrorists and investigators. For their part, Merai and his group tried to procure state-of-the-art documents for the Somali man, but encountered unexpected problems. Ciise, whose fear of being followed by police is surpassed only by his disdain for the inefficiency of Merai's group, divided his time between Milan's two radical mosques (the ICI and Via Quaranta) and Internet cafés, viewing every face around him as a possible police officer tailing him. At the same time, agents were working around the clock to monitor every move made by members of Merai's cell and by the cautious Somali.

As the days went by, Ciise's patience ran short; he kept calling the mysterious Abderrazak, who seemed to be the leader of the entire network. Abderrazak finally put Ciise in contact with another operative based in Italy. The man he called lived in Reggio Emilia, a city just a few kilometers east of Parma, where the Kurds of Ansar al Islam operated. According to Abderrazak, the man, a Moroccan national named Mohammed Daki, was "a specialist" in documents and would solve Ciise's problem. Ciise, having given up on Merai and wishing to leave Italy as soon as possible, traveled right away to Reggio Emilia to meet Daki, a man who was completely unknown to Italian authorities.[25]

Tailing Ciise proved to be an extraordinary challenge for DIGOS, which had to put dozens of agents on the case to get the better of the Somali's brilliant countersurveillance techniques. While in Milan, Ciise used all the tricks that experienced al Qaeda operatives learned in Afghanistan. He would walk up a street, pacing himself, then stop to look back, then enter a phone booth and stay there for few minutes, looking outside. He would go down small side streets, then suddenly walk back in the opposite direction. He went down to the metro platform but did not get into the first train—which the agents were forced to take so that the Somali would not spot them immediately as the only other people still in the station. On one occasion Ciise enlisted the help of another militant who walked twenty or thirty meters behind him, trying to see if anybody was following.[26] While in Reggio Emilia, he became even more cautious, as he and Daki almost never left Daki's dwelling. When they did, they always looked around, staying on any given bus for only a few stops to flush out anyone who might be following them. While riding the bus, they scrutinized the faces of all the passengers.[27]

On March 30, the documents for Ciise were finally ready, but by then, despite the carefulness of the agents, the Somali realized that he was being followed. The entire network panicked and made plans to leave the country. Abderrazak, the mysterious man still coordinating the group's operations from abroad, told Daki to go to France; Ciise prepared to go to Germany, where he would join with other "brothers" to go to Damascus and meet Mullah Fouad. Merai and one of the Kurds in Parma made plans to escape to Syria.[28]

The group's sudden flurry of activity forced DIGOS to close the investigation and arrest all the members before they fled the country. Police in Reggio Emilia and Parma moved to take Daki and the two Kurds into custody, while authorities in Milan arrested Merai and Ciise. No documents were found, as the men managed to hide them inside the Via Quaranta mosque before their arrests. But additional evidence was provided without their knowledge by the two arrested in Milan. Authorities had the forethought to leave Merai and Ciise in a room in the police station in which a microphone had been hidden. Their conversation provided a fuller view both of their activities and of their religious fanaticism and deep hatred.[29]

Ciise: What a situation!

Merai: God sees them. You stay calm.

Ciise: I am calm, but inside of me there is a lot of confusion.

Merai: I tell you again, everything is in the hands of God. Now we are here. Even if they take us to San Vittore . . .

Ciise: What is San Vittore?

Merai: It is a penitentiary, but there we will find the best brothers . . . those brothers who never abandon you.[30]

Ciise: At this point let's pray to God. Where are we now?

Merai: This is the waiting room at DIGOS.

Ciise: Ah, that is what they are called?

Merai: DIGOS. They come right after the security services.

Ciise: If only I had more time today I wouldn't be here, I would be in Paris.

Merai: Don't make me feel guilty.

Ciise: No, no. It's destiny, there have been problems since I came to Italy. I am not blaming you. We are fighters.

Merai: Good, good, for the best.

Ciise: Did they put anything in the food?

Merai: We don't eat the sweets of the enemies of God, because they are sons of dogs.

Ciise: Tell me sincerely, how many times have you been here before?

Merai: Never at DIGOS, I have been to the Foreigners' Office [i.e., the Ufficio Stranieri, where aliens must apply for residence permits].

Ciise: We don't know each other.

Merai: No need to say that. They already asked me if I knew you and I said that I met you at the mosque.

Ciise: OK, let's stick to that version, because they have nothing on me. When they asked me why I was here I told them I came to find my cousin, one of the family that I am desperately trying to find. But, honestly, there is something wrong here. I am surprised about the thing with the bag. How did they know that it was there? How did they bring me the bag? Why are they asking me about the training camps in Syria? I am speechless.

Merai: You know, they are trying to make you speak, they make you believe they know everything but they don't know anything. I have many brothers who are in jail and they got five to fifteen years, in Italy, in Bosnia, all over the world.

Ciise: So there is a link. Maybe you are under surveillance!

Merai: Listen, brother, if I had been discovered I wouldn't be here. I would already be in jail. You have to know that, sometimes, spies come to the mosque, a spy comes and . . . when they see a new face they want to know who he is, where he is from . . . they try to collect information and then they go tell them . . .

Ciise: I am telling you that I saw them from the first day, even the day when we got arrested and they put me in the car and they put the gun against me, they told me that they have gathered information on me and they have asked the Americans. I told them they were enemies of God, to take their hands off of me. Then they asked me what my real nationality was.

Merai: Fool them, tell them you are Egyptian. Thank God they did not find the passports. At home I have just a few things, I just have money, but the rest is hidden, but . . . at home I just have a few euros . . .

Ciise: They don't scare me, you always have to keep the faith in God.

Merai: I recited the Quran the whole night.

Ciise: So did I.

Merai: They just wait for us to say that we are mujahideen and they are happy, but since they have nothing let's fool them.

Ciise: The Moroccan passports?

Merai: Nothing, when they got us I had nothing on me, I had passed everything to Brahim.[31]

Ciise: Of all those you introduced me to, he is the smartest.

Merai: He is smart and generous, quiet and good, he knows how to behave in these situations.

Ciise: And what about the Moroccan passport they had prepared for you and that they passed you while we were sitting?

Merai: Brahim has it, he knows what to do. I am not stupid, I did not keep it with me. When we get out of here you disappear immediately and so do I. If you need help, Brahim knows where the money is hidden. I never had anything on me. If you want to take the passports, take them. He knows all my safe houses and my movements. Sometimes even we forget the places where we hide things. He is a tomb.

Ciise: First of all let's get out of here. Then I'll try to go to Romania, because I have support there. Sorry if I ask you this question again, but are you sure this is the first time they've taken you here? You are not under surveillance?

Merai: I would know if I were under surveillance. I know most of them. And the youth also watches the mosque for me and keeps me informed.

Ciise: I have doubts about the damned phones. If it is so it is a big problem because the others are waiting for me . . . Abderrazak, Abu Zaied, Abdelkarim, these are wanted by the majority of secret services, especially Abu Zaied by the French.

Merai: I don't think so. Because I don't use the telephone a lot, I change the card continuously, and the phone calls we made together we made them from outside.

Ciise: I hope it is so, that they don't have any phone calls, because otherwise it would be a big problem for the brothers, but I think everything is under control.

Merai: It could be. Who isn't under surveillance? It's enough that they see you once and they check your movements.

Ciise: No, brother. Now that I remember well I remember one who told me that it is better to go Afghanistan or Iran rather than Quaranta [i.e., the mosque on Via Quaranta]; this is the most dangerous place after London, because it is known in the world for the preparation of terrorists and for logistical and financial support, it is known because it is targeted. The whole world knows Quaranta.

Merai: Where are you coming from? From Great Britain. And so? Don't worry, they don't have anything. They asked me about Lotfi, Adel, Hammada, Mullah Fouad, Amin, most of them are either in jail or dead. I think their target is Mullah Fouad.

Ciise: I am not worried for myself, I am worried for the others, for the brothers there who are waiting for me. I'll never go to London again because I am flagged over there.

[Short pause.]

Merai: The enemies of God, sons of dogs, stupid questions. Have you been to Iran? Yes, so what? Where is the problem if I have been to Iran? Have you been to Syria? Stupid questions . . .

Ciise: They told me I was Sudanese.

Merai: Tell them yes, no, maybe, I forgot, make fun of them. These people here . . . servants of the Americans, they are servants!

Ciise: Yes, yes!

Merai: But they are terrorized by us. Sooner or later, maybe tomorrow morning, they'll have news. Because both the Americans and the Israelis, sooner or later, will pay, maybe tomorrow morning, who knows. . . . When they kill it's OK, but if we tell them we are going to Iran or Syria they ask us what we are doing there. Now they put Iraq in the middle, the dogs of the Americans and of the Israelis, may God damn them, also their allies, included the Italian army, whatever they ask them they are at their full disposal, the Americans have them on a leash. . . . If they ask me if I went to fight to Afghanistan I tell them yes. So what? Is there a problem? They are armed and they are afraid of us.

Ciise: They . . . whatever the Americans ask . . . not just them, but any other country, they serve them.

Merai: Very soon they will have news, a good thing to see . . . and they will pay because they are dogs, they are like dogs, they are sons of dogs, they are damned, they are enemies of God . . . the others in front and they are on the leash. They have no value. They are dogs! They are devils! The American power does not scare me. Are you afraid of them? You anyway, whatever they ask you, you don't answer. Or you tell them you don't know. You tell them that the Quran answers.

Ciise: The enemy of God came to touch the Quran.

Merai: And you let him?

Ciise: No.

Merai: Tell him to leave and not to touch it with a finger.

Ciise: He told me he wanted to check it and I told him I was going to open it, page by page. He made me open it three times.

Merai: Enemies of God. I am sure they will ask you about people who went to Afghanistan, they want the head [i.e., the chief]. Damned. They love life, I want to be a martyr, I live for jihad. In this life there is nothing, life is afterward, brother, the feeling that is impossible to describe is dying a martyr. God, help me to be your martyr!

[The men recite verses of the Quran. After a few minutes they start insulting Italy and America again.]

Ciise: How come these people [the Italians] are not ashamed of themselves? Whatever they [the Americans] ask them they do it.

Merai: The Americans are like masters for them. Believe me, even if they ask me something about the Americans I tell them that they are both of the same race. Enemies. They are the masters and you are the dogs. Where they tell you to go, you go. Devils. They are afraid of the Americans, we are not.

[The men keep insulting the Americans and then they recite Quranic verses.]

Merai: Do you know the hymn of jihad against the Americans?

Ciise: Yes!

Merai: Of the sheik Abu Faisal. Come on, let's recite it together!

[The men recite the hymn of jihad.]

Merai: We have freedom and we go to paradise, but they will have only troubles. Come on, brother, we will have paradise! We did not lose a day. We learned many things.

Ciise: But generally, when they arrest two, do they put them together?

Merai: No!

Ciise: And how come they put us together?

Merai: They probably arrested a lot of people and everything is full.

Ciise: Weird . . .

Merai: Oh, brother, nothing is wrong, we are just waiting for the Foreigners' Office. They run a check and then you can go. They didn't find anything, they found 1,500 euros that were at home and the watch, that's it. There is nothing. What do you think they'll do to you? If it were something big they would have evidence, we would not be together.

Ciise: I'm anxious to know what is going on. You tell me that generally they keep them separate?

Merai: I have been caught only by the Foreigners' Office, there are no problems.

Ciise: I don't know. We'll see.

As they talk, the different personalities of the two militants emerge. While Merai shows a level of self-confidence and arrogance that borders on the ridiculous, the more experienced Ciise is more level-headed. Merai, blinded by his hatred, does not realize the seriousness of their situation; Ciise asks the right questions, as he understands that their plans have been discovered. But neither realized the danger of speaking so openly, and their words made the prosecutors' job easier.

As Italian authorities began to question the men and gather more information, they came across unsuspected but chilling links. Magistrates realized that both Ciise and Daki had connections to the German city of Hamburg, where they had lived and had befriended some of the key members of the Hamburg cell—a group of Muslim men who used to worship at the same radical mosque, some of whom participated in the attacks of 9/11. These participants included not just three of the four pilots of the planes hijacked on 9/11—Mohammed Atta, Marwan al Shehhi, and Ziad

Jarrah—but many others who shared in the planning or provided aid. Some of these men, such as the key planner Ramzi Binalshibh and Said Bahaji, left Germany in the days before the attacks, while others remained in Hamburg. German authorities have investigated more than one hundred men who they believe had varying levels of connection to the Hamburg cell, but only two, Mounir El Motassadeq and Abdelghani Mzoudi, have been tried for their involvement in the plot (see chapter 3).

In the wake of the attacks of 9/11, Hamburg came under worldwide scrutiny, as officials and media wondered how a wealthy, quiet German city could produce such a large group of radicals willing to take part in a heinous terrorist act. Hamburg became a case study in failed integration and successful jihad recruitment. As investigators, journalists, and social scientists uncovered more information on how the Hamburg cell was formed, they realized that its constituent elements could be found in any European city.

The Hamburg cell was an explosive mixture of individuals who happened to gather at the same place, the al Quds mosque. Most of the worshipers at the mosque were lonely young immigrants from Muslim countries who had come to Germany for work or study. Some were unskilled laborers, but many were the sons of their country's upper middle classes who had come to Hamburg to study at the city's prestigious technical universities. Most of them were not, by Muslim standards, particularly religious when they arrived at Hamburg; they saw the al Quds mosque more as a place where they could meet other young men from the Middle East and feel at home than as a place of worship. But the mosque was also the meeting place of a small group of older men who had dedicated their life to jihad. Revered by other Muslims for their battlefield experience and driven by their extreme commitment, these men viewed recruiting youths for the cause of Allah as their duty. The seasoned jihadis know their ideal targets are young men living in a foreign society very different from that of their home country, often at its margins, unable to adapt to their new reality, and easily influenced by the words of charismatic figures. One of the key figures at the al Quds mosque was a Moroccan imam, Mohammed Fazazi, who gave weekly sermons at the mosque and whose tapes were watched by radicals throughout Europe. Fazazi strongly believed that democracy and Western values must be rejected by Muslims living in the West, who should respect only their own Quranic laws. He often preached that European countries were conducting a war against Islam and that "smiting the head of the infidels" was the duty of all Muslims, mandated by God.[32] Fazazi, who left Hamburg before 9/11, is believed to be the spiritual leader of the Moroccan terrorist group Salafia Jihadia and is serving a thirty-year sentence in a Moroccan prison for his role in the Casablanca attacks.[33]

Mohammed Daki, the Moroccan who had been tasked to provide Ciise with a document, knew some of the key members of the Hamburg cell well and admitted to worshiping at the al Quds mosque. Like most of the members of the cell, he had come to Hamburg to study. Among those he befriended were Said Bahaji, Mounir El Motassadeq, and Ramzi Binalshibh. In fact, he had allowed Binalshibh to claim to be living at his home address in Hamburg between 1997 and 1998, a connection that led German authorities to question him in the wake of the attacks of 9/11.[34] Ciise's link to Hamburg was also strong, though not as recent (Daki had left the city only a few weeks before his arrest in Italy). He had lived in Germany from 1991 until October 1999, when he moved to Great Britain, and while in Hamburg he had worshiped at the al Quds mosque and befriended the same group as Daki. According to witnesses questioned by German authorities, Ciise became a close associate of Ramzi Binalshibh, with whom he often watched videos about Chechnya and talked about religion. Ciise became friendly as well with the hijacker Mohammed Atta and a Yemeni named Mohammed Rajih, whom German authorities have also investigated for terrorist ties. In 1998 Ciise's apartment in Hamburg was raided by German police, who found forged Italian documents, proving the role of Italian cells in supplying false documents to militants worldwide.[35]

Even though Ciise and Daki lived in Hamburg at the same time and had common acquaintances, they never crossed paths in Germany. Their meeting in Reggio Emilia was orchestrated by another Hamburg resident—the mysterious Abderrazak, whom Ciise had frantically called on his first day in Milan. Though Italian authorities at first did not know who the man was, Daki's interrogation and information gathered from their German counterparts enabled them to identify him as an Algerian whose full name was Abderrazak Mahdjoub. Daki confessed that while in Hamburg he had become acquainted with Abderrazak, who had instructed him to give Ciise the documents he needed. The investigation revealed that Abderrazak was in fact the head of operations in Europe for the al Tawheed recruiting network and that he was working closely with Mohammed Loqman, the Ansar al Islam leader in Munich, and Mullah Fouad, the network's operational chief in Syria.[36]

In Abderrazak's story, we see the evolution of al Qaeda in Europe after 9/11. After other key operatives had left Hamburg shortly before 9/11, Abderrazak became one of the most important militants operating in the city. Starting from remnants of the old network, now crippled, he built connections with a new group, Ansar al Islam, and redirected the activities of the Hamburg cell toward a new goal. Under his guidance, several members of the Hamburg cell with ties to the planners and executors of 9/11 were now directing their efforts toward recruiting militants to fight American forces in Iraq. Indeed, investigators found that Abderrazak himself had led a group of Muslims from Hamburg to Syria on March 20, 2003, the day after the first American bombs fell on Baghdad. While in Damascus, Abderrazak met with Mullah Fouad, probably to better coordinate their activities. When he took Ciise's phone call from Milan's Central Station, Abderrazak was, in fact, in Damascus with Mullah Fouad and the two made calls together to militants in Italy, urging them to help Ciise with whatever he needed.[37] The old (Hamburg) and the new (Ansar al Islam) were cooperating to fight their common enemy, the United States.

German authorities believe that a few weeks into the conflict, Abderrazak and the other men from Hamburg attempted to cross into Iraq in order to join the fighting against US forces. Reportedly, Abderrazak and four other militants were arrested by Syrian authorities, held in a Damascus hotel for forty days, and released on May 20. Two days later the men made their way back to Europe. Abderrazak and his top lieutenant, a French citizen named Naamen Meziche who had lived in the German city for a few years (and received benefits from the local government), returned to Hamburg. Meziche, who used to regularly attend services at the al Quds mosque, had married the daughter of the mosque's imam, Mohammed Fazazi. He was a friend of some of the 9/11 hijackers and worked as a baggage handler at Hamburg Airport with the only two men charged in Germany with involvement in the attacks, El Motassadeq and Mzoudi.[38] Meziche was, like Abderrazak, another example of the old al Qaeda network being incorporated into the new organization.

Because Abderrazak and Meziche had committed no crime under German law, local authorities had to let them back into the country, and they continued their activities undisturbed in Hamburg. Another member of the group that had been arrested in Syria, Abdellahi Djaouat, settled in the Spanish coastal town of Lloret de Mar. Djaouat, a professional judoka who had been convicted in France for drug-related offenses, began working as a bouncer in a local club run by fellow Algerians and kept a low profile.[39] Nevertheless, Spanish authorities, aware of Djaouat's ties to extremists, began monitoring his phone conversations. Djaouat stayed in contact with several radicals in Spain and with Abderrazak in Hamburg, whose telephone was also bugged.[40]

A joint Spanish and German investigation determined that Abderrazak and Djaouat were likely planning an attack for the month of August. Specifically, they intended to bomb tourist facilities on Spain's Costa del Sol during the peak of the summer season, when the beautiful coastal towns are crowded with thousands of European vacationers. The attack, perhaps a forerunner of the March 11 attacks in Madrid, was meant to punish Spain for its support of the US invasion of Iraq.[41] Spanish authorities also discovered that Djaouat was involved in a string of robberies and had trafficked in drugs with another Algerian, Samir Ait Mohammed. Authorities believe that the profits of these illegal activities were laundered through clothing shops in the Spanish city of Bilbao. The businesses were owned by Samir and Farid Mahdjoub—the younger brothers of Abderrazak. The Mahdjoubs in Spain apparently funneled money to their older brother in Hamburg, closing the complicated web of links between the two countries.[42] Another man allegedly involved in the Lloret cell is Hedi Ben Youssef Boudhiba, a forty-five-year-old Tunisian man. Boudhiba's ties are astonishing and show the extent of the Algerian network. Spanish authorities accuse him of being part of a cell that helped some of the 9/11 hijackers from Spain.[43] Boudhiba left Hamburg a few days before 9/11 and reached Istanbul. He later returned to Europe, and authorities believe he moved between Spain, Portugal, and the United Kingdom. His picture was found on a fake Portuguese passport in the apartment of Kamel Bourgass, the ricin-maker sentenced to life for the killing of Manchester police officer Stephen Oake. Boudhiba, who is currently fighting extradition to Spain from London's Belmarsh jail, had also a role in Abderrazak's efforts to send fighters from Europe to Iraq.[44]

On July 25, 2003, police in Hamburg arrested Abderrazak, whom they considered the mastermind of the operation; a few days later, Spanish police detained Djaouat in Lloret de Mar. The news of Abderrazak's arrest was received with understandable satisfaction in Italy. Immediately on discovering who the mysterious Abderrazak was, Italian authorities had transmitted the information they had collected on him and his network—evidence that he was the leader of Ansar al Islam's recruiting efforts in Europe—to their German counterparts, hoping to thereby trigger his arrest. Abderrazak's detention came for different reasons, but the Italians were nonetheless pleased. Yet their happiness soon turned to shock: on August 27, after exactly a month of detention, Abderrazak was released by German authorities for lack of evidence on his involvement in the plot to attack tourist resorts in Costa del Sol. Officials in the Italian parliament and at the Ministry of Foreign Affairs lodged a formal complaint about Germany's move, which was interpreted as lack of cooperation in the war on terror.

But, as usual, German authorities' hands were tied. Abderrazak's attempt to go to Iraq and his recruiting efforts were not crimes under German law, and no charges for those acts could possibly have been filed against him. Heino Vahldieck, the head of the security agency for the state of Hamburg, attempted to justify his country's inaction: "If he said, 'I'm going to Iraq to kill nonbelievers,' we would have arrested him, but if he says he's going to support his brothers, we can do nothing."[45] And while German jurists debated the differences between "supporting the brothers" and "killing unbelievers" (at a time when Abderrazak's "brothers" were indeed "killing unbelievers" in Iraq), Abderrazak walked free in the streets of Hamburg.

Abderrazak's case exemplifies a problem common across Europe. In many countries, the high threshold of evidence needed to press charges often prevents authorities from charging known terrorists unless they are caught in the final stages of preparing an attack. On occasion, militants with proven connections to terrorist groups have been recorded talking about their desire to "die as martyrs" and "kill the infidels." But until a specific target is mentioned or a weapon is found, all authorities can do is keep a close watch on the would-be martyrs.

And finding legal justification to detain militants who have either trained or fought abroad is even more difficult. Most European countries do not punish individuals who join terrorist groups or guerrilla bands outside their borders. Therefore, hundreds of European Muslims who fought and trained in such places as Afghanistan, Chechnya, and Bosnia were able to return to their home countries without being charged with any crime. In some cases their experience in jihad made them targets of surveillance from intelligence agencies, which tracked their movements on their return to Europe. But today, hundreds of battle-hardened jihadis are living on the Continent and there is still nothing authorities can do to detain them. Though the events of 9/11 spurred some countries to legislative reform, others have retained a system that hampers their ability to take firm action—as the helplessness of German authorities in Abderrazak's case illustrates.

Abderrazak's legal uncertainties ended in November 2003, when Italian authorities, despairing of the possibility that Berlin would act, officially charged him and issued an international warrant for his arrest. On November 28, German police took him into custody in Hamburg; on March 19, Abderrazak was extradited to Italy, where he is expected to stand trial. As happened in the Ganczarski case (discussed in chapter 5) and in many others, the German legal system proved itself to be incapable of dealing with the threat of Islamic terrorism and had to be rescued by another country.

NOTES

1. Deposition of Shadi Abdallah, Federal High Court, Karlsruhe, Germany, November 18, 2002.

2. ABC News, March 28, 2005; *Wall Street Journal*, February 10, 2004.

3. Jonathan Schanzer, "Ansar al Islam: Back in Iraq," *Middle East Quarterly* 11, no. 1 (Winter 2004).

4. Tribunal of Milan, Indictment of Muhamad Majid and others. November 25, 2003.

5. Ibid. Abu Taisir's real name is Abdal Hadi Ahmad Mahmoud Daghlas; he is a Jordanian national who has reportedly married a relative of Zarqawi's.

6. Christopher Dickey, "Jihad Express," *Newsweek*, March 21, 2005.

7. Tribunal of Milan, Indictment of Merai and others. March 31, 2003.

8. The mention of Abu Qatada, al Qaeda's spiritual leader in Europe in the 1990s, underscores that this new organization contains individuals who have had a key role in Europe for years.

9. The man is probably referring to the Sahabah mosque in Vienna, an important stronghold of the Egyptian Gamaa Islamiya that played a key role during the war in the Balkans. Austrian authorities have been investigating it for years.

10. Tribunal of Milan, indictment of Merai and others.

11. Indictment of Nasr Osama Mustafa Hassan, Tribunal of Milan, June 23, 2005.

12. Tribunal of Milan, indictment of Merai and others.

13. Ibid.

14. Ibid.

15. Ibid.

16. Merai's real name is El Ayashi Radi Abdel Samie Abu El Yazid; he was born in Egypt on January 2, 1972.

17. Tribunal of Milan, indictment of Merai and others.

18. Ibid.

19. Tribunal of Milan, Indictment of Muhamad Majid and others.

20. Ibid.

21. Tribunal of Milan, Indictment of Mohamed Daki, April 4, 2003.

22. Tribunal of Milan, Indictment of Muhamad Majid and others.

23. Ibid.

24. Tribunal of Milan, Indictment of Mohamed Daki.

25. Ibid.

26. Tribunal of Milan, Indictment of Muhamad Majid and others.

27. Stefano Dambruoso, *Milano Bagdad: Diario di un magistrato in prima linea nella lotta al terrorismo islamico in Italia* (Milan: Mondadori, Milan, 2004), p. 53.

28. Tribunal of Milan, Indictment of Muhamad Majid and others.

29. Tribunal of Milan, Evidence on Mohamed Daki.

30. By "the best brothers," Merai means the militants arrested in the earlier Italian investigations that led to the arrests of members of the Ben Khemais cell and of Remadna and Chekkouri. Most individuals convicted for terrorism-related crimes serve their sentences in the San Vittore penitentiary in downtown Milan.

31. Brahim was later identified as the Guinean national Bah Ibrahima, the librarian of the Via Quaranta mosque.

32. Tribunal of Milan, Indictment of Muhamad Majid and others.

33. John Leicester, "Madrid Bombing Probe Sharpens Focus on al-Qaida Connection amid Reports of Five Moroccan Suspects," AP, March 16, 2004.

34. Tribunal of Milan, Evidence on Mohamed Daki.

35. Tribunal of Milan, Indictment of Muhamad Majid and others.

36. Ibid.

37. Ibid. According to intelligence reports, Mullah Fouad left Syria in 2004. British and Turkish authorities are thought to believe that Mullah Fouad's network in Syria was actively involved in planning the November 2003 bombings in Istanbul of two synagogues, a British bank, and the British consulate.

38. Tribunal of Milan, Indictment of Muhamad Majid and others.

39. Carlos Fonseca, "Fresh Clues about Al-Qa'idah's 'Spanish Network,'" *Tiempo de Hoy*, September 1, 2003. Accessed via FBIS.

40. Indictment of Reda Zerroug and others, Audiencia Nacional, Madrid, January 14, 2005.

41. Fonseca, "Fresh Clues about Al-Qa'idah's 'Spanish Network.'"

42. Indictment of Reda Zerroug and others.

43. Ibid.

44. Sean O'Neill, "Extradition for 9/11 Suspect Linked to London Ricin Flat," *Times of London*, June 3, 2005.

45. Victor L. Simpson, "European Militant Network Shut Down," AP, December 19, 2003.

CHAPTER 10
THE IRAQI JIHAD

God favored the [Islamic] nation with jihad on His behalf in the land of Mesopotamia.[1]

—Abu Musab al Zarqawi (January 2004)

As the United States came closer to launching its attack, Ansar al Islam and the situation in Iraq began to attract the attention of Islamists based in Europe. Many Kurdish and Arab sympathizers donated money to Ansar al Islam before the beginning of the Iraq war. The group even had a Web site (www.ansarislam.com) that posted information on its activities in Kurdish, Turkish, Arabic, and English. But while money was important for its operations, what Ansar al Islam needed most were fighters—particularly suicide bombers, as the conversation in which Mullah Fouad requested kamikazes, "those who were in Japan," showed.

Another telling phone call was intercepted on March 16, just three days before the beginning of the hostilities in Iraq. A militant named Yahia in Kurdistan called Mohammed Hammid, one of the Kurds based in Parma:[2]

Yahia: When are you coming?
Hamid: I hope by the end of May. I wanted to come sooner but I have problems with work.

Yahia: Did you know that Abdallah was killed in Kurdistan?

Hamid: Yes, yes, I was told.

Yahia: How is the situation of the Muslims over there [in Europe]? What do they think of the situation [i.e., the upcoming war in Iraq]?

Hamid: Now that the Americans have decided to go to war against Iraq there are many communities of Moroccans and Tunisians that are getting ready to go and fight against the Americans . . . their blood is hot . . . this thing that they [the Americans] want to do [i.e., invading Iraq] will be a good thing for the future of the Muslims!

Hammid's assessment at the eve of war would be confirmed by the events on the ground in Iraq in the following months. Though some young Muslims living in Europe reached the Kurdish camps before the war to train with Ansar al Islam, the number of European Muslims who decided to travel to Iraq soared as the war began. "Iraq is the motor. . . . It's making them all go crazy, want to be shaheed [martyrs]," commented a French counterterrorism official.[3]

In the first days of war, American forces pounded suspected Ansar al Islam facilities in northern Iraq and destroyed its training camps. After the bombings, American Special Forces and the *peshmerga* (the Kurdish fighters allied to the United States) combed the Kurmal training camp, looking for clues on the group's activities. The evidence uncovered in Kurmal showed the extent of Ansar al Islam's recruitment efforts outside Iraq. American forces and their Kurdish allies found bags of documents belonging to militants from Saudi Arabia, Egypt, Qatar, Sudan, United States, and several European countries. Soldiers also found copies of training manuals that had commonly been used by al Qaeda in its Afghan camps.[4]

The American operation against Ansar al Islam can be considered only a partial success. The massive bombardment unquestionably destroyed the group's sanctuary and killed many of its operatives. Yet hundreds of other Ansar al Islam members, anticipating the American attack, had left the camps before the bombings started. The complacency of Iranian border guards allowed most of them to cross into Iran, where they regrouped near the border.

Early in the conflict, when Saddam Hussein was still in power and the regular Iraqi army was trying to resist the pressure of the American infantry, the allied forces seemed to be engaged in a conventional war. Members of Ansar al Islam were trying either to blend in with the civilian population in Kurdistan or to regroup in Iran. Foreign volunteers had been seen in Baghdad before the war, but they did not carry out any significant attack in the first weeks of the war. Only after the fall of Saddam's regime, when American forces thought that the difficult part was over, did the activities of the terrorists begin. According to American military intelligence, Ansar al Islam members crossed the border from Iran back into Iraq and began spreading in small groups throughout the country. While some remained in the group's original area, Kurdistan, many made their way to Baghdad and the so-called Sunni Triangle—the central part of the country, where American forces have encountered the stiffest resistance. The terrorists who had trained in the Kurdish camps before the war were joined by more foreign volunteers, who crossed the border into Iraq from Jordan and Syria to fight US forces.

Militants from throughout the Middle East streamed into the country with the intention of waging jihad against "the infidel occupier." Most of the volunteers came from neighboring countries, with Jordan, Syria, and Saudi Arabia reportedly sending the largest number of fighters. Estimates vary, but reliable reports put at about two thousand the total number of foreign fighters present in Iraq in January 2005, just before the country's landmark elections. Muslims from Europe represent just a small fraction of the total number of jihadis, but they, too, have been reported fighting in Iraq.

Evidence gathered by American and Italian military intelligence in Iraq has revealed the effectiveness of the Milan network in recruiting suicide bombers, those "who can hit the ground and make the iron come out of it," as Mullah Fouad called them. According to military reports, at least five militants who had left Milan for Iraq have died in suicide attacks against US forces. One of them was Lotfi Rihani, a Tunisian who was well known to Italian authorities, as he had been indicted in Italy for his role in the cell headed by Essid Sami Ben Khemais. Rihani had lived in Milan and worshiped at the city's Islamic Cultural Institute; he had been photographed outside the ICI by DIGOS in August 2002, when he met with Hammid and Mohammed Amin Mostafa, the two Kurds from Parma, and with Mullah Fouad, two months before Mullah Fouad left for Syria. Authorities believe that Rihani arranged the details of his journey to Iraq at that time. Rihani died in September 2003, when, accompanied by two other Tunisians, he drove a car laden with explosives against US forces.[5] Another man recruited by Merai in Milan, Fahdal Nassim, apparently also died in Iraq in a suicide attack. An uncorroborated intelligence report suggests that Nassim may have participated in the August 2003 bombing of the UN headquarters in Baghdad that killed twenty-two people, including Sergio Vieira de Mello, the UN's special envoy to Iraq.[6]

Another Milan-based militant who died in Iraq is Morchidi Kamal. The twenty-four-year-old Moroccan, another member of the Ben Khemais cell, reportedly was killed in October 2003 during an attack on Baghdad's Rashid Hotel. The likely target was US Undersecretary of Defense Paul Wolfowitz, who was staying at the hotel on the night the terrorists struck. Kamal's documents were found in the rubble of the Ansar al Islam camp in Kurmal after the facility was bombed by US forces, along with the passports of two other militants who had lived in Milan, Hamsi Said and Yousfi Ben Tijani.[7] And the shipment of documents continued even after the war began. Months after the start of the conflict, a Tunisian man arrested by Kurdish forces in the northern part of the country was found to be carrying a bag full of Italian documents, most of them issued in Milan.[8] Authorities believe that, even though the main players have been caught, militants in Milan are still actively recruiting young Muslims to fight in Iraq. Working from what they think is incomplete knowledge of their activities, Italian officials estimate that the network recruited no fewer than two hundred militants throughout Europe, seventy of them from Italy alone.[9]

The ongoing Italian investigation of the Ansar al Islam recruiting network uncovered several important links to Germany. Not only was the alleged leader of the network, Abderrazak Mahdjoub, based in Hamburg, but the wiretaps and the confessions of the two Kurds arrested in Parma made clear that Ansar al Islam had its European base in Germany—

specifically, in Munich. One of the Kurds from Parma admitted to Italian interrogators that on several occasions, he had traveled to Munich and given money to a man named Omeid Adnan Bamarni, also known as "Doctor Omeid." Further investigation proved that Doctor Omeid was the moneyman of the organization, collecting the funds gathered by various groups of Ansar al Islam sympathizers spread throughout Europe. The money, transported to Kurdistan by young Kurdish immigrants claiming to be returning their native country in order to visit their families, was used mostly to finance Ansar al Islam's camps.[10]

Other evidence confirmed that Munich was the decision-making as well as the financial hub for the group's European operations, hosting a key logistics cell. Under the leadership of a thirty-year-old Kurd named Mohammed Loqman, the group organized safe houses, recruited volunteers, and raised money for "the brothers" in Kurdistan. Investigators found that a major source of its financing was the smuggling of illegal Kurdish immigrants into Europe. The Munich group worked closely with the two Kurds living in Parma, who ran a safe house there for immigrants. After paying thousands of dollars to the smugglers, the Kurds entered Europe from Greece and Italy, and then were sent to settle in wealthier countries, such as Germany, Great Britain, and Switzerland. The profits of this scheme, often the life savings of young Kurds, were sent back to Kurdistan to finance the activities of Ansar al Islam.[11] Ironically, the immigrants were unwittingly financing the very activities that some of them had left Kurdistan to escape.

The information provided by the Italians on the group operating in Munich led German authorities to open an investigation into Loqman's cell. A first round of arrests hit the Munich cell in March 2003. German authorities charged Bamarni, the moneyman of the group, and a dozen other Kurds with facilitating illegal immigration into Germany. The Bavarian minister of the interior said that, before his arrest, Bamarni had raised almost a million euros.[12] As German authorities began to gather evidence for their case against the key players of the cell, they uncovered new information on the network's activities.

Months of intercepted conversations and tailing confirmed that

Munich was the headquarters of Ansar al Islam's operations in Germany and also revealed that the network's reach across the country, as other cells were active in Stuttgart, Berlin, Hamburg, Duisburg, Cologne, Ulm, and Frankfurt.[13] Investigators estimate that at least one hundred members of Ansar al Islam are currently active in Germany.[14] The number of Muslims who have been recruited by the group to fight in Iraq is unclear, but they believe that from Bavaria alone, between ten and fifty militants have left the region to join Ansar al Islam in Iraq. Among them reportedly was a twenty-seven-year-old courier who traveled twenty times between Germany and Iraq before his March 2004 arrest by Iraqi authorities.[15] German authorities believe that at least two of the militants recruited by the network went to Iraq determined to die as suicide bombers.[16]

After months of investigation, on December 3, 2003, Bavarian police arrested Loqman, the leader of the cell, inside Munich Central Station, as he was trying to leave Germany. The charges against Loqman are serious: he is accused of being a high-ranking member of Ansar al Islam and of having recruited volunteers to fight coalition forces in Iraq, as well as raising funds and procuring medical equipment for militants fighting in Iraq. Loqman was also involved in smuggling Kurds into Europe—and not merely innocent asylum seekers. According to German federal prosecutors, Loqman was responsible for smuggling members of Ansar al Islam who had been wounded in Iraq into western Europe for medical treatment. For example, in September 2003, Loqman organized the smuggling in of a severely wounded senior official of the group from Iraq via Italy and France to Great Britain.[17] The senior official was later identified as Ali Fadhil, a bomb expert who lost his hand in an explosion in Iraq. Loqman allegedly arranged for his treatment in a British clinic, using the same routes that network used to smuggle illegal Kurdish immigrants. Authorities have been unable to locate Fadhil and do not know if the Ansar al Islam official is still in Europe.[18]

Three days after Bavarian police arrested Loqman, another key member of the European network of Ansar al Islam was arrested in Amsterdam: Mullah Braw, Loqman's right-hand man in Munich, who had repeatedly traveled back and forth between Germany and Kurdistan before and after the war began. The thirty-two-year-old Kurd had managed to avoid arrest in Germany and had purchased a one-way ticket from Amsterdam's Schiphol Airport to Istanbul under the name Aziz Hassan, intending to make his way to Iraq. He was detained by Dutch police as he was boarding the aircraft.[19]

As authorities quietly closed in on the two leaders of the Munich cell of Ansar al Islam, a plot linked to the German network of the group made headlines worldwide. On December 6, German authorities arrested three men accused of planning to kill Iraq's interim prime minister, Iyad Allawi, during his visit to Germany. Authorities believe that the unsophisticated plot was hatched on the spur of the moment, but as Michael Ziegler, spokesman for Bavarian security authorities, noted, "the foiled attack on Allawi shows that this group must be considered dangerous also for Europe."[20] The attack was thwarted because the members of Ansar al Islam involved, who had been under surveillance by German police for months, were overheard in late November planning to gather information about Allawi's schedule in Germany and to obtain weapons for a possible operation. On December 2, one day before Allawi's arrival in Berlin, Rafik Y., one of the three men arrested, received authorization from the cell's leader to carry out the attack. Authorities suspected that he intended to murder Allawi at a meeting between the prime minister and a group of exiled Iraqis living in Germany, and the event was canceled at the last minute.[21]

In the following days, police continued to intercept conversations between Rafik Y. and the other two men. Their use of coded language did not prevent investigators from learning that the men planned to carry out an attack on December 6, when Allawi was supposed to meet with German officials at the Berlin headquarters of the Deutsche Bank. On December 5, police observed Rafik Y. walking around the Deutsche Bank building; later, he was overheard informing his accomplices that he had "viewed the building site."[22] In the early hours of December 6, special operations police stormed nine apartments in Berlin, Stuttgart, and Augsburg and arrested Rafik Y. and two of his accomplices. On the 7th a fourth man, a Lebanese national, was arrested in Berlin on suspicion of supporting Ansar al Islam.[23]

The revelation of the plot against Prime Minister Allawi shocked Germany. Whereas once Ansar al Islam had used the country as a logistical base of operation, now it was planning attacks inside the country. And though the target this time was an Iraqi, there was no guarantee that in the future the group would not aim for Germans. "If someone is involved in an attack in Iraq, I am virtually 100 percent convinced that he'll also carry out an attack over here if ordered to do so," said Guenter Beckstein, the top state security official in Bavaria.[24] This fear drove German authorities to act with unprecedented firmness and they decided to dismantle the Ansar al Islam network in the country. On January 12, more than seven hundred police officers raided dozens of apartments, businesses, and mosques in Munich, Frankfurt, Ulm, Bonn, Duesseldorf, and Freiburg. Twenty-two members of Ansar al Islam were arrested and charged with such crimes as raising money for a terrorist organization and forging documents.[25] And again, in June 2005, three Iraqis linked to the individuals who planned to assassinate Allawi were arrested in southern Germany and accused of raising funds for Ansar al Islam.[26]

Europeans are increasingly coming to understand that Iraq may become the new Afghanistan, a place where militants gain military and terrorist experience before they travel back to their home countries. France, the country that more than any other in Europe has monitored the movements of Islamists leaving its borders, has formally opened an investigation on French Muslims fighting in Iraq. French magistrates fear that Iraq, along with Chechnya, might become the terrorists' new playground, and that Iraqi-trained jihadists might use their newly acquired skills to strike in France. "We consider these people dangerous because those who go will come back once their mission is accomplished," said a top French counterterrorism official interviewed by the *New York Times* in October 2004. "Then they can use the knowledge gained there in France, Europe or the United States. It's the same as those who went to Afghanistan or Chechnya. Now the new land of jihad is Iraq. There, they are trained, they fight and acquire a technique and the indoctrination sufficient to act on when they return."[27] Though France has strongly opposed the US intervention in Iraq, French authorities have taken strong actions to dismantle the networks of recruiters attempting to send French Muslims to fight in Iraq. To be sure, those actions are motivated by a desire to protect France, not to help US forces on the ground in Iraq; nevertheless, by aggressively pursuing militants who were planning to join the conflict, the French government has indirectly lent a hand to the United States.

French magistrates began investigating a possible network of recruiters operating in France in the fall of 2004, after American and Iraqi authorities informed their French counterparts that between July and October 2004, three young Parisians of North African descent had died while fighting US forces in Iraq. The first one was Hakim Redouane, a nineteen-year-old who was killed during the bombardment of the insurgency's stronghold of Fallujah on July 17. On September 20, American forces shot dead Tarek Ouinis, also nineteen and from Paris. Finally, on October 20, another nineteen-year-old from Paris, Abdelhalim Badjoudj, carried out a bold suicide attack on the road to Baghdad's airport, injuring two American soldiers and two Iraqi police officers. In addition, the magistrates learned that three French citizens were being detained by US forces in Iraq. Two of them, twenty-two-year-old Peter Cherif and twenty-year-old Chekou Diakhabi, had been arrested in Fallujah during the violent battle between US forces and insurgents in the city over the last weeks of 2004. A third Frenchman, twenty-year-old Faras Howeini, was arrested by Iraqi forces in the city of Mosul in April 2004 and accused of murdering an Iraqi police officer.[28]

As they began their investigation, French authorities realized that the three French "martyrs" and the three detainees all came from the same Paris suburb, the 19th arrondissement, an area in the north east of the French capital heavily populated with North African immigrants.[29] Moreover, they discovered that the six young men, all unemployed, had left France in March 2004 for Syria. There they enrolled in the al Fateh al Islami Institute, a religious school in Damascus known for its radicalism, where they stayed only briefly before crossing the border into Iraq. Clearly, some kind of network was recruiting young French Muslims for jihad, and investigators wanted to understand, in the words of a French Interior Ministry official, "how it is that Parisian youngsters of 19 go to sacrifice themselves in Iraq."[30]

As they began to search in the past of the young men, French authorities found similarities in their backgrounds. Relatives described them as quiet and normal youths who were not particularly religious. "Abdelhalim drank beer, he smoked hashish a lot," said the uncle of Badjoudj, a suicide bomber.[31] Other relatives of the young jihadists painted a picture of Westernized young Muslims who wore jeans and listened to rap. But in the months following the beginning of the Iraqi war, the young Parisians had fallen under the spell of radicals who had sensed their weakness and lured them into their world of fanaticism. Exploiting the Iraqi conflict, recruiters living in the neighborhood persuaded the impressionable young men to abandon everything and defend the life and pride of the Muslim nation. "They go to the mosque, discuss, they receive radical prayers, they hear a lot of things, and most of the time they are unemployed. And it's a kind of adventure. They go because it's an honor to go. They become like stars," said Giles Leclair, the head of the French internal intelligence agency, the DST (Direction de la Surveillance du Territoire).[32]

The story of Hakim Reduoane, the first Frenchman killed in Fallujah, is particularly telling. Hakim, a nineteen-year-old of Tunisian origin, grew up in the 19th arrondissement with his mother and his four siblings. While working odd jobs in the neighborhood, Hakim, whom friends characterized as "easygoing," fell under the influence of his older brother Boubaker, a twenty-one-year-old committed Salafist who worshiped at the Iqra mosque.[33] The Iqra mosque, a radical prayer hall in the northern Paris suburb of Levallois-Perret, is suspected of being fertile ground for recruiters; authorities closed it in June 2004, after a man who used to worship there received a text message from Iraq saying, "Group has arrived. I will contact you if I need help."[34] False documents, plastic laminating materials commonly used in forging official papers, and a pistol were found in the raids connected with the closure of the mosque.[35]

Bombarded with speeches about the suffering of fellow Muslims, Hakim gave in to his older brother and Boubaker's radical friends at the mosque. In the spring of 2004, he traveled with five other young men from the neighborhood to Syria and then to Iraq. Boubaker also traveled to Syria, but was arrested by Syrian border police in August 2004 while attempting to cross the border into Iraq.[36] One of the men, Abdelhalim Badjoudj, returned to Paris to marry his Moroccan girlfriend. After less than a month, Badjoudj went back to Syria, reportedly telling his relatives: "God willing, I will be going to Iraq."[37] A few weeks later he died while driving an explosive-laden vehicle into an American convoy on the road to Baghdad airport.

Within a few months, the French investigation uncovered the network that had recruited the six Parisians. After the Iqra mosque was shut down, the group of radicals that used to convene there moved to the Addawa mosque, a former warehouse located in their own neighborhood, the 19th arrondissement.[38] It became Paris's main recruiting center for Iraq. A group of about forty or fifty young men of North African descent, all childhood friends who had attended the same schools, began to worship at the mosque, attracted by the fiery sermons of the local imams.

The spiritual leader of the group, whose average age was no older than twenty, was a twenty-three-year-old Islamic fundamentalist named Farid Benyettou, whose fiery speeches about jihad inflamed the hearts of the young worshipers. His prominent position was due largely to his connections—his mentor was a well-known veteran of Afghanistan, Mohammed Karimi, whom French authorities had deported to his home country, Morocco.[39] Benyettou also benefited from the high regard in which radicals held his Algerian brother-in-law, Mohammed Zemmouri; a leader of the GSPC (Groupe Salafiste pour la Predication et le Combat, or Salafist Group for Preaching and Combat), Zemmouri was deported by French authorities for his involvement in a plot to carry out terrorist attacks during the 1998 soccer World Cup, hosted by France.[40] French authorities began to monitor Benyettou and his group during the 2003 street protests against the Iraq war. After noticing their radicalism, agents snapped several pictures of them praying on the sidewalks of downtown Paris.[41]

In January 2005, French authorities acted against the group and arrested eleven individuals, including Benyettou. Most of those arrested were young North African men with dual nationality, childhood friends of the Redouane brothers and the other men detained or killed in Iraq. One was a French convert to Islam, and two were women.[42] The arrests came in reaction to information uncovered by the DST: two of Benyettou's recruits, Thamer Bouchnak and Cherif Kouachi, were about to depart for Iraq. According to French authorities, Bouchnak had already traveled to Syria, where he had studied in a religious school. He had returned to Paris, where Benyettou encouraged him to do the hajj, Islam's annual pilgrimage to Mecca. Bouchnak was supposed to meet with Kouachi at Benyettou's apartment and to travel to Iraq with him. They were arrested (along with the others) before they could board their flight to Syria.[43]

With the arrests of Benyettou and his closest collaborators, French authorities believe they have completely dismantled the network operating in the 19th arrondissement. The lingering question is how many other such neighborhoods there are in France. Recent intelligence reports are not encouraging. The agency in charge of security outside the country's border, DGSE (Direction Générale de Sécurité Extérieure), has indicated that around December 2004, a group of twenty fighters was operating in the Fallujah area under the command of a Frenchman.[44] The man, known only as Fawzi D., is believed to be a French citizen in his twenties from a middle-class Algerian family.[45] France's top antiterrorism judge, Jean-Louis Bruguière, is conducting the sprawling investigation on the *filière irakienne* and is convinced that dozens of young Frenchmen have reached Iraq since the summer of 2004.[46] In June 2005 French authorities detained seven individuals in the cities of Montpellier and Limoges, accusing them of having recruited French Muslims for jihad in Iraq. Unlike those arrested in the 19th arrondissement, which constituted a spontaneous movement, in this case authorities allege that the men were working closely with Ansar al Islam leadership in Iraq and with other cells of the group in Germany, Spain, and Italy.[47]

Recruitment for jihad in Iraq has touched almost every European country with a large Muslim population. The archbishop of Canterbury, on a visit to Jordan in November 2003, met a group of young British men who claimed they were about to cross the border into Iraq "to be part of the battle against the evil occupying forces."[48] The encounter was widely reported by the country's media, which immediately saw a repeat of the events of 2001, when dozens of British Muslims left the country and went to Afghanistan to fight alongside the Taliban and against UK forces. Recognizing the likelihood that British Muslims were actually battling British soldiers, the nation's tabloids raised disturbing questions about young Muslims' attachment to their home country. The issue will surface again after the July 7, 2005, attacks in London, which were carried out by British-born Muslims.

Confirmation that British Muslims were indeed involved in the fighting in Iraq soon followed. In mid-November, the Yemeni newspaper *Al Ayyam* reported that the parents of a twenty-two-year-old Yemeni national who lived in Sheffield had received a congratulatory phone call from Islamic fighters in Iraq, informing them that their son had been killed in a suicide operation. Wail al Dhalei, a young asylum seeker who had married a British woman and was training to fight with the British Olympic tae kwon do team, was said to have traveled from Sheffield to Iraq, where he fought alongside the local insurgents.[49]

Another British Muslim was arrested by American forces in Iraq in January 2005. Mobeen Muneef, a twenty-five-year-old Londoner of Pakistani descent, was apprehended by US Marines in the Iraqi city of Ramadi, a stronghold of the insurgency. Capt. Brad Gordon described the arrest:

> The gentleman was detained after Marines spotted men passing a weapon over a wall in Ramadi. When Marines approached the house, two men began to flee the house and were subsequently detained when they were found hiding in a shack near by. According to one report, in their possession was an Iraqi pistol and four AK-47s. When he was detained he was found to have an Iraqi ID card which he admitted was fake. When questioned about his reason for being with other foreign fighters, he stated he was there to assist a humanitarian relief organization. He had no other identification at the time of his detention and could not produce any credentials belonging to or the name of the relief organization. He was given a gun-powder residue test. He tested positive for gun powder residue, further indicating that he did have a weapon in his possession.[50]

As of June 2005, British authorities estimate that about seventy volunteers have left the United Kingdom to join the Iraqi insurgency. While at

MAP 10.1. RECRUITMENT FOR THE IRAQI JIHAD IN EUROPE

least three have been killed in combat, one man, a forty-one-year-old Manchester resident named Idris Bazis, is known to have died in a suicide attack.[51] Sunni Muslims have made up the majority of those traveling to Iraq, as most of the groups actively fighting coalition forces are Sunni and often have strong anti-Shia feelings. Nevertheless, at the peak of the conflict between coalition forces and militias loyal to radical Shia clerics, some Shia Muslims, too, left Europe for Iraq—including, according to various uncorroborated reports, small groups from the United Kingdom. Some of them allegedly joined the militias of the Iraqi Shia cleric Moqtada al Sadr and engaged British and American forces in the south of the country.

Spanish authorities have also dismantled a network that was recruiting volunteers for the Iraqi battlefield. On June 15, 2005, more than five hundred policemen raided locations in Madrid, Andalucía, Cataluña, Levante, and Ceuta and arrested eleven individuals, including Samir Tahtah and Fouad Dkikar, the two leaders of a Barcelona-based cell with close links to Zarqawi's network in the United Kingdom and Iraq.[52] Investigators also believe that a young Moroccan man with deep connections to the March 11 Madrid train bombers, Mohammed Afalah, reached Iraq after escaping capture in Spain and died in a suicide attack there.[53]

Even countries with a small Muslim community have been affected. European intelligence agencies believe that one of the leaders of Ansar al Islam, known by the nom de guerre Abu Mohammed Lubnani, is a Lebanese citizen who lived for fourteen years in Denmark under his real name, Mustafa Darwish Ramadan. According to Danish officials, Ramadan served three and a half years in a Danish prison for a robbery committed in 1997. Upon his release, he robbed a money-transfer store in Copenhagen and fled to Jordan or Lebanon. Authorities believe that Ramadan then joined the ranks of Ansar al Islam, becoming one of its leaders.[54]

Members of Ansar al Islam have also been active in Sweden. A few days before they arrested him, German authorities recorded a conversation in which Mohammed Loqman, the Ansar al Islam leader operating in Munich, was asked by a man to smuggle twelve men into Iraq, presumably with the intention of joining the local insurgency. The man requesting Loqman's assistance was a Kurd living in Sweden, Shahab Shabab. Both Shabab and Loqman had grown up in the Kurdish village of Chamchal, which they had left together to immigrate to Europe. Loqman had chosen Germany; Shabab had settled in Stockholm.[55] German authorities relayed this to their Swedish counterparts, who began investigating Shabab. The results of the probe came in April 2004, when Shabab and three others—two Iraqis and one Swede of Lebanese descent —were arrested in separate raids in Stockholm and in the southern city of

Malmö. Under recently introduced Swedish counterterrorism laws, the men were charged with crimes involving "murder and devastation endangering the public," crimes that, according to Swedish authorities, were "directed at the state of Iraq and were aimed at striking grave terror into a population." Swedish prosecutors believe that the men participated in some way in a suicide operation carried out in February 2004 in the Kurdish city of Irbil, when two kamikazes simultaneously blew themselves up at the offices of Kurdistan's two main secular parties during the celebration of the Muslim holiday of Eid al Adha, killing more than one hundred people.[56] Shahab and another suspect have been freed by an appellate judge for lack of evidence, but Swedish authorities continue to investigate what they believe was an Ansar al Islam cell operating on their territory. In May 2005, the two Iraqi Kurds arrested in 2004, Ali Barzengi and Ferman Abdalla, were found guilty by a Swedish court of collecting and transferring more than $148,000 to Ansar al Islam.[57]

The presence of Ansar al Islam has been far more pronounced in another Scandinavian country, Norway. Since 1991, the prosperous and isolated country has hosted the undisputed star of Kurdistan's Islamic fundamentalism, Najmuddin Faraj Ahmad. Ahmad, better known as Mullah Krekar, escaped Iraq after the Gulf War and received political asylum in Norway, where he has been based ever since. Even after obtaining asylum, Krekar, whose extended family also resides in Norway, never abandoned the fundamentalist cause in Kurdistan; he often journeyed back to northern Iraq to guide various local Islamist factions. When, in 2001, Ansar al Islam was formed after the merger of other radical groups, Krekar became its undisputed leader.[58] Enjoying the freedoms granted by Norway, Krekar also traveled extensively throughout Europe, building alliances with other extremists operating on the Continent and raising funds for militants operating in Kurdistan.

American authorities accuse Krekar of having a direct role in preparing attacks against US forces in Iraq, even though he claims not to have had any contact with Ansar al Islam since May 2002 and has not been in Iraq since September of that year.[59] The US government believes Krekar has kept closely in touch with militants in Iraq through the Internet and has provided ideological inspiration to suicide bombers there. Norwegian authorities also interviewed several Ansar al Islam members detained in Kurdish prisons who confirmed that Krekar had told them killing nonbelievers in suicide actions was their religious duty. But Krekar has never hidden his views. Interviewed by the Dutch television network NOS on the eve of war, Krekar said that Ansar al Islam's suicide commandos were ready to strike US forces. "We believe it's America's war against Islam," said the fiery mullah. "Let them come. Now they bring more than 300,000 [troops]. We believe our God—Allah—will be with us."[60]

Mullah Krekar was detained in Holland in September 2002, on his way back to Oslo from Iraq. Dutch authorities were acting on an extradition request filed by Jordan for drug-related crimes. When arrested, Krekar was carrying documents detailing the history of Islamist groups in Kurdistan, the charter of Ansar al Islam, and a notebook with more than two thousand names.[61] Because the evidence provided by Jordan was judged insufficient to grant extradition, Holland deported Krekar to Norway in January 2003. Two months later, after his televised interview threatening the use of suicide commandos, he was arrested by Norwegian authorities; he was released after a few weeks.

In January 2004, Krekar, while fighting a deportation order from the Norwegian government, was arrested again and charged by Norwegian prosecutors with conspiracy, attempted murder of political rivals in Iraq, and inciting criminal activity.[62] Briefly detained, he was released in February while the investigation proceeded. Finally, in June, Norwegian authorities dropped all charges against Krekar, admitting they did not have enough evidence against him. Currently, Krekar is living in Oslo with his family. In April 2004, he won a lawsuit against the Dutch government for his 2002 detention and was awarded 45,000 € by a Dutch appeals court.[63] While the Norwegian government has stripped Krekar of his refugee status, his family still receives benefits from the country's welfare system. The self-professed leader of Ansar al Islam supplements the family's income by his frequent appearances on talk shows on Norwegian television and by the sales of his April 2004 autobiography, *In My Own Words*.[64]

The difficulties experienced by Norway in detaining Krekar have been repeated across Europe as countries have tried to deal with other members of Ansar al Islam and with volunteers who want to join the jihad in Iraq. Manfred Murck, deputy chief of Hamburg's security services, revealed his frustration in an interview with the German magazine *Der Spiegel*: "There is nothing that can be legally done to prevent anyone from going to Iraq, possibly in order to shoot American soldiers there."[65] In many European countries, joining a terrorist organization outside the country's territory is not a crime, and therefore those who travel to Iraq to fight do not break the law. In certain cases authorities have taken an approach similar to that used successfully by the FBI against Al Capone, detaining militants for lesser crimes such as document forging or illegal immigration. Nevertheless, most European prosecutors must work within legal systems that do not provide them with effective tools to tackle recruitment networks.

And even when prosecutors do have the legal tools they need, sometimes their case falls apart because of the judges' interpretation of the law and of events in Iraq. In January 2005, Italy was shocked by the sentence returned in the trial of Mohammed Daki, the Moroccan who was supposed to provide Maxamed Cabdullah Ciise with the passports to go to Iraq, and of other minor players in the Milan Ansar al Islam recruiting network. The Milan judge, Clementina Forleo, decided that the men were indeed part of a network that was recruiting fighters for the Iraqi conflict, but that the operations taking place in Iraq constituted "guerrilla warfare" and not terrorism. In her view, "Ansar al Islam was structured as an Islamic combatant organization, with a militia trained for guerrilla activities and financed by groups in Europe and orbiting in the sphere of Islamic fundamentalism, without having goals of a terrorist nature, goals probably shared by only some of its members."[66] Because one of the men on trial, Mohammed Tahir Hammid, conveniently declared that he did not agree with Ansar al Islam's tactic of using suicide bombers, Forleo considered Ansar al Islam to be a "heterogeneous" organization whose members had conflicting opinions on the valid means to use in fighting enemy forces. Therefore, according to the judge, Ansar al Islam could not be considered a terrorist organization as a whole and those who recruit and raise funds for it cannot be considered terrorists. The men, while found guilty of minor crimes such as document forging, were acquitted of all the charges involving terrorism.

The sentence, which was immediately appealed by Italian prosecutors, caused an uproar in Italy. Many politicians expressed their strong disapproval. Franco Frattini, a former foreign minister and currently EU commissioner for justice and security, commented: "This sends a devastating signal. Cells of Islamic fundamentalists can now think that they have safe haven in Europe."[67] Several Italian politicians accused Forleo of having been influenced by her own political views, as they considered the ruling a slap at the Italian government's support for the US war in Iraq. Public fury grew in the following days when Italian media played a homemade video shot in a training camp in Kurdistan by Hammid, the man who had repudiated the use of suicide bombers before the judge. In the seventy-eight-minute video that he had brought to Italy to use as a recruiting tool, he was shown handling automatic weapons and singing jihad hymns with other Ansar al Islam members.[68] The Italian public, who had watched the funerals of an Italian soldier killed in action in Iraq on the same day the sentence was published, was outraged to know that the Kalashnikov-brandishing Hammid and his associates were now free.

Political considerations aside, the ruling was considered legally flawed by most analysts. Stefano Dambruoso, an Italian prosecutor who led most of the terrorism investigations in Milan and currently serves as a legal adviser for the United Nations in Vienna, commented that it is "impossible to distinguish between guerrilla and terrorist activities."[69] Dambruoso also pointed out that because Ansar al Islam had been designated a terrorist organization by the UN Security Council, Italy was bound to view it as such.

While European authorities struggle to make charges against recruiters stick or debate whether Ansar al Islam is a terrorist organization, the events on the ground in Iraq offer undisputable proof of the group's true nature. In the months after the war began, several radical Islamist insurgent groups were formed throughout Iraq, mostly by former members of

Ansar al Islam. As Ansar al Islam kept fighting Kurdish and US forces and became, in the words of a senior Pentagon official, America's "principal organized terrorist adversary in Iraq," other groups composed of Kurdish, Iraqi, and foreign fighters joined its efforts.[70] Sunni terrorist bands such as Ansar al Sunna, active mostly in the north of the country; Tawhid wa'el Jihad, led personally by Abu Musab al Zarqawi; and other minor outfits sharing a radical Salafi ideology have carried out daily attacks against coalition forces and Iraqi civilians. The differences among these groups are often blurred, as they regularly join forces to carry out operations and plan their strategy. Abu Musab al Zaraqwi is commonly reputed to be the brains behind the religiously motivated insurgency, though analysts debate whether his role has been unduly magnified by the media.

Aside from a common ideology, these groups are characterized by the support they all receive from networks that have traditionally worked with al Qaeda. The same networks that for years had supported al Qaeda turned their attention to Iraq and began recruiting operatives and raising funds for the jihadi groups operating there. The pattern was evident in the Middle East and, as has been shown above, in Europe, where established al Qaeda networks such as those in Milan and Hamburg began to operate in support of Ansar al Islam and its affiliated groups.

The events in Iraq turned Ansar al Islam from a small, mostly Kurdish, virtually unknown Islamist group whose goals were limited to establishing an Islamic state in remote northern Iraq to an outfit operating globally and daily making news worldwide. Realizing that Iraq was the main "field of jihad," the cause that could rally millions of Muslims against "the American aggressor," al Qaeda turned its attention there and decided to use Ansar al Islam and its offshoots as its proxies in the country. Abu Musab al Zarqawi became a jihad star, and Ansar al Islam grew beyond recognition, only because well-organized Islamist networks set up by al Qaeda throughout the world over the past fifteen years gave their backing.

The evidence collected in Europe and in the Middle East about the cooperation between Zarqawi and Osama bin Laden simply confirms what the two have been publicly saying for months, as both have openly expressed their mutual admiration and cooperation. In January 2004, coalition forces arrested a courier who was carrying a letter that authorities believe was written by Zarqawi to al Qaeda's masterminds Osama bin Laden and Ayman al Zawahiri. The letter, in which Zarqawi explained his vision of the Iraqi conflict and his need for support from al Qaeda, clearly showed that Zarqawi considered himself their subordinate:

> You, gracious brothers, are the leaders, guides, and symbolic figures of jihad and battle. We do not see ourselves as fit to challenge you, and we have never striven to achieve glory for ourselves. All that we hope is that we will be the spearhead, the enabling vanguard, and the bridge on which the [Islamic] nation crosses over to the victory that is promised and the tomorrow to which we aspire. This is our vision, and we have explained it. This is our path, and we have made it clear. If you agree with us on it, if you adopt it as a program and road, and if you are convinced of the idea of fighting the sects of apostasy, we will be your readied soldiers, working under your banner, complying with your orders, and indeed swearing fealty to you publicly and in the news media, vexing the infidels and gladdening those who preach the oneness of God. On that day, the believers will rejoice in God's victory. If things appear otherwise to you, we are brothers, and the disagreement will not spoil [our] friendship. [This is] a cause [in which] we are cooperating for the good and supporting jihad. Awaiting your response, may God preserve you as keys to good and reserves for Islam and its people. Amen, amen.[71]

Bin Laden's public response came in December 2004, in an audiotape played by al Jazeera television. In the message, the Saudi millionaire officially appointed Zarqawi as his man in Iraq: "The brother mujahid Abu Musab al Zarqawi is the emir of the al Qaeda organization in the land of the two rivers. . . . The brothers in the group there must listen to him and obey him for what is good. . . . We in the al Qaeda organization strongly welcome their joining hands with us."[72] Bin Laden's message finally made official the de facto merger between Zarqawi's group and al Qaeda. This move enabled bin Laden, whose prominence has been partially obscured by Zarqawi's brazen operations in Iraq, to benefit from Zarqawi's popularity and make the Iraqi insurgency's successes his own. At the same time, the alliance brings Zarqawi additional financial and logistical support from the worldwide al Qaeda network—and the official endorsement, by demonstrating that Zarqawi has the support of the undisputed leader of worldwide jihadi movement, adds to his prestige.

After the message was broadcast, Zarqawi's group changed its name to "Al Qaeda's Jihad Committee in Mesopotamia," making the alliance explicit. In reality, not much changed, as the cooperation between the two organizations was complete even before their exchange of praises. Iraq has become a new major field of jihad where thousands of al Qaeda members, sympathizers, or wannabes fight and get experience. The consequences for the West are easy to imagine. "The Iraqi conflict, while not a cause for extremism, has become an extremist cause. Those jihadists who survive will leave Iraq experienced in and focused on acts of urban terrorism," said CIA director Porter Goss in his January 2005 testimony before the US Senate Intelligence Committee.[73] Director Goss's statement is based on concrete evidence that al Qaeda is training militants—including some with Western passports—in Iraq and sending them back to their home countries to form sleeper cells.

Europe, given its geographical proximity to the Middle East and the number of European Muslims currently fighting in Iraq, is feeling the effects of this problem most acutely. "We are determined to stop young people going to make jihad in Iraq because if they come back they will have greatly enhanced prestige and be in a position to recruit more people to the cause—or even mount terrorist operations," declared a senior French counterterrorism official.[74] The fears of French security officials were confirmed by the January 2005 arrests of the militants operating in Paris's 19th arrondissement. Investigators soon realized that the men, originally detained just because they were recruiting volunteers to go to Iraq, were "drawing up plans for attacks in France against French and foreign interests."[75] Veterans of the conflicts in Afghanistan, Bosnia, and Chechnya have either attempted or successfully carried out terrorist attacks in Europe. It may be just a matter of time before a veteran of Iraq will strike the Continent.

NOTES

1. Zarqawi letter, February 2004. Translated into English by the Coalition Provisional Authority.

2. Tribunal of Milan, Indictment of Muhamad Majid and others. November 25, 2003.

3. Sebastian Rotella, "Europe's Boys of Jihad," *Los Angeles Times*, April 2, 2005.

4. Tribunal of Milan, Indictment of Muhamad Majid and others.

5. Ibid.

6. Paolo Biondani, "Pestaggi dei Camorristi contro i Detenuti Islamici," *Corriere della Sera*, December 10, 2004.

7. Tribunal of Milan, Indictment of Muhamad Majid and others.

8. Stefano Dambruoso, *Milano Bagdad: Diario di un magistrato in prima linea nella lotta al terrorismo islamico in Italia* (Milan: Mondadori, 2004), p. 63.

9. Victor L. Simpson, "European Militant Network Shut Down," AP, December 19, 2003.

10. Tribunal of Milan, Indictment of Muhamad Majid and others.

11. Ibid.

12. Florian Meesman, Ahmed Senyurt, "Ansar al Islam—Terror in Deutschland?" *Mitteldeutscher Rundfunk*, December 13, 2004.

13. Annette Rameisberger, "Islamistische Terrorzelle in Muenchen Zerschlagen," *Sueddeutsche Zeitung*, December 3, 2003.

14. Tony Czuczka, "Militants Said to Send Fighters to Europe," AP, January 8, 2005.

15. Craig Whitlock, "In Europe, New Force for Recruiting Radicals. Ansar al Islam Emerges as Primary Extremist Group Funneling Fighters into Iraq," *Washington Post*, February 18, 2005.

16. Elaine Sciolino, "French Detain Group Said to Recruit Iraq Rebels," *New York Times*, January 26, 2005.

17. Tony Czuczka, "Germany Cites Link to Islamic Group's Command in Alleged Allawi Plot, Charges Group Member," AP, December 7, 2004.

18. Whitlock, "In Europe, New Force for Recruiting Radicals."

19. "Terrorist with One-Way Ticket to Istanbul Caught," *Hurriyet*, December 10, 2003. Accessed via FBIS.

20. Tony Czuczka, "Militants Said to Send Fighters to Europe," AP, January 8, 2005.

21. "Chronicle of a Foiled Plot—How Iraqis Were Tailed," *Deutsche Presse-Agentur*, December 8, 2004.

22. "Schnelles Eingreifen Verhinderte Anschlag auf Allawi," *Tagesschau*, December 7, 2004.

23. "Berlin Building Searched in Probe of Alleged Attack Plan on Iraqi Prime Minister," AP, December 8, 2004.

24. Tony Czuczka, "German Authorities Say Islamic Militants behind Allawi Assassination Plot Are Sending Fighters from Iraq to Europe," AP, January 8, 2005

25. "Islamic Terrorist Suspects Held after Police Raids," *Deutsche Presse-Agentur*, January 12, 2005.

26. Geir Moulson, "Terror Suspects Arrested in Germany," AP, June 14, 2005.

27. Craig S. Smith and Don van Natta Jr., "European Muslims Joining War against U.S. in Iraq," *New York Times*, October 26, 2004.

28. Jean Chichizola, "Le Troisième Français Capturé en Irak a Eté Identifié," *Le Figaro*, February 5, 2005.

29. "Sept Suspects Arrêtés à Paris," *Le Parisien*, January 26, 2005.

30. Jean Chichizola, "Four Recruiters for Jihad in Iraq Arrested," *Le Figaro*, January 26, 2005. Accessed via FBIS.

31. Scheherazade Faramarzi, "Leaving Slums of Paris, Two Muslim Teens Turn to Waging Jihad," AP, November 26, 2004.

32. Ibid.

33. "France Detains 11 Suspected 'Recruits' to War in Iraq," AFP, January 26, 2005.

34. "France Investigates Iraqi Jihad Volunteer Suspects," AFP, September 22, 2004.

35. Piotr Smolar, "Une Enquête Mise à Mal par les Tensions entre Parquet et Juges antiterrorists," *Le Monde*, June 15, 2004.

36. Chichizola, "Le Troisième Français Capturé."

37. Faramarzi, "Leaving Slums of Paris."

38. "France Detains 11 Suspected 'Recruits.'"

39. Karimi is believed to have recruited Brahim Yadel, one of the seven Frenchmen detained in Guantanamo Bay.

40. Pierre-Antoine Souchard, "Arrests Keep Young Would-Be French Militants from Iraqi Battlefields," AP, February 3, 2005.

41. Rotella, "Europe's Boys of Jihad."

42. Elaine Sciolino, "French Detain Group Said to Recruit Iraq Rebels," *New York Times*, January 26, 2005.

43. Craig S. Smith, "U.S. Holding 3 Frenchmen with Ties to Insurgency," *New York Times*, February 5, 2005.

44. Gerard Davet, "Les Filières de Recrutement de la 'Guerre Sainte' Sont en Place," *Le Monde*, December 16, 2004.

45. Elaine Sciolino, "French Detain Group Said to Recruit Iraq Rebels."

46. Don van Natta Jr. and Desmond Butler, "Calls to Jihad Are Said to Lure Hundreds of Militants into Iraq," *New York Times*, November 1, 2003.

47. Jean Chichizola, "Coup de filet de la DST a Limoges et Montpellier," *Le Figaro*, June 22, 2005.

48. Nick Pelham, Jordan Antony Barnett, and Mark Townsend, "British Olympic Hope 'Was Iraq Suicide Bomber,'" *Observer*, November 16, 2003.

49. Ibid.

50. Richard Beeston, "Briton 'Caught Red-Handed' over Guns," *Times* (London), January 7, 2005.

51. David Leppard and Hala Jaber, "70 British Muslims Join Iraq Fighters," *Sunday Times*, June 26, 2005.

52. "Operacion en Espana Contra el Terrorismo," *El Mundo*, June 15, 2005.

53. "Interior Sospecha que Afalah se Inmolo' en Irak," *El Mundo*, June 15, 2005.

54. Whitlock, "In Europe, New Force for Recruiting Radicals."

55. Ibid.

56. "4 Sweden Terror Suspects Said to Murder," AP, April 23, 2004.

57. "Iraqi Pair Jailed for Terror Plots," AFP, May 12, 2005.

58. Tribunal of Milan, Indictment of Muhamad Majid and others.

59. Philip Shishkin, "Norway Hits Bumps in Terror Probe," *Wall Street Journal Europe*, March 23, 2004.

60. "Mullah Krekar Warns US," *Aftenposten*, March 20, 2003.

61. Tribunal of Milan, Indictment of Muhamad Majid and others.

62. Nathanael Johnson, "Norway's Dilemma: How to Deal with Mullah Krekar," PBS Frontline Special on Europe. http://www.pbs.org/wgbh/pages/frontline/shows/front/map/krekar.html.

63. Ibid.

64. Jonathan Tisdall, "Bin Laden Turned Him Down," *Aftenposten*, April 22, 2004.

65. Domink Cziesche and Georg Mascolo, "Departure for the Killing Fields," *Der Spiegel*, December 8, 2003. Accessed via FBIS.

66. Tribunal of Milan, Sentence against Maher Bouyahia and others, January 24, 2005.

67. Giuseppe Sarcina, "Frattini: "Ora c'e' il Rischio che l'Italia Diventi Zona Franca per gli Estremisti,'" *Corriere della Sera*, January 25, 2005.

68. Paolo Biondani and Biagi Marsigilia, "Il 'Moderato' Tradito da un Video dove Spara," *Corriere della Sera*, January 26, 2005.

69. "Dambruoso: Guerriglia e Terrore? Indistinguibili," ANSA Agenzia Nazionale Stampa Associata, January 26, 2005.

70. Air Force Lieutenant General Norton Schwartz, Department of Defense briefing, October 23, 2003.

71. Abu Musab al Zarqawi, letter of February 2004, translated into English by the Coalition Provisional Authority.

72. "Bin Laden Hails Zarqawi as Iraq Chief, Calls for Polls Boycott; Tape," AFP, December 27, 2004.

73. Testimony of CIA Director Porter Goss before the US Senate Intelligence Committee, January 16, 2005.

74. "Third Suspected Radical Islamic under Investigation in France," AFP, January 29, 2005.

75. "Islamists Arrested in Paris Planned France Attacks," Reuters, January 28, 2005.

PART IV

MADRID, VAN GOGH, AND THE NEW FACE OF AL QAEDA

CHAPTER 11

THE MADRID
TRAIN BOMBINGS

You have to know that I met other brothers, that little by little I created with just a few things, before they were drug dealers, criminals, I introduced them to faith and now they are the first ones to ask me when it's the moment for jihad. Some of them went to Afghanistan and others are praying and waiting. . . . You have to know that we are emigrants of God. We are for jihad, we believe in God and in his Prophet Mohammed, because everything is allowed, including marrying Christian women because we need the documents. We have to be everywhere, in Germany, Holland, London. We are dominating Europe with our presence.

—Rabei Osman El Sayed Ahmed, alleged mastermind
of the Madrid train bombings (Milan, May 26, 2004)

AL QAEDA ENTERS POLITICS

"We think that the Spanish government could not tolerate more than two, maximum three blows, after which it will have to withdraw as a result of popular pressure."[1] This view was expressed in a very complete and sophisticated political analysis of the war in Iraq circulating on the Internet, titled "Jihadi Iraq, Hopes and Dangers"; it was discovered in December 2003 by the Forsvarets Forskningsinstitutt, a Norwegian research institute. Released by the mysterious "Media Committee for the Victory of the Iraqi People (Mujaheddin Services Center)," the forty-two-page Arabic document resembled previous writings and communiqués of al Qaeda–linked groups in its style and ideology; while its real authorship is unknown, it is to have been written by an astute political analyst within al Qaeda. Initially, authorities paid the text little attention; but a few months later, they realized that it outlined al Qaeda's global strategy.

Starting from the premise that "America cannot be coerced to leave Iraq by military-political means alone, but the Islamist resistance can succeed if it makes the occupation of Iraq as costly as possible—in economic terms—for the United States," "Jihadi Iraq" provided various recommendations on how to make the occupation too expensive. The best solution, the author argued, was to attack the fragile coalition put together by the Bush administration, as he believed that, in the long term, the United States could not afford the occupation alone. After offering an informed and thorough analysis of the internal situation of three of the main European countries providing troops to the coalition, he concluded that the United Kingdom and Poland were unlikely to withdraw their support easily, despite the widespread domestic opposition to the war, and Spain was the alliance's weakest link. The document noted that "[then Prime Minister José María] Aznar's position does not express the Spanish popular stance," and pointed to the weakness of the leftist opposition, the power of the Catholic Church, the youth of the Spanish democracy, and the "lack of direct influence of the event[s] in Iraq on life in Spain" to explain why the Aznar government was still in power despite popular discontent over the US-led war in Iraq. "Therefore we say that in order to force the Spanish government to withdraw from Iraq the resistance should deal painful blows to its forces. This should be accompanied by an information campaign clarifying the truth of the matter inside Iraq. It is necessary to make the utmost use of the upcoming general election in Spain in March next year."[2]

At the time of the document's discovery, Spanish forces in Iraq had already been hit hard by the insurgency. In October 2003, a Spanish diplomat was executed by three gunmen outside his Baghdad house.[3] A month later, seven agents from Spain's National Intelligence Center were massacred after their convoy was attacked about thirty kilometers south of Baghdad.[4] The pictures of Iraqi children kicking the dead bodies of the agents near their burning cars shocked Spain, but Aznar's resolution to keep the country's thirteen hundred troops in Iraq did not falter.

Then came the fatal morning of March 11, 2004. Between 7:37 and 7:42 AM, ten bombs exploded on commuter trains traveling from the eastern suburbs of Madrid to the Spanish capital's city center. Seven bombs went off on two trains about to enter the Atocha Station, in the heart of Madrid, sending body parts through windows of nearby apartments.[5] The Atocha bombs killed nearly a hundred people, but the carnage would have been immensely worse had the explosions occurred only a few minutes later, when the trains had reached the station. According to Spanish authorities, detonation of the bombs inside Atocha would probably have caused part of the old station to collapse, perhaps killing tens of thousands of commuters (more than a quarter of a million pass through Atocha every workday). Two more bombs went off in El Pozo and one in Santa Eugenia, two suburban stations on the route that takes commuters to Atocha from the town of Alcalá de Henares. In a span of less than five minutes, the explosions had killed 191 people and injured more than fifteen hundred.[6]

As emergency workers fought to rescue the injured and collected body parts from the tracks, Spanish authorities tried to understand what had happened. For decades Spain had been battling internal terrorist actions launched by ETA (Euskadi Ta Askatasuna, or Basque Homeland and Liberty), a Basque separatist group. Though the Aznar government's aggressive campaign had recently managed to cripple ETA, remnants of the organizations were still active and, according to Spanish authorities, determined to strike. Just three months earlier, Spanish authorities had arrested two ETA operatives who were planting backpack bombs on trains.[7] ETA seemed the logical culprit, and within hours the Spanish government was publicly announcing that it was behind the attacks. At 1:30 PM, Interior Minister Ángel Acebes declared that with the train attacks, "ETA had achieved its objective." At the same time, Prime Minister Aznar instructed the Spanish delegation at the United Nations to introduce a resolution condemning the Basque terrorist group. [8]

Nevertheless, even before the investigation began, some Spanish officials doubted that ETA could be responsible. ETA's bombing campaigns as rule have had low casualties, because the group routinely telephones authorities to warn that an explosion is about to take place. ETA generally preferred more targeted attacks, attacking government officials and the Spanish elite and sparing members of the working class. Moreover, intercepted phone calls between known ETA members in the immediate wake of the attacks revealed that they came as a surprise to all of them.[9]

In the early afternoon, authorities began to gather information that might have suggested a different lead. At 10:50 AM, a resident of Alcalá de Henares, the station from which all the bombed trains had left, called the police to report a suspicious vehicle parked across the street from the local train station. Agents examining the Kangoo van found out that its plates did not match the vehicle's registration. A quick inspection of the van's interior revealed nothing sensitive, but the vehicle was nevertheless impounded. A few hours later, investigators searching more carefully found a plastic bag with seven detonators under the passenger seat. In addition, the van's cassette player held a tape with Arabic inscriptions on its case that contained recitations of Quranic verses.[10]

By the evening, Aznar had given information about the tape to the opposition's leader, José Luis Rodríguez Zapatero, and to the publishers of the country's main newspapers, while maintaining that ETA was still the primary suspect. A few hours later, the Abu Hafs al Masri Brigades, a group that claimed to speak on behalf of al Qaeda, issued a communiqué proudly asserting its responsibility for the attacks: "The squadron of death has managed to penetrate in the heart of Crusader Europe, striking one of the pillars of the Crusaders and their allies, Spain, with a painful blow. This is part of an old game with Crusader Spain, ally of America in its war against Islam."[11] Its claim was considered "unreliable" by the

Spanish government, which publicly announced that a connection to ETA was the most "logical."[12] There was good reason to be suspicious of claims by the Abu Hafs al Masri Brigades, which is not considered to be a functioning organization; moreover, it had already issued a demonstrably false statement in August 2003, when it claimed responsibility for a major blackout in the northeastern United States that was in fact caused by an overload in the grid and communications failures.

Police had a break in their case early in the morning of March 12, when a young officer sorting through the personal effects of the victims in the El Pozo station found a sports bag. The bag contained a Motorola mobile phone that was connected by two wires to ten kilograms of explosives. The type of explosive found was Goma 2 ECO, a Spanish brand used in the bombs that had detonated.[13] The bag was also filled with nails and screws, objects commonly added to increase the deadliness of an explosion. Once activated from a distance by a second telephone, the cell phone was supposed to send an electronic signal to the detonator. While the other ten bags had exploded, this one did not. Investigators had found the key to solving the case.

The discovery of the bag was initially kept secret, as investigators gathered clues from the SIM card found inside the cell phone and the fingerprints on the bag and in the van. Even though ETA sent various media outlets a number of communiqués strongly denying any involvement in the attacks, the Aznar government kept blaming the Basque group. In the meantime, Spain was a country in shock. Spontaneous rallies brought life in Madrid and other cities to a halt, as one in four Spaniards participated in emotional vigils and shows of support for the victims throughout the country. And as Spain was grappling with its sorrow, it was also getting ready for the general national elections, due to take place on Sunday, March 14.

The events of Saturday the 13th changed Spain once again. Early in the morning, police managed to trace the phone card to a shop owned by two Indian immigrants in Alcorcon, a Madrid neighborhood. The Indians told the counterterrorism police that the SIM card found in the unexploded bag was from a stock of thirty cards they had sold to a Moroccan immigrant who owned a small shop in Lavapies, an immigrant neighborhood located not far from the Atocha Station.[14] At 4 PM, Spanish police arrested the owner of the shop, Jamal Zougam, and two other Moroccan citizens, Mohammed Bekkali Boutaliha and Zougam's half-brother, Mohammed Chaoui.[15] They were detained, together with the two Indians, for what Interior Minister Acebes called "their presumed implication in the sale and falsification of the cell phone and cell phone card found in the bag which did not explode."[16] As media began to spread the information that Zougam had been linked in the past to Islamic fundamentalists operating in the Madrid area, more than three thousand protesters began to gather in front of the government party's headquarters in Madrid, shouting that they demanded "the truth before going to vote."[17]

Just before 8 PM, an anonymous phone call informed the TV station Telemadrid that a tape had been left in a trash bin near one of Madrid's main mosques. Alerted by the station, police retrieved the tape. On the tape, a man speaking Arabic with an unmistakable Moroccan accent who identified himself as Abu Dujan al Afgani, the military spokesman for al Qaeda in Europe, claimed responsibility for the attacks.[18] "We declare our responsibility for what happened in Madrid," he declared, "exactly two and a half years after the attacks in New York and Washington. It is a response to your cooperation with the criminal Bush and his allies. . . . You love life and we love death."[19] The tape sent shockwaves through Spain and convinced most Spaniards that Islamic fundamentalists and not ETA, as the government had repeatedly claimed, were behind the attacks.

The general elections of Sunday, March 14, took place in an extremely tense atmosphere. A quiet campaign that was expected to end with a comfortable victory for Aznar's ruling Popular Party had become white-hot after the attacks and the arrests in Lavapies. Thousands of protesters flooded the streets of Madrid, blaming the attacks on the Aznar government's support of the US-led war in Iraq. Graffiti saying "Aznar killer" covered the wall of the El Pozo train station, where two of the bombs had exploded. When Mariano Rajoy, the Popular Party's candidate for prime minister, went to vote at his Madrid polling station, other Spaniards attacked him with screams of "Liar!" and "Get our troops out of Iraq!"[20] A record 77.2 percent of eligible Spaniards voted,[21] giving an unexpected victory to the Spanish Socialist Workers Party (Partido Socialista Obrero Español, or PSOE), whose main electoral goal just one week earlier had been to keep the same number of seats in the Chamber of Deputies.

The Madrid bombings made it clear that Islamic terrorists are not only bloodthirsty criminals willing to kill innocent civilians but also savvy interpreters of Western politics. Choosing to strike right before the elections, the terrorists correctly predicted that Spanish voters would blame the unprecedented carnage on their government's support of the US-led war in Iraq. The Aznar government's insistence on blaming ETA without even looking at the evidence only played into the hands of the bombers, as many Spaniards perceived this behavior as an attempted cover-up. The terrorists succeeded in persuading many that Spain was attacked solely because of its support of the war. Polls showed that a great number of voters believed that the new government's pledge to withdraw Spanish troops from Iraq would leave Spain untouched by Islamic militants in the future. One Spanish citizen who originally supported the Popular Party but voted for the Socialists spoke for many when he told an interviewer that he changed his mind because of the Madrid bombings: "Maybe the Socialists will get our troops out of Iraq, and Al Qaeda will forget about Spain."[22]

While the attacks were clearly timed to influence the outcome of the Spanish elections, there are several indications that Spain had been a target of Islamic terrorism well before its involvement in the Iraqi war. Islamic militants have been active in Spain since the mid-1980s. Al Qaeda's cell in Madrid was one of its most active in Europe, and some of the cell's key members have been charged with direct involvement in the planning of 9/11.[23] Jamal Zougam, one of the Moroccans arrested two days after the March 11 attacks, was closely linked to Abu Dahdah, the leader of the Madrid cell.[24] While the cell never carried out an attack on Spanish soil, it always considered Spain an infidel country suitable for a strike.

Many Islamists call Spain by its ancient Arabic name, Al Andalus, recalling the more than seven centuries of Muslim domination in the Iberian peninsula. Though that period, which ended with the 1492 expulsion of all Muslims from Spain, is ancient history for most Spaniards, the Muslim conquest still evokes inspiring memories of glory for Islamic fundamentalists. Radical preachers such as Abu Qatada and Mohammed Fazazi, the Madrid cell's two main spiritual leaders, often spoke of the day when Al Andalus would return to Muslim rule. And even Ayman al Zawahiri, al Qaeda's second in command, referred to the expulsion of the Arabs from the Iberian peninsula more than five centuries ago as "the tragedy of Al Andalus."[25] Spain has a high symbolic value for Islamic fundamentalists as a place where Muslims have been humiliated and that has to be recaptured by the new Muslim armies. Indeed, as will be seen later, the group that carried out the train bombings called itself "the brigade situated in Al Andalus."[26]

It is the distance that Spain has come from Al Andulus that also explains why it was struck. The country is now a secular democracy with strong Christian roots that supports the modernization and democratization of its southern Muslim neighbors, such as Morocco and Algeria. Historical and geopolitical grievances give Islamic fundamentalists reason to hate Spain; its support for the war in Iraq was a minor factor. Indeed, Spanish investigators believe that the group that carried out the Madrid bombings had been studying the Spanish railway system for a possible attack for almost three years,[27] beginning long before a US war with Iraq even seemed likely. But the war determined its timing, which was masterfully chosen to play on the emotions of the Spanish people.

In the online document "Jihadi Iraq, Hopes and Dangers," radicals had predicted that the Spanish government "could not tolerate more than two, maximum three blows." They were too conservative: one blow was enough in a country where 69 percent of the population opposed a war with Iraq even if it had the support of the United Nations.[28] The voters punished the Popular Party and acclaimed the Socialists, who had strongly opposed the war since the beginning. A few days after he was sworn in, Zapatero, whom the London *Times* dubbed "the accidental premier,"[29] kept his promise to the electorate and began withdrawing the thirteen hundred Spanish troops from Iraq. By mid-May 2004, the last of them returned home. Al Qaeda had achieved its goal: it had become a key player in the political life of a Western democracy, influencing the outcome of an election. Significantly, when Jamal Zougam—later recognized by several eyewitnesses as one of the men who had placed the backpacks filled with explosives on the trains—entered the court after five days incommunicado, his first words were "Who won the elections?"[30]

THE PERPETRATORS

As soon as they realized that the mobile phones that had been used for the bombings had been sold to Jamal Zougam, Spanish authorities knew that Islamic fundamentalists were behind the attacks. The thirty-one-year-old Moroccan immigrant from Tangier, who had moved to Spain in 1983 with his mother, was well known to them for his involvement with radicals in Spain and in at least two other countries.[31] Nevertheless, he had never been charged with a crime and was not under surveillance.

In 2001 Spanish authorities had received an official request to investigate Zougam from their Moroccan counterparts, who believed that Zougam was involved with a network of veterans of Afghanistan operating in Morocco.[32] At the same time, French authorities were also interested in him, as they had information that he had met in a Madrid mosque with David Courtailler, the French convert convicted for his terrorist activities in May 2004. The French antiterrorism magistrate Jean-Louis Bruguière traveled to Spain and interviewed Zougam in June 2001.[33] Acting on the information provided by Paris, Spanish police searched Zougam's apartment in August 2001 and found several tapes of the fighting in Chechnya and speeches of Mullah Krekar.[34] Phone numbers of known radicals operating in Madrid were also discovered.

Spanish investigators also knew Zougam as a marginal figure in the network of Imad Eddin Barakat Yarkas, the leader of an important al Qaeda cell operating in Madrid that had helped provide logistical support for the network. Yarkas had recruited dozens of Muslims residing in Spain for al Qaeda's training camps in Afghanistan, where his associate and former Madrid resident Chej Saleh was working as a trainer.[35] While raising thousands of dollars for the mujahideen in Afghanistan and Chechnya, Yarkas maintained close relationships with al Qaeda militants on four continents, traveling constantly to London to meet with Abu Qatada and to Oslo to meet Mullah Krekar, whom Zougam also allegedly met.[36] In addition, Yarkas and members of his cell are accused of having organized the July 2001 meeting in Spain between Mohammed Atta and Ramzi Binalshibh at which the two former Hamburg residents finalized the plans for the attacks of 9/11.

In the summer of 2001, Spanish authorities began monitoring the conversations of several Islamic fundamentalists operating in the Madrid area, but Zougam's telephone was tapped only briefly. When Yarkas and most of the members of his cell were arrested in November 2001, Zougam was not charged. Even though Yarkas had frequently spoken with him and had often used his shop to make phone calls or to meet other members of the network, there was no evidence that Zougam had committed any crime.[37] It was common knowledge that Zougam was involved in radical activities, but investigators lacked sufficient evidence to charge him or even to maintain a constant tap on his phone. Because the tapes of his conversations were given low priority, they were set aside for months. And since the Spanish counterterrorism authorities had only seven part-time Arabic translators, who were overwhelmed by their workload, most of the tapes were not translated at all.[38]

Zougam's name surfaced again after the May 2003 Casablanca bombings, which had been carried out by young suicide bombers recruited in the slums of the Moroccan city by experienced veterans of Afghanistan. Even though he appeared to be happily integrated into the mainstream in Spain, where he ran a fairly profitable business and drove a fancy red car, Zougam stayed closely tied to his native Morocco; he returned to Tangier frequently to stay with his father, a muezzin in one of the city's mosques.[39] It was in Tangier, a hotbed of radicalism separated from Spanish territory only by the narrow Strait of Gibraltar, that Zougam began to befriend local radicals and was introduced to fundamentalism.

Zougam became a close associate of the Beniyach brothers, three Tangier natives who are equivalent to royalty in al Qaeda. Abdullah

Beniyach died in December 2001 in Afghanistan fighting American forces in the battle of Tora Bora. His brother Abdelaziz is a veteran of Bosnia and Chechnya who met repeatedly with Abu Musab al Zarqawi and was arrested in Spain after the Casablanca bombings.[40] Authorities believe that Zougam met with Abdelaziz Beniyach in Morocco a month before the Casablanca bombings. Zougam was also friends with a third Beniyach brother, Salahuddin, a one-eyed fighter who is shown in a Chechen video attending a briefing for commanders led by Ibn ul Khattab. Salahuddin is currently detained in Morocco, accused of taking part in a conspiracy to blow up a French refinery.[41]

In Tangier, Zougam also became fascinated with the fiery sermons of Mohammed Fazazi, the Moroccan imam who had preached at Hamburg's al Quds mosque to the future 9/11 hijackers and had moved back to Morocco before the United States was attacked. Fazazi, who in 2003 was sentenced to thirty years in jail by a Moroccan court for his role as a spiritual leader of Salafia Jihadia, the group responsible for the Casablanca bombings, played a large part in Zougam's radicalization. Spanish wiretaps recorded Zougam telling Yarkas he had offered Fazazi financial support from the Madrid cell.[42] "You should speak to him," Zougam told Yarkas in August 2001. "I told him that if he needed contributions we could get them from where the brothers are."[43]

After the Casablanca bombings, Moroccan authorities cracked down on Islamic fundamentalists operating in the country. Fazazi, the Beniyachs, and several other associates of Zougam were either arrested or investigated. Zougam, who had returned to Madrid three weeks after the bombings, was also investigated, but there was not enough evidence to charge him. "Morocco informed the Spanish that he went to Spain and that he was a quite dangerous person. There was no evidence against him in Morocco, but they asked Spain to investigate him," said frustrated a Moroccan official.[44] For the third time, Spanish authorities received intelligence detailing Zougam's dangerous ties and views, but since he technically had committed no crime, no action could be taken. Zougam provides one of most dramatic examples of the current inability of European legal systems to effectively deal with the threat of Islamic terrorism.

Zougam's was just the first in a long series of arrests: in the year following the attacks more than seventy individuals have been detained in connection with the train bombings.[45] In the early hours of March 25, police arrested five more men involved in the plot. One of them, the Moroccan national Hamid Ahmidan, was a known drug trafficker; in his apartment police found a stash of more than twenty kilograms of hashish and cocaine. Another man arrested on the same day was Basel Ghalyoun, a Syrian who had been involved with Yarkas's cell and was well-known to Spanish counterterrorism authorities.[46] Ghalyoun is believed to have been one of the men who placed the bags filled with explosives on the trains. A victim of the attacks who recognized Ghalyoun's picture gave a disturbing account of his cold-bloodedness. The young Romanian immigrant was commuting to the Atocha station with a fellow countrywoman when she and her friend noticed a young, good-looking man sitting near them. The three exchanged quick "flirtatious smiles" before the man rushed off the train. When the women yelled to him that he had forgotten his backpack, he pretended not to hear. A few minutes later, the bomb in the backpack went off, killing one of the Romanians and injuring the other. The survivor recognized Ghalyoun as the handsome man who had smiled at her. "She identified him right away," said a Spanish investigator. "She said she would never forget that face, that smile, as long as she lived."[47]

The Spanish investigation was progressing quickly; by the end of March, almost twenty people connected to the attacks had been detained, including at least two of the men who had physically placed the backpacks on the trains. José Luis Rodríguez Zapatero, the newly elected prime minister, had ordered the withdrawal of Spanish troops from Iraq, leading many Spaniards to hope that "al Qaeda would forget about Spain." But their hopes were illusory. At 11 AM on April 2, a Spanish railway worker spotted a supermarket bag some sixty kilometers south of Madrid on the tracks of the high-speed train that connects the Spanish capital to Seville. It contained twelve kilograms of Goma 2 ECO, the same explosive used in the March 11 attacks.[48] That the bag was dry despite an overnight rain indicated that it had been placed on the tracks that morning.[49] The explosives were connected to a detonator by a one-hundred-thirty-meter cable but lacked a trigger, making an explosion impossible.[50] Apparently, the terrorists had been interrupted before they could finish the device. The entire line was closed, reopening only after every tie of the tracks was checked. Three days earlier, workers had surprised five men digging a hole on the tracks of the high-speed train that connects Madrid to Lerida. The men fled immediately, but authorities believe that the March 11 bombers were behind both incidents.[51] Spain had not yet been "forgotten" by the terrorists.

Meanwhile, Spanish authorities were continuing their investigation of the March 11 bombings. The stock of thirty SIM cards sold by the two Indians to Zougam proved to be essential to the probe. While half of them had been employed in the attacks, the other fifteen were still being used by terrorists linked to Zougam. And though authorities could not determine the individuals using the cards, they could locate with some precision where the cards were being used.[52] On April 3, electronic signals brought investigators to Leganes, a bleak commuter neighborhood on the outskirts of Madrid. After methodically showing pictures around and asking questions to locals, investigators homed in on a five-story building at number 40, calle de Martín Gaite.[53]

After police officers buzzed the apartment where they believed the terrorists were hiding, a voice with a thick Moroccan accent answered. They were clearly on the right track. As soon as they entered the building, a young North African man who was taking out the trash spotted them and ran away. Agents tried to chase him, but the man—later determined to be Abdelmajid Bouchar, a local track champion—was faster.[54] A few seconds later, voices from the upper floors yelled "Allah u Akhbar!" (God is great) and began spraying the officers with bullets fired from a machine gun.[55] It was the beginning of the "siege of Leganes," a dramatic operation that led to the death of seven of the perpetrators of the March 11 attacks. The men barricaded themselves inside the apartment; when contacted by police negotiators, they threatened to blow themselves up with the entire building. By 8 PM, authorities had evacuated the residents of adjacent apartment buildings and cordoned off the area, laying siege to the apartment with hundreds of men.[56]

While the authorities' attention was focused on the Leganes siege, the Madrid offices of the Spanish daily newspaper *ABC* received a fax hand-written in Arabic. It was signed by Abu Dujan al Afgani, the same man who had claimed responsibility for the train bombings on the tape found near a Madrid mosque two days after the attacks. In the fax, al Afgani said his organization, which he called "al Qaeda in Europe," had already showed its force by carrying out the "blessed attacks of March 11" and by planting a bomb on the tracks of the Madrid–Seville railway. He therefore demanded the immediate withdrawal of Spanish forces not only from Iraq but also from Afghanistan, where the Zapatero government was planning on redeploying some of the returning troops. "If these demands are not met," threatened al Afgani, "we will declare war on you and . . . convert your country into an inferno and your blood will flow like rivers."[57] Simply distancing Spain from the conflict in Iraq was clearly not enough.

Meanwhile, the situation inside and outside the Leganes apartment was becoming more tense by the minute. The seven men who had been cornered by Spanish authorities were some of the planners of the train bombings, associates of Zougam who were now willing to die. On that Saturday afternoon, the group had intended to carry out more attacks, with a local shopping center and a Jewish center in Avila as the likely targets. Seeing the unusual movements of police in the quiet suburban community of Leganes, the terrorists thought they had been identified and returned to their apartment, waiting to face the police in a final standoff.[58] "We will die killing," they shouted from the windows of their second-floor apartment.[59] Inside, they donned traditional white robes and began drinking water from Mecca, acts of purification before death. They chanted Islamic songs and recited verses from the Quran. They also telephoned their families in North Africa and Spain, telling them about their plans to kill themselves rather than be caught by the "infidels." One of them, Jamal Ahmidan, called his mother in Morocco and said, "Mom, I'm going to paradise. I am ready."[60] The men were getting ready to die as martyrs. Reportedly, they even called Belmarsh prison, the London penitentiary where Abu Qatada, al Qaeda's spiritual leader in Europe, was then being detained, possibly seeking a religious edict to justify suicide.[61]

One of the men inside the apartment, Abdennabi Kounjaa, had previously written a letter to his son in Morocco in which he announced his plans to die. "I ask God to give me the martyrdom so I can be reunited with you in paradise," wrote the thirty-four-year-old, who authorities believe to have been one of the men who left backpacks on the trains on March 11 and placed the unexploded bomb on the tracks of the Seville–Madrid railway. Kounjaa told his young son, "I don't stand living like a weak and humiliated person under the watch of the infidels. I prefer death to life." He added, "I ask you to have faith in God and that you follow the mujaheddin brothers in the world and maybe one day you'll be one of them, because that's what I expect from you."[62]

After hours of fruitless negotiations, at 9 PM Spanish police decided to storm the apartment: they tore down the front door and fired tear gas inside. It was the sign that the terrorists were expecting, and a few seconds later they detonated twenty kilograms of explosives, killing themselves and mortally injuring Francisco Javier Torronteras, an officer of the special forces who had entered the apartment. The walls of three floors of the buildings were shattered by the explosion, which was so violent that the body of one of the terrorists, Jamal Ahmidan, was hurled into a swimming pool in the building's courtyard.[63]

In the rubble of the apartment, police found a badly damaged tape that forensic experts were nevertheless able to reconstruct. It showed three men wearing balaclavas and white robes and holding automatic weapons as they read a statement to the camera, following a style commonly used by suicide bombers around the world. The video, which authorities believe was shot on the day of the apartment siege, contained new threats against Spain. The men promised to continue their "jihad until martyrdom" if Spain did not "leave Muslim lands," and threatened: "You are not safe and you know that Bush and his administration will bring only destruction. We will kill you anywhere and in any manner." Even as the terrorists linked their actions to Spain's alliance with the Bush administration, they also looked to the past as they claimed to be ready to achieve "martyrdom in the land of Tarek Ben Ziyad."[64] Ben Ziyad was the Moorish general who began the invasion of the Iberian peninsula in the eighth century, conquering the southern regions of Spain. The group also revealingly called itself "the brigade situated in al Andalus."[65]

The men who immolated themselves inside the Leganes apartment were the operational leaders of the March 11 bombings and of the failed attacks that followed. Most of them, like Zougam, were young North African immigrants who lived a double life in Europe. While immersing themselves in the more mundane aspects of Western life, dating women, pursuing successful careers, and going to clubs with friends, the men also flirted with radicalism, worshiping in one of Madrid's main mosques and creating a radical subgroup within it. They entertained casual relationships with known radicals and were all known to counterterrorism officials as marginal figures in the Islamist underworld. The men were an odd mix of petty criminals, students, small entrepreneurs, and drug dealers whom few suspected of harboring such deep hatred for the West. Undetected by authorities, the men planned one of the bloodiest terror attacks in Europe's history.

The story of Jamal Ahmidan, the man whose body was hurled into the empty pool of the Leganes complex after the apartment's explosion, is typical. The thirty-four-year-old Moroccan, whose cousin Hamid had been arrested two weeks after the attacks and found with twenty kilograms of drugs, had helped lead the entire operation. According to Spanish authorities, Ahmidan, using a false Belgian passport, had rented a house in the countryside outside Madrid where the terrorists had assembled the explosives and built the bombs. And investigators also believe that it was Ahmidan who procured the explosives used in the attacks, purchasing them from a Spanish miner he had met while trafficking drugs.[66] As a criminal, Ahmidan seemed not to fit the classic profile of the Islamic fundamentalist, if there is such a thing. He left his native Tetuan, a poor town in northern Morocco, in 1993 to escape a conviction for murdering his accomplice in a robbery.[67] Ahmidan moved to Madrid, where his brothers owned a small shop in Lavapies, a melting pot neighborhood where immigrants from various homelands live and work side by side. Falling back immediately and comfortably into a life of crime, continuing to sell ecstasy and hashish, Ahmidan adopted the nicknames "Mowgli" and "El Chino." At the same time, he began to befriend some of the radicals that gravitated toward Yarkas. In 1999 he was detained for drug-related offenses; sent to a detention center in Mortalez to await deportation, Ahmidan showed all his charisma. "He set himself up as an imam and told guards he would come back and kill them," recounted a Spanish official. "No one took him seriously then, but he already had quite a following."[68] Like K, the Algerian terrorist described in chapter 6 who managed to escape a British facility housing asylum seekers that detainees burned down, Ahmidan started a small fire and escaped from Mortalez. He was subsequently captured and finally deported to Morocco.[69]

Back in his native Tetuan, he was arrested for the crime he had committed in 1993 and spent two and a half years in jail.[70] There Ahmidan met many Islamic fundamentalists, veterans of Afghanistan who had been detained by the Moroccan government for their subversive activities and who were recruiting young, disaffected men. Fascinated by them, he slowly embraced their fanatic and militant interpretation of Islam. When he came out of jail in 2002, he was a completely changed man. In the summer, he decided to leave Morocco and return to Madrid using a forged Belgian passport.[71]

Back in Lavapies, Ahmidan lived as he had before, frequenting clubs and dating a Spanish woman who favored provocative outfits.[72] Nor did he stop trafficking with drugs, as he and his brothers allegedly smuggled large stocks of hashish from Morocco to Spain. "We all knew that Ahmidan was a drug trafficker," said an official at the Madrid mosque where Ahmidan and most of the March 11 bombers used to worship, "but we would have never imagined that he was also a terrorist."[73] But Mowgli lived a double life. Though he continued to sell drugs, he stopped using them himself.[74] He began attending services at the mosque where some of the followers of Yarkas used to meet and befriending other radicals. Following the teachings of Takfir wa'l Hijra, Ahmidan hid his true feelings to deceive "the infidels"; deep within, his religious fanaticism was growing.

Lavapies was the ideal place for Ahmidan to meet like-minded Muslims. He became friends with other young men from his native Tetuan, including Rachid and Mohammed Oulad, two brothers who bounced from odd job to odd job in the neighborhood. Another Tetuan native was Abdennabi Kounjaa, the man who wrote the letter to his son before dying; he had grown up a few yards from Ahmidan, and the two became good friends in Madrid.[75] Kounjaa had close ties to a network that specialized in smuggling stolen cars from Spain to Morocco. In 1999 Kounjaa himself was arrested at the Spanish border while attempting to cross the Moroccan border with a car that had been stolen in Italy.[76] The four Tetuan natives, who had known each other since childhood and had spent their young adulthood on the streets of Madrid, became radicalized together in Lavapies and died together in the Leganes apartment.[77]

Ahmidan befriended other Moroccans living in Lavapies as well. Several local Muslims used to meet in the barbershop of Abdelhouahid Berraj, a native of Tangier, where they drank water that Berraj had brought home from his pilgrimage to Mecca. The rite also attracted Jamal Zougam, whose phone shop was located just a few meters from Berraj's, on the same street.[78] A few meters past the barbershop and Zougam's phone store was another meeting point for the men, an Arab restaurant called Alhambra, a name reminiscent of the Moorish heritage in Spain. There, in 2001, Zougam stabbed a man because he attempted to bring a dog inside the restaurant, an act perceived as insulting by Islamic fundamentalists. After the stabbing, Yarkas, the leader of the Madrid cell, was warned by an associate that "the young people got into a fight." Yarkas immediately called Zougam's half-brother, Mohammed Chaoui, and told him to "clean out the shop. "[79]

The decision of Yarkas, an experienced mujahid with connections at the highest levels of al Qaeda, to get involved in this street fight is significant. Though Zougam, Ahmidan, and the other North Africans involved in the fight were little more than young hoodlums, Yarkas recognized in them the next generation of al Qaeda in Spain. The savvy and well-connected recruiter nurtured them for years; as they rediscovered their roots in the streets of Lavapies and embraced radical Islam, he gave them tapes and books on jihad and the righteousness of the mujahideen's cause. The knowledge and the contacts he provided enabled them to continue jihad after his arrest in November 2001.

Among those not captured in the massive Spanish antiterrorism operation of late 2001 was one of Yarkas's most loyal disciples, a young Tunisian man who had immigrated to Spain in 1996. Serhane Ben Abdelmajid Fakhet, the son of middle-class government workers, had obtained a scholarship to study economics at Madrid's Universidad Autonoma, where he developed friendships with Spanish students and settled into a Westernized life. But after his 1998 pilgrimage to Mecca, Fakhet began to embrace radical views and to frequent the Madrid mosque attended by members of Yarkas's cell. "The Tunisian," as he was known in the neighborhood, became a regular at the Alhambra restaurant and often participated in the water rites at Berraj's barbershop. As his relationship with Yarkas grew closer, he became one of the most respected figures among the neighborhood's young Muslims, gaining a reputation as a charismatic and educated man. The Tunisian also began a long-distance relationship with the daughter of Ahmed Brahim, an Algerian who was arrested in April 2002 and is believed to be al Qaeda's moneyman in Spain.[80]

Yarkas's arrest left Fakhet temporarily at a loss. "The situation inspired and infuriated the Tunisian," said a Spanish official familiar with the Madrid cell. "He was the one who kept insisting that the group had to do something here in Spain. Why go to Afghanistan if you can fight jihad here?"[81] But in order to take vengeance in Spain, Fakhet needed expert help. As Spanish investigators continued to uncover more information on the attacks, they became increasingly convinced that the group of young North Africans from Lavapies could not have carried out the bombings alone. The charismatic and intelligent Fakhet had capably handled their logistics, but he lacked the knowledge and experience to plan the whole operation and the connections to carry it out. To Spanish authorities, the timing and the magnitude of the attacks pointed to the involvement of al Qaeda's leadership, who conceived the plan executed by the assembled students, drug dealers, and shopkeepers.

Investigators began scouring their files to see what senior al Qaeda members had been in contact with the bombers. Fakhet, Zougam, and Ahmidan had had close ties to Yarkas and Brahim, two senior operatives, but the two had been in jail for months. One of the men authorities believed could have played a role in the attacks was a mysterious militant who had arrived on the scene a few weeks after the 9/11 attacks; members of Madrid's fundamentalist community called him "Mohammed the Egyptian." He had attracted the investigators' attention shortly after entering Spain, as he immediately created a group of followers inside the mosque at which the radicals from Lavapies gathered. The role of "the Egyptian" increased after November 2001, as he filled the leadership void created by Yarkas's arrest. In December 2001, Spanish authorities began tapping his cell phone, suspecting he might be an important al Qaeda operative.[82]

In a few months, the Egyptian, whose real name was Rabei Osman El Sayed Ahmed, became the leader of the small group of radicals who had been spared by the wave of arrests that hit the Madrid cell in the wake of 9/11. Fakhet, who more than anybody felt the need of guidance after Yarkas's arrest, became very attached to Ahmed, spending entire nights watching tapes about jihad with the Egyptian and Khaled Pardo, an Algerian who had connections to a Barcelona cell of the Salafist Group for Preaching and Combat (Groupe Salafiste pour la Predication et le Combat, or GSPC) dismantled in 2003. Basel Ghalyoun, the handsome Syrian who flirted with the Romanian women on the train before leaving the explosives-filled backpack, and Fouad Amghar, a Moroccan later arrested for his role in the train bombings, also became part of the small group led by Ahmed.[83] According to Spanish authorities, Ahmed was a model recruiter, both supplying the men with tapes and books on jihad and martyrdom and teaching them how to avoid detection by intelligence agencies. Under Ahmed's supervision, Fakhet and others who had been marginal figures in the old Madrid cell led by Yarkas formed the core of a new cell, gaining new prominence following the arrests or flight from the country of more experienced operatives.

Ahmed disappeared from Spain shortly before the train bombings, and authorities' interest in his whereabouts grew as they came to realize that most of the men behind the attacks were part of his group. Ahmed's involvement in the plot was confirmed when a witness identified him as one of the men who used to go to the country house in Morata de Tajuña, where the train bombers met to assemble the explosives. Two weeks after the attacks, Spanish authorities had a breakthrough: While searching the apartment of a suspect, Fouad Amghar, they discovered an electronic notebook containing an Italian cell phone number. The same number was found in the belongings of two of the men who died in the Leganes apartment, who listed it as Ahmed's new cell phone number in Italy.[84]

Spanish authorities passed the information to their Italian counterparts, who immediately began monitoring Ahmed's cell phone. By analyzing the calls made from and to the telephone, Italian intelligence (Divisioni Investigazioni Generali e Operazioni Speciali, or DIGOS) located Ahmed in an apartment in Milan, which he shared with other Egyptians, and began round-the-clock surveillance of his movements. Ahmed was living inconspicuously in Milan, working as a painter and rarely leaving the apartment. The few occasions when he would leave home were on Fridays to go to either the Islamic Cultural Institute (ICI) or the Via Quaranta mosque, Milan's two radical mosques (discussed in part 3). And it was during one of the few times that Ahmed left for Friday services that DIGOS agents managed to enter his apartment and plant listening devices.

On May 24, 2004, a phone call intercepted between Ahmed and Murad, an unidentified Moroccan living in Belgium, proved that Ahmed was involved with the Madrid bombings:

Ahmed: You know what happened there, I don't want to mention the country.

Murad: Yes, yes.

Ahmed: And you know the whole group.

Murad: Yes.

Ahmed: The group, you saw it?

Murad: Yes.

Ahmed: I can't get close to the consulate because . . .

Murad: What happened to the boys there? What happened to them?

Ahmed: You know Murad, you know the news. . . . The boys, our friends, they were behind the problems there.

Murad: They were behind?

Ahmed: They were behind the whole time, Sarhane [Fakhet, "the Tunisian"] and the brothers, and everybody! My brother!

Murad: Oh God!

Ahmed: Fouad [Amghar, one of the men arrested after the bombings] and everybody . . .

Murad: What happened to them?

Ahmed: They went to God!

Murad: So they are all gone now?

Ahmed: Yes, all to God!

Murad: Oh God![85]

But the depths of Ahmed's involvement in the Madrid bombings did not become clear to authorities until two days later. On May 26, the bug inside the Milan apartment recorded a conversation between Ahmed and Yahia, a young Egyptian immigrant whom Ahmed had been "mentoring" since his arrival in Italy.

Ahmed: If one has the desire to sacrifice himself in the name of God he has to be ready. It is a shame. We, the youth, should be the first ones to sacrifice, like for example Mohammed, because God tries all of us and tires us, He tries the faith of all of us, He tries our soul. The solution is one, join al Qaeda. Here we are sleepers, it is our duty to be the first ones to go to jihad, here they are torturing and tiring us. Think about it, we come from our country, from far, to come to the land of the unbelievers, we were wrong, but it's never too late, because our destination should be for example Chechnya, Kashmir. . . . We see death every day, let's hope God will give us the courage to win; the reward for those who choose death has no limit. Because one has to stay like this, then they take you and you go to jail, why not tak, tak, tak and you are a martyr, you serve God.

Yahia: Stay be my side always; unfortunately I was blocked at the beginning, but stay by my side and you'll see how I rise, with the strength of God, and I end up inside.

Ahmed: We need just one blow, you see what they do to our brothers in Iraq, you see what they do to the Arabs, you see the prisons, you see the humiliations. Isn't it better to die than to be imprisoned there? What do the Americans think they are going to do, stop us? There are other ways, they'll see . . . [. . .] God is great . . . I am very honest with you, you have to know it, listen to me carefully, I am sincere, you have to know that I have many friends that died as martyrs in Afghanistan, that also died in jail, there is one thing, there is one thing that I am not going to hide from you: [lowering his voice] the attack in Madrid was my project and those who died martyrs are my very dear friends.

Yahia: Ahhh!

Ahmed: I am the thread of Madrid, when the deed happened I wasn't there, but I'll tell you the truth, before the operation, on the 4th, I had contacts with them . . . keep your mouth shut . . . I go around alone, they worked in group.

Yahia: They all died martyrs?

Ahmed: Five died martyrs and eight have been arrested; they are the best friends, dearest friends, very loyal . . . beware . . . already on the 4th I began to plan, but to plan at a high level, I wanted to plan it in order that it was something unforgettable, including me, because I wanted to blow up too, but they stopped me and we obey the will of God. I wanted a big load but I couldn't find the means. This plan cost me a lot of study and patience, it took me two and half years . . . beware . . . beware!! Don't you ever mention anything and never talk to Jalil, in any way, not even on the phone.

Yahia: Not even with the phone card?

Ahmed: No, nothing, in no way. You have to know that this information that I have given you . . . nobody in the world knows it. All my friends are dying one after the other. Some of them blew themselves up in Afghanistan, and there are many people that I know that are ready, I am telling you that there are two groups ready for martyrdom, the first group leaves the 25th, the 20th of the next month for Iraq, through Syria, there are four ready for martyrdom. You don't have to say anything to Mohammed, even though he knows everything, and knows those that are leaving on the 20th, but you don't know anything, OK?

Yahia: OK, and Ahmed?

Ahmed: Yes, he is there.

Yahia: The passports?

Ahmed: Everything is ready, the passports are not a problem, they are already ready.

Yahia: Egyptian passports?

Ahmed: The Egyptian passports are not OK. They were already bought in Spain for two or three hundred euros, it depends on the color. Passports from France, Morocco, Syria, England, and Pakistan, you can find them at the market, it's not a problem. Listen, your brother Mohammed knows everything, but I tell you again, beware, this is the first lesson I give you, I have meant to tell you this for a long time: nothing on the phone.

Yahia: Not even the call centers?

Ahmed: Nothing, nothing, when the moment comes you don't have to use anything, it's the first lesson, if you have a phone card throw it away.

Yahia: My Egyptian passport is not worth anything?

Ahmed: No, the Egyptian passport doesn't work.

Yahia: I am ready to sacrifice myself.

Ahmed: Brother Yahia, I appreciate your enthusiasm, but you have to keep calm, consider yourself already in paradise just for the fact that you are ready to sacrifice your life.

[The men recite verses of the Quran together.]

Ahmed: You have to know that jihad has different mechanisms, different components. There is knowledge, information, study. . . . Why don't you take care of obtaining information on the [Egyptian] Embassy and on the different movements of the diplomats and the employees? Try to get to know somebody from the embassy, because we need to know, always, if our brothers have to come in or out. You have to know that our brothers need information on the consulates in Europe. We have to develop this issue. Anyways, if you make a commitment, don't forget that you already have a commitment with God. I met several brothers of jihad, may God bless them, and they didn't have documents, anything, but they are ready for jihad, they don't have money, they don't have anything . . . oh my God . . . oh my God. . . . You have to know that there was a group that was ready in Holland, then, for different reasons, the knot was untied and now there is just one who is ready, he is worried, he just got out of jail, but everything at due time. You have to know that I met other brothers, that little by little I created with just a few things, before they were drug dealers, criminals, I introduced them to faith and now they are the first ones to ask me when it's the moment for jihad. Some of them went to Afghanistan and others are praying and waiting . . . [. . .] You have to know that we are emigrants of God. We are for jihad, we believe in God and in his Prophet Mohammed, because everything is allowed, including marrying Christian women because we need the documents. We have to be everywhere, in Germany, Holland, London. We are dominating Europe with our presence. We need the women to obtain the documents, because we are for the cause of God and with time you'll learn many things.[86]

Italian investigators apparently had been given the confession of the mastermind of the Madrid bombings on a silver platter. A few days later, on June 7, police arrested Ahmed and Yahia inside their Milan apartment and charged them with belonging to a terrorist organization.[87] While the words of Ahmed cannot be taken as completely truthful—they are intended, at least in part, to impress his young recruit—without question his arrest took off the streets a man deeply involved with terrorist activities across Europe. Moreover, Ahmed was the perfect recruiter, a lone wolf who traveled throughout Europe and spotted young radical Muslims who could serve the needs of the organization: "before they were drug dealers, criminals, I introduced them to faith and now they are the first ones to ask me when it's the moment for jihad." His relationship with Yahia provides revealing insights into the process of recruiting young Muslims living in Europe for terrorist activities.

Ahmed was born in Egypt in 1971; for five years he served in the Egyptian army, where he joined the specialized Explosives Brigade in Port Said. Because Ahmed had a degree in electronics from an Egyptian technical school as well, he was skilled in the two areas most essential for making bombs. According to Egyptian authorities, Ahmed was also a member of the Islamic Jihad, and, in the mid-1990s he served time at the Abu Za'abal jail, a facility that the Egyptian government uses to detain Islamic fundamentalists and other political prisoners.[88] He is first known to have been in Europe in 1999, when he was arrested by French authorities as he attempted to cross the French border from Germany without documents. He was detained for a few months and then sent to a camp in Lebach, a small town near the French border, where German authorities place asylum seekers while they process their applications.[89]

Ahmed immediately applied for political asylum, claiming to be a Palestinian—a tactic common among Middle Eastern immigrants, since most European governments give Palestinians preferential treatment. Because Ahmed had no documents, his claim could not be verified. Nevertheless, German authorities granted him temporary asylum and allowed him to stay in Lebach, even though Palestinian representatives who had interviewed him reported their doubts about his story.[90] A conversation between Ahmed, Yahia, and another guest in the Milan apartment reveals other sophisticated methods that the Egyptian used to hide his real identity from German officials:

Hussam: Have you been to Germany?

Ahmed: Yes, I lived in Germany

Hussam: Is Germany a nice place?

Ahmed: Yes, they are organized, if you work or study and they are not after you, they respect you. They are people who wake up early, they are workers, at 8 they are already at work, did you hear that, Yahia? But, unfortunately, half of my friends in Germany have been arrested. In Germany if you have documents you live well; I had a lot of Palestinian friends. For them it's easy to get the documents, they ask for political asylum. I also lived with them, in a refugee center. The police are very strict there, especially since they have begun taking fingerprints.

Yahia: Were you wanted?

Ahmed: Yes. Once I scratched my fingers, once I used transparent glue and another time, when I was at the refugee center and I claimed to be Palestinian, I used a product . . . there is a special product that modifies fingerprints. I drove them crazy. In Germany I had to be ready because every two or three months they took your fingerprints, so you should keep the product with you. This way they never find you, you confuse them, they will never find out your nationality.

[The men laugh together.]

Ahmed: In Germany the thing was repetitive, they came by surprise every month, two months, three months . . . but I drove them crazy, one day they arrested me and then they freed me, they told me, "It's not you." I know a way that allows me to change my fingerprints continuously, they are never the same. They had this law and they would get me every two, three months and I continuously changed my fingerprints. By now they erase by themselves, not even the American services will find me, they cannot find me [in their database].

Yahia: What do you mean, even if they take your fingerprints they cannot find you?

Ahmed: Yes, if you want I can show you that now I have certain fingerprints and tomorrow a different set. I know a technique that does not ever lead to your fingerprints. I know who I am, they don't know who I am; you are illegal but you go around legally.[91]

In Lebach, Ahmed immediately emerged as a leader. Fluent in English and Spanish, he became the spokesman for the more than two thousand asylum seekers living in the camp, dealing with German authorities on their behalf. Ahmed also became the main imam of the camp, preaching his radical views to hundreds of Muslim detainees. His sermons attracted the attention of local authorities, who began to monitor him sporadically.[92] The surveillance was not very tight, however, and a couple of weeks before the attacks of 9/11, Ahmed disappeared from the camp. "Each month, a lot of people disappear here," commented one employee. "I don't know how they do it, but each month we have to close a lot of files." The "disappearances" might be explained by the camp's lack of any guards or barriers to prevent the asylum seekers from leaving.[93] Illegal aliens—and in this case, terrorists—are free to "escape" whenever they want.

From Lebach, Ahmed moved to Madrid, where, as already noted, he befriended Fakhet and his group. He then moved to Paris, where he became involved in forging documents to facilitate the immigration of other militants. He returned to Madrid, but left the Spanish capital for Italy shortly before the March 11 attacks. In Milan, he began to plan new operations. Conversations were intercepted by DIGOS between Ahmed and two North Africans, one in Paris and one in Brussels, who apparently were receiving his orders for an attack. Italian authorities, afraid that a sequel to the Madrid attacks was in process, shared the content of the wiretapped conversations with their French and Belgian counterparts in real time, and arrests were made in both countries.[94]

But in Milan, the Egyptian also continued his recruiting efforts, and Yahia, his young roommate and fellow countryman, was the ideal recruit. The twenty-one-year-old, who had immigrated illegally to Italy just a few months earlier, immediately developed a morbid fascination with Ahmed's tales of jihad and martyrdom. Day and night, the two watched gruesome videos and listened to radical tapes. The following conversation taped by DIGOS is particularly telling:

> Ahmed: When you see brother Mohammed [the librarian of a Milan mosque, either the ICI or Via Quaranta], ask him to show you the material. There you'll find what you want; if you are interested in culture there are the books and more.
>
> Yahia: Yes.
>
> Ahmed: Tell Mohammed to introduce you to the great culture, it will teach you everything, in the library there is everything you are interested in, if you are really interested in jihad, if you want to see movies of all the operations, they have been all documented, only Spain is missing.
>
> Yahia: All?
>
> Ahmed: All, all. And you also see the brothers, you see the movies from Chechnya, Afghanistan, Algeria, thousands of things, thousands . . .
>
> Yahia: And where does all this stuff come from?
>
> Ahmed: After September 11 I was forced to move everything from Spain to Paris because in Spain there was too much movement of secret services . . . [inaudible] . . . I began with the normal things up until the very important things.
>
> Yahia: Good.
>
> Ahmed: Look, you watch them and start studying for jihad, for jihad and martyrdom.

Yahia: Is there also audio material about this?

Ahmed: There is everything, but I think that for you it would be better to read, so that each page enters inside you and explains the meaning to you. There are about 2,000 pages that teach you what is the meaning of jihad. Then you can listen. Look at me, I always have the cassette on martyrdom, I always listen to it.

Yahia: Do you have it here?

Ahmed: Yes, yes, I have it here right now, "The strength of the martyr." I also have other ones that talk about martyrdom, many others. But listen to me, you also have to start watching the videos, watch and learn, there are about 300 tapes of actions of the mujahideen in Chechnya, Afghanistan, Algeria, Kashmir, and in other countries. Technically they are very interesting tapes, there you can learn many things, they are particular tapes.

Yahia: Can I listen to this? So that I start to memorize.

Ahmed: Please.

[Ahmed turns the stereo on and they listen to the tape.]

Ahmed: Go to Mohammed and learn![95]

Ahmed spent hours showing Yahia how to activate mobile phones via computer, focusing specifically on software with which a user can send the same text message to a number of previously selected mobile phones. The technology-savvy Ahmed introduced his disciple to "Oxygen Phone Manager 2," a program that enables a computer to command all the functions of a Nokia cell phone. The importance of this lesson is obvious: The bombs on the Madrid trains were set off by mobile phones activated from a distance.[96]

While under constant surveillance by Italian authorities, the two men read books and watched tapes about jihad. Ahmed was also obsessed with the Internet, spending hours surfing the Web for Islamist sites. Together, he and Yahia watched online clips of Western hostages being murdered by Zarqawi's group in Iraq. "Watch closely. This is the policy of the sword. Slaughter him! Cut his head off! God is great!" cheered Ahmed like a soccer fan at a game during the footage of the beheading of Nicholas Berg, the twenty-six-year-old American businessman beheaded by Zarqawi in May 2004. And when Yahia, horrified by the guttural noises made by the American as his captors chopped at his neck, asked if such killing was not a sin, Ahmed was quick to respond: "It's never a sin! It's never a sin for the cause. Everyone must end up like this."[97]

Ahmed was brainwashing Yahia, turning the already-radicalized young man into the weapon that has made Islamic terrorism so successful: a suicide bomber. As another conversation proved, he had done similar work in Madrid months earlier, showing the same tapes and giving the same speeches to Fakhet and the other train bombers who blew themselves up in Leganes:

> Ahmed: These are very particular tapes . . . they teach the direction of the martyr. These make everything easier, when you listen to them they enter inside your body, but you have to listen to them continuously. I listen to them continuously. . . . Even now that I am working during the break, I use both the CD and the cassette . . . while for you it is better if you listen to the cassettes first and then to the CD.
>
> Yahia: Fine.
>
> Ahmed: In particular, this tape has an amazing voice . . . it enters inside your veins. Everybody in Spain learned this cassette by heart. It gives you a lot of security and tranquillity. It takes away your fear.
>
> Yahia: Come on, come on, give me one so that I can learn it.
>
> Ahmed: Yes, but you have to learn it by heart.
>
> Yahia: No, no . . . I will learn it by heart.[98]

MORE AL QAEDA LINKS, MORE ATTACKS

The evidence incriminating Ahmed, who was extradited to Spain in December 2004,[99] is solid. But Spanish authorities are convinced that Ahmed is not the attacks' only mastermind and are still pursuing other leads. One man who might have had a leading role in the bombings is Amer Azizi, whose fingerprints were found in the country house used by the cell to fabricate the bombs.[100] The experienced Moroccan jihadi, who married a Spanish woman and lived in Spain for almost a decade, is believed to be the link between the loose-knit group of immigrants from Lavapies and al Qaeda's leadership. "Without a doubt, he was more important that the Tunisian," commented a Spanish official. "Azizi was the brains, he was the link between the Moroccans and the rest of al Qaeda."[101]

Born in Morocco in 1967, Azizi is a battle-hardened militant who fought in Bosnia and, in the late 1990s, trained in the Afghan camp of Martyr Abu Yahyia, where hundreds of other Moroccan fundamentalists received instruction.[102] The graduates of the camp later formed the nucleus of the Moroccan Islamic Combatant Group (Groupe Islamique Combattant Marocain, or GICM), one of the organizations believed to be behind the 2003 Casablanca bombings. Operating out of Madrid, where he established close relations with Yarkas, Azizi is a true globe-trotter of jihad, having met with known terrorists on four continents. He is also believed to have had close connections with some of the key players in the 9/11 attacks; Spanish magistrates have accused him of organizing the crucial July 2001 meeting between Mohammed Atta and Ramzi Binalshibh in Cambrils, a Spanish coastal town. Moreover, his phone number was found in the possession of the would-be "twentieth hijacker," Zacarias Moussaoui, when the French native was arrested in Minnesota in August 2001.[103]

In Madrid, Azizi, who was also known as Othman al Andalusi, frequented the Alhambra restaurant and drank water from Mecca with the other Moroccans at Berraj's barbershop, becoming friends with Fakhet and Zougam.[104] While some reports indicate that he had a reputation of being a drug addict, his religious zealotry was well-known to Spanish counterterrorism officials, who had monitored him since the end of the 1990s.[105] Azizi had fully displayed his fanaticism on June 10, 2000, after the death of Syria's president, Hafiz al-Assad. When the ambassadors from Arab countries went to the Madrid mosque attended by Yarkas's cell, Azizi attacked them, decrying their mourning for an "apostate ruler" and yelling, "Why do you come to pray for an infidel?"[106]

Three months later, Azizi traveled to Istanbul, where he met with other leaders of the Moroccan network to set up new routes by which recruits could travel to the Afghan training camps.[107] It was after the Istanbul meeting that Azizi crossed paths with Abu Musab al Zarqawi, who was then running a camp near Herat, a few kilometers from the Iranian border. Azizi apparently began sending the militants he had recruited to Afghanistan via Iran; at least two of them stayed to train in Zarqawi's camp. [108] And when Azizi managed to escape the November 2001 antiterrorist crackdown, leaving Spain two days before the wave of arrests that dismantled much of the Madrid cell, he found refuge in Iran, where Zarqawi was also reportedly hiding after the fall of the Taliban.[109]

Spanish authorities have repeatedly searched for a link between Abu Musab al Zarqawi and the Madrid bombings. Azizi could be this link—an operative who had extensive ties to Spain, knew most of the perpetrators, and had been in close contact with Zarqawi. Investigators believe that Azizi may have sneaked back into Spain shortly before the attacks to coordinate the operation under Zarqawi's orders. A senior Spanish official told the *Los Angeles Times*, "There are people who have seen Azizi in Spain after the attacks. It looks like he came back and may have directed the others. If he was here, his background would make it likely that he was the top guy. We have reliable witness accounts that he was here in significant places connected to the plot. The idea of Azizi as a leader has become more solid."[110]

In Spain, Azizi's most trustworthy contacts were two Syrian brothers, Mouhannad and Moutaz Almallah. The men were detained in the immediate aftermath of the attacks, but soon released. The men were re-arrested in the spring of 2005, when Spanish authorities realized that, "according to all we know to this point," without the "recruiting, indoctrination and direction of the Almallah brothers, the March 11 attacks possibly would not have occurred."[111] But the importance of the Almallah brothers was not initially fully grasped by Spanish authorities, who had also received a very detailed tip on them a year before the attacks. On February 12, 2003, the wife of Mouhannad Almallah entered a Madrid police station and told officers that her husband was planning a car bomb attack in Madrid and that the likely targets were the towers of Plaza de Castilla, a modern and imposing structure located on one of Madrid's busiest arteries. The woman told officers that her Madrid apartment was often visited by men who watched jihadi tapes, and she identified a few of them as key players in the March 11 plot such as Fakhet and Ghalyoun.[112] The story, which constitutes another example of how Spanish authorities did not pursue Islamist terrorists aggressively enough before March 11, is also extremely important in showing that attacks in Spain had been planned well before the country landed its support to the US invasion of Iraq, since the conflict had not even begun when Mrs. Almallah tipped Spanish authorities off.[113]

Another hypothesis advanced by investigators is that Azizi was acting as the deputy not of Zarqawi but of Abu Musab al Suri, the former editor of the *Al Ansar*, the newsletter of the GIA (Groupes Islamiques Armés, the Armed Islamic Group) mentioned in chapter 4. Al Suri, a longtime resident of Spain who had obtained citizenship by marrying a Spanish convert to Islam, had developed close contacts with Yarkas and other members of the "old" Madrid cell before moving to London and then to Afghanistan, where he worked as a trainer in an al Qaeda camp.[114] At the time of the Madrid attacks, al Suri was believed to be operating out of Iran; authorities suspect that he was the one who, in December 2003, dispatched Azizi to Spain to supervise the operation.[115]

In fact, in November 2004, the FBI told Spanish authorities of intelligence indicating that the individual who had assisted Atta and Binalshibh in their July 2001 meeting was the same person who activated the Madrid cell that carried out the bombing. While the FBI is not wholly certain that this man was Amer Azizi, it is convinced that he was acting on behalf of al Suri. In November 2004, the US State Department offered a $5 million reward for information leading to the capture of al Suri, who (according to some sources) could have recently spent some time fighting beside Zarqawi's insurgents in Iraq.[116]

Even as authorities explore the strong connection to al Qaeda, they are led by the backgrounds of the perpetrators to investigate their links to Moroccan terrorist groups such as the Moroccan Islamic Combatant Group and Salafiya Jihadia. As already noted, most of the March 11 bombers were Moroccans, and most had significant ties to both groups.

Drawing on the evidence they have collected over more than two years, Spanish and Moroccan investigators see the Madrid attacks of March 2004 as the second large operation conceived by the same network that carried out the Casablanca bombings in May 2003. The links between the two operations are multiple.

One of the men who, along with Ahmed, assumed a leadership role in the Madrid cell after Yarkas's arrest was a Moroccan, Mustafa al Mauymouny. He is considered to be one of the top leaders of Salafia Jihadia, and he spent time in Madrid before being arrested in Morocco for his role in the Casablanca bombings.[117] In a change that could be interpreted as symbolizing a switch in the Madrid cell's affiliation, in 2003 Fakhet broke up with the daughter of Ahmed Brahim, the jailed moneyman of the "old" al Qaeda cell in Spain, and married Mauymouny's sixteen-year-old sister. Mauymouny also paid the rent of the countryside house where the bombers assembled the explosives.[118] Another connection between Casablanca and Madrid is a thirty-five-year-old Moroccan imam, Hicham Temsamani, who during his time in Madrid became one of the spiritual leaders of the group that met at Berraj's barbershop in Lavapies, leading the prayers and water drinking.[119] Temsamani served as imam at a mosque in Toledo as well, and he was arrested in June 2003 by Spanish authorities for his alleged involvement in the Casablanca bombings and in a plot to blow up a refinery in France.[120] Temsamani also provides one of the links between Moroccan Islamic fundamentalism and drug trafficking, as his brother Rachid is one of Morocco's most famous drug lords, controlling the shipment of tons of hashish, cocaine, and Ecstasy from his native Tetuan to Spain and the rest of Europe.[121] Indeed, a powerful alliance was forged between drug kingpins and religious fanatics in Tetuan, a smuggling paradise in northern Morocco. This was the hometown of Jamal Ahmidan, who financed the March 11 bombings by drug trafficking. According to Spanish authorities, Ahmidan, a known drug dealer, obtained the explosives from a Spanish miner who had been convicted of drug-related offenses in exchange for thirty kilograms of hashish.[122] And Ahmidan also flew to the island of Mallorca shortly before March 11 to arrange the sale of hashish and Ecstasy, planning to use the profits for additional attacks.[123] His scheme was hardly new—Moroccan groups used drug money to finance both the thwarted attacks against American ships in Gibraltar in 2002 and the Casablanca bombings—but terrorists' use of drug trafficking is viewed with growing alarm by European authorities; they believe that terrorist organizations have infiltrated around two-thirds of the Moroccan hashish trade, worth about $12.5 billion annually.[124]

Following Takfir's ideology of "necessity permits the forbidden," the Madrid bombers used any means available to achieve their murderous goals. They dated women, drank wine, and even sold drugs. But everything was done for the cause, and their behavior had the approval of senior figures in the network, respected leaders with more religious knowledge. One of those leaders, a Spanish official revealed, was Yarkas: "We know that when Barakat [Yarkas] had been consulted in the past, he justified drug trafficking if it was for Islam. He saw it as part of jihad."[125] According to Moroccan intelligence, the sale of drugs for the Madrid bombing was legitimized by a fatwa issued "within the organization responsible for the attacks," which "provided religious legality to the use of criminal acts, such as drug trafficking, to finance the perpetration of any action aimed at destroying the infidel enemy."[126]

The Madrid plot is a puzzle that will be difficult to solve in its entirety. Authorities are sure that no single group ordered the attacks. Those involved were Moroccan Islamists belonging to local terrorist groups, remnants of the pre–9/11 al Qaeda network operating in Europe, experienced jihadis linked to Abu Musab al Zarqawi, and drug traffickers with newly acquired sympathy for fundamentalist Islam—a combination that represents the new face of al Qaeda in Europe. A year after the attacks, more than seventy individuals have been arrested and almost forty thousand pages of evidence collected.[127] Yet authorities still do not have the full picture: "The great majority of the perpetrators are identified, dead or in prison," said a senior Spanish counterterrorism official interviewed by the *New York Times* on the one-year anniversary of the attacks. "But we cannot say that we have all of them. There are questions that remain unclear. The most important is: Who masterminded March 11?"[128]

And even as Spanish investigators are trying to find all the answers about March 11, new threats continuously emerge. On the night of April 19, the body of Francisco Javier Torronteras, the Spanish agent who had died in the explosion of the Leganes apartment, was pulled from his tomb in a Madrid cemetery, dragged for six hundred meters, mutilated, doused with gas, and burned.[129] The barbaric act, which the Spanish Interior Ministry called an "Islamic rite of revenge,"[130] showed that Islamic fundamentalists were still active in the country. More evidence came in the following six months that despite Spain's withdrawal from Iraq, the terrorists had not "forgotten about Spain."

In September, police in Barcelona broke up a cell of ten Pakistanis, accusing them of providing logistical support to al Qaeda and other groups. According to Spanish authorities, the cell raised money by falsifying documents and selling drugs. More than one hundred eighty grams of heroin were discovered in the raids, together with radical Islamist tapes and 18,000 €.[131] The group, which is believed to have sent money to the Pakistani militants who killed *Wall Street Journal* reporter Daniel Pearl in 2002, also possessed videos showing details of two Barcelona high-rises commonly referred to as "Spain's twin towers." Investigators suspect the tapes were surveillance for future attacks.[132]

The confirmation that Islamic terrorists were planning new attacks on Spanish soil came in October 2004, when a two-pronged police operation netted more than forty militants throughout the country. Spanish authorities reported that the group was planning to deploy a suicide bomber to drive a van loaded with five hundred kilograms of explosives inside the Audiencia Nacional, the country's most important criminal court, where all the cases related to Islamic fundamentalism are investigated and prosecuted. The men were charged with the attempted murder of four hundred people, the estimated average number of individuals who work and visit the building every day.[133] Authorities also suspect that the group was planning an additional wave of suicide bombings aimed at the headquarters of the Popular Party, the Atocha train station, and the famous Santiago Bernabéu stadium, where more than one hundred thousand soccer fans attend each home game of Real Madrid.[134]

The group dismantled in the fall of 2004 bore striking resemblances to the cell that carried out the March 11 train bombings. Led by Mohammed Achraf, an Algerian who had taken up radical Islam in jail while serving two stints for credit card fraud between 1999 and 2002, the group was an odd mixture of drug dealers, document forgers, and experienced Islamic fundamentalists who had come together almost by chance in various Spanish prisons.[135] The core of the group was patiently put together by Achraf between 2001 and 2002, when frequent fights between Spanish and Muslim inmates in the Salamanca prison led the latter to organize themselves in a group that named itself "Martyrs of Morocco." And like the Madrid train bombers, the Martyrs of Morocco began planning their deadly operation well before Spain became involved in the Iraqi war; investigators believe that the attack against the Audiencia Nacional was conceived in 2002.[136]

The history of the Martyrs of Morocco reveals how European prisons serve as a breeding ground for Islamic fundamentalism. In Salamanca, Achraf's constant and aggressive indoctrination radicalized scores of North African immigrants who had pursued a life of crime and "unbelief" in Spain, turning them into Islamic fundamentalists and volunteers for suicide operations. Achraf personally recruited dozens of Muslim prisoners, following their movements even after they had been released. According to Spanish authorities, Achraf kept meticulous tabs on his recruits inside and outside of jail, establishing a tight-knit network that covered various Spanish cities and jails. The men stayed in touch via personal contact, telephone, or e-mail, and Achraf and his lieutenants made sure to constantly correspond with recruits so that "their fundamentalist point of views would not be extinguished."[137]

The Martyrs of Morocco also included some experienced jihadis, members of the Algerian GIA and GSPC who had operated in Spain for years. One of Achraf's closest helpers, for example, was Abdelkrim Bensmail, a GIA member who had been convicted in 1997 for terrorist activities; he was an associate of Allekema Lamari, one of the seven men who blew themselves up in Leganes.[138] The combination of young disenfranchised Muslim criminals and hardened Islamic radicals, confined together for months in the harsh prison environment, proved to be explosive. By 2003, when Achraf was already out of Salamanca, the group was ready. "I give you the good news that I have formed a group of good brothers who are willing to die at any given moment for the project of God, they and we are only waiting to be released," he wrote to Said Afis, a twenty-three-year-old Algerian who had originally been detained in Salamanca for theft. "We are yearning for this and we have the weapons and you will be with us."[139]

While the more experienced jihadis provided the cell with ideological support, the recruits put their criminal skills to use for their new cause. Thus the Mauritanian inmate Kamara Bidahima Diadie obtained the explosives from one of his contacts in the Spanish criminal under-world.[140] Experienced forgers procured false documents and other felons committed additional crimes to raise money. Funds for the attacks were allegedly raised through robberies carried out in Switzerland, where Achraf had moved after his release from Salamanca.[141] In a phone call intercepted by Spanish authorities a few months before the arrests, Achraf told one of his associates, "It's not a problem to find the money necessary to buy the explosives. There is plenty of it in Switzerland and we only have to take it from the infidels."[142]

Authorities throughout Europe fear that the Martyrs of Morocco are a harbinger of things to come and acknowledge that prisons constitute fertile territory for the efforts of experienced recruiters. And while in Spain Muslims represent only 12 percent of the general penal population[143]—though low, a number still disproportionally higher than in the general population—in other countries the percentages are much higher; in France, they constitute more than half of those in prison. Recruiters know that inmates represent the perfect targets and exploit their weaknesses. According to Spanish authorities, the Martyrs of Morocco "focused on people sentenced for petty crimes who then are introduced to this extremist vision of Islam as a manner to expiate their sins, to reject a previous way of life, and which would purify them, in this case, through martyrdom."[144]

September 11, 2001, brought about "a radical change in Muslim prisoners," observed Juan Figueroa, the vice president of the Spanish prison employees union. "After Sept. 11, the inmates radicalized. . . . Groups of hard-core Muslims began to form, and they pressured other Muslims." Information gathered about the Martyrs of Morocco triggered significant changes in the internal procedures of Spanish jails. Hundreds of radical Muslim inmates were either transferred or isolated, and prison guards were instructed to pay particular attention to the activities of Muslim inmates.[145] But Spain is hardly the only Western country where fundamentalists operate undetected inside prisons. Indeed, this particular case featured terrorists detained in two other countries who were free to communicate and plot while behind bars.

Swiss authorities admitted that Achraf, the leader of the group, had been allowed to make phone calls and send uncensored e-mail while detained in a Zurich facility before the November arrests. Though he was being held for immigration violations, he was known to Swiss intelligence as a suspected terrorist; yet he was able to continue preparing for the attacks while in custody. In fact, because of his good conduct and the overcrowding of the detention facility, Achraf was scheduled to be released a few days after the plot was discovered.[146]

Even more shockingly, Spanish authorities discovered that Achraf had received letters from Mohammed Salameh, who is serving a life sentence in the Supermax, America's most secure federal prison, for his part in the 1993 World Trade Center bombing. He wrote several times to Achraf, wishing him luck in his future endeavors. "Oh God!" wrote Salameh in February 2003. "Make us live with happiness, make us die as martyrs, may we be united on the Day of Judgment."[147] Behind the bars of the West's most secure jails, the old guard was symbolically passing on the baton to a new generation of Islamic terrorists.

NOTES

1. Norwegian Defense Research Establishment (Forsvarets Forksninginstitutt, or FFI) "FFI Explains al Qaida Document," March 19, 2004.

2. Ibid.

3. "Spanish Diplomat Killed in Iraq," CNN, October 9, 2003.

4. "Spanish Agents, Japanese Diplomats Killed in Iraq," CNN, November 29, 2003.

5. Lawrence Wright, "The Terror Web," *New Yorker*, January 17, 2005.

6. El Mundo special report, "11-M. Masacre en Madrid," http://www.el-mundo.es/documentos/2004/03/espana/atentados11m/index.html.

7. Wright, "The Terror Web."

8. El Mundo, "11-M. Masacre en Madrid."

9. Wright, "The Terror Web."

10. El Mundo, "11-M. Masacre en Madrid."

11. "Quien os Protegerá de Nosotros?" *El Mundo*, March 12, 2004.

12. El Mundo, "11-M. Masacre en Madrid."

13. Ibid.

14. Casimiro García-Abadillo, *11-M. La Venganza* (Madrid: La Esfera de los Libros, 2005), pp. 115–19.

15. Spanish Ministry of the Interior, *Actividad Antiterrorista,* Summary of Anti-Terrorist Activities, 2004, pp. 113–14.

16. Keith B. Richburg, "Five Held in Madrid Blasts; Tape Asserts Al Qaeda Responsibility," *Washington Post*, March 14, 2004.

17. El Mundo, "11-M. Masacre en Madrid."

18. "Al Qaeda 'Claims Madrid Bombings,'" BBC, March 14, 2004.

19. "Transcripcion del video en el que Al Qaeda reivindica el 1-M," *El Mundo*, March 14, 2004.

20. Wright, "The Terror Web."

21. El Mundo, "11-M. Masacre en Madrid."

22. Elaine Sciolino, "Following Attacks, Spain's Governing Party Is Beaten," *New York Times*, March 15, 2004.

23. Indictment of Reda Zerroug and others, Audiencia Nacional, Madrid, January 14, 2005.

24. Indictment of Imad Eddin Barakat Yarkas, Juzgado Central de Instruccion n. 005, Proceeding 35/2001, Madrid, September 17, 2003.

25. Wright, "The Terror Web."

26. "Coping with the Past," *Guardian*, July 28, 2004.

27. Italian intelligence officer, interview with the author, Milan, March 2005.

28. Giles Tremlett, "Supporters Desert Aznar as Spaniards Reject Conflict," *Guardian*, February 18, 2003.

29. David Sharrock, "The Accidental Premier," *Times* (London), September 19, 2004.

30. García-Abadillo, *11-M. La Venganza*, p. 120; Zougam is quoted in Tim Golden, Desmond Butler, and Don Van Natta Jr., "Suspect in Madrid Carnage Not an Unknown," *New York Times*, March 22, 2004.

31. Keith Johnson, John Carreyrou, David Crawford, and Karby Leggett, "Islamist's Odyssey: Morocco to Madrid, a Bomb Suspect Grew Radicalized," *Wall Street Journal*, March 19, 2004; Spanish Ministry of the Interior, *Actividad Antiterrorista*, pp. 113–14.

32. Spanish Ministry of the Interior, *Actividad Antiterrorista*, pp. 113–14.

33. Wright, "The Terror Web."

34. Johnson et al., "Islamist's Odyssey."

35. Indictment of Imad Eddin Barakat Yarkas.

36. Ibid.; Keith Johnson, David Crawford, and Craig Karmin, "Spain's Bomb Probe Traces Web of al Qaeda Links," *Wall Street Journal*, March 16, 2004.

37. Johnson et al., "Islamist's Odyssey."

38. García-Abadillo, *11-M. La Venganza*, p. 119.

39. Ibid., p. 116.

40. Peter Finn and Keith B. Richburg, "Madrid Probe Turns to Islamic Cell in Morocco," *Washington Post*, March 20, 2004.

41. Tim Golden and Don Van Natta Jr., "Suspect in Madrid Was under Scrutiny in 3 Countries," *New York Times*, March 17, 2004.

42. Johnson et al., "Islamist's Odyssey."

43. Mark Townsend, John Hooper, Greg Bearup, Paul Harris, Peter Beaumont, Anthony Burnett, Martin Bright, Jason Burke, and Nick Pelham, "The Secret War," *Observer*, March 21, 2004.

44. Golden and Van Natta, "Suspect in Madrid."

45. Spanish Ministry of the Interior, *Actividad Antiterrorista*.

46. Indictment of Imad Eddin Barakat Yarkas.

47. Sebastian Rotella, "Terrorists at the Table; Islamic Militants in Europe Blend Political Sophistication and Crude Violence to Influence Events, as the Bombings in Madrid Show," *Los Angeles Times*, March 6, 2005.

48. Spanish Ministry of the Interior, *Actividad Antiterrorista*, p. 122.

49. García-Abadillo, *11-M. La Venganza*, p. 259

50. "Bomb Found on Spain Rail," BBC, April 2, 2004; Spanish Ministry of the Interior, *Actividad Antiterrorista*, p. 122.

51. García-Abadillo, "*11-M. La Venganza*," pp. 258–64.

52. Ibid., p. 265.

53. Wright, "The Terror Web."

54. García-Abadillo, "*11-M. La Venganza*," p. 262.

55. Wright, "The Terror Web."

56. El Mundo, "11-M. Masacre en Madrid."

57. "Inferno Terror Threat to Spain," CBS News, April 5, 2004.

58. EFE, March 10, 2005; Giles Tremlett, "Madrid Bombers Planned More Attacks: Video Found in Flat of Dead Terrorists Gave Ultimatum," *Guardian*, April 9, 2004.

59. Wright, "The Terror Web."

60. García-Abadillo, *11-M. La Venganza*, p. 265.

61. Wright, "The Terror Web."

62. Mar Roman, "Madrid Terror Suspect Left a Goodbye Note for His Family Saying He Wanted to Become a Martyr," AP, February 16, 2005; for the authorities' view of his role, see Spanish Ministry of the Interior, Summary of Anti-Terrorist Activities, 2004.

63. El Mundo, "11-M. Masacre en Madrid."

64. Tremlett, "Madrid Bombers Planned More Attacks."

65. "Coping with the Past," *Guardian*, July 28, 2004.

66. Spanish Ministry of the Interior, *Actividad Antiterrorista*, p. 121.

67. García-Abadillo, *11-M. La Venganza*, p. 132.

68. James Graff, "Morocco: The New Face of Terror?" *Time*, March 21, 2005.

69. García-Abadillo, *11-M. La Venganza*, pp. 132–33.

70. Ibid., p. 133.

71. Graff, "Morocco: The New Face of Terror?"

72. Sebastian Rotella, "Jihad's Unlikely Alliance," *Los Angeles Times*, May 23, 2005.

73. "Cinco de los Terroristas del 11-M Estaban Fichados y Varios Fueron Vigilados y Filmados por la Policia," *El Pais*, April 18, 2004.

74. Graff, "Morocco: The New Face of Terror?"

75. García-Abadillo, *11-M. La Venganza*, p. 134.

76. "Cinco de los Terroristas del 11-M."

77. Spanish Ministry of the Interior, Summary of Anti-Terrorist Activities, 2004.

78. García-Abadillo, *11-M. La Venganza*, p. 118.

79. Johnson et al., "Islamist's Odyssey."

80. García-Abadillo, *11-M. La Venganza*, pp. 136–39; "Spain Holds al-Qaeda Finance Suspect," BBC, April 23, 2002.

81. Sebastian Rotella, "Jihad's Unlikely Alliance."

82. Tribunal of Milan, Indictment of Rabei Osman Ahmed El Sayed and others, June 5, 2004.

83. Ibid.

84. Ibid.

85. Ibid.

86. Ibid.

87. Ibid.

88. Ibid.

89. H. Gude, J. Hufelschulte, E. Kallinger, T. Staisch, C. Sturm, "The Trail of a Preacher: Suspected Mastermind of Madrid Attacks Lived in Germany for Years as Rejected Asylum-Seeker," *Focus*, June 14, 2004. Accessed via Foreign Broadcast Information Service (FBIS).

90. Tribunal of Milan, Indictment of Rabei Osman Ahmed El Sayed and others.

91. Ibid.

92. Gude et al., "The Trail of a Preacher."

93. Craig Whitlock, "A Radical Who Remained Just out of Reach; Suspect in Madrid Attacks Moved Freely in Europe," *Washington Post*, November 14, 2004.

94. Tribunal of Milan, Indictment of Rabei Osman Ahmed El Sayed and others.

95. Ibid.

96. Ibid.

97. "Al Qaeda's New Front," *Frontline,* PBS, January 25, 2005, http://www.pbs.org/wgbh/pages/frontline/shows/front/.

98. Tribunal of Milan, Indictment of Rabei Osman Ahmed El Sayed and others.

99. "Al Qaeda's New Front."

100. "'El Tunecino' Empezo a Pensar en la Guerra Santa ante de los Atentados del 11-S," EFE, January 24, 2005.

101. Keith Johnson and David Crawford, "Madrid Bombing Suspect Is Key al Qaeda Liaison," *Wall Street Journal*, April 7, 2004.

102. García-Abadillo, *11-M. La Venganza*, pp. 142–44; Rotella, "Terrorists at the Table."

103. Johnson and Crawford, "Madrid Bombing Suspect."

104. Indictment of Imad Eddin Barakat Yarkas; García-Abadillo, *11-M. La Venganza*, pp. 142–44.

105. Wright, "The Terror Web"; "Cinco de los Terroristas del 11-M."

106. Wright, "The Terror Web."

107. García-Abadillo, *11-M. La Venganza*, pp. 142–44.

108. Johnson and Crawford, "Madrid Bombing Suspect."

109. "Cinco de los Terroristas del 11-M"; Tribunal of Milan, Indictment of Muhamad Majid and others.

110. Sebastian Rotella, "Al Qaeda Fugitive Sought in Bombings," *Los Angeles Times*, April 14, 2004.

111. "Syrian Brothers Led Madrid Train Bombings," Reuters, August 2, 2005.

112. "La mujer del imputado del 11-M que se afilió al PSOE denunció en 2003 que quería cometer atentados," *El Mundo*, July 28, 2005.

113. Two weeks after the Madrid train bombings, police searched Mouhannad Almallah's apartment and found sketches of New York's Grand Central Terminal. Consequently, federal and local authorities tightened security inside and around the busy railroad terminal.

114. Indictment of Imad Eddin Barakat Yarkas.

115. "Report: FBI Finds Link Between 9/11, Madrid Bombers," Reuters, November 11, 2004.

116. US State Department, "Secretary of State Colin L. Powell Authorizes Reward," press release, November 18, 2004; Italian intelligence officer, interview with the author.

117. "La Policia Siguió a el Tunecino Hasta Poco Dias Antes del 11-M," *El Mundo*, October 6, 2004.

118. García-Abadillo, *11-M. La Venganza*, pp. 144–45.

119. Rotella, "Jihad's Unlikely Alliance."

120. Spanish Ministry of the Interior, Summary of Anti-Terrorist Activities, 2003.

121. "La filière espagnole," *Maroc Hebdo International*, September 12–18, 2003, http://www.maroc-hebdo.press.ma/MHinternet/Archives_571/html_571/lafiliere.html.

122. Spanish Ministry of the Interior, *Actividad Antiterrorista*.

123. Rotella, "Jihad's Unlikely Alliance."

124. Graff, "Morocco: The New Face of Terror?" p. 46.

125. Rotella, "Jihad's Unlikely Alliance."

126. I. Cembrero, "Moroccan Intelligence Report Warns of Possible New Terrorist Strikes," *International Herald Tribune*, March 22, 2005.

127. A. Eatwell, "3/11 Judge Aims for Mass Fall Trial of Terror Suspects," *International Herald Tribune*, February 17, 2005.

128. Elaine Sciolino, "Spain Continues to Uncover Terrorist Plots, Officials Say," *New York Times*, March 13, 2005.

129. El Mundo, "11-M. Masacre en Madrid."

130. Isambard Wilkinson, "Officer's Body Burnt in 'Islamic Revenge,'" *Telegraph*, April 20, 2004.

131. Spanish Ministry of the Interior, Summary of Anti-Terrorist Activities, 2004.

132. Sciolino, "Spain Continues to Uncover Terrorist Plots, Officials Say."

133. Spanish Ministry of the Interior, Summary of Anti-Terrorist Activities, 2004.

134. "El Segundo Commando Suicida Pretendia Volar Atocha, el Bernabeu o la Sede del PP," *Diario Sur*, November 3, 2004.

135. Indictment of Eddebdoubi Taoufik and others.

136. Tracy Wilkinson, "Spain Acts against Prisons Becoming Militant Hotbeds," *Los Angeles Times*, November 2, 2004.

137. Indictment of Eddebdoubi Taoufik and others.

138. Spanish Ministry of the Interiors, Summary of Anti-Terrorist Activities, 2004.

139. Indictment of Eddebdoubi Taoufik and others; Spanish Ministry of the Interior, Summary of Anti-Terrorist Activities, 2004.

140. Spanish Ministry of Interiors, Summary of Anti-Terrorist Activities, 2004.

141. Indictment of Eddebdoubi Taoufik and others.

142. Sylvain Besson, "Un Nouvel Episode d'une Longue Guerre de Polices," *Le Temps*, November 2, 2004.

143. Wilkinson, "Spain Acts against Prisons Becoming Militant Hotbeds."

144. Indictment of Eddebdoubi Taoufik and others.

145. Wilkinson, "Spain Acts against Prisons Becoming Militant Hotbeds."

146. Onna Coray, "Swiss Intelligence Knew Terror Suspect Had Links to Radical Islam," AP, October 27, 2004.

147. Copy of the original letter in possession of the author.

CHAPTER 12

THE VAN GOGH ASSASSINATION

I deem thee lost, O America.
I deem thee lost, O Europe.
I deem thee lost, O Holland.
I deem thee lost, O Hirshi Ali.
I deem thee lost, O unbelieving fundamentalist.
—Mohammed Bouyeri, letter pinned to the body of
Theo van Gogh (Amsterdam, November 2, 2004)

THE HOFSTAD GROUP AND THE VAN GOGH ASSASSINATION

The Madrid attacks represented the first strike on European soil by the Moroccans, a network that had been dangerously underestimated and overlooked by European authorities. The French antiterrorism magistrate Jean-Louis Bruguière has noted somberly, "The Moroccans are much more important than we thought. They have significant financial and logistics cells. And they turn out to be more structured and organized than other networks."[1] Though they played only a marginal role during the 1990s, in the past few years Moroccan groups have gained prominence in the European Islamist scene, filling the void created by the apparent demise of the Algerian network and other al Qaeda–linked structures.

Fundamentalist groups aiming at overthrowing the monarchy have operated in Morocco since the 1970s, but it was only at the end of the 1990s that groups with an extensive organization and strong ties to al Qaeda emerged there and in Europe.[2] Moroccan veterans of the Afghan training camps formed several groups such as the Moroccan Islamic Combatant Group (Groupe Islamique Combattant Marocain, GICM) and Salafiya Jihadia, loosely connected terrorist organizations that quickly established their strongholds in the poverty-ridden slums of the country's large cities and in the conservative rural areas of northern Morocco. The mix of poverty and fundamentalism, often spread by Saudi-financed Wahhabi schools and mosques, created a fertile recruiting pool for the Moroccan groups, whose ranks swelled rapidly.

The May 2003 Casablanca attacks revealed the Moroccan groups' dangerousness. The bombings were carried out by a score of young suicide bombers from the city's poor neighborhoods who had no previous ties to Islamic fundamentalism. Moroccan authorities believe that the men had been spotted, radicalized, and recruited within the span of a few months by experienced GICM members, who saw them as ideal trainees. One of the recruiters—Abdelkarim Mejatti, a veteran of Afghanistan who had studied in the United States—reportedly took the young men to the hills outside Casablanca, teaching them bomb-making skills and Wahhabi philosophy.[3] The Moroccan government's reaction was particularly forceful. More than five thousand suspected Islamic fundamentalists were arrested, and several GICM and Salafiya Jihadia leaders were sentenced to death. Authorities, admitting they had failed to notice the problem, estimate that the country hosts up to one hundred terrorist cells ready to carry out suicide attacks.[4] But Morocco's clampdown came after most of the real masterminds of the network had already left for Europe, where an extensive web of cells provided them with logistical support.

"There are cells in which the Moroccans are well integrated into the population. So they do not seem suspicious," explains the head of France's internal intelligence agency, DST (Direction de la Surveillance du Territoire). "They work. They have kids. They have fixed addresses. They pay rent. The networks are dispersed throughout Europe and are very autonomous."[5] European intelligence officials believe that the GICM and Salafiya Jihadia have meticulously created a web of highly independent sleeper cells throughout the Continent, counting on the fact that authorities were paying more attention to other networks—notably the Algerians' and the Egyptians'. And since Moroccans represent the largest Muslim immigrant group in many European countries, Moroccan militants can more easily hide their clandestine activities in plain sight.

After the Casablanca bombings, Moroccan authorities asked various European countries to extradite a number of Moroccan militants. Unpersuaded by the scant evidence provided by Rabat and afraid that the individuals would have faced torture or the death penalty on their return to Morocco, the countries denied most of the extradition requests. Nevertheless, several investigations of the European bases of the Moroccan network were opened, and authorities soon realized how widespread and well-organized it was. But only after the Madrid bombings, when it was clear that the Moroccan network had decided to bring its jihad to Europe, did most European countries begin to crack down on GICM and Salafiya Jihadia.

A senior GICM member, Youssef Belhadj, was arrested in Belgium a week after the Madrid bombings and charged with membership in a terrorist organization.[6] Released in July on bail, he was arrested again in February 2005 after Spanish authorities issued an international arrest warrant for him. Spanish magistrates believe that Belhadj, who had left his sister's Madrid apartment shortly before the train bombings, had been one of the masterminds behind the attacks—indeed, they think he is Abu Dujan al Afgani, the mystery man who claimed responsibility for the bombings in the tape found on March 13 near the Madrid mosque.[7] The final report by Spanish police on the Madrid bombings alleges that Belhadj chose March 11 as the day of the attacks on October 19, 2003, the day after al Jazeera broadcasted a tape where bin Laden threatened Spain for its involvement in Iraq. That day Belhadj also bought a new Belgian cell phone, providing a false name and

"March 11, 1921" as his date of birth. Knowing that the Spanish elections would have taken place in March, but ignoring the exact day, he decided for the eleventh, so that the Madrid attacks would have taken place exactly two and a half years after those in the United States.[8] Belhadj's sister Safia; her husband, Allal Moussaten; and the couple's two sons have also been arrested by Spanish authorities for their involvement in the train bombings.[9] Proving his close ties to Spain, Belhadj is also suspected of having facilitated the escape of Mohammed Afalah from Europe to Iraq. Afalah, a close associate of Fakhet and other key Madrid bombers who had escaped the Leganes siege, managed to leave Spain in April of 2004 and reached Belgium, where Youssef Belhadj and his brother Moumin gave him shelter in Maaseik, a small border town strategically located near the German and Dutch border.[10] Afalah shared an apartment with a close associate of Rabei Osman El Sayed Ahmed before leaving Belgium for Syria and Iraq. Authorities believe Afalah died in a suicide operation in Iraq in May of 2005.[11]

The small town of Maaseik was also the destination chosen by the El Haski brothers after the fall of the Taliban. The Moroccan nationals settled in the quiet Belgian border town of Maaseik after escaping the American dragnet in Afghanistan, continuing their terrorist activities undisturbed for almost three years. Investigators believe that El Houcine, Mehdi, and Hassan El Haski were key members of the European GICM network, maintaining contacts with militants in Holland, France, and Spain. El Houcine, who had fought in Chechnya and proudly kept a picture of himself taken with Osama bin Laden, turned himself in to Belgian authorities in July 2004.[12] His older brother, forty-one-year-old Hassan, was arrested by Spanish police in the Canary Islands in December 2004 and accused of being involved in planning and preparing the March 11 train bombings.[13]

Since the March 11 Madrid bombings Belgian authorities also netted more than twenty people linked to the Moroccan network; among the high-ranking GICM members they detained was Abdelkader Hakimi, a veteran of Bosnia, Chechnya, and Afghanistan who was directing the network while running a snack bar in a quiet suburb of Brussels.[14]

Other significant operations against the Moroccan network were carried out in Italy and Spain, where dozens of Moroccan militants connected to the

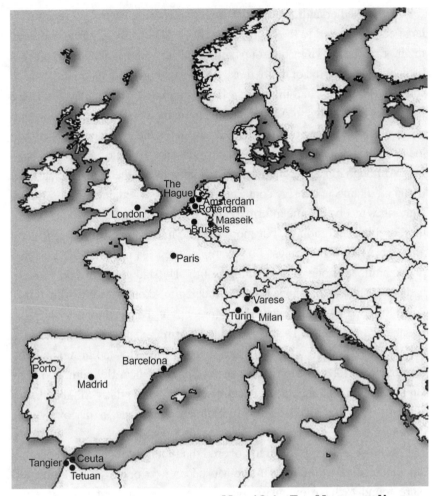

MAP 12.1. THE MOROCCAN NETWORK

Madrid bombers have been detained since March 2004.[15] In France, investigators dismantled a cell that raised hundreds of thousands of euros for the network (see chapter 2). Only England has been reluctant to take rigorous measures against the network; Mohammed al Gharbouzi, whom Moroccan authorities consider the founder of the GICM and one of the chief architects of the Casablanca bombings, still lives in London and enjoys the £1,000 a month that his wife collects from the British government.[16]

In the Netherlands, authorities were well aware of the presence of a large cell connected to the Moroccan network. Dutch intelligence had been monitoring the activities of groups of radicals in various cities for years and had noticed that some of them, mostly Moroccan immigrants or Dutch-born sons of Moroccans, had united in a large group that was regularly meeting in various apartments in Amsterdam, Rotterdam, and The Hague. Since the group used to convene often in The Hague, given the Dutch capital's central location, the group was dubbed by authorities the "Hofstad" (Dutch for *capital*). Although most of its members grew up in the Netherlands, the Hofstad group maintained extensive contacts with militants in other countries. Dutch authorities received some information on these contacts from Morocco after the Casablanca bombings, but more specific intelligence came from Spain after the Madrid bombings. For example, they learned that the encoded phone number of one of the members of the Hofstad group, Ismail Aknikh, had been found in the phone book of Abdeladim Akoudad, a GICM member jailed by Spain and accused by Morocco of being implicated in the Casablanca bombings. Despite Akoudad's firm denial, Spanish authorities believe that Akoudad was one of the leaders of the Hofstad group and had coordinated efforts of Moroccan cells in Spain, France, Belgium, and Holland.[17] Aknikh's phone number was also found in the diary of Abdelkader Hakimi when he was arrested by Belgian authorities, a discovery that demonstrated the circular connections of the network.[18]

Moreover, when Madrid uncovered the plot to blow up the Audiencia Nacional, some of the men in the Moroccan network who were arrested were found to have extensive ties to the Netherlands and the Hofstad group. Two of them, Abdul Ghaffar Hashemi (a Dutch citizen) and Mourad Yala, had lived in Holland and become friendly with some of the members of the group. Yala had earlier been arrested in the town of Geleen by Dutch police, who accused him of falsifying passports. According to Dutch media reports, Yala and Hashemi were suspected of having studied ways to turn laptop computers into time bombs while in the Netherlands. In addition, the mastermind of the Audiencia Nacional plot, Mohammed Achraf, is believed to have wired money to some of the members of the Hofstad group. [19]

The information provided by Madrid and Rabat on the extremists operating in the Netherlands caused Dutch authorities to step up their surveillance of the group. In October 2003, five militants with Hofstad connections were arrested "because there were serious reasons to believe that the group was involved in the preparation of an imminent terrorist attack."[20] Nevertheless, the Dutch legal system's strict rules of evidence prevented authorities from putting together a solid case, and the men were soon released.[21]

The member of the Hofstad group that more than any other had attracted the Dutch authorities' attention because of both his radicalism and his connections was a Dutch-born teenager, Samir Azzouz, a close associate of Akoudad. Azzouz's father, a day laborer, was a Moroccan immigrant; his mother, also Moroccan, suffered from poor health. Azzouz was a shy boy who attended a local Catholic school and lived with his grandmother because of his family's financial straits, but his father used to take him every Friday to the al Tawheed mosque, Amsterdam's most radical place of worship. [22]

Influenced by the sermons heard at al Tawheed and by the vitriolic rhetoric he found in Islamic chat rooms on the Internet, by the age of fifteen Azzouz had already embraced radical Islam. The events of 9/11 only increased his fanaticism, and in the spring of 2002, Azzouz attempted to reach Chechnya to join the mujahideen. His traveling companion was Abdelaziz Beniyach, a Moroccan who was a close associate of Jamal Zougam (see chapter 11). Azzouz and Benyaich were detained by Ukrainian authorities on their way to the Caucasus and eventually sent back to Europe. Upon his return to Holland, Azzouz settled in Rotterdam, where he began to socialize with two militants who belonged to the Hofstad group. [23]

Azzouz was among the militants detained and released in October 2003; by the first months of 2004, freshly married to a Palestinian and seventeen years old, he had become one of the key elements of the Hofstad group. According to Dutch authorities, he had begun surveiling key installations throughout the Netherlands that were suitable targets for attacks. In June, he was arrested in connection with the robbery of the small supermarket where he worked, and police searched his Rotterdam apartment. Investigators found a gun, two ammunition clips, night vision goggles, a bulletproof vest, and chemicals commonly used in making bombs. They also found sketches and floor plans of Amsterdam's Schiphol Airport, the headquarters of the AIVD (Algemene Inlichtingen- en Veiligheidsdienst, or the General Intelligence and Security Service), the parliament and Defense Ministry in The Hague, and a nuclear power plant in Borssele.[24]

Their discoveries caused Dutch authorities to issue a terror alert for the installations Azzouz had surveilled, and he was charged with plotting terrorist attacks. At the trial, held in early 2005, Dutch prosecutors presented the notes that Azzouz had taken on maps of the installations, which they interpreted as planning the use of weapons and a getaway car and thus as confirming that he was planning an attack. The prosecution also introduced footage from a surveillance camera placed outside the headquarters of the AIVD that appeared to show Azzouz scouting the building.[25] Moreover, to prove his radicalism, tapes of phone calls that Azzouz had made while in custody were introduced as evidence. In one conversation with his wife, he described the September 2004 massacre of schoolchildren in the Russian town of Beslan as a "great party."[26]

Dutch prosecutors, who tried Azzouz as an adult, asked for a sentence of seven years. They also demanded that Azzouz be denied his voting rights for twelve years, an unusual request that they argued was justified because he had tried to "attack democracy."[27] But as often happens in terrorism trials in the Netherlands, the Rotterdam court acquitted Azzouz, sentencing him to only three months for illegal possession of firearms, a term he had already served.[28] Exiting the courthouse with his wife, Azzouz celebrated his release by punching a freelance photographer and knocking him unconscious against a parked car.[29]

Azzouz's alleged plans were not the only attacks the group had conceived. In June 2004, Dutch authorities informed their Portuguese counterparts that three members of the Hofstad group had left the Netherlands and had traveled to Portugal, a few days before the kickoff of the European Cup soccer tournament that Portugal was hosting in June and July. Driving a Volkswagen Golf owned by another member of the group, the three had collected a small amount of cash at Lisbon Airport and checked into a hotel in Porto, in the north of the country. Portuguese and Dutch authorities believe that the group was planning to kill Jose Manuel Durão Barroso, a former Portuguese prime minister who was then president-designate of the European Commission, and other important guests at a reception held in Porto the night before the tournament began.[30] Certain that the threat from the Dutch hit squad was imminent, Portuguese police forced Barroso to stay in his hotel the night of the gala and deported the three Hofstad members.[31]

The Portuguese trip demonstrated the dangers posed by the group, but usually its schemes were aimed at the Netherlands. Most of the members of the Hofstad group had grown up in Holland, and although they supported bin Laden's concept of a worldwide jihad, they thought of Dutch society as their primary enemy. And the group even aimed at attacking the system from within. Dutch authorities were shocked to discover that the group had access to classified documents from the AIVD, the country's domestic intelligence agency. Indeed, in 2003 they discovered that a member of the group, Ahmed Hamdi, possessed a transcript of a conversation between militants that the AIVD had taped, and three other men linked to the group were also found to have classified documents. Their investigation later revealed that the documents had been passed to the men by Othman Ben Amar, an audio editor and interpreter in the Islamic Terrorism Center, the small section of the AIVD that investigates the activities of Islamic fundamentalists operating in the Netherlands. In September 2004, Ben Amar was arrested inside the offices of the AIVD and charged with releasing state secrets.[32]

Ben Amar, a Dutch Muslim of Moroccan descent who had set up a nonprofit organization following 9/11 to counter the negative image of Muslims in Holland, is also accused of mishandling other material. According to Dutch prosecutors, he leaked a document listing AIVD's antiterrorism investigations to an Utrecht-based group of Moroccans suspected of possessing explosives.[33] And those investigating Ben Amar's past activities believe that he may have provided an illegal Turkish immigrant with a residence permit when he was working in the Department of

Immigration and Naturalization.[34] The ability of Hofstad group to take advantage of a mole inside Dutch intelligence is particularly disturbing and shows the magnitude of Holland's problem.

Familiar with Dutch language and culture and plugged into the international jihadi network, the Hofstad group thought globally and acted locally. Members spent hours chatting online about the evils of Dutch society and providing authorities with hints of their future plans. These young men were, on average age, in their early twenties; one of the more interesting was Jason Walters. The son of an African American father who worked at the Soesterberg US Air Force Base and a native Dutch mother, Walters grew up in the Netherlands, a quiet and lonely boy whose dreams were simple: "Married with two children," wrote Walters in his high school yearbook. "And a nice job and a nice house." At sixteen, Walters visited a Dutch mosque and quickly converted to Islam, changing his name to Jamal. Within a few months, he traveled to Pakistan and perhaps Afghanistan. Once back, he was the quintessential militant, fighting with officials of a local mosque he deemed too moderate and forbidding his mother and sisters to drink alcohol or even watch television.[35]

Jason Walters was eighteen when he was arrested with other members of the Hofstad group in October 2003; he had been under surveillance for months.[36] Authorities confiscated his computer and found worrying messages on its hard drive. Walters was an active member of several Internet chat rooms, and in some of them he had talked about killing prominent members of the Dutch political establishment. After bragging with his chat partner about the training he had received in Afghanistan, Walters (under the alias "Mujaheed") mentioned a "death list" of people he wanted to kill, including member of parliament Ayaan Hirsi Ali, Prime Minister Jan Balkenende, and other prominent ministers of the Dutch government.[37] Despite these menacing words, Walters, like Azzouz and the others detained, was released by Dutch authorities.

In retrospect, the words of Walters sound ominously prophetic. On November 2, 2004, shortly before 9 AM, the controversial and provocative Dutch filmmaker Theo van Gogh was riding his bicycle on his normal morning route from his house to his production company. On the bike path along Linnaeusstraat, a boulevard in central Amsterdam, a man who appeared to be North African and who was wearing a traditional Arab robe passed him, stopped in the middle of the path, and shot at him four times. Van Gogh ran across the street but his attacker chased him, shooting him again from a close distance while the filmmaker was begging for mercy. In broad daylight, the man pulled out a large butcher knife, stabbed van Gogh several times, and tried without success to behead him. After pinning a letter to the filmmaker's chest with a smaller knife, the attacker calmly reloaded his weapon and walked to a nearby park, which was cordoned off by police agents called to the scene by witnesses. After firing at the police and at bystanders, the man was shot in the leg and taken into custody.[38]

The gruesome and ritualistic killing of van Gogh shocked the Netherlands, one of Europe's most peaceful and tolerant societies, yet it could have been foreseen. Theo van Gogh, a descendant of the nineteenth-century painter, was an outspoken critic of Islam; using the same straightforward language in which he also attacked Judaism and Christianity, he accused Islam of being a backward religion. Van Gogh had come under fire after the broadcast of a short TV movie titled *Submission* that he had directed. The film, which aimed at exposing the sufferings of women under Islam, had been written by Ayaan Hirsi Ali, a Somali-born Muslim member of the Dutch parliament who has openly criticized Islam's treatment of women and the reluctance of most Muslim immigrants to integrate into Dutch society. One scene that particularly outraged Holland's Islamists shows Quranic verses justifying violence against women written on the naked body of a young woman, and both Hirsi Ali and van Gogh received numerous death threats.

It was predictable that a member of the Hofstad group would take it upon himself to punish van Gogh for his "offenses" against Islam. The perpetrator of the brutal assassination, Mohammed Bouyeri, was indeed a member of the Hofstad group, and authorities had been surveilling him for months. After chatting online about targeting prominent figures in Dutch public life, the group had finally decided to go into action and attack van Gogh, who had refused police protection.

Dutch intelligence had been aware of Bouyeri for years, though they paid him no particular attention; he was not considered to be one of the one hundred fifty most dangerous Islamists operating in the Netherlands. Bouyeri was known to be a close associate of Akoudad and Azzouz,[39] and the group regularly met in his small Amsterdam apartment. He was also the owner of the Volkswagen Golf used by three members of the Hofstad group to travel to Portugal in June 2004.[40] Bouyeri had been questioned in October 2003, when Dutch authorities first moved against the group, but, like everyone else, he was immediately released. Just as had happened in Madrid with Jamal Zougam, an individual under surveillance who was considered a marginal figure in a wider network executed the attack.

Mohammed Bouyeri was the son of Moroccan immigrants; born in 1978, he grew up in the predominantly immigrant neighborhood of Slotervaart, a western suburb of Amsterdam where Muslims outnumber native Dutch residents. He was an average student at the local high school with many friends in the neighborhood. Before his conversion to radical Islam, Bouyeri gave signs of an internal conflict. He tried to fit into Dutch society, organizing soccer games between local youths and police officials and volunteering at a local community center; he lobbied local authorities and even the national parliament to obtain funding for the construction of a larger center.[41] At the same time, he had a rebellious side. According to media reports, in November 1997 Bouyeri was involved in a heated discussion with police officers outside of an Amsterdam coffee shop. After threatening the officers he was given a five-hundred-guilder fine. The incident caused Bouyeri to lose a position as a security guard at Amsterdam's Schiphol airport for which he had applied. Bouyeri had already begun his training when the police told the security firm about the incident and other unspecified but "well-known and relevant facts" that made Bouyeri an unfit candidate.[42] In June 2000, Bouyeri was involved in a fight in a bar, but he was not arrested. One year later, when four police agents were trying to arrest him after he had hit a fifth officer, he threatened them with a knife. He was sentenced to twelve weeks in jail.[43]

Some of his friends believe it was in jail that Bouyeri embraced radical Islam. Others claim that the attacks of 9/11 shocked him and deepened his faith. The death of his mother in 2002 also had a strong impact on him. By late 2002 Bouyeri had become a fundamentalist, growing a beard and wearing a djellaba and a skullcap rather than jeans and a T-shirt. His changed views caused friction at the community center, as he opposed the sale of alcoholic beverages and discouraged women from participating in the center's events.[44] He also began to worship regularly at Amsterdam's al Tawheed mosque, where he met Azzouz and other members of the Hofstad group. By August 2003 he stopped going to the center; shortly thereafter, he moved from Slotervaart to a small one-bedroom apartment in another district of Amsterdam.[45]

The files from his computer analyzed by Dutch intelligence after his arrest trace Bouyeri's shift to extremism. The e-mails that Bouyeri sent to his Dutch girlfriend before 9/11 are typical of any young European man, who complains about his inability to afford Reebok sneakers and is excited because a store featuring his favorite brand of ice cream, Haagen Dazs, is in his neighborhood. But as Frits van Straelen, the Dutch magistrate who prosecuted Bouyeri, said, "It is on the Internet that his radicalization took place: in the story of Mohamed Bouyeri the influence of the 'online jihad' counts more than anything else." After 9/11 and his mother's death, Bouyeri visited Islamic sites and posted frequently in radical chat rooms. On a Web site he painted Holland red and drew a flag inscribed with the Islamic sword and the phrase "Victory is ours." He added the faces of Hirsi Ali and Theo van Gogh, writing, "The infidels attack us, but they will be defeated."[46]

After moving away from Slotervaart, Bouyeri lost touch with his friends from the neighborhood and began to spend time only with his new friends from the mosque. He dropped out of the polytechnic where he had been studying accounting and began collecting unemployment benefits.[47] The apartment that Bouyeri shared with other radicals became one of the meeting points of the Hofstad group. Following a common pattern, the Hofstad group took shape at a mosque (the al Tawheed and others throughout Holland) and then, when its radicalism and level of involvement with illegal activities became too pronounced, it left the mosque to meet in members' residences. And like many other clusters, the young

Dutch Muslims formed a terrorist cell once they fell under the tutelage of experienced jihadis.

Though the members of the Hofstad group were, on average, very young, it had a few older and charismatic leaders. As noted above, Azzouz attempted to travel to Chechnya with a thirty-six-year-old veteran of Bosnia, Abdelaziz Beniyach. Other members of the group had close contacts with Abdeladim Akoudad, a man with ties to senior al Qaeda operatives.[48] After Beniyach and Akoudad left the Netherlands, the group's guide was a forty-three-year-old Syrian named Reduoane al Issar, whom the group called Abu Khaled. Al Issar, a former member of the Syrian army, had shuttled between Germany and Holland for almost ten years before becoming the undisputed spiritual leader of the Hofstad group, teaching the young men about the importance of jihad and the beauty of martyrdom.[49] When Dutch authorities clamped down on the group in October 2003, al Issar was deported to Germany but he managed to reenter the Netherlands, thanks to the absence of border controls between the countries.[50]

Under the influence of al Issar, Bouyeri, Azzouz, and Walters quickly were wholly caught up in the group and its murderous goals. The men spent days chatting online and meeting in various apartments in Amsterdam, The Hague, and Rotterdam. As Dutch authorities continued to keep a close eye on them, the militants held nightlong meetings where they watched cassettes of mujahideen endeavors and listened to tapes of radical scholars. Neighbors reported seeing dozens of young Muslim men at Bouyeri's Amsterdam apartment: "They came and went every day until two in the morning, all dressed in traditional robes."[51] Dutch authorities also monitored the online activities of the group. While Walters was expressing his desire to decapitate members of Holland's political elite, Bouyeri focused his anger on the events in Iraq, declaring that American troops deserved to be beheaded.[52]

In the wake of the assassination, the Dutch Interior and Justice Ministries published a joint letter defending their failure to anticipate it, asserting that "The information about [Bouyeri] that the intelligence services received did not alter the image they had of him that he was not a key figure in the network. Up until the attacks on Van Gogh the intelligence services had no information that indicated that [Bouyeri] was preparing a violent action."[53] Yet officials had repeatedly received hints of Bouyeri's nature, as he had been detained for minor violent crimes on various occasions. When Bouyeri and one of his roommates, Noureddine El Fathni, were arrested in October 2003, the search of their apartment turned up a "martyr's testament" under El Fathni's name. Questioned, El Fathni told investigators that the testament was Bouyeri's. Unable to ascertain the truth and having no recourse under Dutch law, authorities had to release El Fathni, Bouyeri, and the other men.[54]

Moreover, on September 29, 2004, Bouyeri was detained after he attacked transportation officials who caught him riding a tram without a ticket. Taken to the Amsterdam West police station, he kept spitting at the officers who were interrogating him. In his pockets, police found a note in which Bouyeri praised the beheadings of Westerners by Zarqawi in Iraq; he was also carrying the addresses of other known members of the Hofstad group. The police could do nothing more than book him and release him by evening. As he left, he shouted, "I hate you! I hate you! Sooner or later I will kill some of you!"[55] Five weeks later he kept his word and murdered Theo van Gogh.

Bouyeri's deep radicalism is evident in the martyr's testament that he carried with him when he killed Theo van Gogh. The letter, titled "Baptized in Blood," showed Bouyeri's desire to die as martyr: "So these are my last words. . . . Riddled with bullets. . . . Baptized in blood. . . . As I had hoped."[56] Even more chilling words were written on the five-page letter he pinned to Van Gogh's body after killing him. This "Open letter to Hirshi Ali" is a long string of invective against the Somali-born intellectual and her alleged apostasy:

Since your entrance into the political arena of Holland you have been constantly terrorizing Muslims and Islam with your words. You are not the first and you won't be the last to join the crusade against Islam.

With your apostasy, you have not only turned your back on the truth, but you also march along the ranks of the soldiers of evil. You mince no words about your hostility against Islam, and for this your masters have rewarded you with a seat in parliament. They have found in you a companion in their crusade against Islam and Muslims. A companion that gives them the "gunpowder" so they don't have to do the dirty work.

After accusing Hirsi Ali at length of hating Islam, Bouyeri concluded his letter with ominous threats:

Islam will conquer by the blood of the martyrs. It will spread its light to every corner of this Earth and it will, if necessary, drive evil to its dark hole by the sword.

This unleashed battle is different from previous battles. The unbelieving fundamentalists have started it and Insha Allah the true believers will end it.

There shall be no mercy for the unjust, only the sword raised at them. No discussion, no demonstrations, no parades, no petitions; merely DEATH will separate the Truth from the LIE. . . .

I deem thee lost, O America.

I deem thee lost, O Europe.

I deem thee lost, O Holland.

I deem thee lost, O Hirshi Ali.

I deem thee lost, O unbelieving fundamentalist.[57]

As Dutch police identified Bouyeri and examined his testament and the letter he had pinned on van Gogh, they rushed to the five apartments where the Hofstad group used to meet and arrested eight individuals.[58] Early in the morning of November 10, police officers attempted to raid an apartment house in a quiet working-class neighborhood of The Hague; they were looking for two suspects connected to the Hofstad group, Ismail Aknikh (the man whose telephone number had been found in possession of Abdelkader Hakimi in Belgium and Abdeladim Akoudad in Spain) and Jason Walters, the teenage son of an American airman. "We will decapitate you," the two shouted, throwing a hand grenade at the officers and injuring four.[59] It was the beginning of a drawn-out siege that led

Dutch authorities to evacuate five blocks around the house and to ban air traffic over The Hague. Fourteen hours later, after the intervention of Dutch Special Forces, the radicals barricaded inside the house surrendered and were arrested.[60] Jason Walters's brother Jermaine was arrested a few hours later in Amersfoort.[61]

A total of fifteen members of the Hofstad group, excluding Bouyeri, have been arrested and charged in a Rotterdam court with various crimes following van Gogh's assassination.[62] Many of them, whose ages at the time they were apprehended ranged from eighteen to twenty-seven, possessed copies of the letter that Bouyeri had pinned on the filmmaker's body and handbooks on how to perform murders according to Islamic rituals. Some of them had received military training in Pakistan and were recorded in intercepted phone calls discussing slaying infidels like "sacrificial lambs."[63] Authorities are certain that the group was planning follow-up operations targeting Ayaan Hirsi Ali; the Dutch politician Geert Wilders; Amsterdam's mayor, Job Cohen; and the city's Moroccan-born alderman, Ahmed Aboutaleb.[64] In June of 2005, Amsterdam police arrested Noureddine El Fathni, Bouyeri's former roommate, and found him in possession of a fully-loaded machine pistol and loose ammunition. El Fathni, who had been briefly arrested twice before (but always released), is now believed to be a key member of the Hoftsad and of having facilitated the escape of Issar from the Netherlands.[65]

But even if the arrested members of the Hofstad group are convicted, others are ready to replace them. Authorities estimate that the group contained more than fifty members and that there are at least a few hundred radical Islamists living in the Netherlands.[66] And the next attack might be carried out by a woman. In February 2005, the Dutch newspaper *Volkskrant* interviewed three women, Naima, Fatima, and Khadisja, who claimed to be members of the Hofstad group. The women were adamant in their determination to carry on the jihad that the men had begun. And as one of them—Naima, the wife of Mohammed el Murabit, one of the men on trial in Rotterdam observed—"If Hirsi Ali is murdered by a woman it would have a much larger impact." Authorities are well aware of the women's intentions. Shortly after the assassination of van Gogh, a young Muslim woman showed up at the Dutch parliament asking to discuss with Hirsi Ali a book she was carrying. The book, *The True Muslim*, had been written by Mohammed Bouyeri under a pseudonym. Authorities suspect that the woman might have been a member of the group attempting to attack the legislator. "She will not escape her punishment: death," Naima told the *Volkskrant* reporters. "Even if it takes ten years."[67]

Confirming the important role played by females in the Hofstad group, when Noureddine El Fathni was arrested in June 2005, he was accompanied by two women, his wife, Soumaya S., and twenty-six-year-old Dutch convert Martine van den Oever. The two women, who are close friends, are accused of being deeply involved in the group's activities. At the moment of her arrest Martine van den Oever, who had converted to Islam in high school and had progressively radicalized, was found in possession of a farewell letter in which she asked her friend Soumaya S. to inform her mother in case she died or something happened to her.[68] And authorities believe that Soumaya S. had tried to obtain the private addresses of prominent Dutch politicians.[69] Reportedly, on the day of their arrest, her husband Noureddine El Fathni was found in possession of what authorities call a "death list" with the names, among others, of Justice Minister Piet Hein Donner and People's Party leader Jozias van Aartsen.[70]

THE CAUSE AND THE REACTION

"It's a Dutch plot, homegrown terrorism," observed a spokesman for the AIVD after van Gogh's assassination.[71] The statement is true on a number of levels. The operation was conceived, planned, and executed in the Netherlands. Bouyeri was a Dutch-born Muslim, as were most of the members of the Hofstad group. "What's disturbing," commented the Dutch justice minister, "is that the suspect, born and raised in the Netherlands, went through a radicalization process here that brought him to this unimaginable deed."[72]

More significantly, the motivations that drove Bouyeri and his associates to act were homegrown. Prosecutors have stated that the group's aims were to "terrorize Dutch society" and to "drive a wedge between different sections of Dutch society."[73] Even though the group sympathized with bin Laden, the Iraqi insurgency, and the struggle of the Palestinians, its targets were Dutch, proving that its main enemy was secular Dutch society. In a bulletin he wrote in 2003, Bouyeri linked the situation in Iraq to the status of the Muslim community in Holland: "The Netherlands is now our enemy, because they participate in the occupation of Iraq. We shall not attack our neighbors but we will those who are apostates and those who are behaving like our enemy. Ayan Hirshi Ali is an apostate and our enemy."[74] In online Islamic chat rooms, he called Holland a "democratic torture chamber" and described his dream of overthrowing the Dutch parliament and replacing it with an Islamic court.[75]

Though international events may have contributed to the men's radicalization, their rage was directed toward individuals they perceived as their immediate enemies: local figures who (they believed) were fighting Islam in the Netherlands. The letter that Bouyeri pinned on van Gogh's body—written in a traditional rhyming Dutch verse form, which itself demonstrated Bouyeri's apparent assimilation into Dutch society[76]—is full of references to events and characters of Dutch political life; no "global" Islamic issues are mentioned. The Hofstad group was completely immersed into Dutch society, and members therefore fully understood that targeting intellectuals and politicians would deal that society a painful blow.

The dangers of the radicalization of parts of the Dutch Muslim community had been thoroughly exposed and analyzed by the AIVD, Holland's internal security agency. In its 2003 annual report, the AIVD had warned that "small groups of young Muslims, mainly of North African origin, have appeared to be susceptible to radical views and expressed their preparedness to take part in the violent jihad in speech and action."[77] The agency also clearly identified the reason of this radicalization: the spread of Salafism, the puritanical and violent strain of Islam embraced by growing numbers of fundamentalists worldwide. According to the AIVD, "present-day Salafism works like a magnet on some sections of the Muslim communities in Western countries, in particular on some groups of Muslim youngsters, the main reason being that it offers seemingly simple solutions to the problem of identity that many of them struggle with."[78]

A key role in the spread of Salafism in Holland, as elsewhere in Europe, has been played by mosques, charities, Islamic schools, and organizations linked to Saudi Arabia. By giving millions of dollars to individuals and organizations that have agreed to spread its rigorous interpretation of Islam, the oil-rich kingdom has contributed greatly to the radicalization of segments of the Dutch Muslim community. The AIVD reports that in some cases, the Saudi embassy has directly financed Dutch Salafi imams. In others, Saudi-based charities that are officially considered nongovernmental organizations (NGOs) but that in reality "maintain close ties with parts of the Saudi establishment" have been a crucial influence on "those segments of Muslim communities in the Netherlands that have shown to be susceptible to manipulative activities deployed from Saudi Arabia."[79]

The Dutch mosques that receive support from Saudi Arabia have often been linked to radical or terrorist activities. The al Tawheed mosque, which has been a headquarters of radical activities in the Netherlands, is closely linked to Al Haramain, a Saudi charitable organization whose branches in the Netherlands and in other six countries have been designated as terrorism financiers by the US Treasury Department.[80] According to Dutch authorities, Al Haramain underwrote the construction of the al Tawheed mosque, located in a multiethnic district of central Amsterdam, and Al Haramain founder Aqeel al Aqeel and his assistant, Mansour al Qadi, held positions on its board.[81] The joint US-Saudi document that designated al Aqeel as a terrorism financier notes that under al Aqeel's leadership Al Haramain became "one of the principal Islamic NGOs providing support for the al Qaida network and promoting militant Islamic doctrine worldwide."[82]

Thanks to its large Saudi funding, al Tawheed became one of the most prominent mosques in Europe's Islamist underworld. The mosque often organized events and conferences attended by radicals from across the Continent. For example, investigators believe that Mohammed Atta, Ramzi Binalshibh, and Marwan al Shehhi traveled from Hamburg to Amsterdam in 1999 to attend a conference on Salafism organized at al Tawheed.[83] The mosque's imam, Mahmoud El Shershaby, preaches that Islam is under attack and that Jews, Christians, and other unbelievers are "fuel for the fires of hell." And the mosque's bookstore recently came under scrutiny after newspapers revealed that it sold books that advocated throwing homosexuals headfirst off high buildings.[84] Not surprisingly, given the mosque's radical teachings, investigators believe that Mohammed Bouyeri and Samir Azzouz there first met their mentor, Reduoane al Issar.[85]

But al Tawheed is hardly an isolated case. Saudi-funded Islamic schools and institutions throughout Holland have been under scrutiny since before the van Gogh assassination. In The Hague, the imam of the As Soennah mosque preaches the superiority of Muslims over all other people and teaches his congregation that women must not leave their houses unless they are going to the mosque or shopping for groceries.[86] As we say in chapter 3, Eindhoven's al Furqan mosque is frequented by known terrorists and organizes radical seminars that the AIVD has judged "damaging to the Dutch democratic order."[87] Both mosques have strong ties to the al Waqf al Islami Foundation, a Saudi "charitable" organization whose real purpose is to spread radical Islam.[88] The values preached by these mosques are clearly incompatible with the basic principles of a Western democracy; yet thousands of the almost one million Muslims living in the Netherlands have embraced them, creating a direct threat to the Netherlands' stability.

"It's a group of radicals who see us as the enemy, and with whom we've actually been drawn into a war," said Jozias van Aartsen, a member of Hirsi Ali's People's Party for Freedom and Democracy, a few days after van Gogh's tragic murder. "There's a jihad in the Netherlands. Ayaan Hirsi Ali indicated this danger a year and a half ago, and now we've crossed a threshold."[89] In the wake of the van Gogh assassination, mainstream Dutch politicians began saying what few "enlightened" public figures had dared saying before. Hirsi Ali, member of parliament Geert Wilders, and, in his provocative way, Theo van Gogh had warned about the dangers posed by the failed integration and subsequent radicalization of parts of the Dutch Muslim community, but most had ignored them, labeling their words racist or "Islamophobic."

But similar warnings had also come from the AIVD, which had repeatedly informed authorities about the dangerous repercussions for the country of the radicalization of Dutch Muslims. In 2002 the AIVD provided an accurate analysis of the challenges facing Holland.

The recruitments for the Islamic war which took place in the Netherlands over the past year, can therefore not be seen as mere isolated incidents. They are rather the first tangible illustrations of a tendency,
closely related to a stealthy entrance of a violent radical Islamic movement in Dutch society, which is also taking place in the rest of the
western world.

The outlined development is a significant threat for the Dutch
society. People who can be included in this radical Islamic movement
are positioning themselves explicitly outside and opposite the democratic legal order. They are not only willing to support or use violence
if they deem it necessary to defend "true Islam," they are also decidedly
trying to discourage the full participation of Muslims in Dutch society.
By employing a strategy of provocation they are trying to drive a wedge
between Muslims and non-Muslims.[90]

And if the goals of Islamists in the Netherlands, as the AIVD and
prosecutors in the van Gogh case claim, is "to drive a wedge between
Muslims and non-Muslims," the assassination of the filmmaker brought
them nearer to that goal. The brutal killing of van Gogh brought turmoil
to the Netherlands, traditionally one of Europe's most tolerant and open
societies. In the tense days following the assassination, mosques and
Islamic schools were firebombed by angry Dutch youngsters; a poll conducted after the attack revealed that 40 percent of the Dutch hoped that
Muslims "no longer felt at home" in Holland.[91] In retaliation, groups of
Dutch Muslims attacked churches, intensifying the spiral of hatred.

"We were tolerant to the intolerants and we only got intolerance
back," commented Geert Wilders on the country's lenient attitude toward
fundamentalism.[92] In the days after the van Gogh assassination Dutch
politicians of all colors rushed to declare that Holland was at war against
radical Islam and that extraordinary measures would be taken to defeat it.
Nevertheless, six months after the attacks, not much had changed. In
March 2005, a Dutch court rejected a request from public prosecutors to
ban the activities of Al Haramain, stating that it had seen no evidence that
the charity supported terrorism, despite being designated a terrorist financier by the United States and the United Nations. As already recounted,

in April a Rotterdam court acquitted Samir Azzouz, the child prodigy of the Hofstad group. The sentence caused strong emotions in the country; according to the public broadcasting channel NCRV, 82 percent of the respondents to its opinion program were opposed to Azzouz's acquittal and many declared they wanted to take the law into their hands.[93] And while Wilders and Hirsi Ali are forced to live under round-the-clock surveillance and must sleep, for security reasons, in a high-security jail and on a naval base, respectively, more than one hundred known Islamic fundamentalists live undisturbed in the country, with Dutch authorities powerless to do anything beyond watching them.

At the same time, the radicalization of the Dutch Muslim community is still taking place. Reportedly, Bouyeri has become a hero for young Moroccan children living in the Netherlands, and many of them even display his picture on their backpacks or notebooks.[94] His appeal among young radicals has only grown after his conviction to life in prison decreed by an Amsterdam court in July 2005. Wearing a traditional robe and brandishing a Quran, a defiant Bouyeri refused to speak during the trial, claiming he recognized only the justice of Allah. He opened his mouth only once to address the mother of Theo van Gogh, Anneke, who had given a moving speech about her son. "I don't feel your pain," he said coldly, "I don't have any sympathy for you. I can't feel for you because you're a non-believer." He added remorselessly: "If I ever get free I would do it again."[95]

If the situation in Holland is representative of things to come for the rest of Europe, and many think it is, then al Qaeda needs no effort to send terrorists to Europe—the Continent is growing its own. The July 2005 attacks in London are just further confirmation of this new reality. He was "an average, second-generation immigrant," said the chairman of the parliamentary commission that reviewed the immigration history of Mohammed Bouyeri.[96] He was the new face of al Qaeda in Europe.

NOTES

1. Sebastian Rotella, "Terrorists at the Table; Islamic Militants in Europe Blend Political Sophistication and Crude Violence to Influence Events, as the Bombings in Madrid Show," *Los Angeles Times*, March 6, 2005.

2. US Department of State, *Patterns of Global Terrorism, 2003*, http://www.state.gov/s/ct/rls/pgtrpt/2003/.

3. Rotella, "Terrorists at the Table."

4. Daniel Wools, "Spain: Militants Threaten Morocco Gov't," AP, March 8, 2005.

5. Elaine Sciolino, "Morocco Connection Is Emerging as Sleeper Threat in Terror War," *New York Times*, May 16, 2004.

6. "Spanish Judge Starts Questioning Moroccan Suspect in Train Bombings," AP, April 8, 2005.

7. Daniel Wools, "Spain Arrests Four Moroccan Suspects in Madrid Train Bombings, Belgium Detains Moroccan Man Sought by Spain," AP, February 1, 2005; "Al-Qaidah Spokesman in Europe Travelled to Madrid at End of 2003 to Order 3/11 Massacre," ABC, February 28, 2005 (accessed via Foreign Broadcast Information Service, or FBIS).

8. "La fecha del ataque del 11-M fue fijada al día siguiente de que Bin Laden amenazara a España," *El Pais*, August 5, 2005.

9. Al Goodman, "Family Charged in Madrid Bombings," CNN, February 5, 2005.

10. Spanish investigators have carried out an in-depth investigation on who helped Afalah leave Spain. On July 15, 2005, Spanish daily *El Mundo* reported that authorities arrested a Moroccan man, Abdeneri Essebar, for his role in facilitating Afalah's escape. What is shocking is that Essebar had lost his stepdaughter, thirteen-year-old Sanae ben Salah, in the Madrid train bombings.

11. "Interior Sospecha que Afalah se Inmolo' en Irak," *El Mundo*, June 15, 2005.

12. Mark Eeckhaut, "The El Haski Connection—Three Brothers Are Muslim Terrorist Leaders," *De Standaard*, December 21, 2004 (accessed via FBIS).

13. Piotr Smolar, "Implique dans les Attentats de 11 Mars, Hassan El Haski a Eté Incarceré," *Le Monde*, December 24, 2004.

14. "Reports List Names of Madrid-Linked Terror Suspects Arrested in Belgium," *Le Soir*, March 11, 2005 (accessed via FBIS).

15. Spanish Ministry of the Interior, Summary of Anti-Terrorist Activities, 2004.

16. Jean-Pierre Tuquoi, "Un Franco-Marocain suspecté dans les Attentats de Casablanca et Madrid," *Le Monde*, March 24, 2004; Evan Stretch, "Terror in UK Atrocity Fear," *Sunday Mirror*, April 4, 2004.

17. Jean-Pierre Stroobants, "Le Reseau Islamiste 'Hofstad' Etait Solidement Ancré en Europe," *Le Monde*, December 10, 2004.

18. Mark Eeckhaut, "Van Gogh Investigation Leads to Brussels," *De Standaard*, December 15, 2004 (accessed via FBIS).

19. Craig Smith, "Dutch Look for Qaeda Link After Killing of Filmmaker," *New York Times*, November 8, 2004.

20. AIVD (Algemene Inlichtingen- en Veiligheidsdienst, or General Intelligence and Security Service), *Annual Report 2003*, p. 17.

21. Sebastian Rotella, "2 Held after Dutch Standoff," *Los Angeles Times*, November 11, 2004.

22. David Crawford and Keith Johnson, "New Terror Threat in EU: Extremists with Passports," *Wall Street Journal*, December 27, 2004.

23. Crawford and Johnson, "New Terror Threat in EU."

24. "Teen Terror Suspect Stays Silent," *Expatica*, February 24, 2005.

25. "Terror Suspect Faces Seven Years," *Expatica*, March 23, 2005.

26. "Teen Terror Suspect Stays Silent."

27. "Terror Suspect Faces Seven Years."

28. "Dutch Court Acquits Teenager of Terrorism," *Guardian*, April 6, 2005.

29. "Ex-Terror Suspect Accused of Assault," *Expatica*, April 8, 2005.

30. João Pedro Fonseca, "Police Give Details of Attack Planned on Portugal by Dutch-Based Islamist Cell," *Diario de Notocias*, November 15, 2004 (accessed via FBIS).

31. Ambrose Evans, "Islamic Terrorists 'Plotted Attack at Finals of Euro 2004,'" *Telegraph*, November 16, 2004.

32. "AIVD Secrets 'Leaked to Van Gogh Accomplice," *Expatica*, January 10, 2005.

33. Stephen Castle, "Secret Service Link to Film-Maker's Killing," *Independent*, January 11, 2005.

34. "Mol' Lekt naar Hofstadgroep," *Volkskrant*, January 11, 2005.

35. Keith B. Richburg, "From Quiet Teen to Terrorist Suspect," *Washington Post*, December 5, 2004.

36. "Terrorism Suspect Bragged on Internet about Killing Dutch Prime Minister," Agence France-Presse, January 28, 2005.

37. Sebastian Rotella, "Europe's Boys of Jihad," *Los Angeles Times*, April 2, 2005; "Terrorism Suspect Bragged on Internet."

38. "Van Gogh Murder Designed to 'Terrorise Dutch Society,'" *Expatica*, January 26, 2005.

39. "Al-Qa'idah Member with Spanish Passport Held in Netherlands," *El Pais*, November 12, 2004 (accessed via FBIS); Smith, "Dutch Look for Qaeda Link."

40. Fonseca, "Police Give Details of Attack."

41. Glenn Frankel, "From Civic Activist to Alleged Terrorist; Muslim Suspect in Dutch Director's Killing Was Caught between Cultures," *Washington Post*, November 28, 2004.

42. Frank Hendrickx and Ferdi Schrooten, "Mohammed B. Bijna Bewaker Schiphol," *Rotterdams Dagblad*, August 5, 2005.

43. "L'Assassin presumé de Theo van Gogh déjà Condamné pour Agression," *Le Monde*, January 25, 2005.

44. Frankel, "From Civic Activist to Alleged Terrorist."

45. Craig S. Smith, "Dutch Try to Thwart Terror without Being Overzealous," *New York Times*, November 25, 2004.

46. Marco Imarisio, "Vi Uccidero' come Al Zarkawi'; Il Diario del Killer di Van Gogh," *Corriere della Sera*, April 15, 2005.

47. Frankel, "From Civic Activist to Alleged Terrorist."

48. "Al-Qa'idah Member with Spanish Passport."

49. Stroobants, "Le Reseau Islamiste 'Hofstad' Etait Solidement Ancré en Europe."

50. Smith, "Dutch Try to Thwart Terror without Being Overzealous."

51. Smith, "Dutch Look for Qaeda Link."

52. Frankel, "From Civic Activist to Alleged Terrorist."

53. "Dutch Investigation Reveals Suspected Terror Cell with International Links," Agence France-Presse, November 12, 2004.

54. Smith, "Dutch Try to Thwart Terror without Being Overzealous."

55. Imarisio, "Vi Uccidero' come Al Zarkawi'."

56. As translated by Nesser Petter in "The Slaying of the Dutch Filmmaker—Religiously Motivated Violence or Islamist Terrorism in the Name of Global Jihad?" Norwegian Defense Research Establishment (Forsvarets Forskningsinstitutt, or FFI), February 2, 2004.

57. As translated by Petter in "The Slaying of the Dutch Filmmaker."

58. "Acht Arrestaties in Onderzoek Moord Van Gogh," *De Telegraaf*, November 3, 2004.

59. Rotella, "2 Held after Dutch Standoff."

60. "Netherlands Police Operation Ends with Arrest of Two Terrorist Suspects," AFP, November 10, 2004.

61. Richburg, "From Quiet Teen to Terrorist Suspect."

62. Among the individuals arrested in connection to the Hofstad group there are two Chechen men. One, Bislan Ismailov, was arrested in Tours (France) in May 2005. His fingerprints were found on a copy of Bouyeri's testament. The other Chechen, twenty-three-year-old Marat J., was arrested in southern Holland (*Le Monde*, May 27, 2005).

63. Anthony Deutsch, "Alleged Dutch Terror Network Case Starts," AP, February 7, 2005.

64. "Terror Arrests 'Prevented' Attacks, Court Refuses Bail," *Expatica*, February 7, 2005.

65. "Dutch Minister Says Arrest of Terrorist Suspects May Have Prevented Attacks," Radio Netherlands, June 24, 2005. According to Dutch authorities, El Fathni purchased the ticket for Issar to fly to Syria, while another member of the group, Rachid Belkacem, drove the Syrian to the Brussels airport. Belkacem was arrested in London a few hours before El Fathni's arrest.

66. Dutch official, interview with the author, Amsterdam, July 2005.

67. Janny Groen and Annieke Kranenberg, "Van Onze Verslaggeefsters," *Volkskrant*, February 5, 2005.

68. "Radicale bekeerde moslima had afscheidsbrief," *Algemeen Dagblad*, July 24, 2005.

69. "Soumaya S. ontkent zoeken adressen politici," *Reformatorisch Dagblad*, August 4, 2005.

70. Dutch official, interview with the author, Amsterdam, July 2005.

71. Frankel, "From Civic Activist to Alleged Terrorist."

72. Sebastian Rotella and Douglas Heingartner, "Suspect in Slaying of Filmmaker Faces Terrorism Charges; Dutch Authorities Are Looking into Possible Links to International Militant Groups," *Los Angeles Times*, November 6, 2004.

73. "Van Gogh Murder Designed to 'Terrorise Dutch Society,'" *Expatica*, January 26, 2005.

74. Petter, "The Slaying of the Dutch Filmmaker."

75. Imarisio, "Vi Uccidero' come Al Zarkawi'."

76. Petter, "The Slaying of the Dutch Filmmaker."

77. AIVD, 2003 annual report, p. 17.

78. AIVD report, "Saudi Influences in the Netherlands: Links between the Salafist Missions, Radicalisation Processes and Islamic Terrorism," January 2005, p. 5.

79. AIVD, "Saudi Influences in the Netherlands," p. 1.

80. US Treasury Department, "Additional Al-Haramain Branches, Former Leader Designated by Treasury as Al Qaida Supporters Treasury Marks Latest Action in Joint Designation with Saudi Arabia," press release JS-1703, June 2, 2004, http://www.treas.gov/press/releases/js1703.htm.

81. AIVD, "Saudi Influences in the Netherlands," p. 4.

82. US Treasury Department, "Additional Al-Haramain Branches."

83. Andrew Anthony, "When Theo van Gogh Was Slaughtered in the Streets for His Attacks on Islamic Fundamentalism, It Was Also a Knife to the Heart of the Dutch Liberal Dream," *Observer* magazine, December 5, 2004.

84. "Moskee als Broeinest van Haat," *Algemeen Dagblad*, November 5, 2004.

85. Petter, "The Slaying of the Dutch Filmmaker."

86. "Radicale Imams Prediken Materlaarschap," *Volkskrant*, June 14, 2002.

87. Ian Johnson and David Crawford, "A Saudi Group Spreads Extremism in 'Law' Seminars," *Wall Street Journal*, April 15, 2003.

88. "AIVD, Saudi Influences in the Netherlands," p. 4.

89. Rotella and Heingartner, "Suspect in Slaying of Filmmaker Faces Terrorism Charges."

90. AIVD, "Recruitment for the Jihad in the Netherlands; from Incident to Trend," December 2002, pp. 31–32.

91. Justin Sparks, "Muslim Mole Panics Dutch Secret Service," *Times* (London), November 14, 2004.

92. Gareth Harding, "Netherlands on Edge after Slaying," UPI, December 2, 2004.

93. "Ex-Terror Suspect Accused of Assault," *Expatica*, April 8, 2005.

94. "Mohammed B. Is de Held," *Amsterdams Stadsblad*, March 16, 2005.

95. Notes taken by the author during the trial.

96. Andrew Higgins, "Van Gogh Killing 'Highlights Risk from Home-Grown Terrorists,'" *Wall Street Journal*, November 22, 2004.

APPENDIX: ISLAMIC EXTREMISM IN EUROPE

TESTIMONY OF LORENZO VIDINO

Before the House Committee on International Relations
Subcommittee on Europe and Emerging Threats

"Islamic Extremism in Europe"
April 27, 2005

Lorenzo Vidino
The Investigative Project
5505 Connecticut Avenue NW, Suite 341
Washington, DC 20015
Phone: 202-363-8602
stopterror@aol.com

Good afternoon, Mr. Chairman and Mr. Vice-Chairman, and thank you for the opportunity today to discuss the threat posed to Europe by Islamist extremism.

The deadly train bombings that killed almost two hundred commuters in Madrid on March 11, 2004, shocked most Europeans, as the attacks represented the first massive strike by Islamist terrorists on European soil.

The Madrid bombings, nevertheless, did not surprise security officials on both sides of the ocean, as the intelligence community was well aware that it was just a matter of time before Europe, one of the terrorists' favorite bases of operations, could become a target.

Over the last ten years, in fact, Europe has seen a troubling escalation of Islamist terrorist and extremist activities on its soil. This disturbing phenomenon is due to a combination of several factors and chiefly to:

- lax immigration policies that have allowed known Islamic radicals to settle and remain in Europe,
- the radicalization of significant segments of the continent's burgeoning Muslim population, and
- the European law enforcement agencies' inability to effectively dismantle terrorist networks, due to poor attention to the problem and/or the lack of proper legal tools.

Given these premises, it should come as no surprise that almost every single attack carried out or attempted by al Qaeda throughout the world has some link to Europe, even prior to 9/11. A Dublin-based charity provided material support to some of the terrorists who attacked the US embassies in Kenya and Tanzania in 1998. Part of the planning for the thwarted millennium bombing that was supposed to target the Los Angeles international airport was conceived in London. False documents provided by a cell operating between Belgium and France allowed two al Qaeda operatives to portray themselves as journalists and assassinate Ahmed Shah Massoud, the commander of the Afghan Northern Alliance, just two days before 9/11. And, as we well know, the attacks of 9/11 were partially planned in Hamburg, Germany, where three of the four pilots of the hijacked planes had lived and met, and from where they received extensive financial and logistical support until the day of the attacks.

After 9/11, as the al Qaeda network became less dependent on its leadership in Afghanistan and more decentralized, the cells operating in Europe gained even additional importance. Most of the planning for the April 2002 bombing of a synagogue in the Tunisian resort town of Djerba that killed twenty-one mostly European tourists was done in Germany and France. According to Moroccan authorities, the funds for the May 2003 Casablanca bombings came from Moroccan cells operating between Spain, France, Italy, and Belgium. And cells operating in Europe have also directly targeted the Old Continent. Only after 9/11, attacks have been either planned or executed in Madrid, Paris, London (in at least four different circumstances), Milan, Berlin, Porto, and Amsterdam.

However, while investigations in all these cases revealed that different cells operating throughout Europe were involved in the planning of the operation, the role of these cells extends beyond the simple planning or execution of attacks. European-based Islamists raise or launder money, supply false documents and weapons, and recruit new operatives for a global network that spans from the United States to the Far East. Within the last decade, their role has become essential to the mechanics of the network. It is, therefore, not far-fetched to speak of Europe as "a new Afghanistan," a place that al Qaeda and others have chosen as its headquarters to direct operations.

ORIGINS AND DEVELOPMENTS OF ISLAMIST TERRORISM IN EUROPE

The foundations for this security disaster were laid in the 1980s, when many European countries either granted political asylum or allowed the entrance to hundreds of Islamic fundamentalists, many of them veterans of the war in Afghanistan against the Soviets facing persecution in their home countries. Moved by humanitarian reasons, for decades countries like Britain, Sweden, Holland, and Germany have made it their official policy to welcome political refugees from all over the world. But blinded by their laudable intentions of providing protection to all individuals suffering political persecutions from autocratic regimes throughout the world, most European countries never really distinguished between opponents of dictatorships who wanted to spread democracy and Islamic fundamentalists who had bloodied their hands in their home countries with heinous terrorist acts. As a consequence, some of the world's most radical Islamists facing prosecutions in the Middle East found not only a safe haven but also a new convenient base of operation in Europe.

Many European governments thought that, once in Europe, these committed Islamists would have stopped their violent activities. Europeans also naively thought that, by giving the mujahideen asylum, they would have been spared their murderous wrath. All these assumptions turned out to be completely wrong. In fact, as soon as they settled on European soil, most Islamic radicals exploited the Continent's freedom and wealth to continue their efforts to overthrow Middle Eastern governments, raising money, and providing weapons and false documents for their groups operating in their countries of origin.

And it was in Europe that Islamic radicals from different countries converged and forged strategic alliances. Originally intending only to fight the secular regimes of their own countries, top members of various Islamist terrorists groups, drawn to the radical mosques of Europe, joined forces with their colleagues who all adhered to the same Salafi/Wahhabi ideology and shared the common dream of a global Islamic state. It was between London and Milan, for example, that the strategic alliance between Algerian and Tunisian terrorist groups was conceived. Europe, along with al Qaeda's Afghan training camps, was the place where bin Laden's project of "global jihad" came to realization, as various Islamist groups progressively abandoned their local goals and embraced al Qaeda's strategy of attacking America and its allies worldwide.

Moreover, the mosques and networks established by radicals who had been given asylum played a crucial role in what could be considered Europe's biggest social and security problem, the radicalization of its growing Muslim population. Europe is facing monumental problems in trying to integrate the children and grandchildren of Muslim immigrants who have come to the continent since the 1960s. Dangerously high percentages of second- and third-generation Muslim immigrants live at the margins of European societies, stuck between unemployment and crime. While they hold French, Dutch or British passports, they do not have any attachment to their native land, feeling like foreigners in their home countries.

"After things didn't work out with work, I decided to devote myself to the Koran," explained an Islamic fundamentalist interviewed by the German magazine *Der Spiegel*.

As they perceive themselves with no economic future, trapped in a country that does not accept them and without a real identity, many young European Muslims turn to their fathers' religion in their quest for direction. While some of them find solace in their rediscovered faith, others adopt the most belligerent interpretation of Islam, embarking on a holy war against their own country. According to a French intelligence report, radical Islam represents for some French Muslims "a vehicle of protest against—problems of access to employment and housing, discrimination of various sorts, the very negative image of Islam in public opinion."

Whether this troubling situation is due to the European societies' reluctance to fully accept newcomers or on some Muslims' refusal to adapt to new customs is hard to say.

Nevertheless, given the burgeoning numbers of Muslim immigrants living in Europe, currently estimated between fifteen million and twenty million, the social repercussions of these sentiments are potentially explosive.

While it is true that the situation in the immigrant suburbs of many European cities is dramatic and that it is difficult for the children of Muslim immigrants to emerge in mainstream European society, the popular paradigm that equates militancy with poverty is simplistic and refuted by the facts. An overview of the European-born Muslim extremists that have been involved with terrorism, in fact, shows that many of them came from backgrounds of intact families, with financial stability and complete immersion in mainstream European society. The example of Omar Sheikh—the British-born son of a wealthy Pakistani merchant who attended some of England's most prestigious private schools, led a Pakistani terrorist group and was jailed for his role in the beheading of *Wall Street Journal* reporter Daniel Pearl—shows that the causes of radicalization are deeper for many individuals.

Nevertheless, it is undeniable that young, disaffected Muslims living at the margins of European societies are the ideal recruits for terrorist organizations. The recruitment takes place everywhere, from mosques to cafés in Arab neighborhoods of European cities to the Internet. As in the United States, European prisons are considered a particularly fertile breeding ground for radicalism, a place where young men already prone to violence can be easily turned into terrorists. In France, for example, where unofficial estimates indicate that more than 60 percent of the inmates are Muslims (while Muslims represent only 10 percent of the total French population), authorities closely monitor the activities of Islamic fundamentalists, aware of the dangers of the radicalization of their jail population.

Officials, who estimate that three hundred militants are active in the Paris prisons alone, have seen cases of radicals who seek to get arrested on purpose so that they can recruit new militants in jail.

Similarly, in Spain, where one in ten inmates is of Moroccan or Algerian descent, Islamic radicals have been actively recruiting in jail for the last ten years. In October of 2004, Spanish authorities dismantled a cell that had been planning a bloody sequel to the March 11 Madrid bombings, intending to attack the Audiencia Nacional, Spain's national criminal court. Most of the men, who called themselves "The Martyrs of Morocco," had been recruited in jail, where they had been detained for credit card fraud and other common crimes and had no prior involvement with Islamic fundamentalism.

CURRENT TRENDS OF TERRORISM FINANCING IN EUROPE

If the European criminal underworld provides an excellent recruiting pool, crime also constitutes a major source of financing for terrorist organizations. Islamic terrorist groups operating in Europe have resorted to all kinds of crimes to finance their operations, including robberies, document forging, fraud, and the sale of counterfeited goods. But more alarming is the fact that Islamist groups have built strong operational alliances with criminal networks operating in Europe.

Over the last few years, Islamic terrorists have been actively involved in one of Europe's most profitable illegal activities, human smuggling. The GSPC, a radical Algerian Islamist group operating in the desert areas of North Africa, is actively involved in smuggling large groups of Sub-Saharan migrants across the desert and then to Europe, where the group can count on an extensive network of cells that provides the illegal immigrants with false documents and safe houses. In 2003 German authorities dismantled a network of Kurdish militants linked to Ansar al Islam, the terrorist group led by Abu Musab al Zarqawi that is battling US forces in Iraq. The Kurdish cells had organized a sophisticated and profitable scheme to smuggle hundreds of illegal Kurdish immigrants into Europe, raising hundreds of thousands of dollars. Considering that, on average, a migrant pays about $4,000 to his smugglers and that around half a million illegal immigrants reach Europe every year, terrorist groups have all the reasons to get involved in the human smuggling business.

Likewise, the terrorists' use of drug trafficking is also considered a particularly serious problem by European authorities, which believe that terrorist organizations have infiltrated around two-thirds of the $12.5 billion-a-year Moroccan hashish trade.

Evidence from recent terrorist operations reveals that profits from drug sales have directly financed terrorist attacks. According to Spanish authorities, Jamal Ahmidan, a known drug dealer and one of the operational masterminds of the Madrid train bombings, obtained the two hundred twenty pounds of dynamite that were used in the attacks in exchange for sixty-six pounds of hashish. And Ahmidan also flew to the island of Mallorca shortly before March 11 to arrange the sale of hashish and Ecstasy, planning to use the profits for additional attacks. The scheme is not new to Moroccan groups, which have used profits from the drug sales to finance the thwarted attacks against American ships in Gibraltar in 2002 and the Casablanca bombings.

European authorities are confronting criminal activities with relative success, but are facing an uphill battle when they have to prove the links to terrorism. Severe evidentiary requirements and the secretive nature of terrorism financing have prevented Europeans from effectively tackling known networks that financed terrorist activities. The most commonly used legal tool, the designation as a "terrorism financier," has had only modest results. In fact, since the various terrorism financing resolutions allow authorities only to freeze the bank accounts of suspected terrorism financiers, businesses, residential and commercial properties belonging to the designated individual cannot be touched.

The case of Youssuf Nada and Ahmed Idris Nasreddin is illustrative. Nada and Nasreddin operated a bank, Bank Al Taqwa, and a network of companies between Italy, Switzerland, Liechtenstein, and the Bahamas. The US Treasury Department, which designated Al Taqwa and both men as terrorism financiers in the aftermath of the 9/11 attacks, claims that, since its foundation in 1988, Al Taqwa financed groups such as the Palestinian Hamas and the Algerian GIA. Moreover, according to the Treasury Department, Al Taqwa provided funding to al Qaeda until September of 2001 and granted a clandestine line of credit to "a close associate of Usama Bin Laden." European authorities have also designated the bank and the two financiers, but with scant results.

Both men, financial experts with decades of experience, have devised a system of front companies, figureheads, and secret bank accounts in offshore banking paradises that allowed them to circumvent resolutions and shelter their finances from the authorities' action. And while Nada still maintains business interests in Switzerland and Liechtenstein, Nasreddin still owns a luxurious hotel in downtown Milan.

LEGAL OBSTACLES

The problems faced by European authorities in tackling terrorism financing are the same that prevent them from successfully prosecuting and dismantling terrorist networks operating on the Continent. In many European countries, laws prevent intelligence agencies from sharing information with prosecutors or law enforcement agencies unless they follow a lengthy and complicated procedure. With few exceptions, the monitoring of individuals has to be authorized by a judge based on extremely strong evidence of the suspect's guilt presented to secure the order. Severe evidentiary requirements often prevent prosecutors from using information obtained by intelligence agencies in their cases. And prosecutors also have to prove the specific intent of an accomplice in a terrorist act, showing that he knowingly provided support to the person who carried out a terrorist attack.

These provisions are the product of centuries of democratic legal tradition and are meant to defend the citizen from the creation of a police state. They epitomize Europe's success in creating a civil society where the government cannot unduly interfere with its citizens' lives. But, at the same time, they create an ideal shelter for the terrorists. European laws need to be adapted to the new threat that it is facing.

"There has to be a balance between individual liberty on one hand and the efficiency of the system to protect the public on the other. In an ideal world, I would choose the first, but this is not an ideal world, and when dealing with Islamic extremists we have to be brutal sometimes," is the view of Alain Marsaud, a member of the French parliament and an antiterrorism magistrate. Marsaud's views represent France's attitude toward terrorism, as the French legal system provides investigators and antiterrorism magistrates with powers that have no equal in Europe and in the United States as well.

But France is an isolated case. The aftermath of 9/11 showed that most European legal systems are not prepared to efficiently face the new legal issues that have arisen with the war on Islamic terrorism. The excellent work done by European intelligence agencies and law enforcement has often been thwarted by the courts, which are forced to enforce laws that do not adequately punish individuals that associate themselves for terrorist purposes.

The German trials of Abdelghani Mzoudi and Mounir El Motassadeq, two of the accomplices of Mohammed Atta and the other hijackers in Hamburg, revealed how Europe often finds itself legally impotent against terrorism.

Mzoudi and Motassadeq, the only two men to go on trial in Europe in connection with the 9/11 attacks, have been engaged in a complicated legal battle against German authorities for more than three years. According to prosecutors, Mzoudi's Hamburg apartment served as the meeting place for a group of Islamic radicals who, bound by a common hatred for the United States and Jews, planned an attack that would shock the world. After countless meetings at Mzoudi's apartment, some members of the Hamburg cell went to the United States to attend flight schools and carry out the lethal 9/11 plan; others remained in Hamburg providing logistical help and wiring them money.

Prosecutors assert that while the men who worked from Germany may not have known every detail of the plot, they were well-aware of the fatal intentions of their US-based cohorts. For instance, Mounir Motassadeq allegedly told a friend, "[The 9/11 hijackers] want to do something big. The Jews will burn and we will dance on their graves."

Motassadeq and Mzoudi were charged in Hamburg with being accessories to the murder of more than three thousand people and being members of a terrorist organization. Motassadeq was initially found guilty and sentenced to fifteen years. Mzoudi's trial was more complicated, as, by the time it began, Ramzi Binalshibh, one of the key members of the Hamburg cell, had been arrested in Pakistan. Mzoudi's lawyers demanded that they could examine Binalshibh, whose testimony they alleged was essential to uncover Mzoudi's real role. Since the US government, which has detained Binalshibh since his arrest, refused to even disclose Binalshibh's location, German judges reluctantly acquitted Mzoudi. "Mr. Mzoudi, you are acquitted, but this is no reason to celebrate," said the presiding judge, adding that the court was not convinced he was innocent and that he had been acquitted only because the prosecution had failed to prove its case. A month after Mzoudi's acquittal, an appeal court ordered a retrial for Motassadeq, claiming that he had been denied a fair trial because the United States had refused to allow the testimony of Binalshibh.

The difficulty faced by German prosecutors in the case of both Mzoudi and Motassadeq lies in the fact that the two were facilitators, sending money and providing apartments to terrorists but not actually carrying out terrorist acts themselves. Indeed, the lawyers for both men have argued that their clients believed they were simply helping fellow Muslims. When asked why he wired money to 9/11 pilot Marwan al-Shehhi, Motassadeq explained: "I'm a nice person, that's the way I am."

Great Britain, America's closest ally in Afghanistan and Iraq, has similarly tied its own hands. Radical imams openly preach hatred for the West and incite worshipers in the mosques of London to carry out attacks inside England. And recruiters have operated freely in Britain for more than a decade, as the story of Hassan Butt proves. With British forces still battling the Taliban in Afghanistan, the British public was shocked to read in the tabloids the interview with Hassan Butt, a British-born Muslim who bragged: "I have helped to bring in at least 600 young British men. These men are here to engage in jihad against America and its allies— That there are so many should serve as a warning to the British government. All of them are prepared to die for the cause of Islam." Despite his activities and his not-so-veiled threats to the British government, Butt was allowed to return to England undisturbed.

Upon his return to England, Butt was contacted by a reporter from the *Mirror* and agreed to be interviewed for the price of £100,000. When the *Mirror*'s reporter informed British counterterrorism officials of the meeting and asked them if they wanted to interview Butt themselves, their response was shocking: "I know this sounds ridiculous," said a detective from the Anti-Terrorist Squad, "But we can't get involved. All our checks, all our intelligence, show that he is not wanted for any offences in the UK." Since recruiting for a foreign terrorist organization operating overseas was not a crime in Britain, Butt could not be charged with any crime.

Another example of this frustrating situation and of its dangerous consequences is represented by the results of a 2003 Dutch intelligence investigation on a group of forty to fifty young North African radicals. Dutch intelligence had collected important information on the men, revealing their ties to some of the masterminds of the May 2003 Casablanca bombings and other terrorists throughout Europe. Moreover, some of the men had expressed their desire to die as martyrs and to kill prominent members of the Netherlands' political and cultural establishment. In the fall of 2003, some of the men were arrested. Nevertheless, the men had committed no crime, and the Dutch legal system forbade the use of information obtained by intelligence agencies in a trial. As a consequence, the men had to be released.

Predictably, after a few months, the group decided to go into action. Last November, one of its members, Mohammed Bouyeri, who had been under surveillance for months, gunned down and tried to ritualistically behead in the middle of one of Amsterdam's busiest streets Theo van Gogh, a popular Dutch filmmaker who, according to Islamists, had dared to offend Islam with a controversial movie about the treatment of Muslim women.

A similar situation occurred in Spain, as some of the key planners and perpetrators of the Madrid train bombings had been known to Spanish intelligence as radical Islamists with ties to terrorism since 1999. Some of them had had their phone conversations intercepted and their apartments searched, but no charge could be brought against them since, technically, they had committed no crime.

Unfortunately, the results in the cases in Britain, Holland, and Spain are not the exception, but the rule. The legal systems of most European countries do not have provisions that provide authorities with preemptive measures that can be taken against a known fundamentalist who is overheard saying he wants to "die as a martyr," unless evidence of a specific plan is also uncovered. Moreover, the laws of few European countries adequately punish activities that, while not directly harming people, are instrumental and necessary to the execution of a terrorist attack. Enabling a terrorist to enter the country by supplying him with a false document is equally important as providing him with the explosives, but few countries punish the two crimes with the same severity.

THE IRAQI CONFLICT AND OTHER REPERCUSSIONS FOR THE UNITED STATES

Before 9/11, recruiting individuals for a terrorist organization, as long as the group operated outside of the country, was not a crime in most European countries. While some countries have recently changed their laws to allow prosecution, the phenomenon of recruitment in Europe is taking place with even greater intensity than it did prior to 9/11, and its consequences are dire for both Europe and the United States. Shielded by the fact that recruitment for a terrorist organization is difficult to prosecute, and exploiting the widespread opposition to the Iraqi war within Muslim communities in Europe, recruiters have been sending hundreds of European Muslims to Iraq, joining the ranks of the insurgency that is fighting US and Iraqi forces on the ground.

In 2003 an investigation launched by Italian authorities dismantled a network that recruited more than two hundred young Muslims in Germany, France, Sweden, Holland, and Italy to train and fight with Ansar al Islam, the al Qaeda–linked group led by Abu Musab al Zarqawi that has carried out dozens of attacks against American and Iraqi civilian targets.

Reportedly, five young Muslims recruited in Milan have died in suicide operations in Iraq, including the attack against the Baghdad hotel where US deputy secretary of defense Paul Wolfowitz was staying. The investigation revealed that the network that had sent the volunteers to Iraq was the same that had recruited hundreds of militants before 9/11 for the al Qaeda training camps in Afghanistan, showing the continuity and adaptability of terrorist networks that have been operating in Europe for more than a decade.

The Iraqi war is also presenting evidence of a different phenomenon, the involvement of extremely young European Muslims who do not belong to any organized network or terror group, but who, nevertheless, feel the sudden urge of fighting "the infidels." While the Italians dismantled a very sophisticated network that had close links to Zarqawi and al Qaeda's leadership, investigators throughout Europe have noticed that many of the volunteers who leave for Iraq are groups of teenagers, high-school students, and petty criminals from the Continent's poor immigrant neighborhoods with no connections to a terrorist group, who seemingly decide to act on their own.

This phenomenon is the direct consequence of the social crisis that is affecting Europe, as local governments are struggling to integrate the Continent's soaring Muslim population.

And while it is true that only a minority of the millions of Muslims living in Europe espouse radical views or support violent activities, the dangerous consequences of the actions of this minority cannot be overstated.

Every act of violence or foiled terrorist plot increases the rift between Muslims and the native European population. The brutal killing of Van Gogh, for example, brought turmoil to the Netherlands, traditionally one of Europe's most tolerant and peaceful societies. Mosques and Islamic schools were firebombed in the wake of the filmmaker's assassination and a poll conducted after the attacks revealed that 40 percent of Dutch hoped that Muslims "no longer felt at home" in Holland. In retaliation, groups of Dutch Muslims attacked churches, igniting a spiral of hatred.

The spread of Islamic radicalism and terrorism in Europe needs to be closely monitored by the United States and not only for the historical and cultural links between the United States to Europe. Hundreds of Islamist terrorists have, either by birth or through naturalization, European passports and can, therefore, enter the United States without a visa and with just a summary scrutiny once they attempt to enter the US borders. It is not a coincidence, for example, that the three men who have been charged just two weeks ago for their role in a plot to attack various financial institutions in the United States were all British citizens whom al Qaeda had dispatched on several surveillance missions to the States, counting on the fact that their British passports would have made their entrance into the United States easier.

As the attacks of 9/11 have painfully shown, events that occur overseas can have a direct impact on the security of this country and its interests abroad. It is therefore crucial for the United States to follow carefully the events taking place in Europe and to closely cooperate with its European counterparts, as only a global effort can defeat this global enemy.

INDEX